I.C. Entertainment Presents:

Vampire Princess Miyu
Volume Two: "Encounters"

Story and Art by Narumi Kakinouchi

Domestic Credits
ART TOUCH-UP: Steven R. Bennett IV
COVER DESIGN: Doug Smith
TRANSLATOR: Duane Johnson
EDITING: Stephanie Brown

Dedicated in memory of "Shogun Pop," Steven Bennett III.
This volume contains Vampire Princess Miyu Volume 2 in its entirety.

I.C. Entertainment
1005 Mahone
Fredericksburg, VA 22401
Website: www.ic-ent.com

Translator's Note: Miyu's name means "beautiful evening."

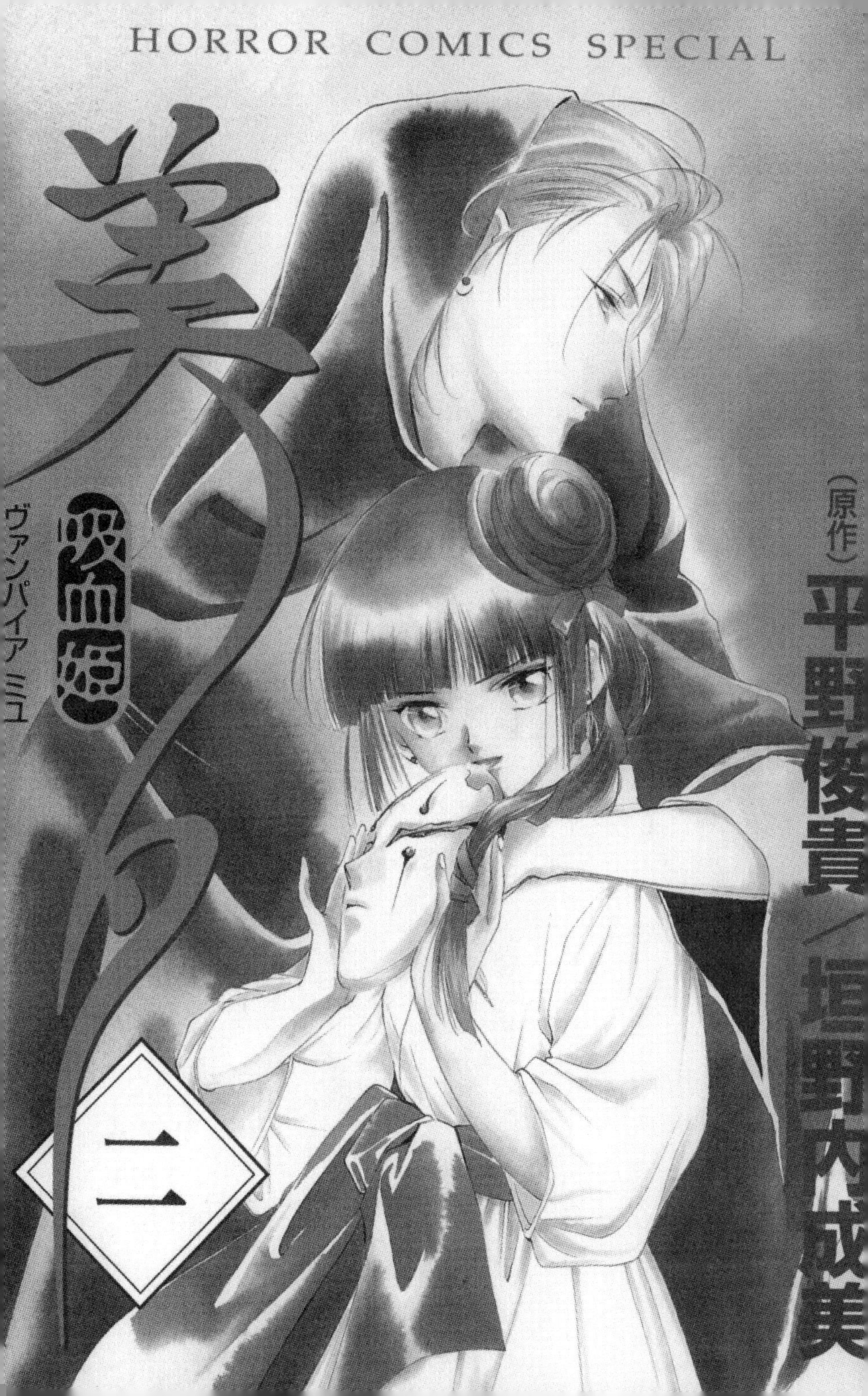
HORROR COMICS SPECIAL
吸血姫美夕
ヴァンパイアミユ
二
（原作）平野俊貴／垣野内成美

Table of Contents

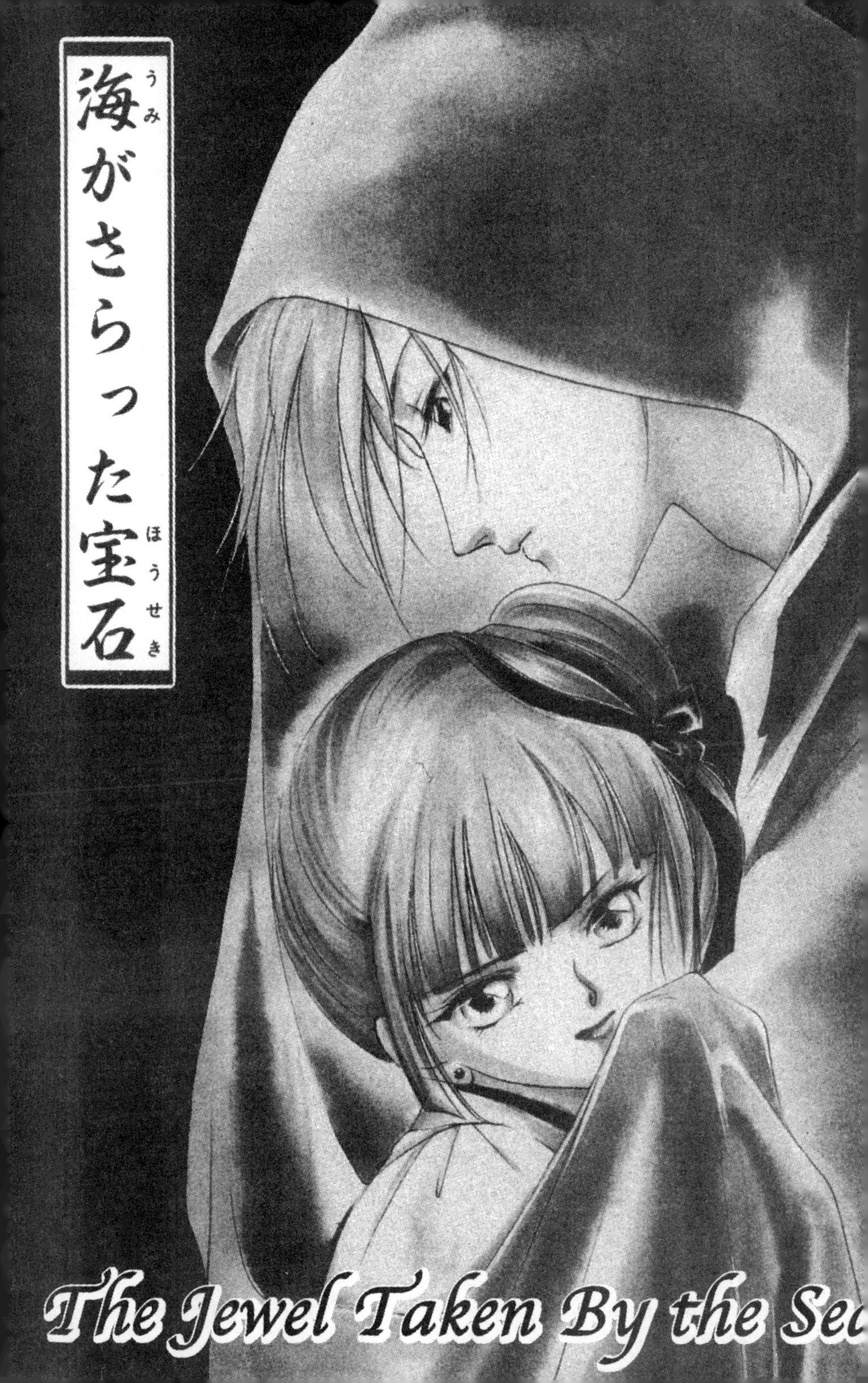
海がさらった宝石
The Jewel Taken By the Sea

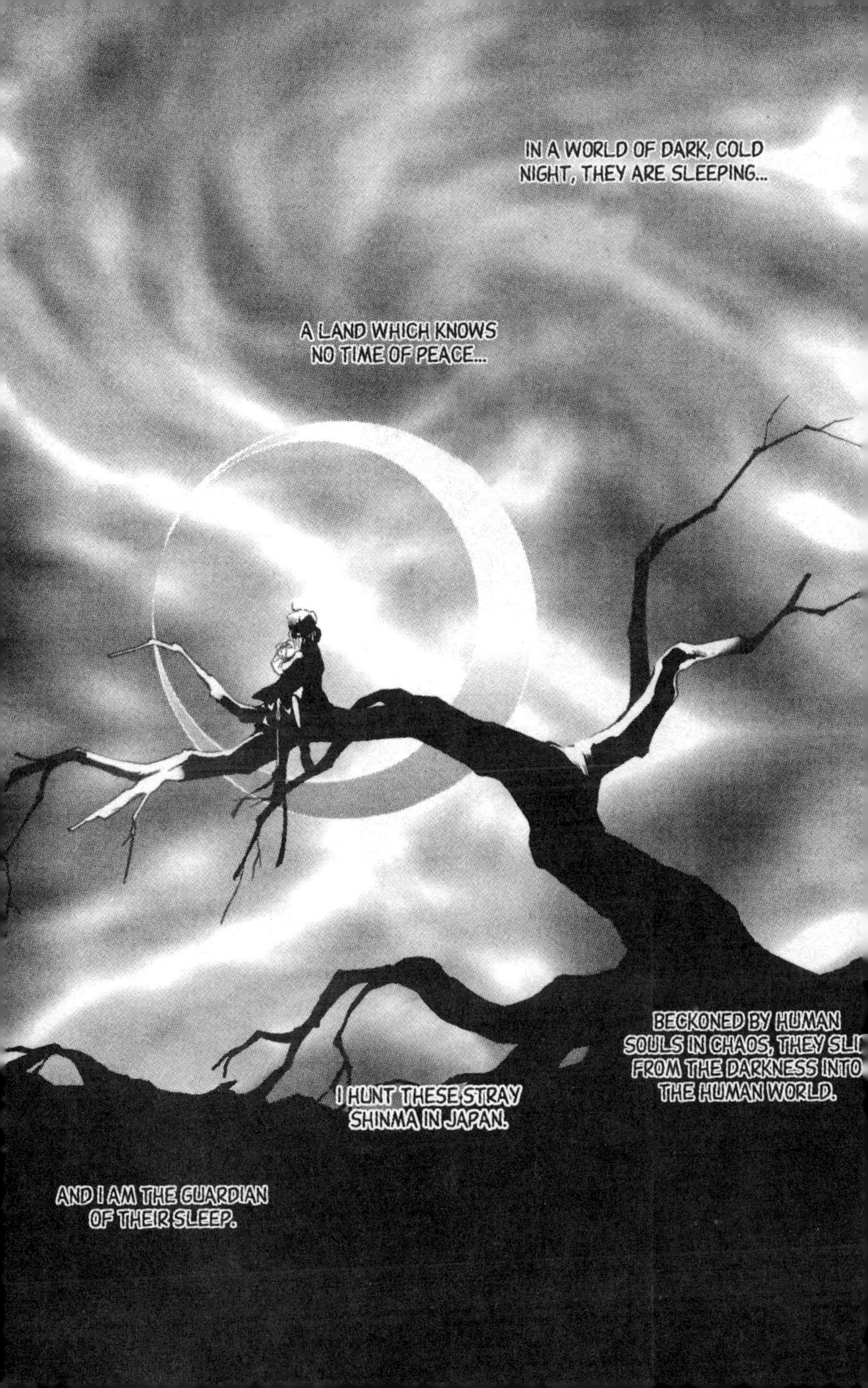
IN A WORLD OF DARK, COLD NIGHT, THEY ARE SLEEPING...
A LAND WHICH KNOWS NO TIME OF PEACE...
BECKONED BY HUMAN SOULS IN CHAOS, THEY SLI FROM THE DARKNESS INTO THE HUMAN WORLD.
I HUNT THESE STRAY SHINMA IN JAPAN.
AND I AM THE GUARDIAN OF THEIR SLEEP.

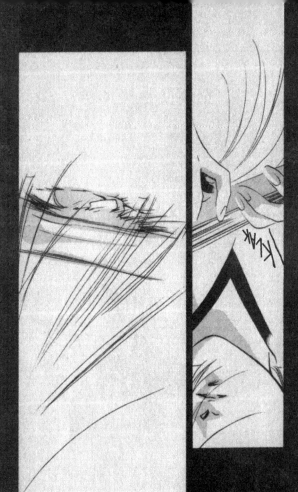

...MIYU...

VAMPIRE PRINCESS MIYU...

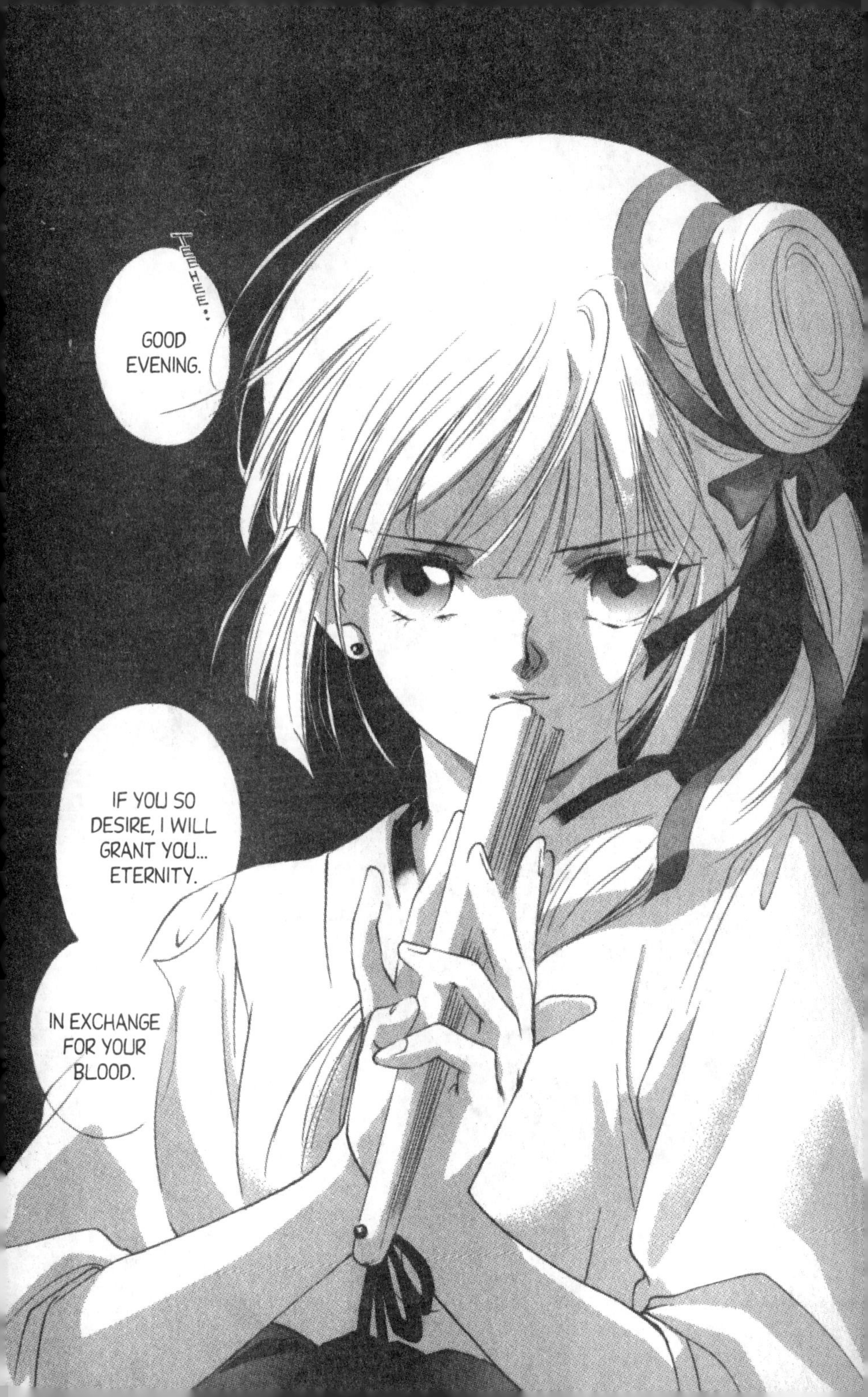
TEEHEE..
GOOD EVENING.
IF YOU SO DESIRE, I WILL GRANT YOU... ETERNITY.
IN EXCHANGE FOR YOUR BLOOD.

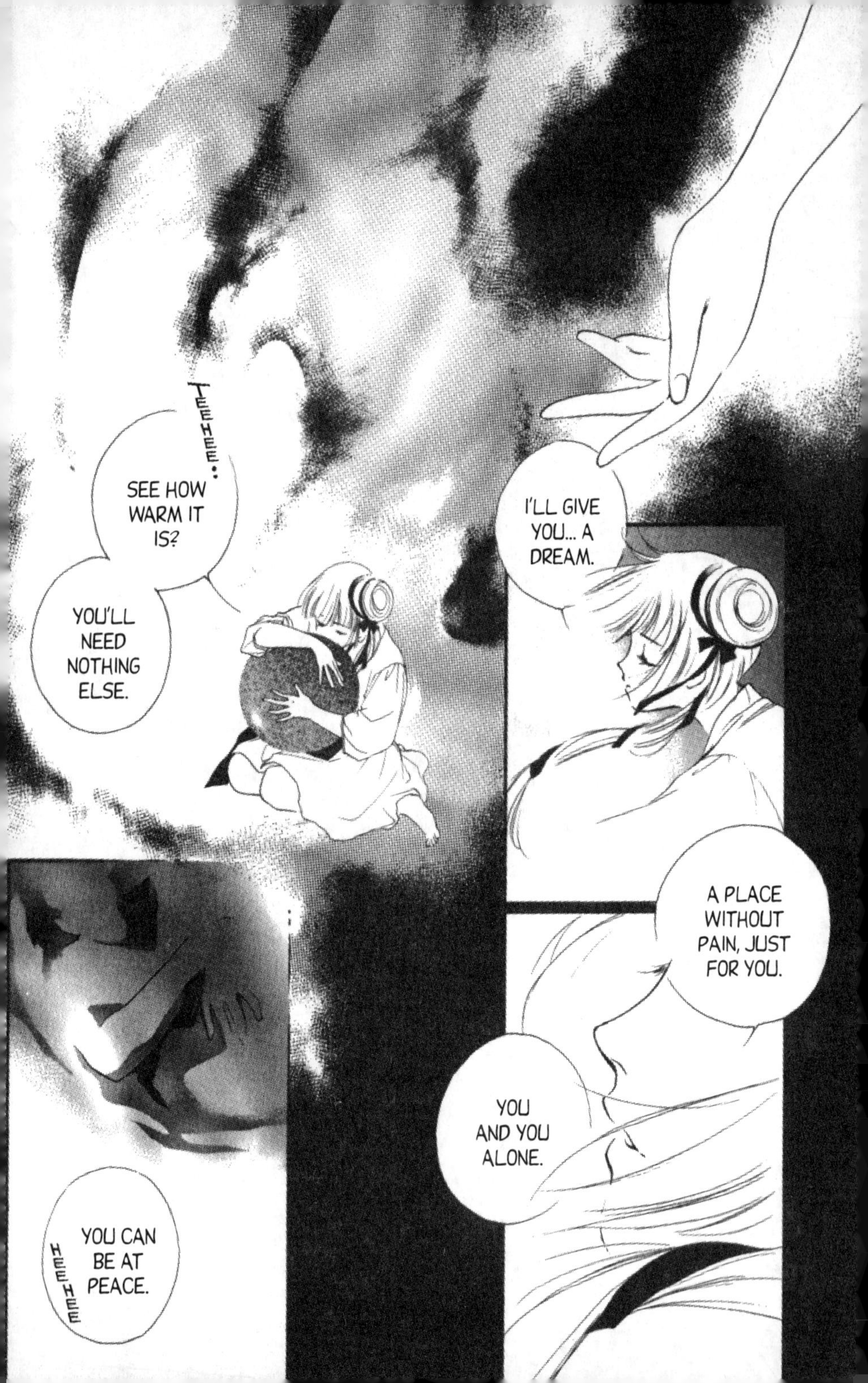
I'LL GIVE YOU... A DREAM.
A PLACE WITHOUT PAIN, JUST FOR YOU.
YOU AND YOU ALONE.
TEEHEE...
SEE HOW WARM IT IS?
YOU'LL NEED NOTHING ELSE.
YOU CAN BE AT PEACE.
HEEHEE

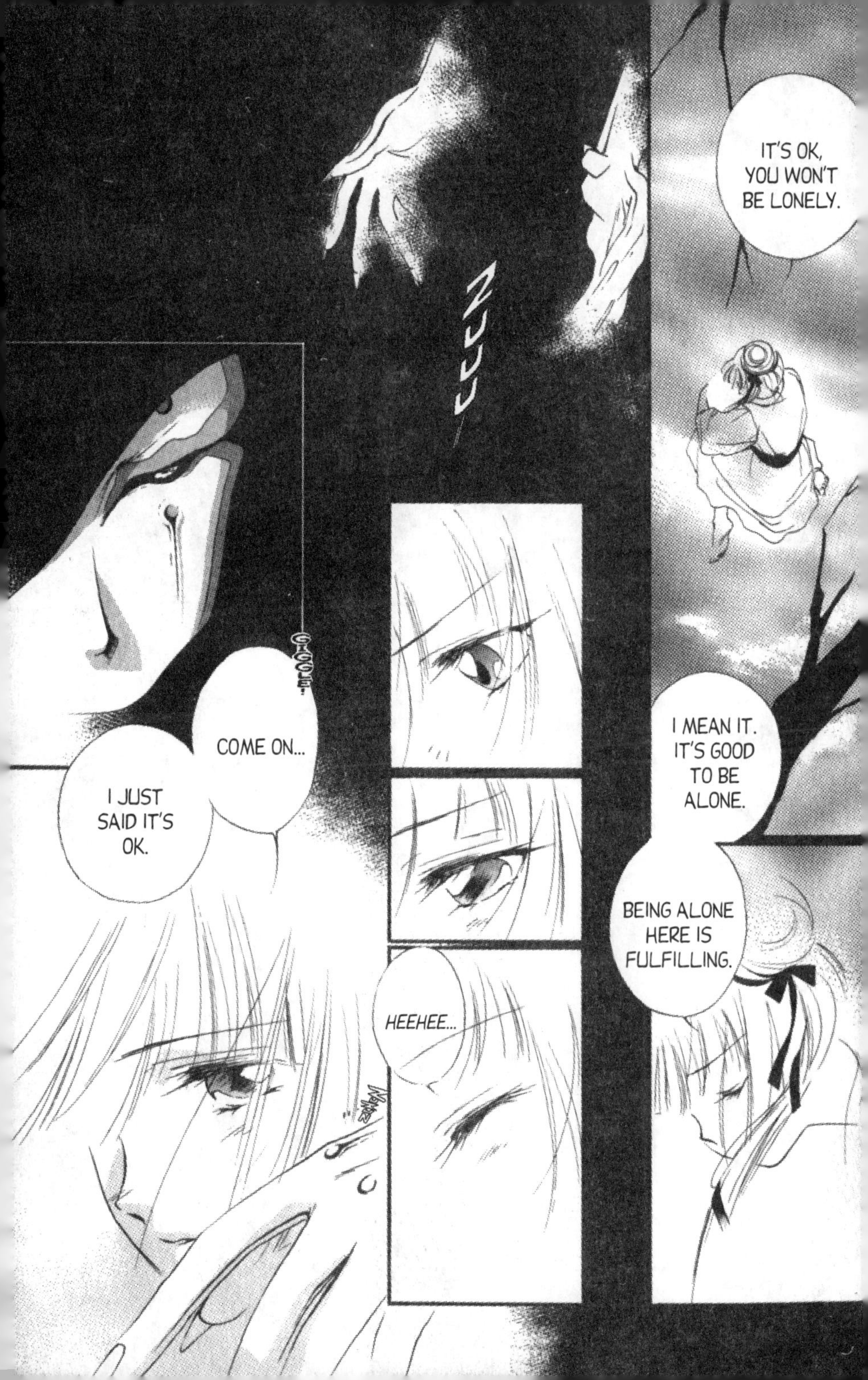
IT'S OK, YOU WON'T BE LONELY.
ZUJJU
I MEAN IT. IT'S GOOD TO BE ALONE.
BEING ALONE HERE IS FULFILLING.
GIGGLE
COME ON...
I JUST SAID IT'S OK.
HEEHEE...

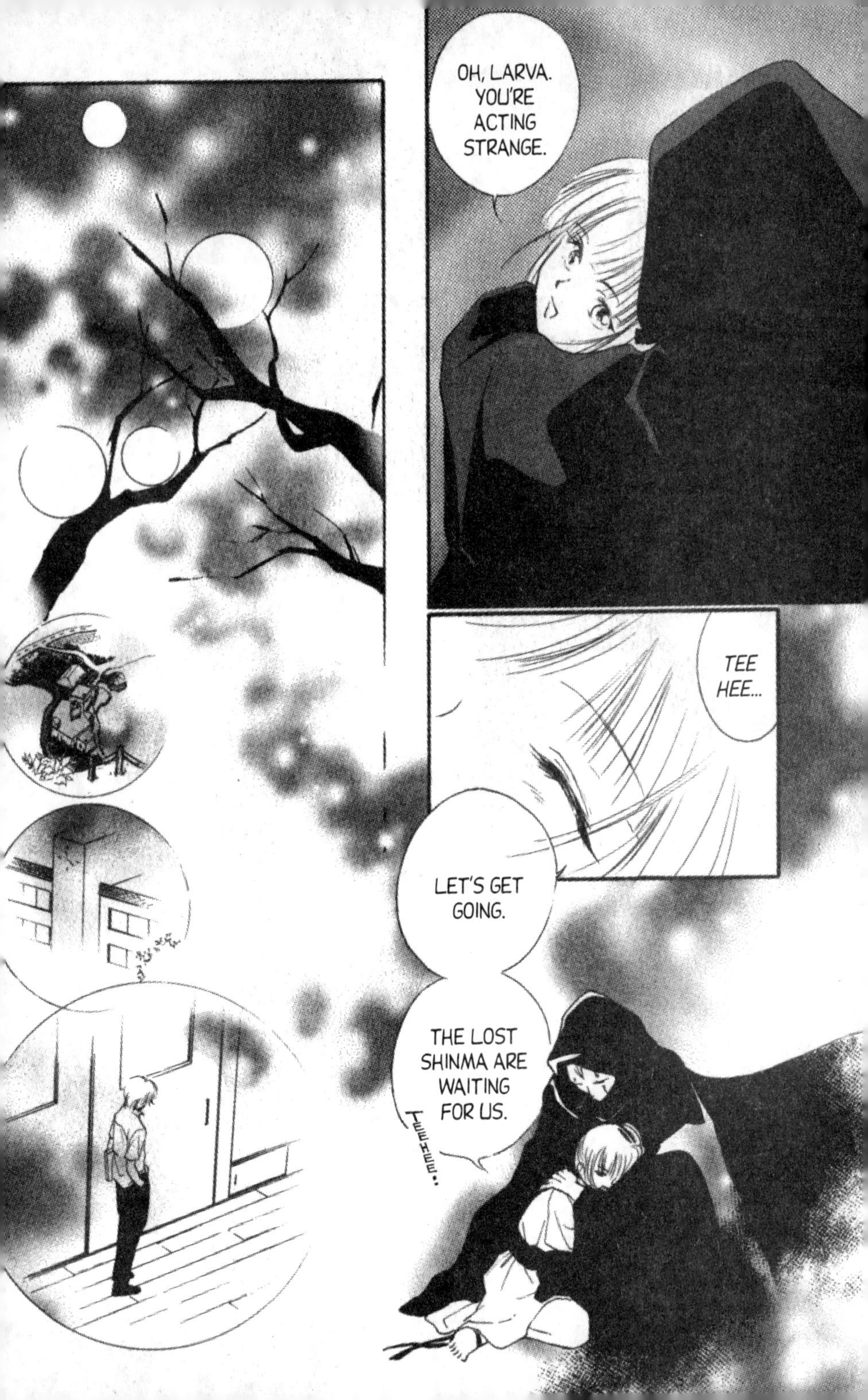
OH, LARVA. YOU'RE ACTING STRANGE.
TEE HEE...
LET'S GET GOING.
THE LOST SHINMA ARE WAITING FOR US.
TEEHEE...

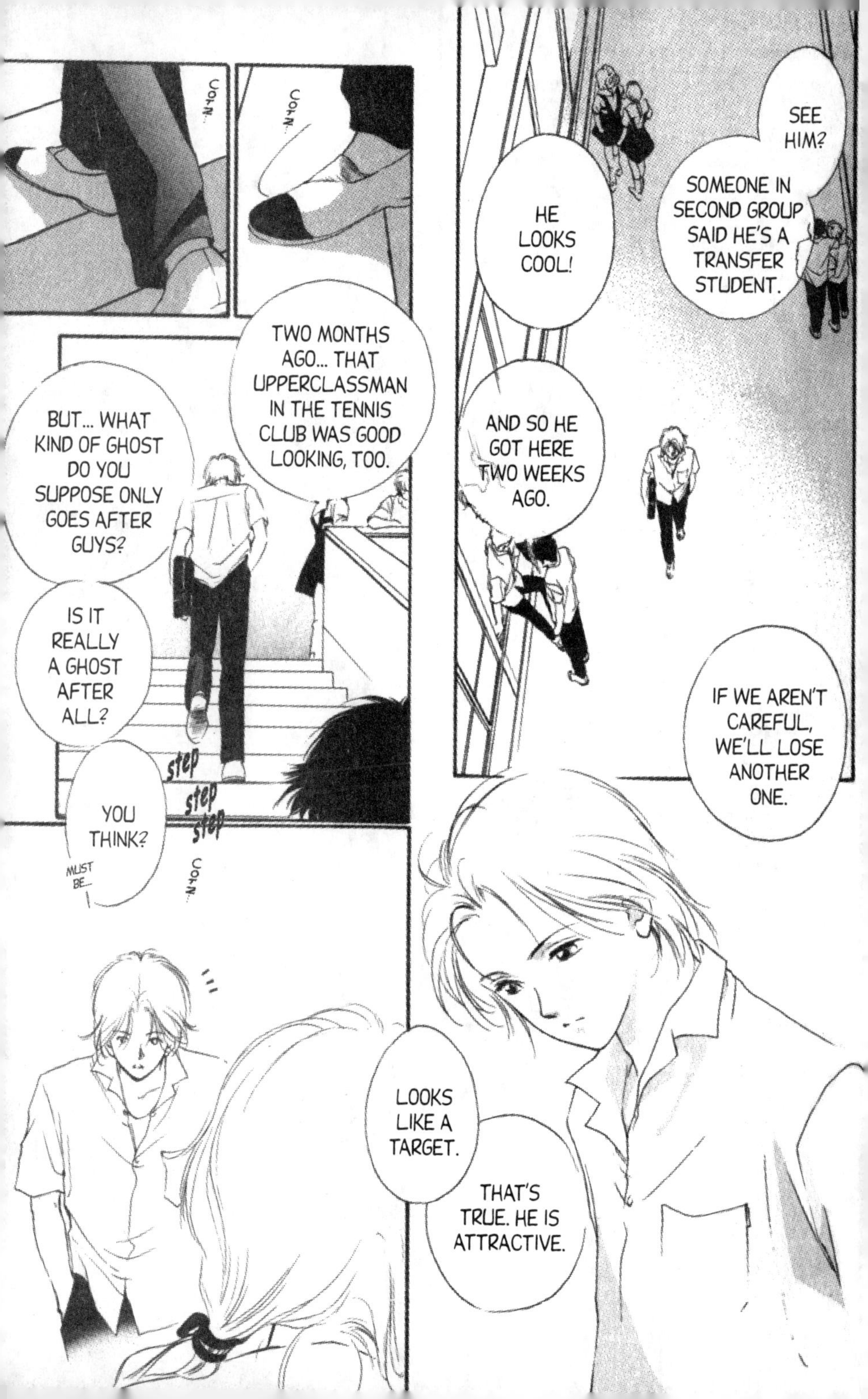
SEE HIM?
SOMEONE IN SECOND GROUP SAID HE'S A TRANSFER STUDENT.
HE LOOKS COOL!
AND SO HE GOT HERE TWO WEEKS AGO.
IF WE AREN'T CAREFUL, WE'LL LOSE ANOTHER ONE.
LOOKS LIKE A TARGET.
THAT'S TRUE. HE IS ATTRACTIVE.
TWO MONTHS AGO... THAT UPPERCLASSMAN IN THE TENNIS CLUB WAS GOOD LOOKING, TOO.
BUT... WHAT KIND OF GHOST DO YOU SUPPOSE ONLY GOES AFTER GUYS?
IS IT REALLY A GHOST AFTER ALL?
step
step
step
YOU THINK?
MUST BE...

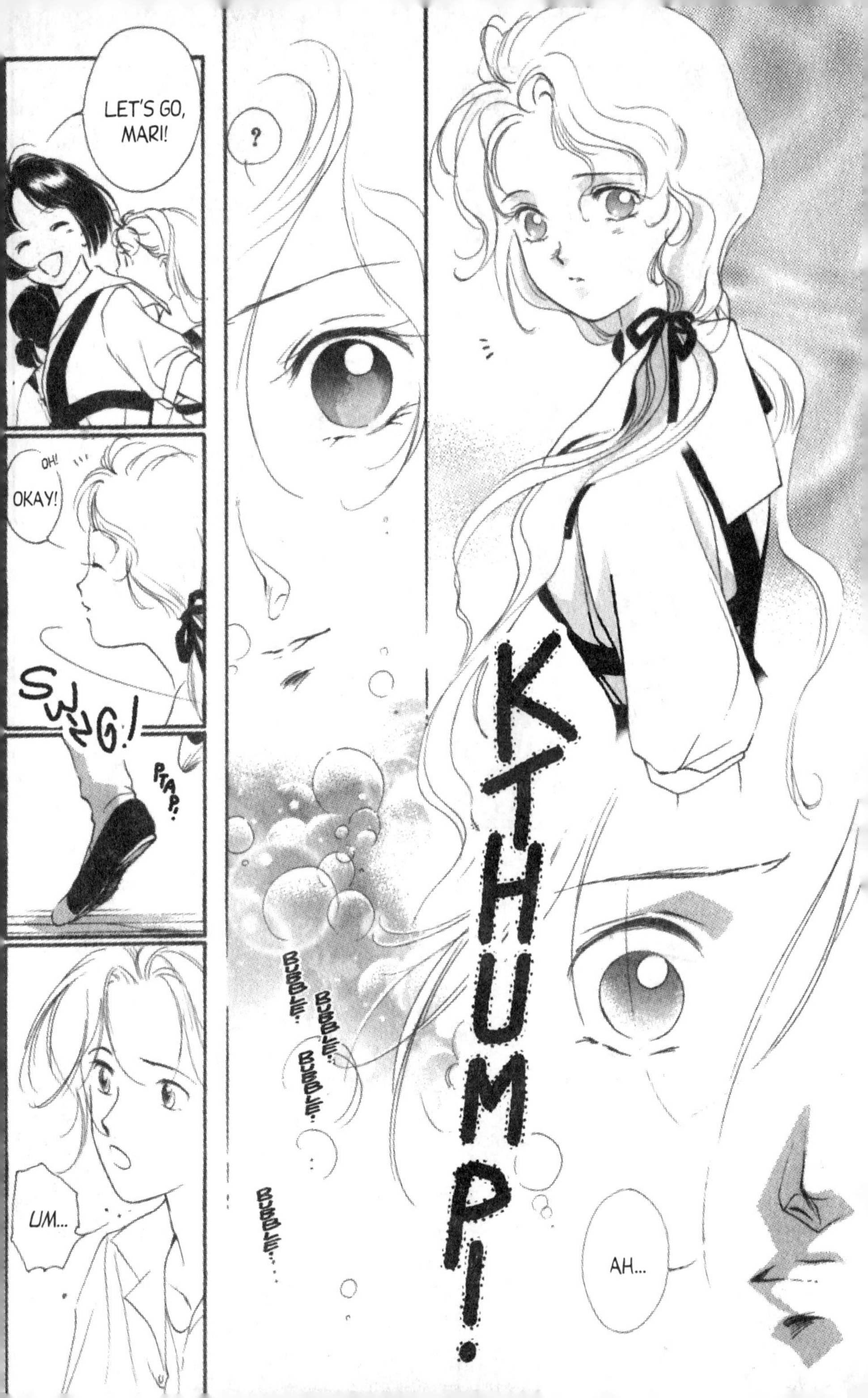
KTHUMP!
AH...
?
BUBBLE... BUBBLE... BUBBLE...
BUBBLE...
LET'S GO, MARI!
OH!
OKAY!
SWING!
PTAP.
UM...

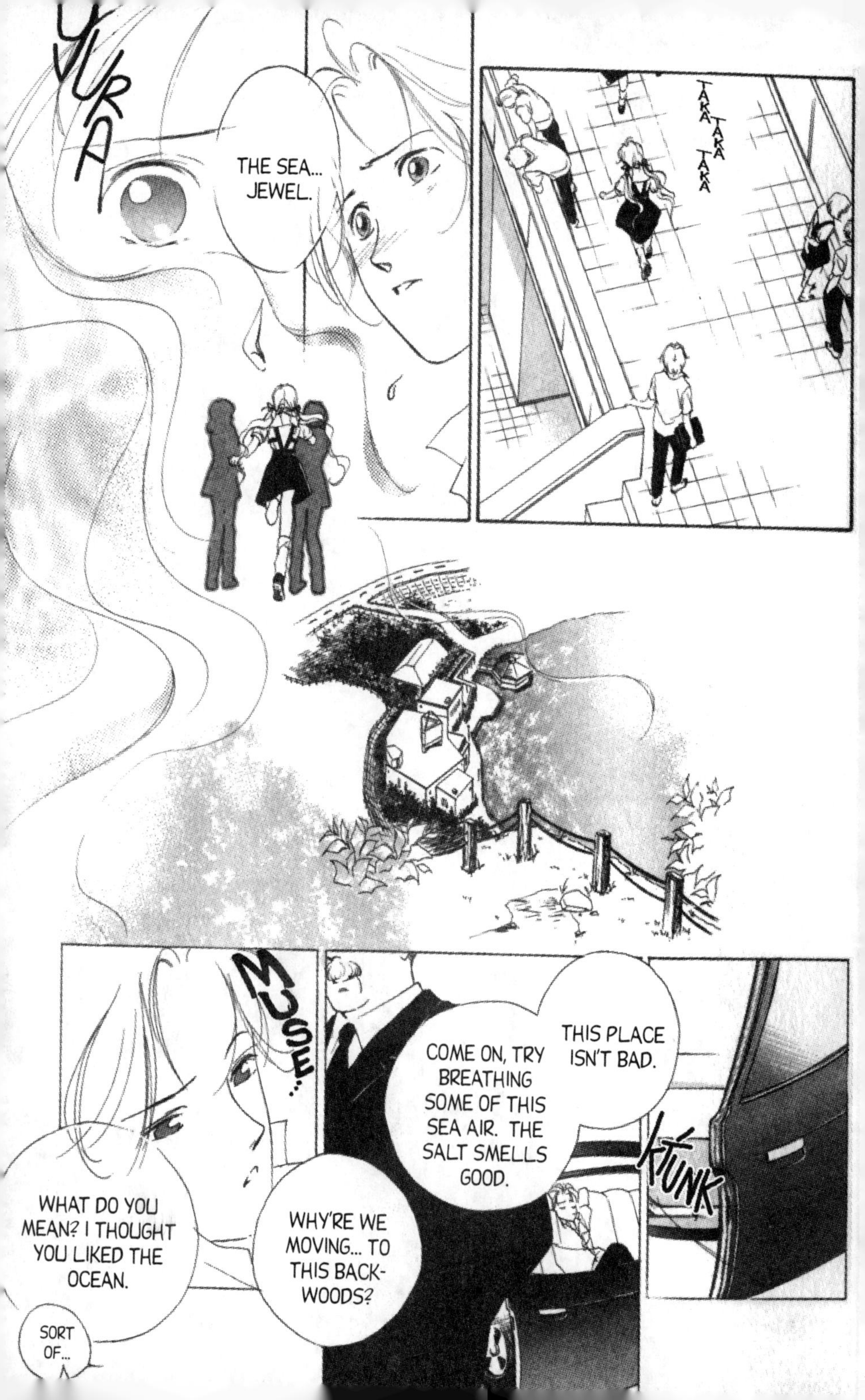
TAKA TAKA TAKA
YURA
THE SEA... JEWEL.
KTUNK
THIS PLACE ISN'T BAD.
COME ON, TRY BREATHING SOME OF THIS SEA AIR. THE SALT SMELLS GOOD.
WHY'RE WE MOVING... TO THIS BACK-WOODS?
MUSE...
WHAT DO YOU MEAN? I THOUGHT YOU LIKED THE OCEAN.
SORT OF...

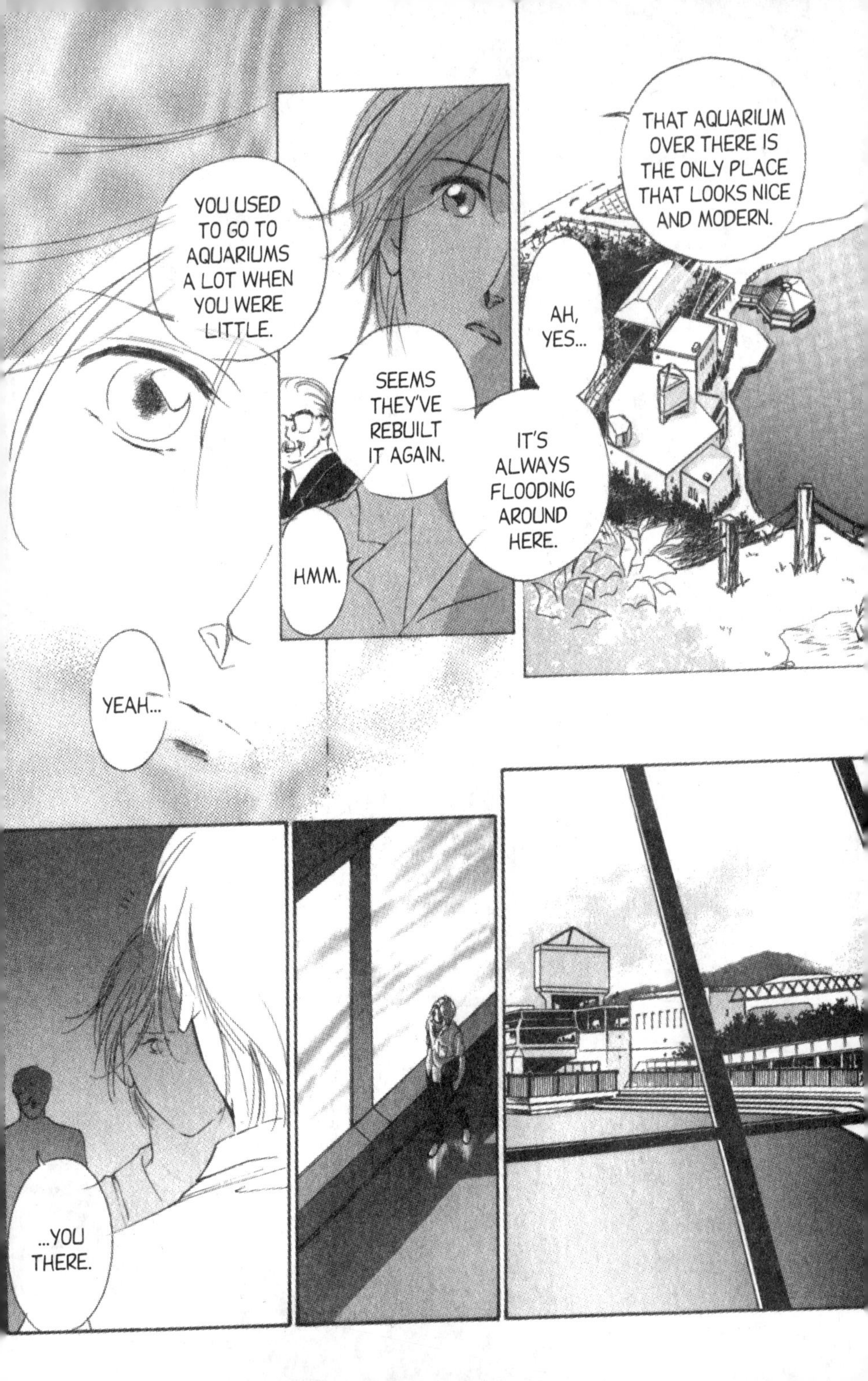
THAT AQUARIUM OVER THERE IS THE ONLY PLACE THAT LOOKS NICE AND MODERN.
AH, YES...
IT'S ALWAYS FLOODING AROUND HERE.
SEEMS THEY'VE REBUILT IT AGAIN.
HMM.
YOU USED TO GO TO AQUARIUMS A LOT WHEN YOU WERE LITTLE.
YEAH...
...YOU THERE.

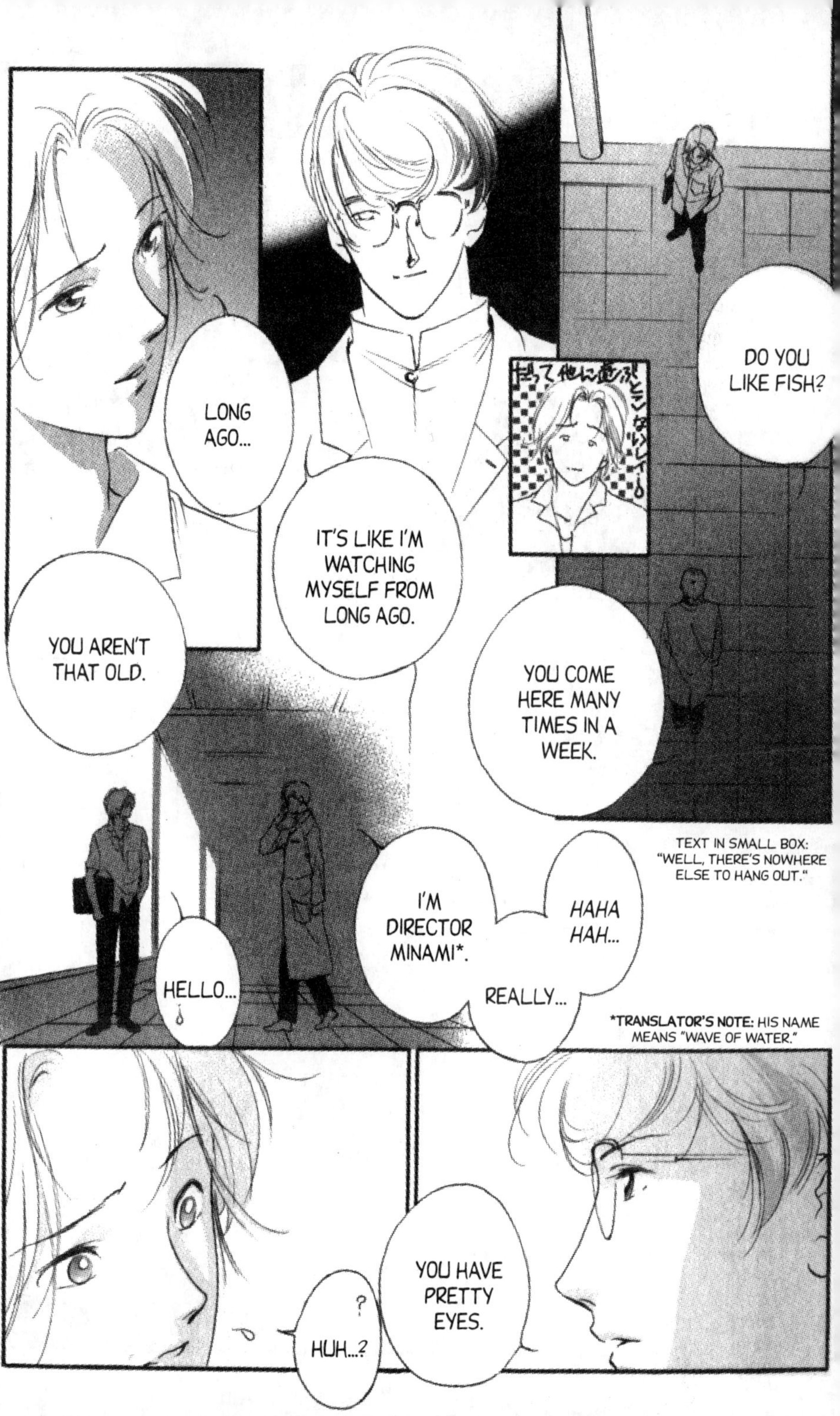
DO YOU LIKE FISH?
YOU COME HERE MANY TIMES IN A WEEK.
LONG AGO...
IT'S LIKE I'M WATCHING MYSELF FROM LONG AGO.
YOU AREN'T THAT OLD.
HAHA HAH...
I'M DIRECTOR MINAMI*.
REALLY...
HELLO...
YOU HAVE PRETTY EYES.
HUH...?

TEXT IN SMALL BOX: "WELL, THERE'S NOWHERE ELSE TO HANG OUT."

***TRANSLATOR'S NOTE:** HIS NAME MEANS "WAVE OF WATER."

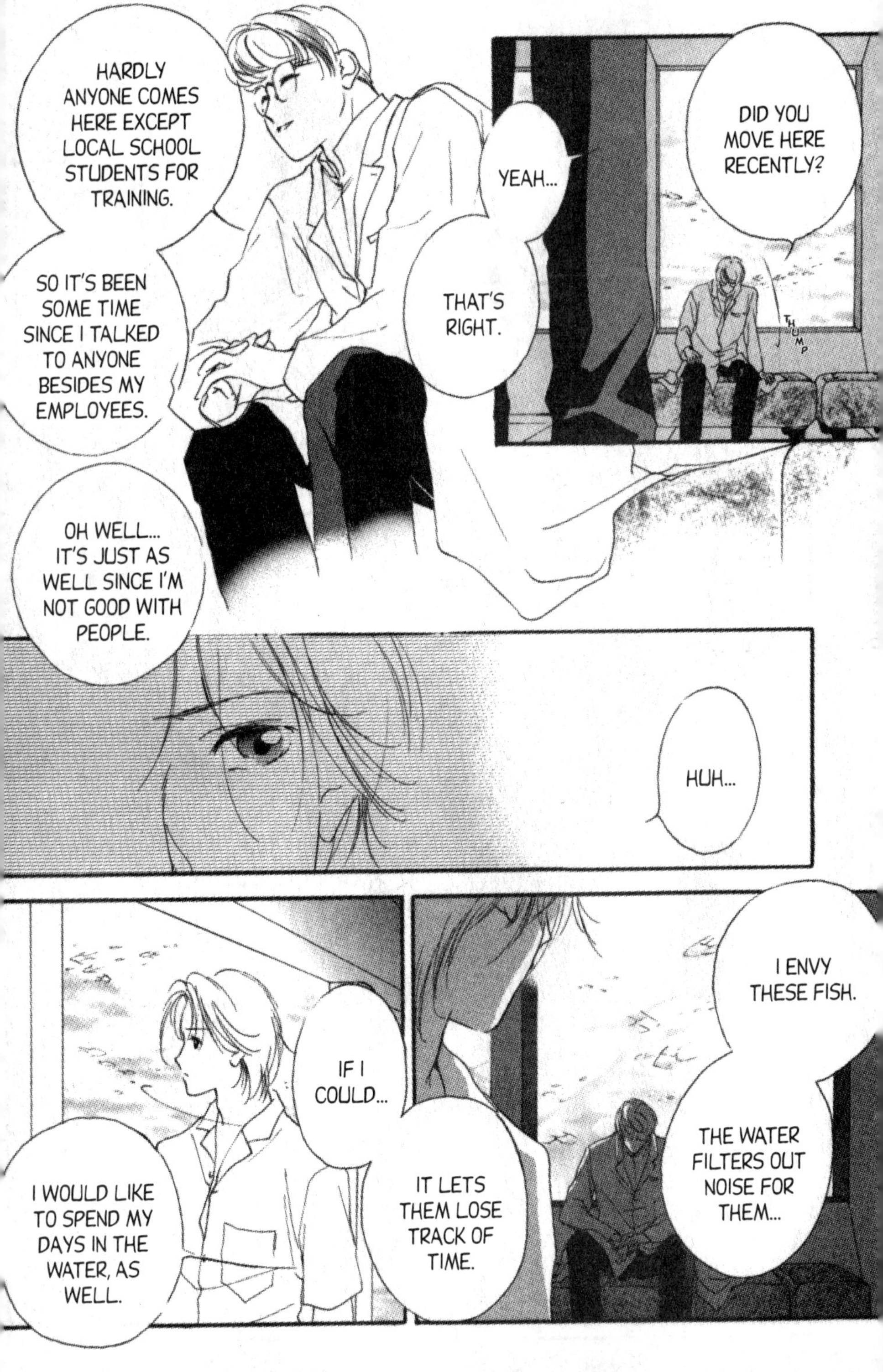
DID YOU MOVE HERE RECENTLY?
THUMP
YEAH...
THAT'S RIGHT.
HARDLY ANYONE COMES HERE EXCEPT LOCAL SCHOOL STUDENTS FOR TRAINING.
SO IT'S BEEN SOME TIME SINCE I TALKED TO ANYONE BESIDES MY EMPLOYEES.
OH WELL... IT'S JUST AS WELL SINCE I'M NOT GOOD WITH PEOPLE.
HUH...
I ENVY THESE FISH.
THE WATER FILTERS OUT NOISE FOR THEM...
IT LETS THEM LOSE TRACK OF TIME.
IF I COULD...
I WOULD LIKE TO SPEND MY DAYS IN THE WATER, AS WELL.

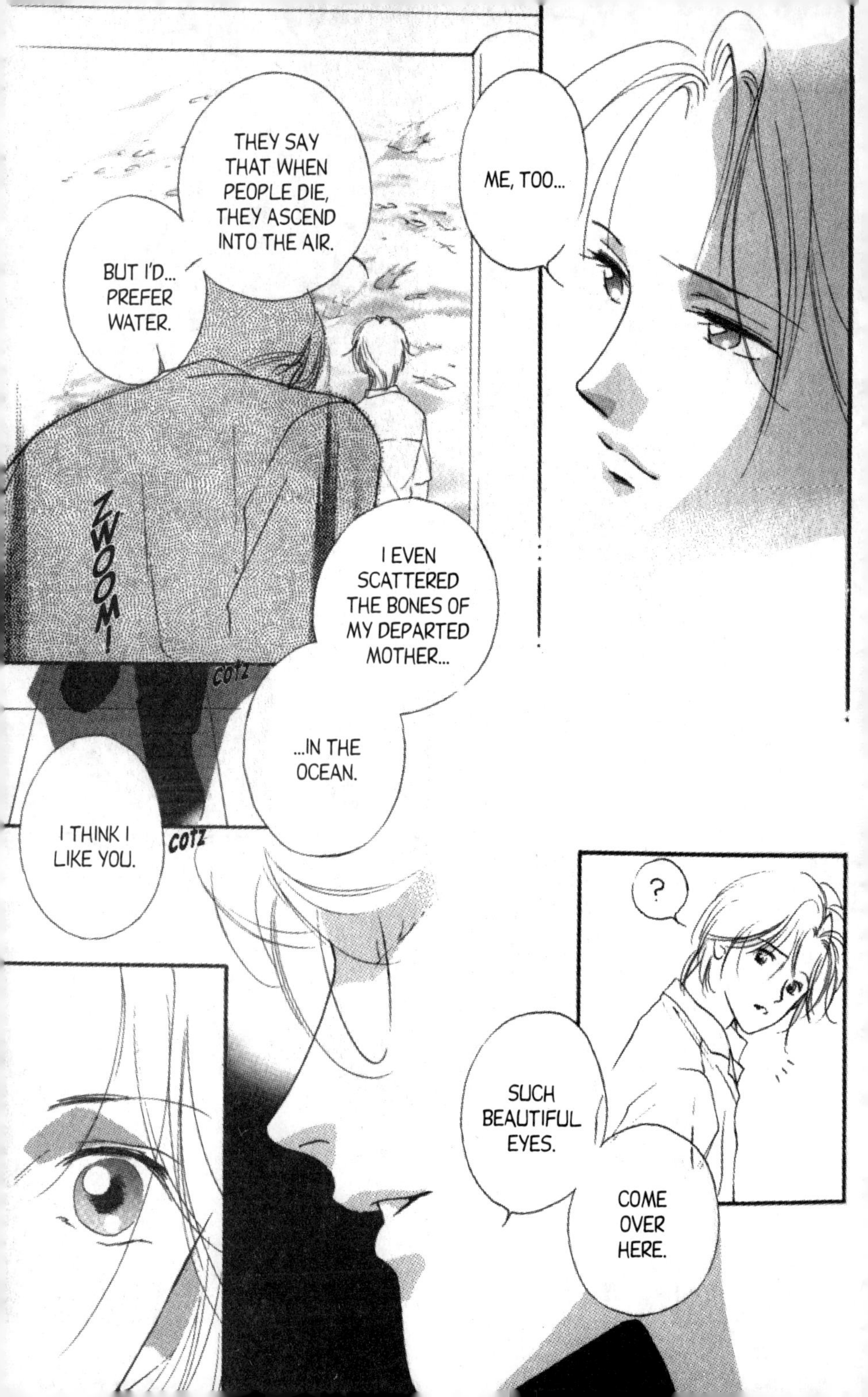
ME, TOO...
THEY SAY THAT WHEN PEOPLE DIE, THEY ASCEND INTO THE AIR.
BUT I'D... PREFER WATER.
ZWOOM!
I EVEN SCATTERED THE BONES OF MY DEPARTED MOTHER...
...IN THE OCEAN.
COTZ
COTZ
I THINK I LIKE YOU.
?
SUCH BEAUTIFUL EYES.
COME OVER HERE.

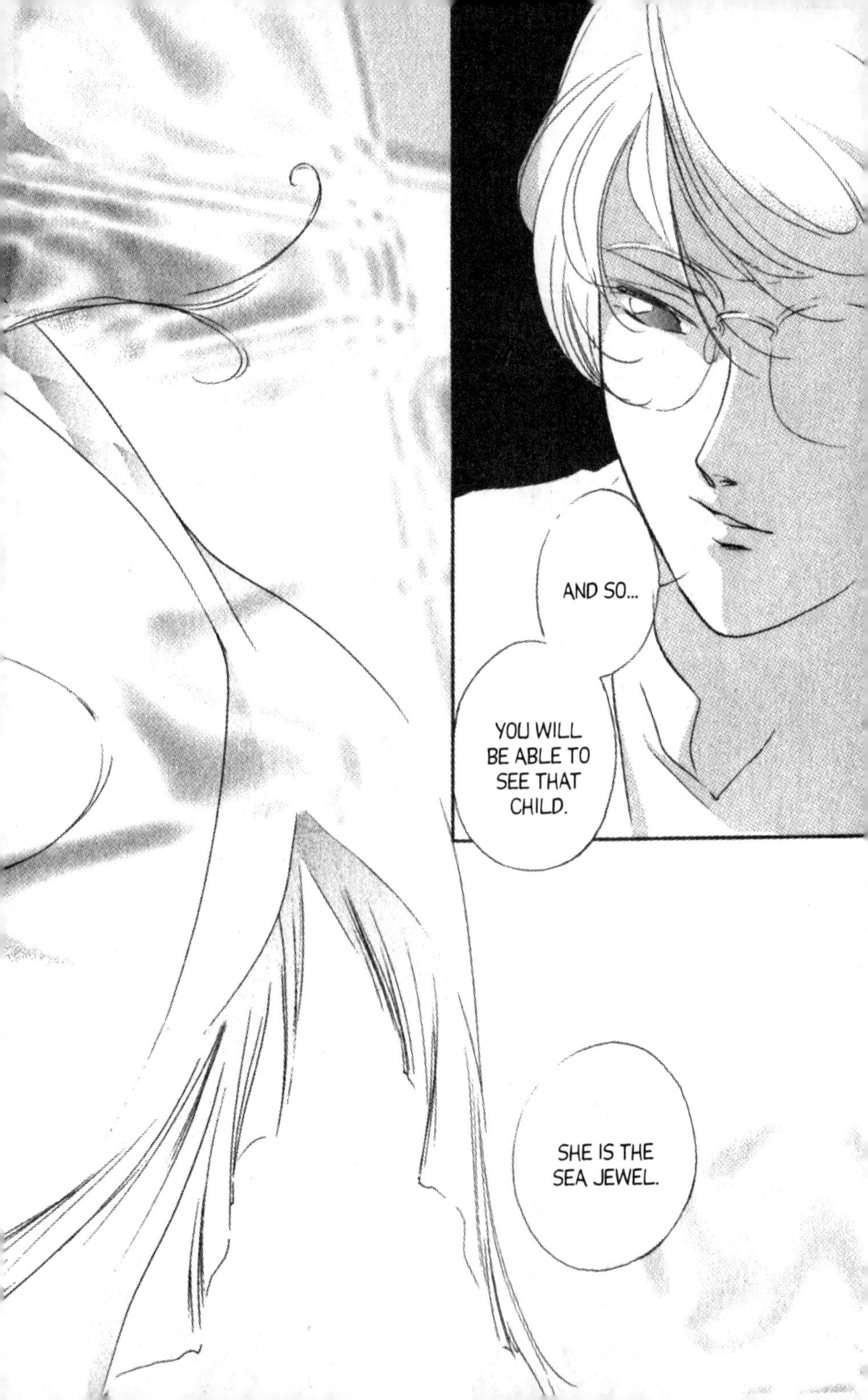
AND SO...
YOU WILL BE ABLE TO SEE THAT CHILD.
SHE IS THE SEA JEWEL.

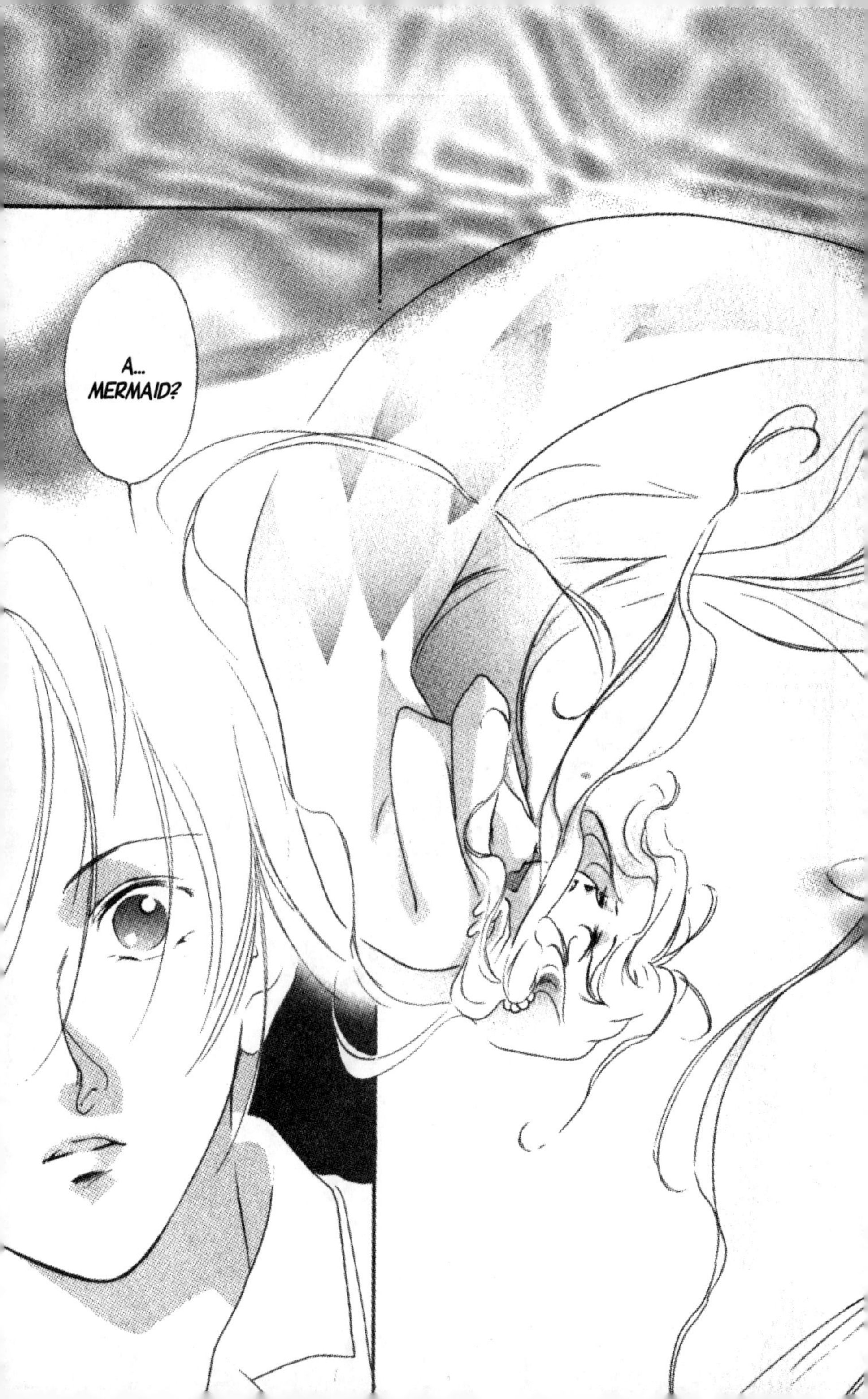
A... MERMAID?

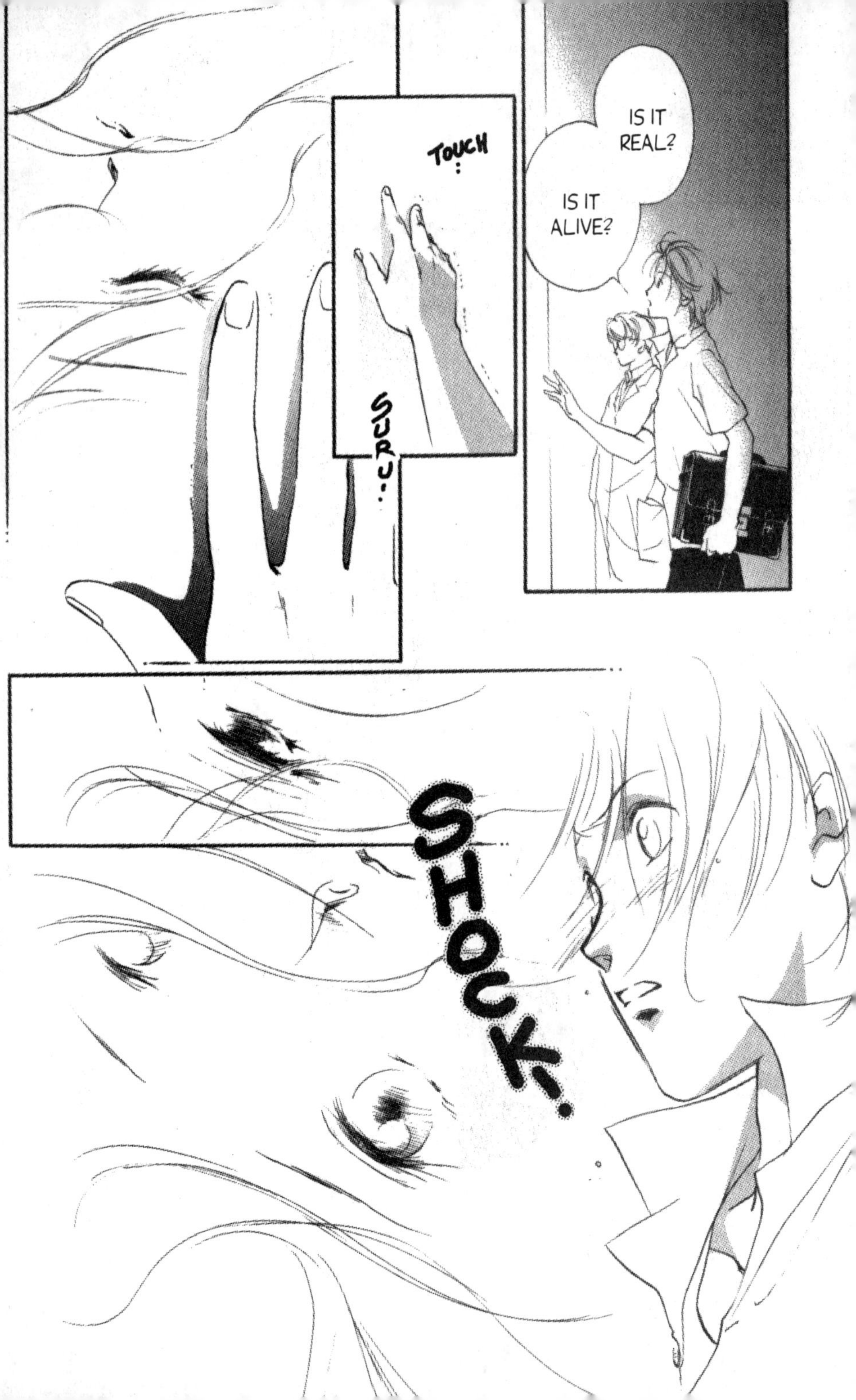
IS IT REAL?
IS IT ALIVE?
TOUCH
SURU..
SHOCK!

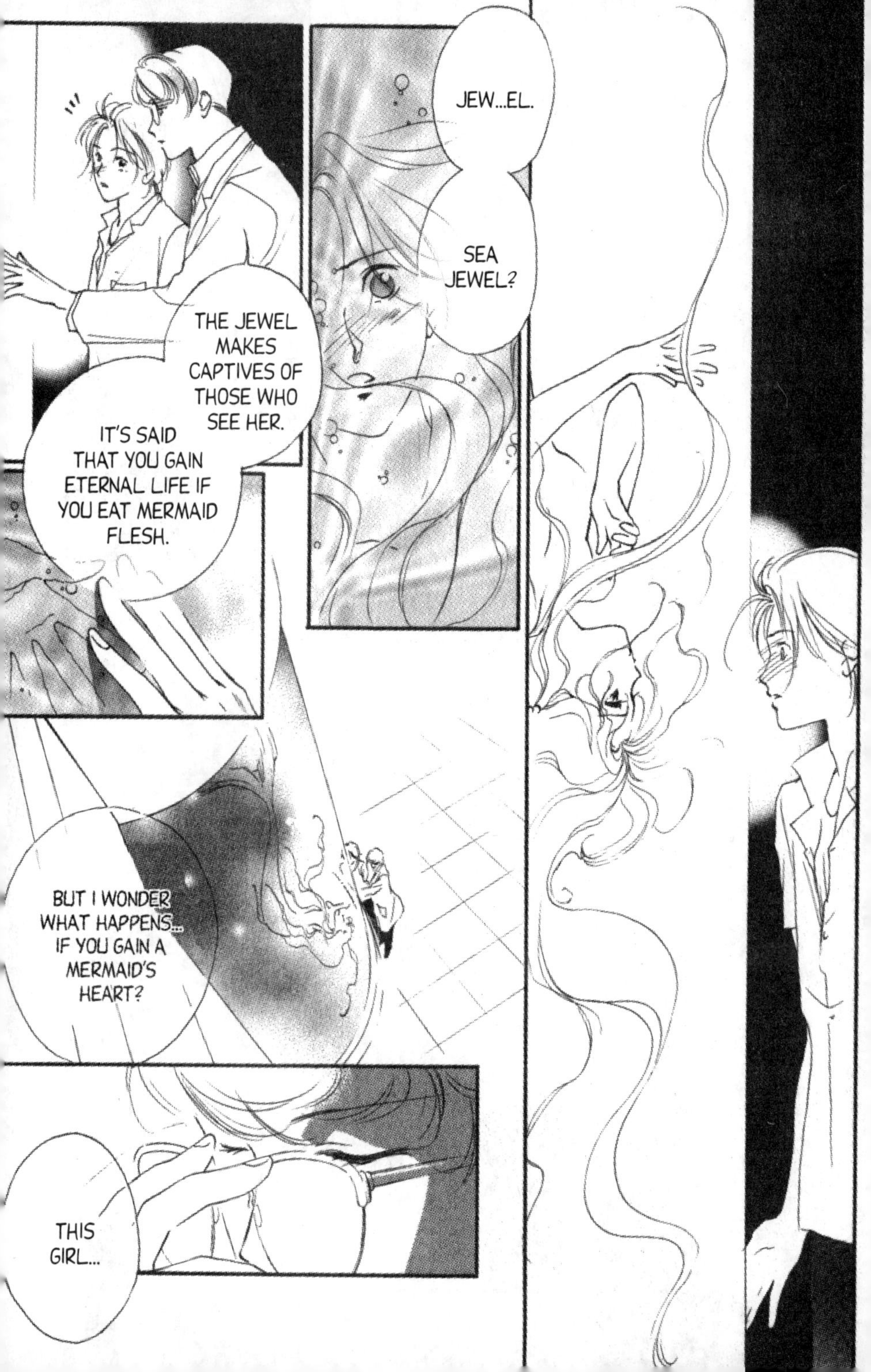
JEW...EL.
SEA JEWEL?
THE JEWEL MAKES CAPTIVES OF THOSE WHO SEE HER.
IT'S SAID THAT YOU GAIN ETERNAL LIFE IF YOU EAT MERMAID FLESH.
BUT I WONDER WHAT HAPPENS... IF YOU GAIN A MERMAID'S HEART?
THIS GIRL...

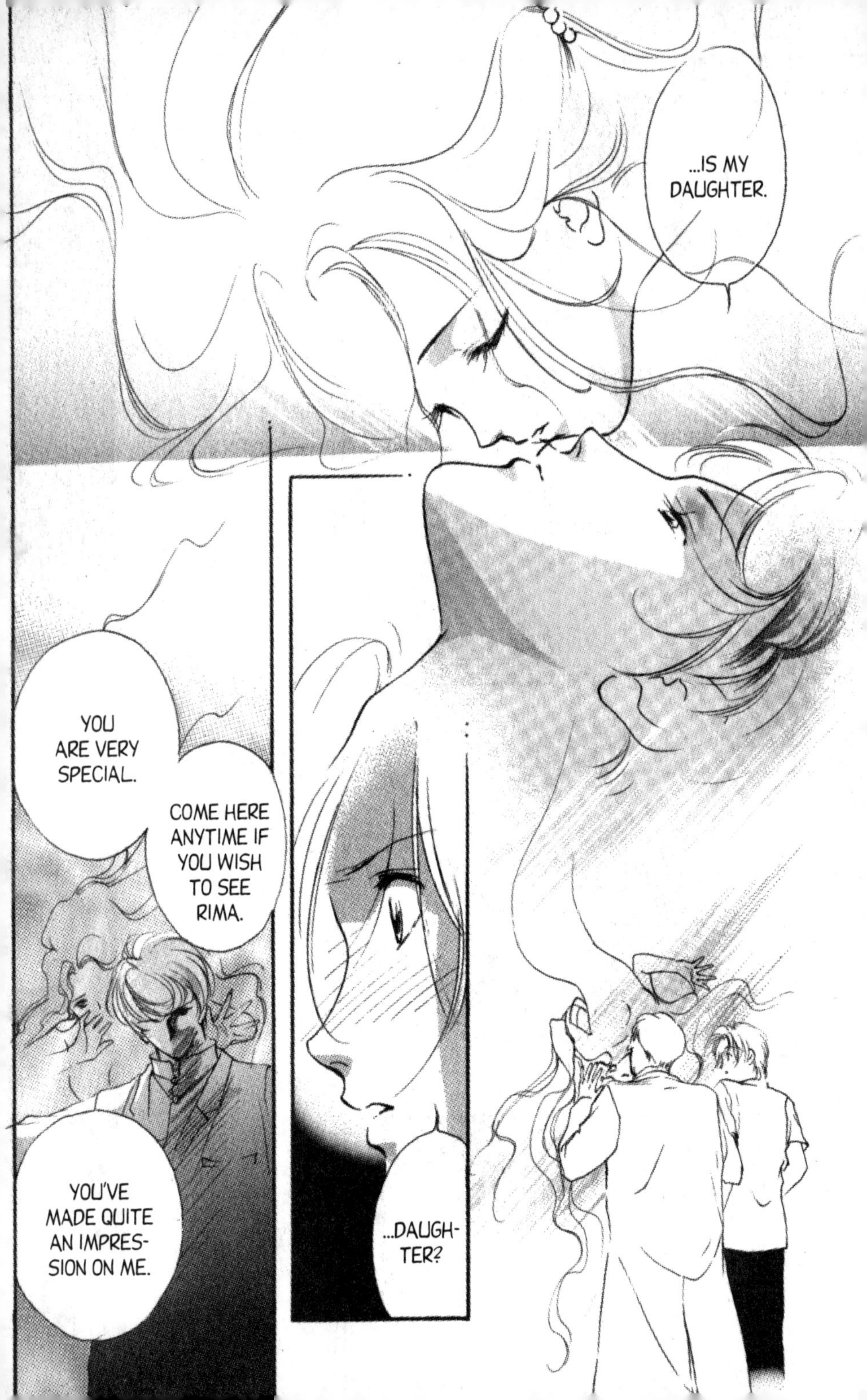
...IS MY DAUGHTER.
...DAUGHTER?
YOU ARE VERY SPECIAL.
COME HERE ANYTIME IF YOU WISH TO SEE RIMA.
YOU'VE MADE QUITE AN IMPRESSION ON ME.

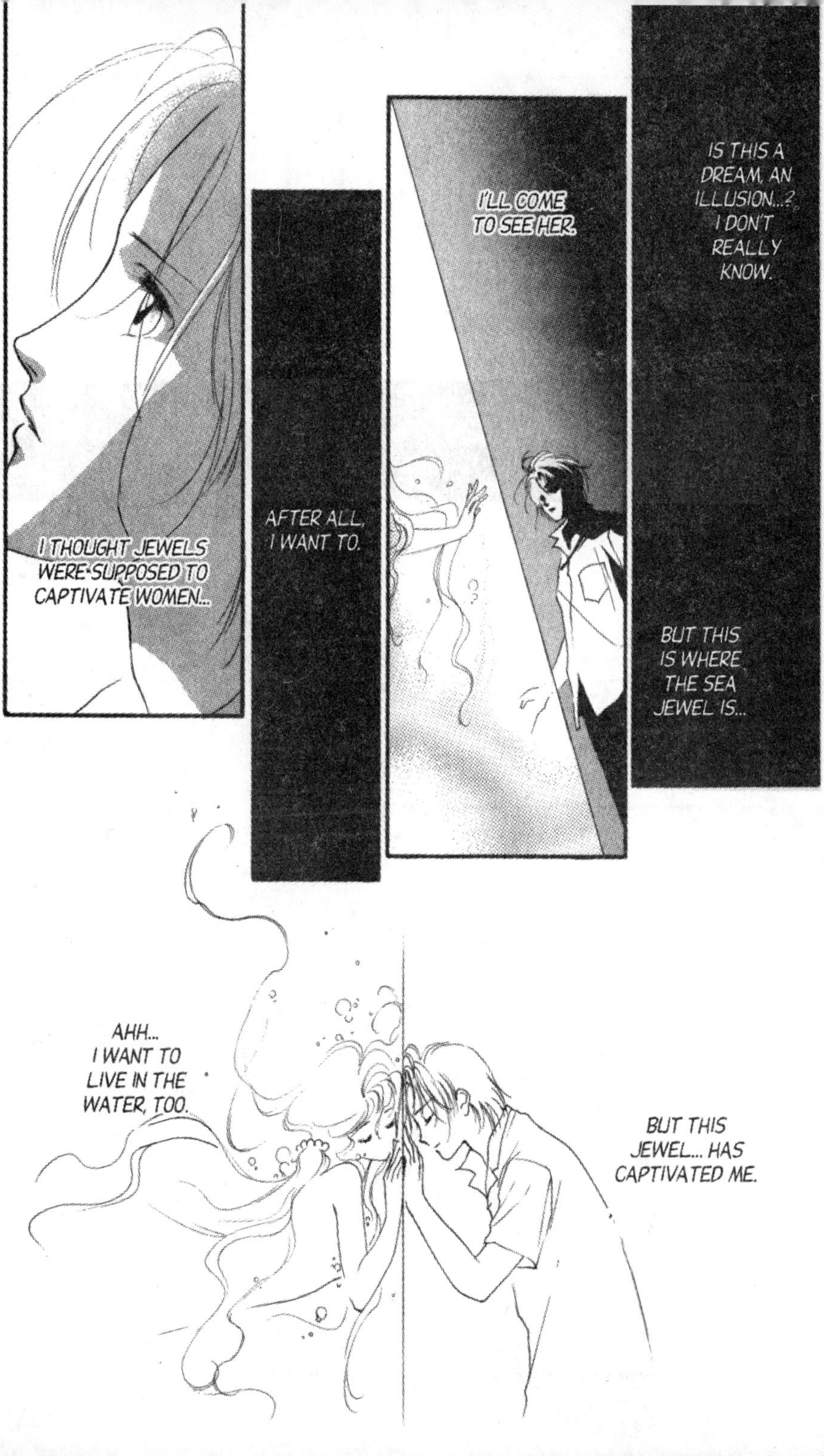
IS THIS A DREAM, AN ILLUSION...? I DON'T REALLY KNOW.
BUT THIS IS WHERE THE SEA JEWEL IS...
I'LL COME TO SEE HER.
AFTER ALL, I WANT TO.
I THOUGHT JEWELS WERE SUPPOSED TO CAPTIVATE WOMEN...
BUT THIS JEWEL... HAS CAPTIVATED ME.
AHH... I WANT TO LIVE IN THE WATER, TOO.

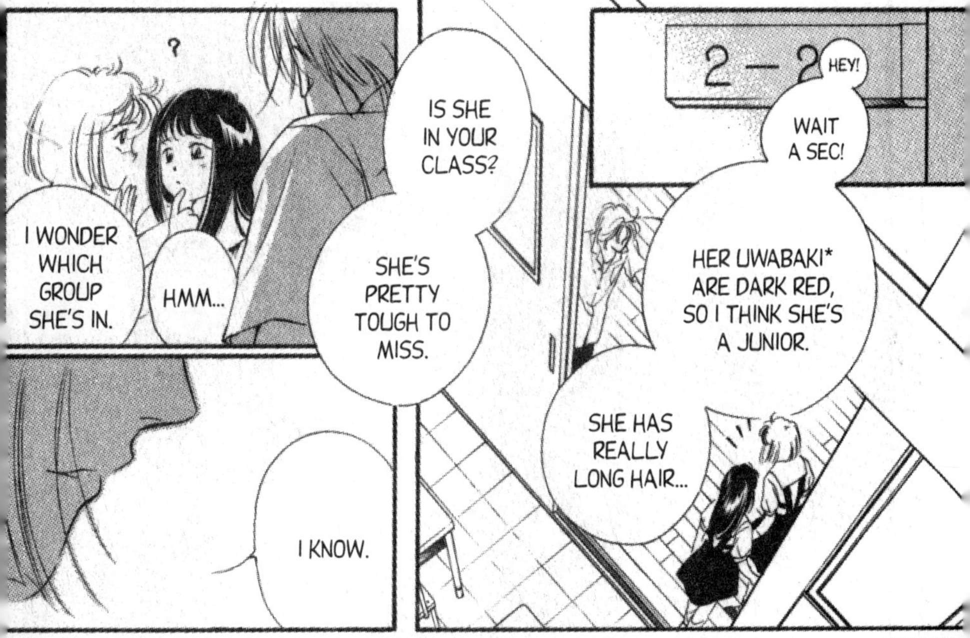
HEY!
WAIT A SEC!
HER UWABAKI* ARE DARK RED, SO I THINK SHE'S A JUNIOR.
SHE HAS REALLY LONG HAIR...
IS SHE IN YOUR CLASS?
SHE'S PRETTY TOUGH TO MISS.
I WONDER WHICH GROUP SHE'S IN.
HMM...
I KNOW.

TRANSLATOR'S NOTE: UWABAKI ARE SLIPPER-TYPE SHOES WORN BY JAPANESE STUDENTS WHILE INSIDE THEIR SCHOOL BUILDING. AS PART OF THE UNIFORM, THEY OFTEN HAVE VARIOUS COLOURED TRIMS TO DENOTE A STUDENT'S GRADE LEVEL. IN THIS CASE, KYO SURMISES THAT MARI IS A SECOND-YEAR STUDENT.

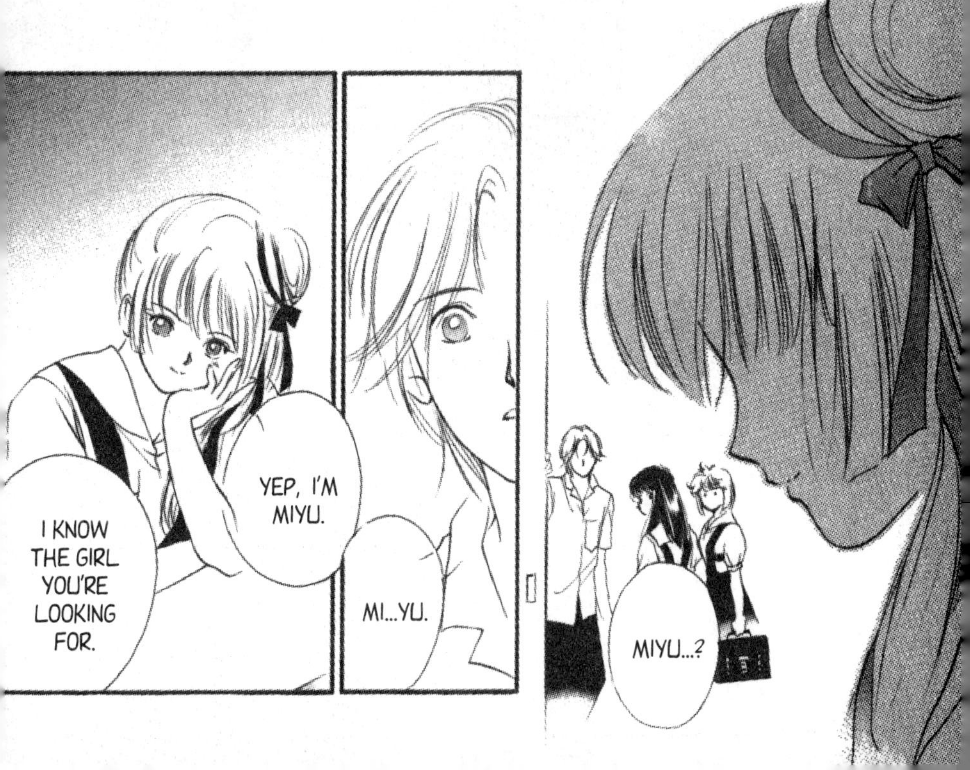
MIYU...?
MI...YU.
YEP, I'M MIYU.
I KNOW THE GIRL YOU'RE LOOKING FOR.

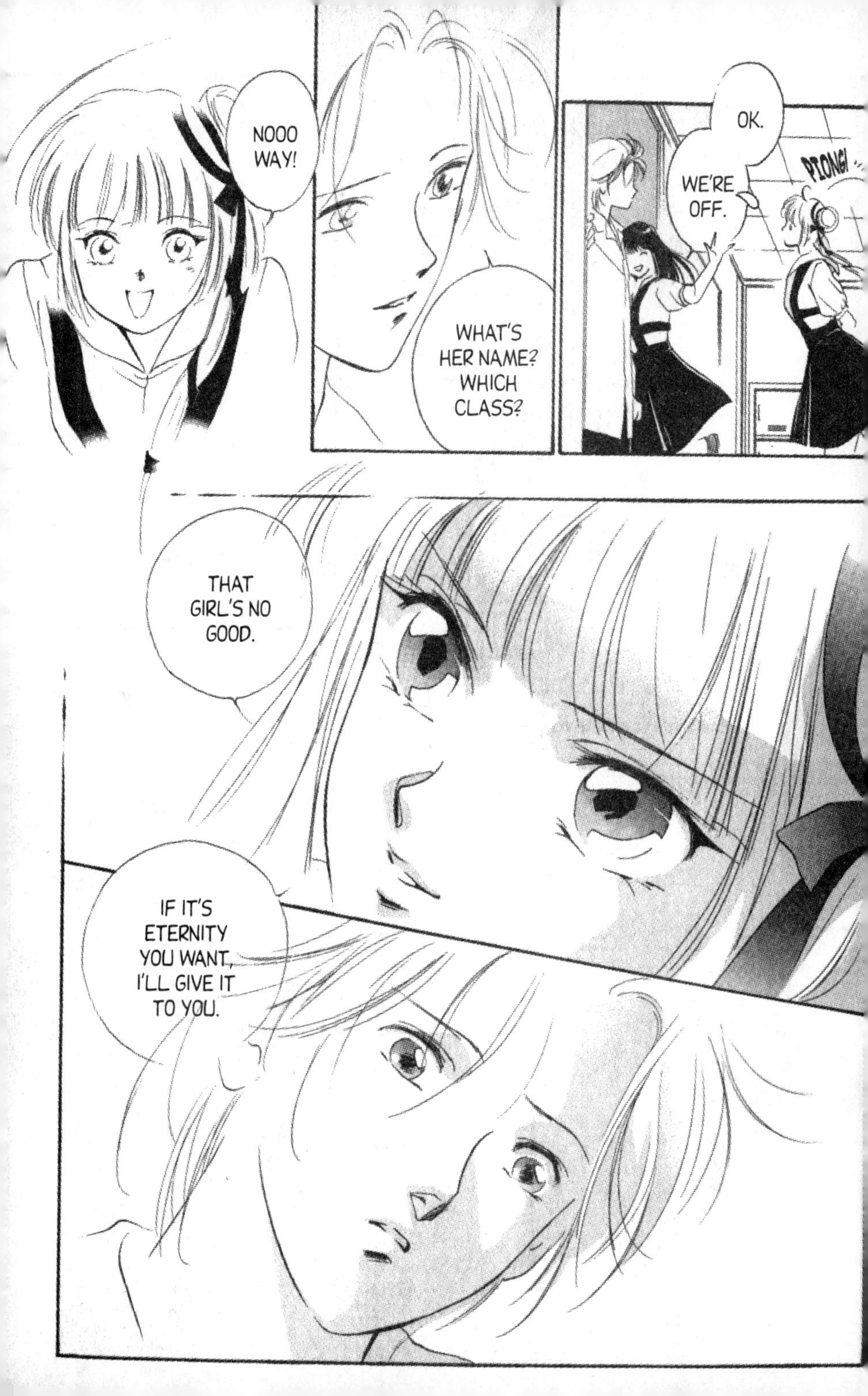
OK.
WE'RE OFF.
PIONG!
WHAT'S HER NAME? WHICH CLASS?
NOOO WAY!
THAT GIRL'S NO GOOD.
IF IT'S ETERNITY YOU WANT, I'LL GIVE IT TO YOU.

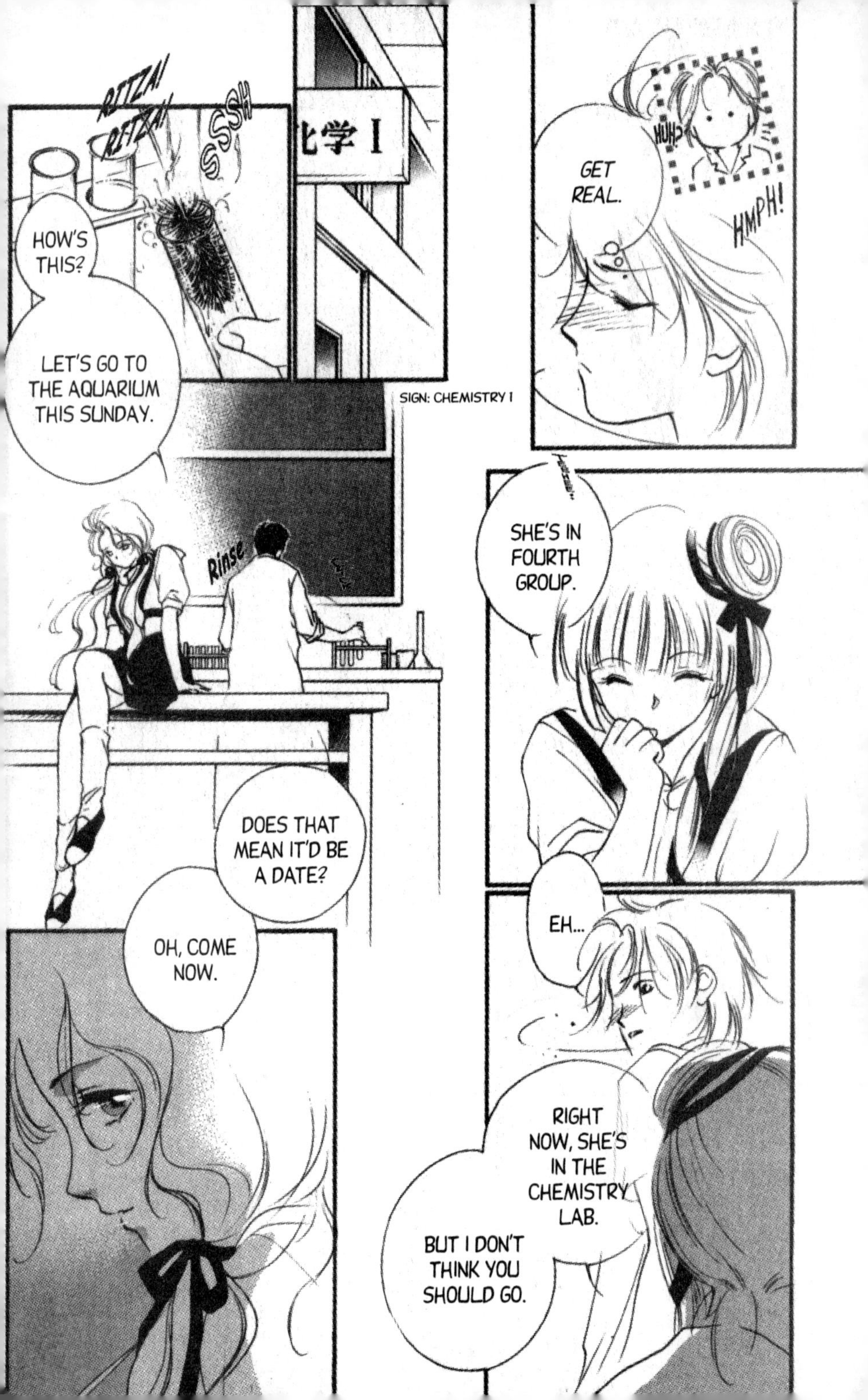
GET REAL.
HUH?
HMPH!
SHE'S IN FOURTH GROUP.
EH...
RIGHT NOW, SHE'S IN THE CHEMISTRY LAB.
BUT I DON'T THINK YOU SHOULD GO.
化学 I
SIGN: CHEMISTRY I
RITZA! RITZA!
SSSH
HOW'S THIS?
LET'S GO TO THE AQUARIUM THIS SUNDAY.
Rinse
DOES THAT MEAN IT'D BE A DATE?
OH, COME NOW.

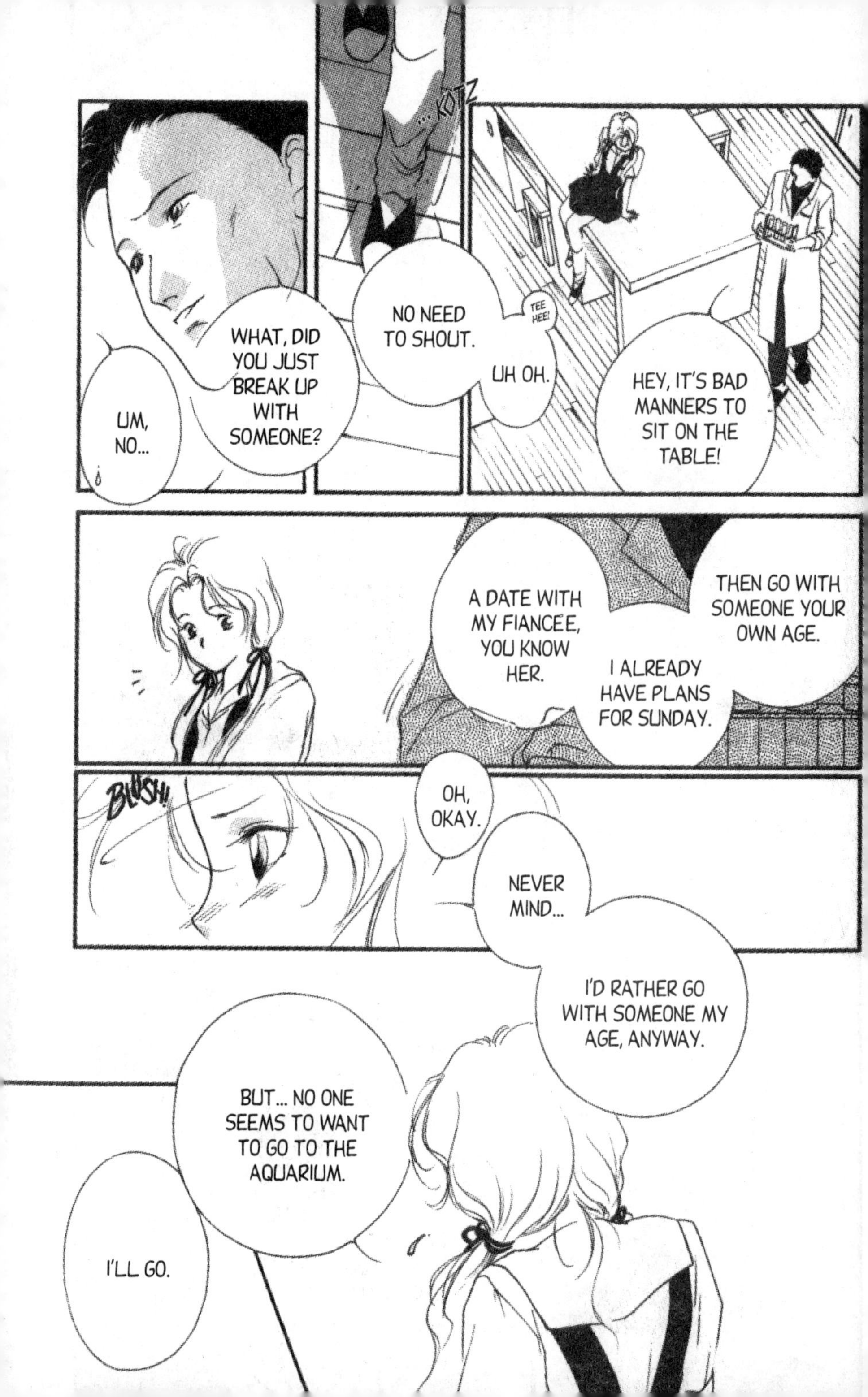
HEY, IT'S BAD MANNERS TO SIT ON THE TABLE!
TEE HEE!
UH OH.
NO NEED TO SHOUT.
...KOTZ
WHAT, DID YOU JUST BREAK UP WITH SOMEONE?
UM, NO...
THEN GO WITH SOMEONE YOUR OWN AGE.
A DATE WITH MY FIANCEE, YOU KNOW HER.
I ALREADY HAVE PLANS FOR SUNDAY.
OH, OKAY.
BLUSH!
NEVER MIND...
I'D RATHER GO WITH SOMEONE MY AGE, ANYWAY.
BUT... NO ONE SEEMS TO WANT TO GO TO THE AQUARIUM.
I'LL GO.

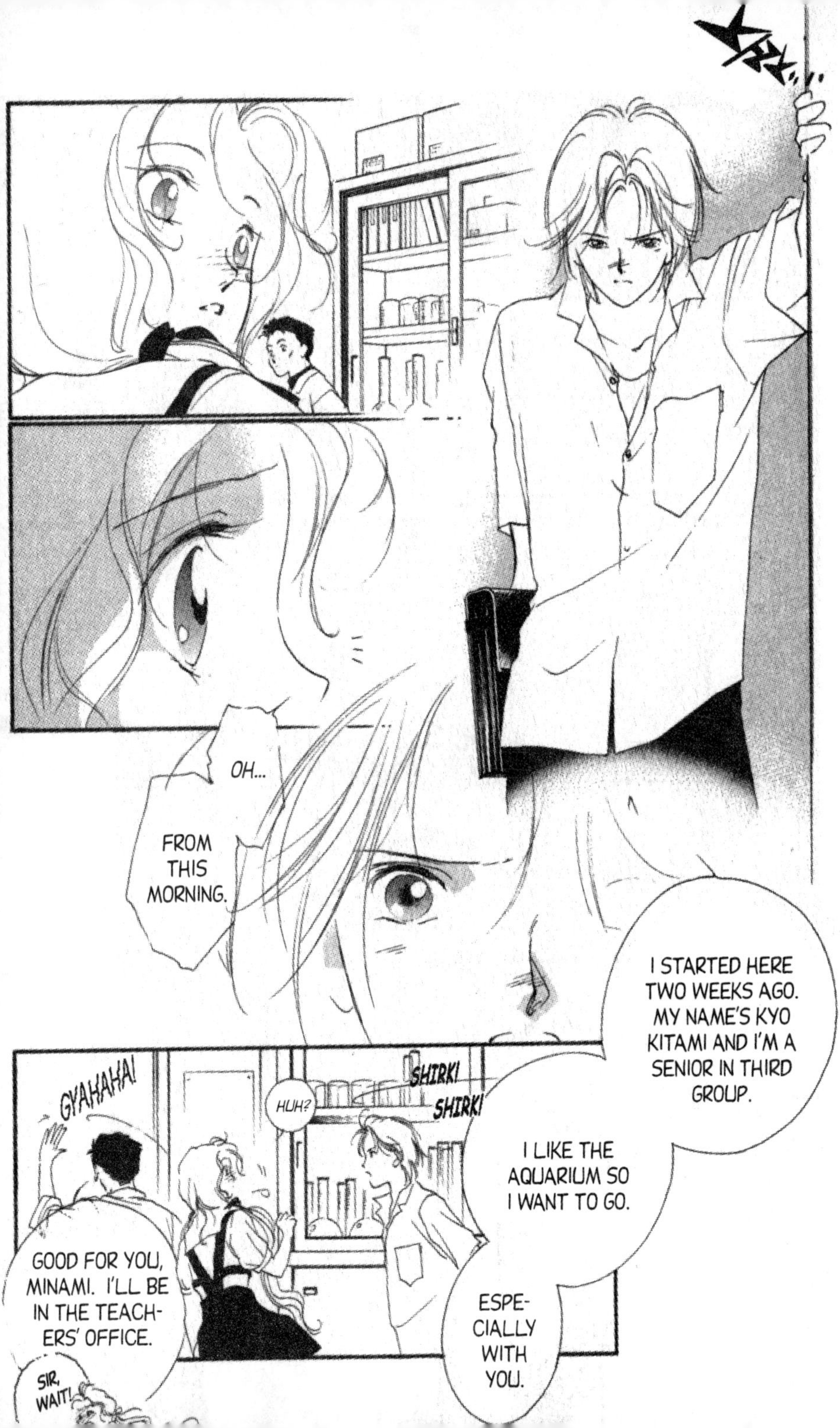
OH...
FROM THIS MORNING.
I STARTED HERE TWO WEEKS AGO. MY NAME'S KYO KITAMI AND I'M A SENIOR IN THIRD GROUP.
I LIKE THE AQUARIUM SO I WANT TO GO.
ESPE-CIALLY WITH YOU.
SHIRK!
SHIRK!
HUH?
GYAHAHA!
GOOD FOR YOU, MINAMI. I'LL BE IN THE TEACH-ERS' OFFICE.
SIR, WAIT!

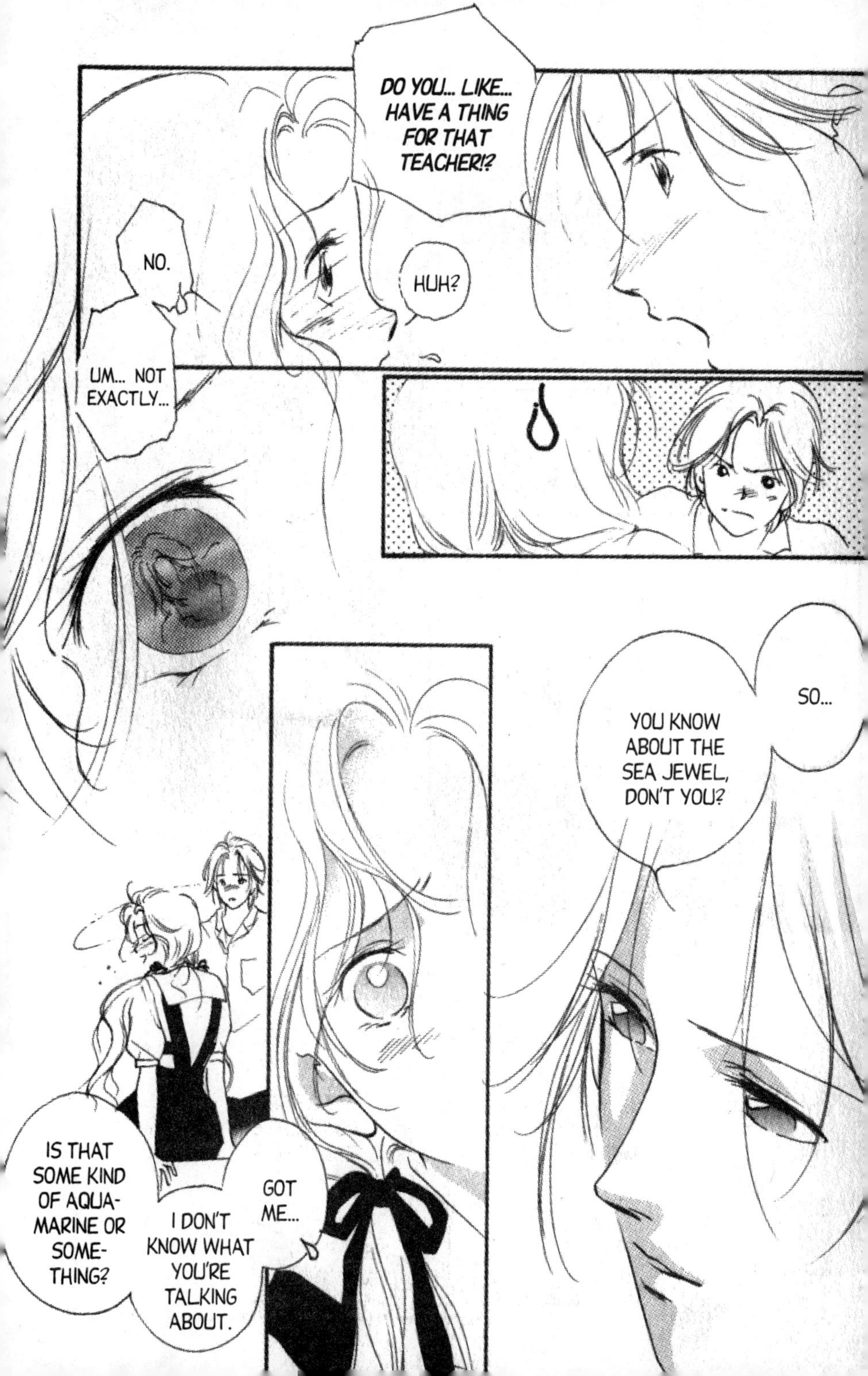
DO YOU... LIKE... HAVE A THING FOR THAT TEACHER!?
HUH?
NO.
UM... NOT EXACTLY...
SO...
YOU KNOW ABOUT THE SEA JEWEL, DON'T YOU?
GOT ME...
I DON'T KNOW WHAT YOU'RE TALKING ABOUT.
IS THAT SOME KIND OF AQUA-MARINE OR SOME-THING?

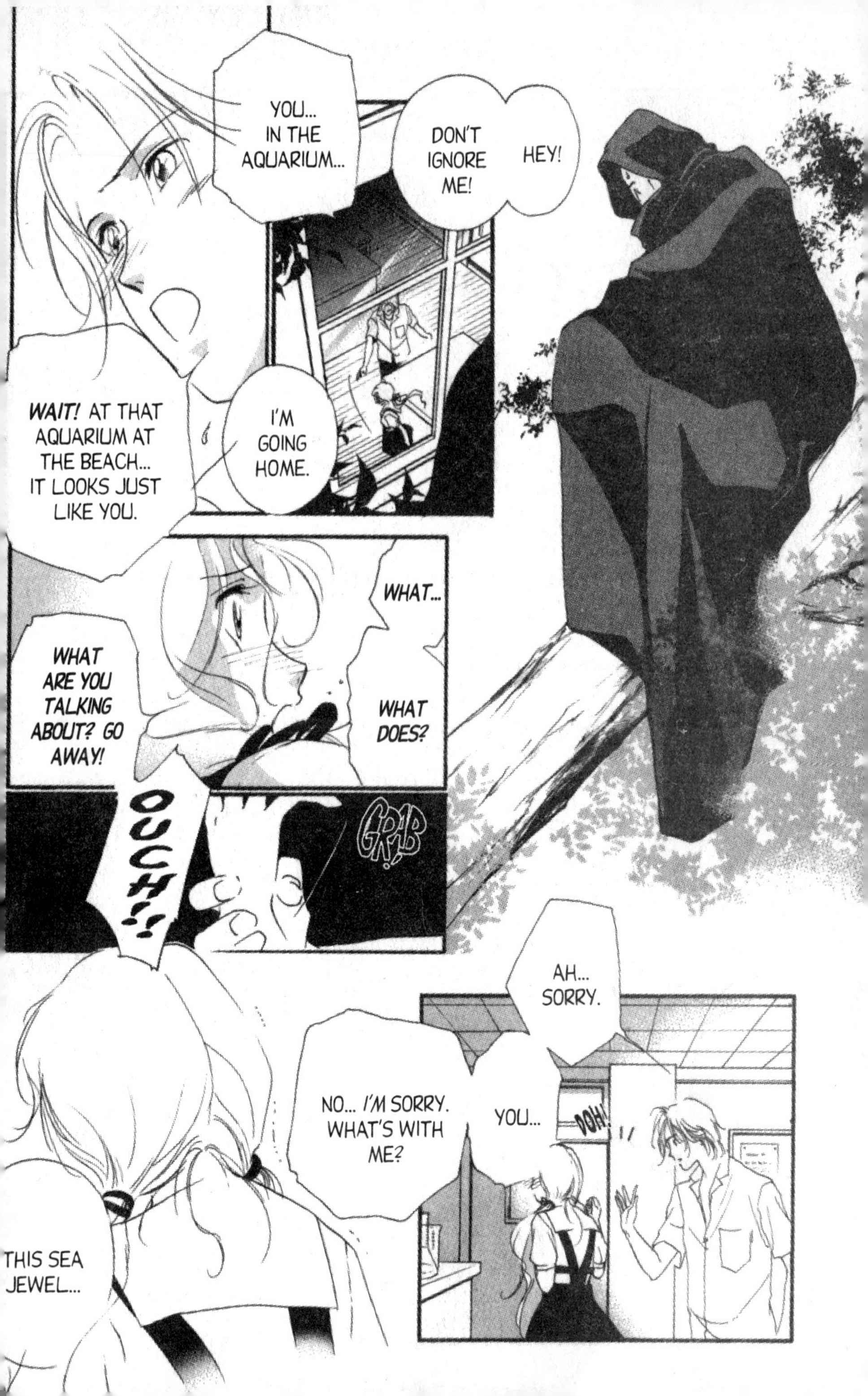
HEY!
DON'T IGNORE ME!
YOU... IN THE AQUARIUM...
I'M GOING HOME.
WAIT! AT THAT AQUARIUM AT THE BEACH... IT LOOKS JUST LIKE YOU.
WHAT...
WHAT DOES?
WHAT ARE YOU TALKING ABOUT? GO AWAY!
GRAB
OUCH!!
AH... SORRY.
YOU...
DOH!
NO... I'M SORRY. WHAT'S WITH ME?
THIS SEA JEWEL...

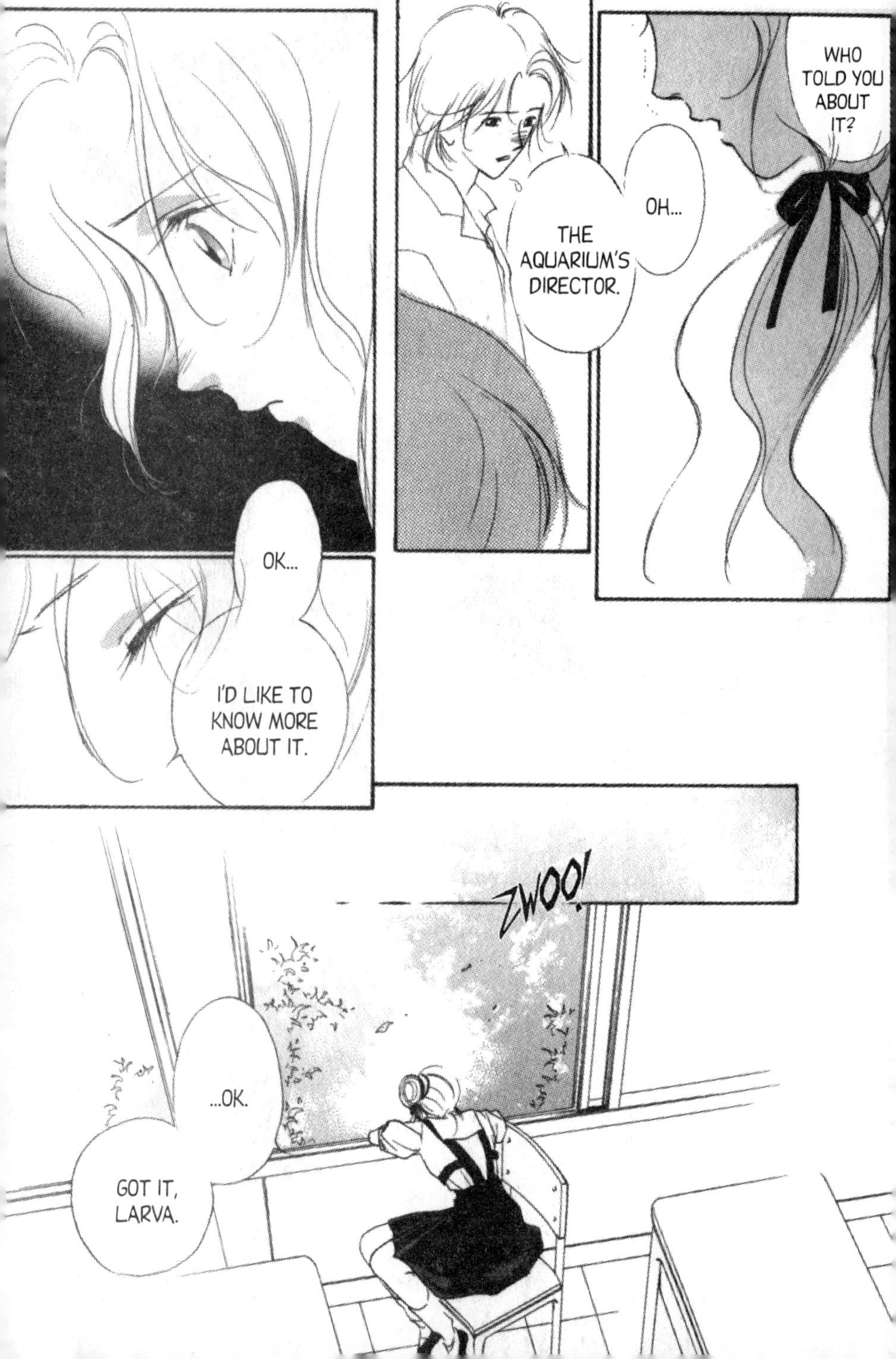
WHO TOLD YOU ABOUT IT?
OH...
THE AQUARIUM'S DIRECTOR.
OK...
I'D LIKE TO KNOW MORE ABOUT IT.
ZWOO!
...OK.
GOT IT, LARVA.

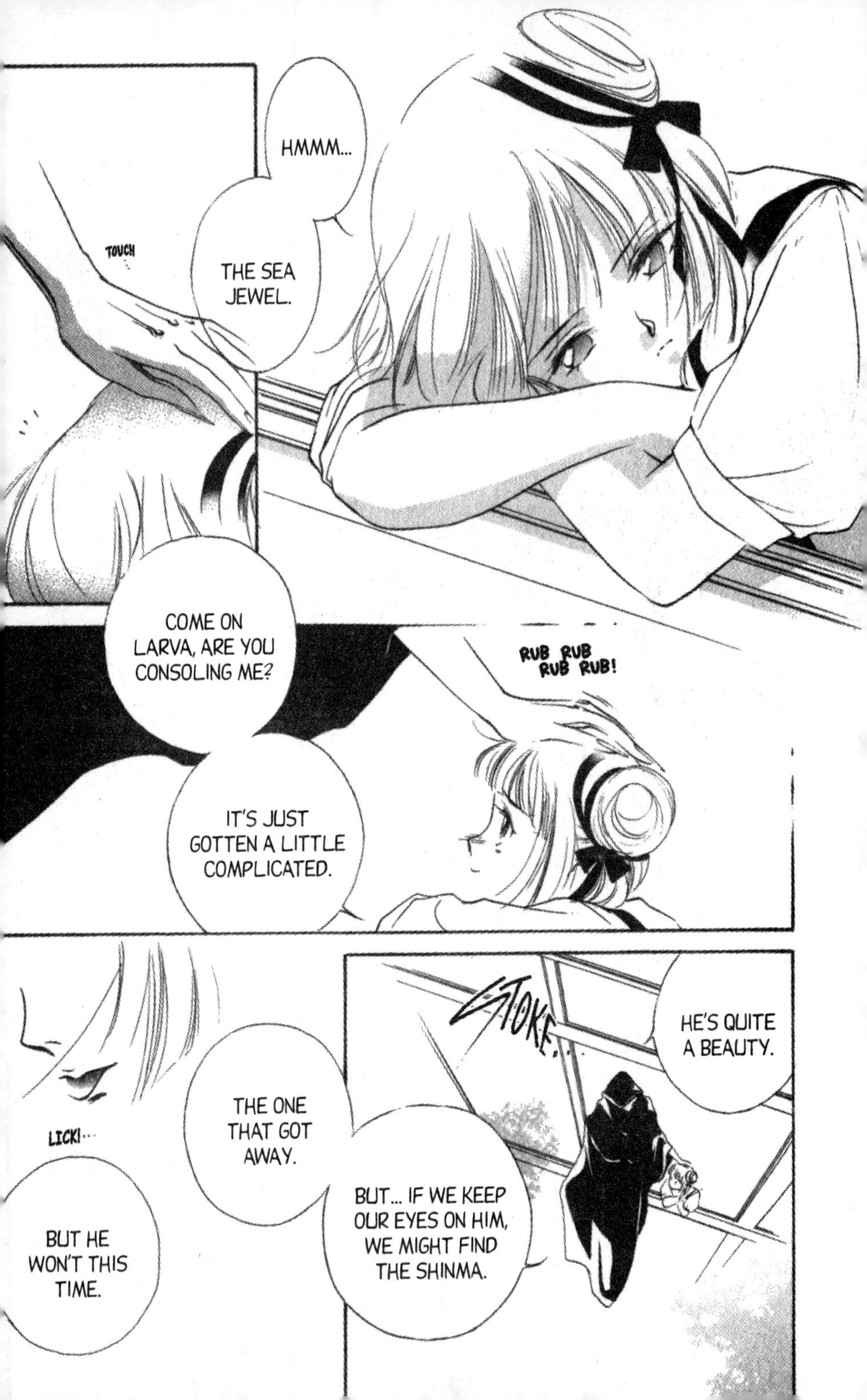
HMMM...
THE SEA JEWEL.
TOUCH
RUB RUB RUB RUB!
COME ON LARVA, ARE YOU CONSOLING ME?
IT'S JUST GOTTEN A LITTLE COMPLICATED.
STOKE...
HE'S QUITE A BEAUTY.
BUT... IF WE KEEP OUR EYES ON HIM, WE MIGHT FIND THE SHINMA.
THE ONE THAT GOT AWAY.
LICK!...
BUT HE WON'T THIS TIME.

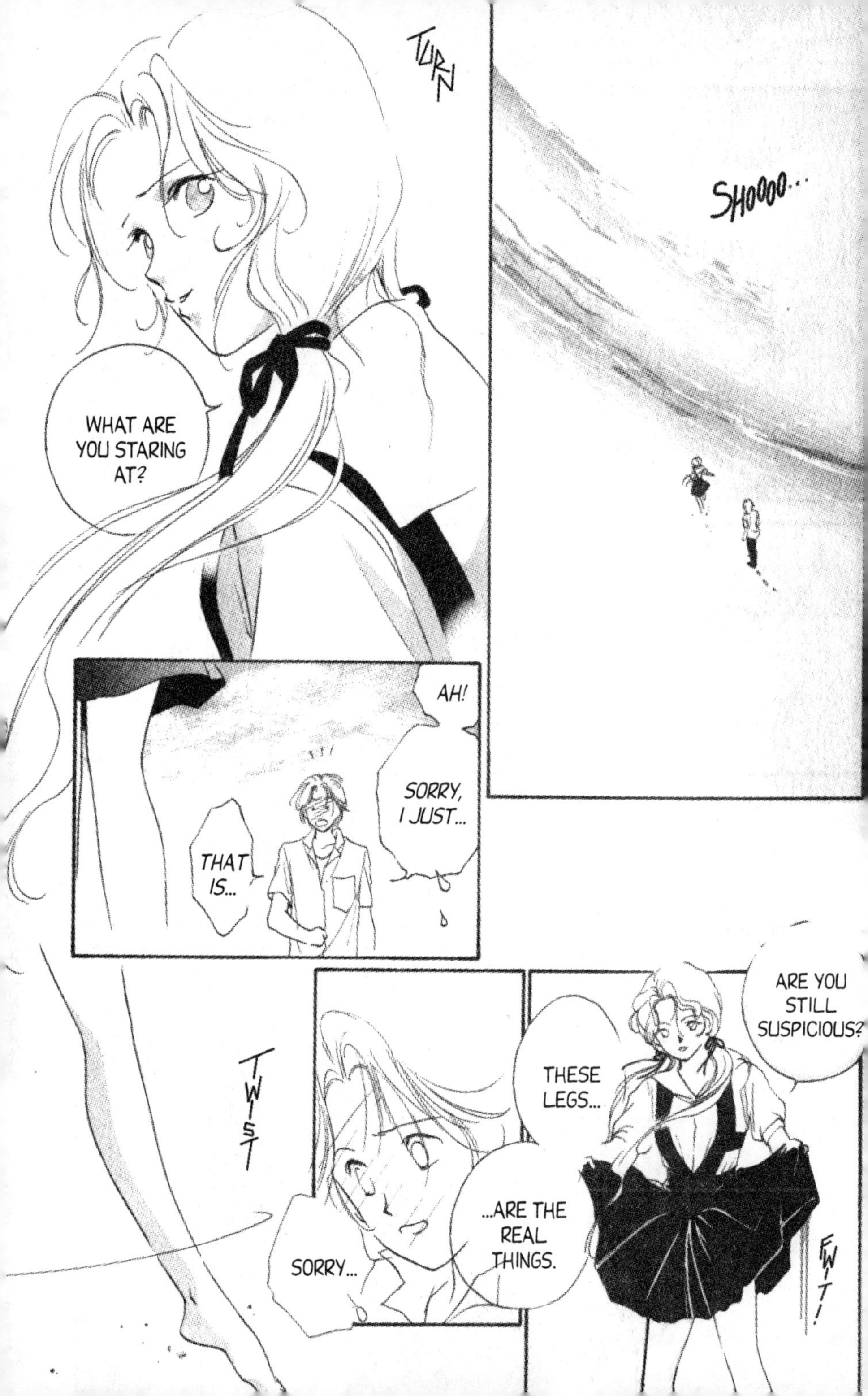
SHOOOO...
TURN
WHAT ARE YOU STARING AT?
AH!
SORRY, I JUST...
THAT IS...
ARE YOU STILL SUSPICIOUS?
THESE LEGS...
...ARE THE REAL THINGS.
FWIT!
SORRY...
TWIST

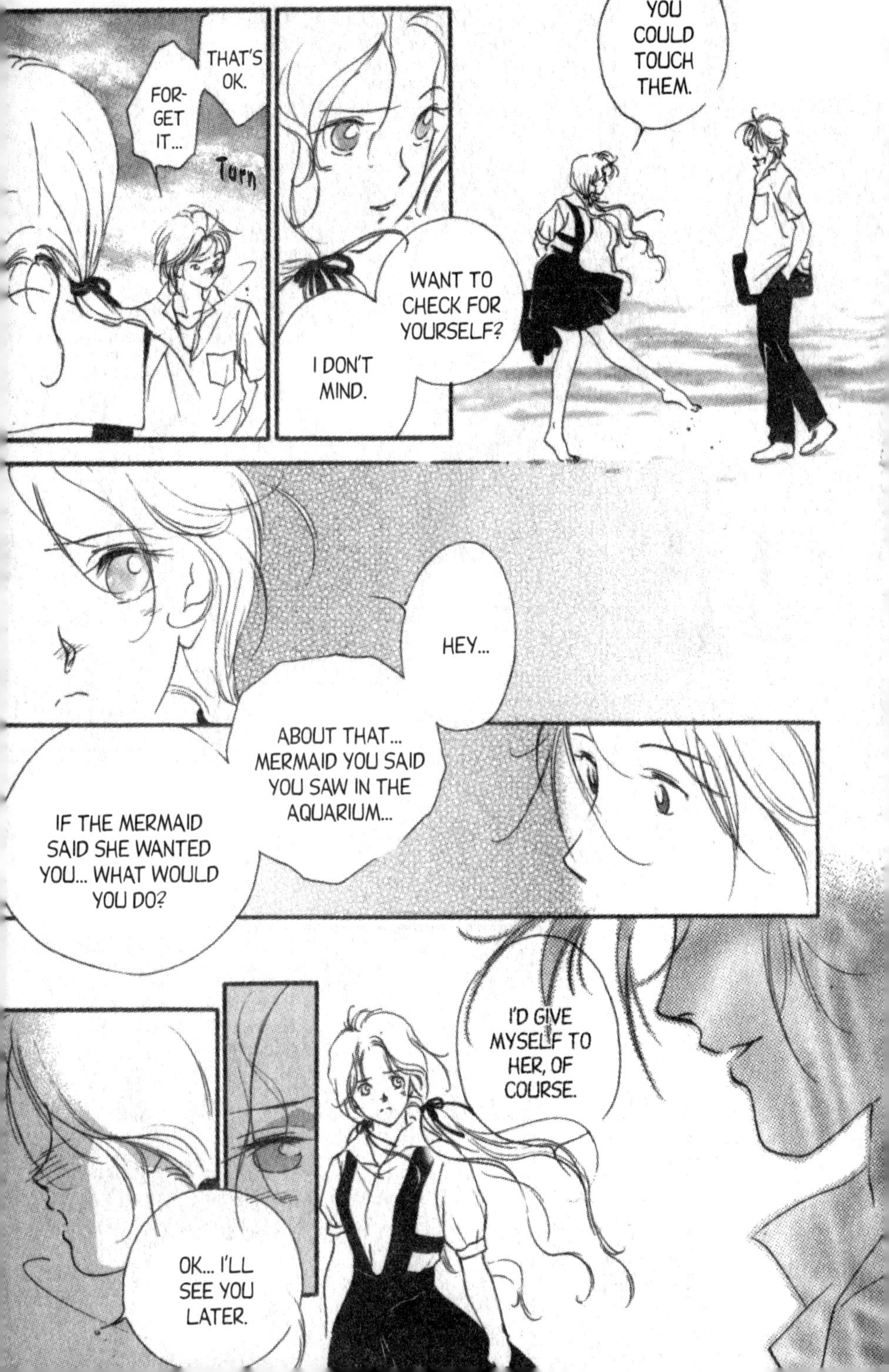
YOU COULD TOUCH THEM.
WANT TO CHECK FOR YOURSELF?
I DON'T MIND.
THAT'S OK.
FOR-GET IT...
Turn
HEY...
ABOUT THAT... MERMAID YOU SAID YOU SAW IN THE AQUARIUM...
IF THE MERMAID SAID SHE WANTED YOU... WHAT WOULD YOU DO?
I'D GIVE MYSELF TO HER, OF COURSE.
OK... I'LL SEE YOU LATER.

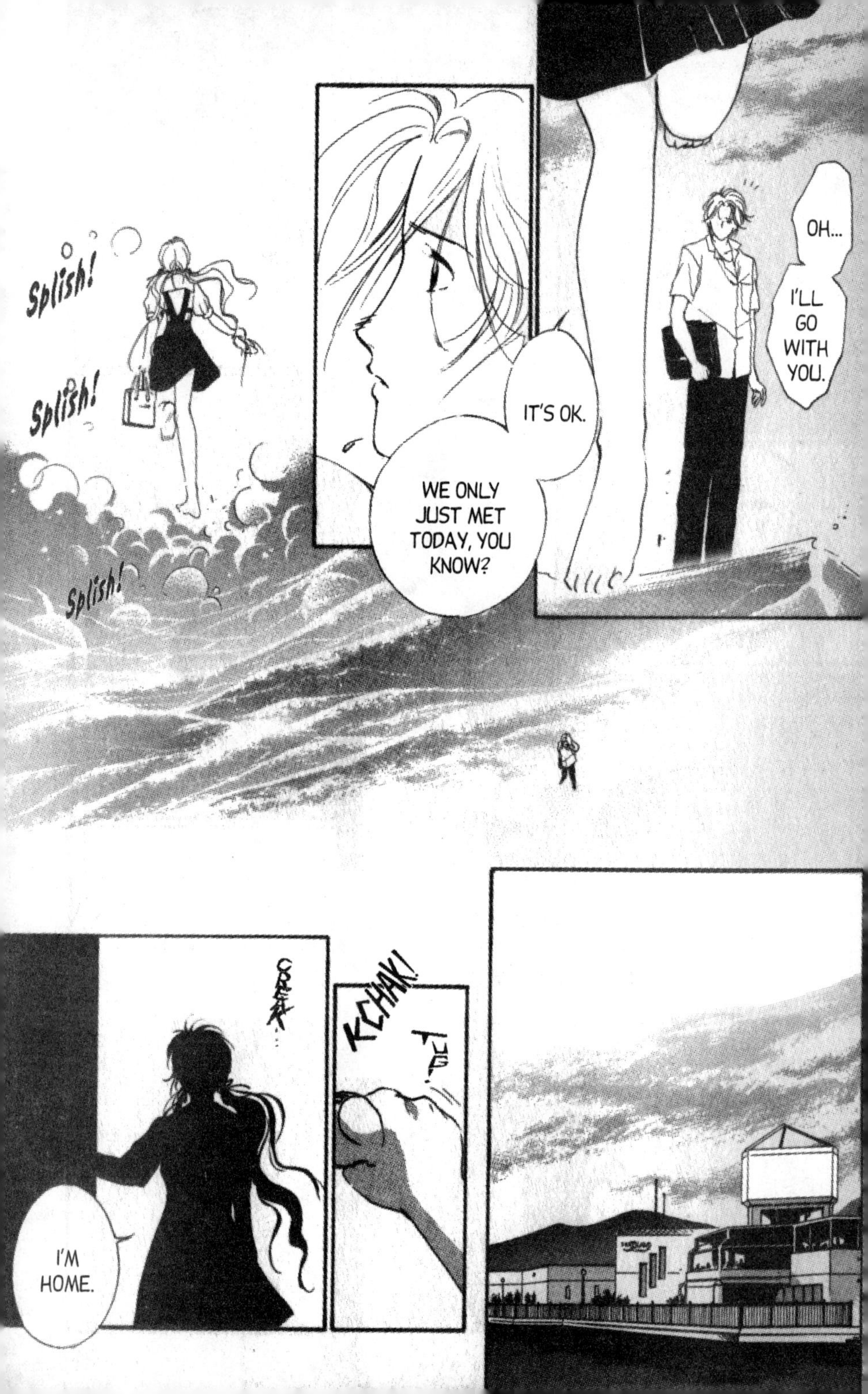
OH...
I'LL GO WITH YOU.
IT'S OK.
WE ONLY JUST MET TODAY, YOU KNOW?
Splish!
Splish!
Splish!
KCHAK!
TUG!
CREAK...
I'M HOME.

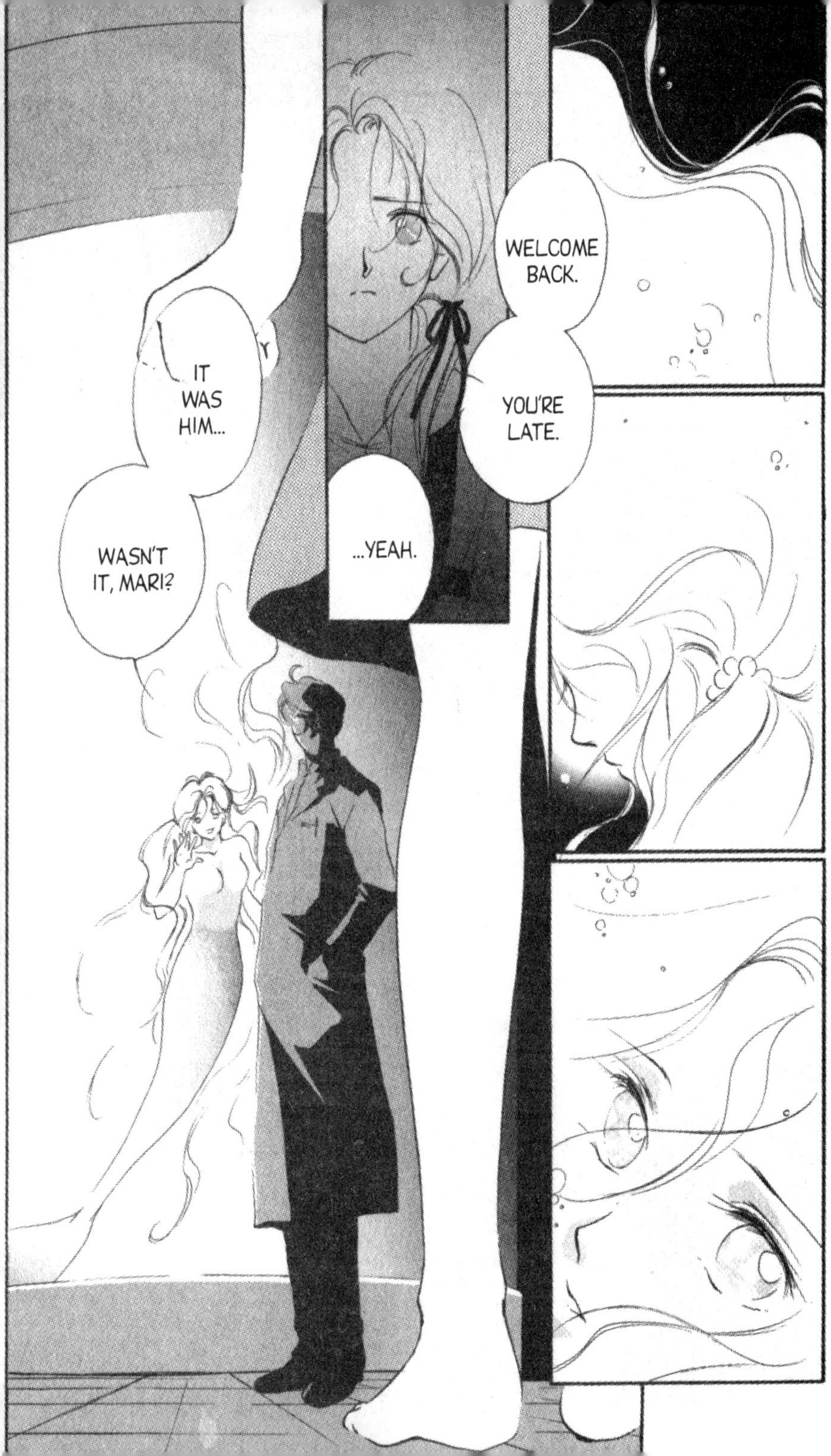
WELCOME BACK.
YOU'RE LATE.
...YEAH.
IT WAS HIM...
WASN'T IT, MARI?

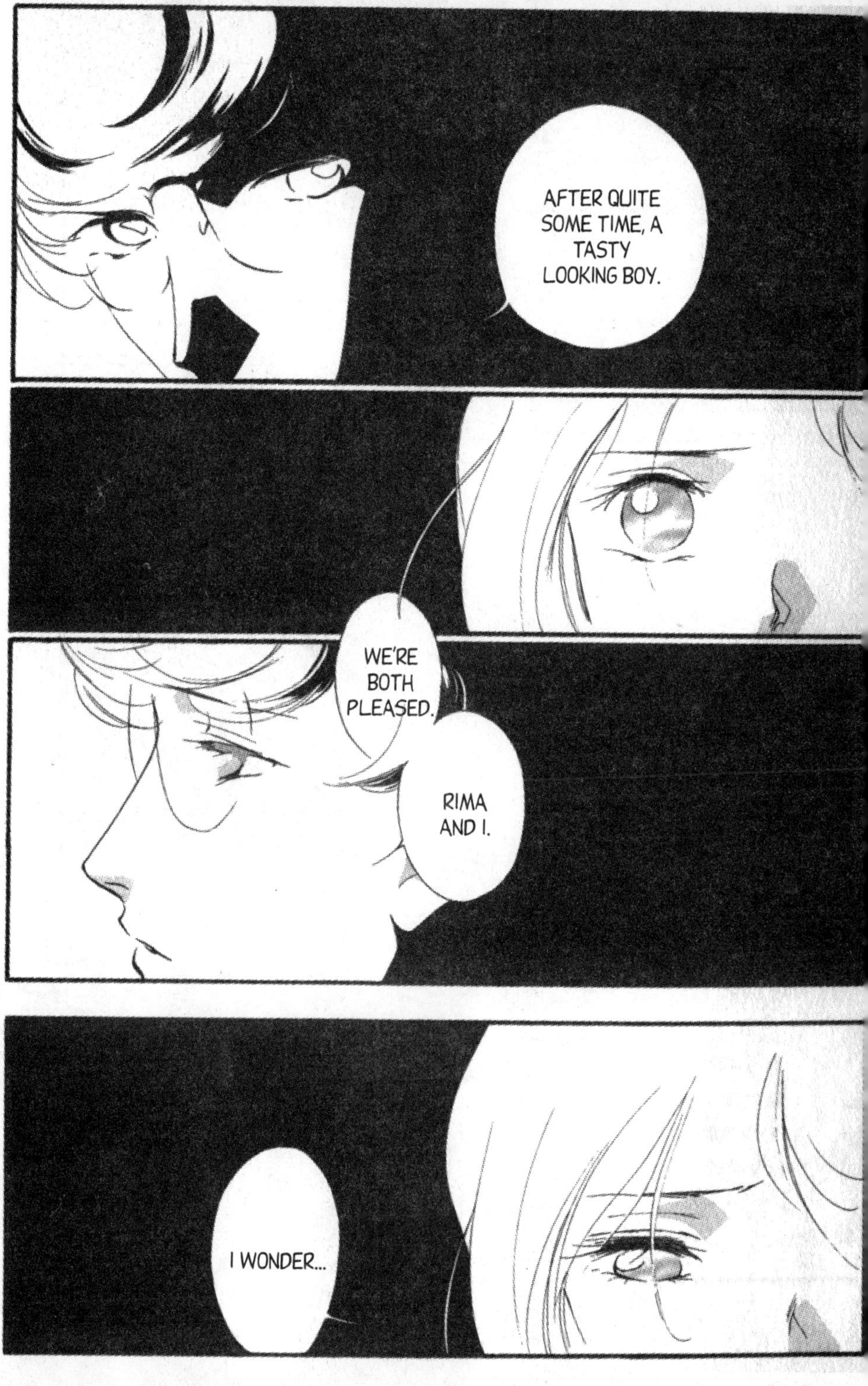
AFTER QUITE SOME TIME, A TASTY LOOKING BOY.
WE'RE BOTH PLEASED.
RIMA AND I.
I WONDER...

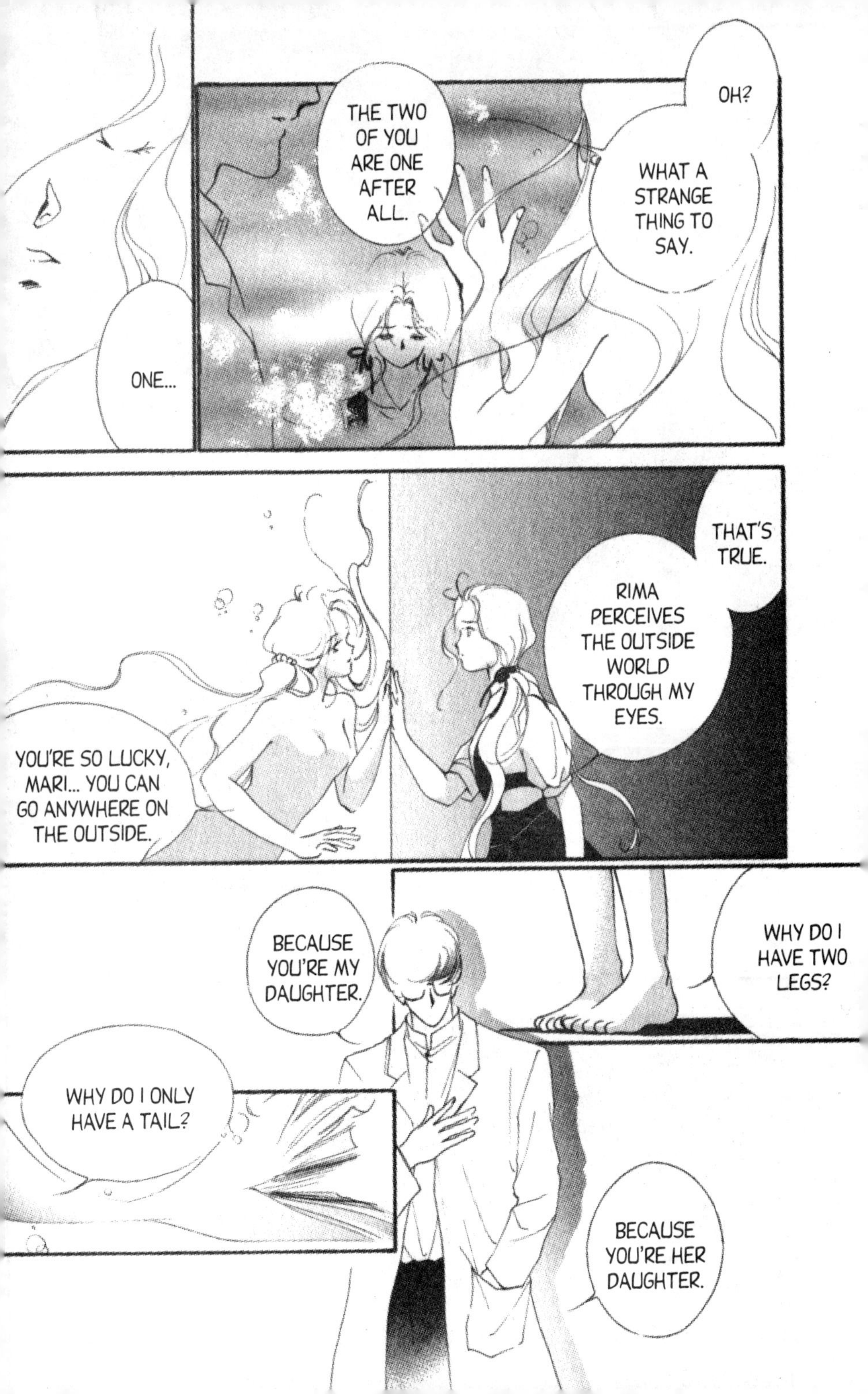
OH?
WHAT A STRANGE THING TO SAY.
THE TWO OF YOU ARE ONE AFTER ALL.
ONE...
THAT'S TRUE.
RIMA PERCEIVES THE OUTSIDE WORLD THROUGH MY EYES.
YOU'RE SO LUCKY, MARI... YOU CAN GO ANYWHERE ON THE OUTSIDE.
WHY DO I HAVE TWO LEGS?
BECAUSE YOU'RE MY DAUGHTER.
WHY DO I ONLY HAVE A TAIL?
BECAUSE YOU'RE HER DAUGHTER.

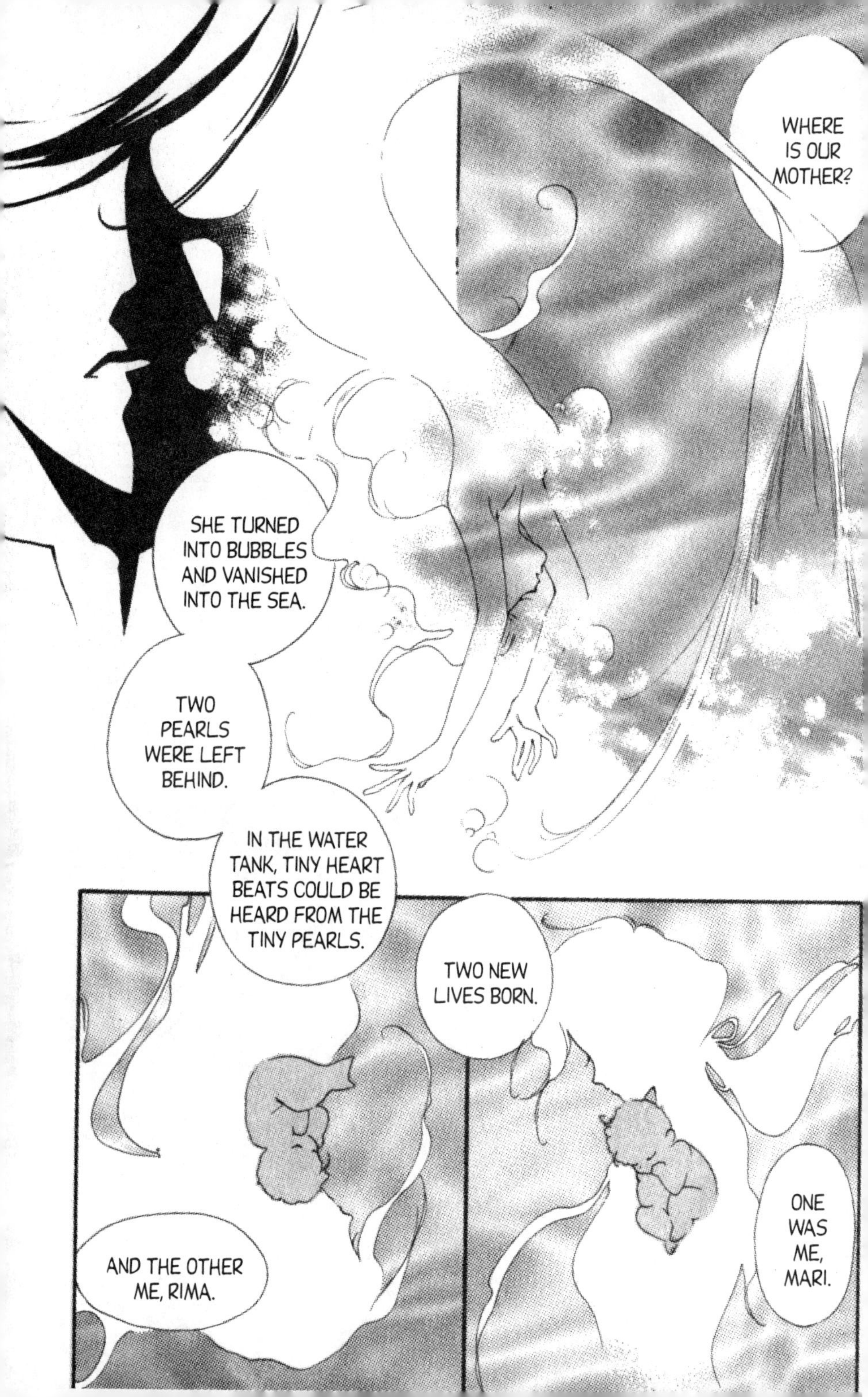
WHERE IS OUR MOTHER?
SHE TURNED INTO BUBBLES AND VANISHED INTO THE SEA.
TWO PEARLS WERE LEFT BEHIND.
IN THE WATER TANK, TINY HEART BEATS COULD BE HEARD FROM THE TINY PEARLS.
TWO NEW LIVES BORN.
ONE WAS ME, MARI.
AND THE OTHER ME, RIMA.

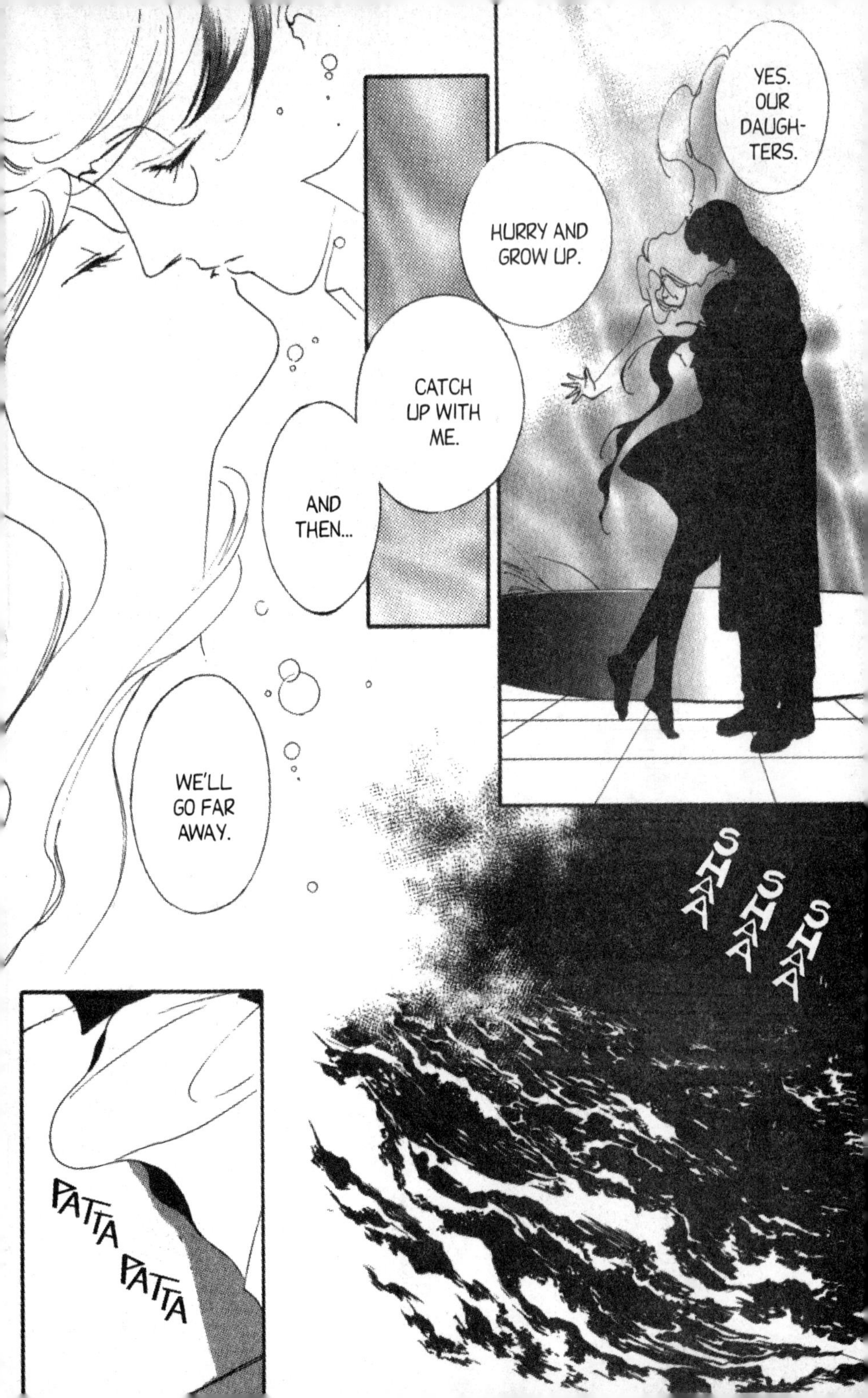
YES. OUR DAUGH-TERS.
HURRY AND GROW UP.
CATCH UP WITH ME.
AND THEN...
WE'LL GO FAR AWAY.
SHAA SHAA SHAA
PATTA PATTA

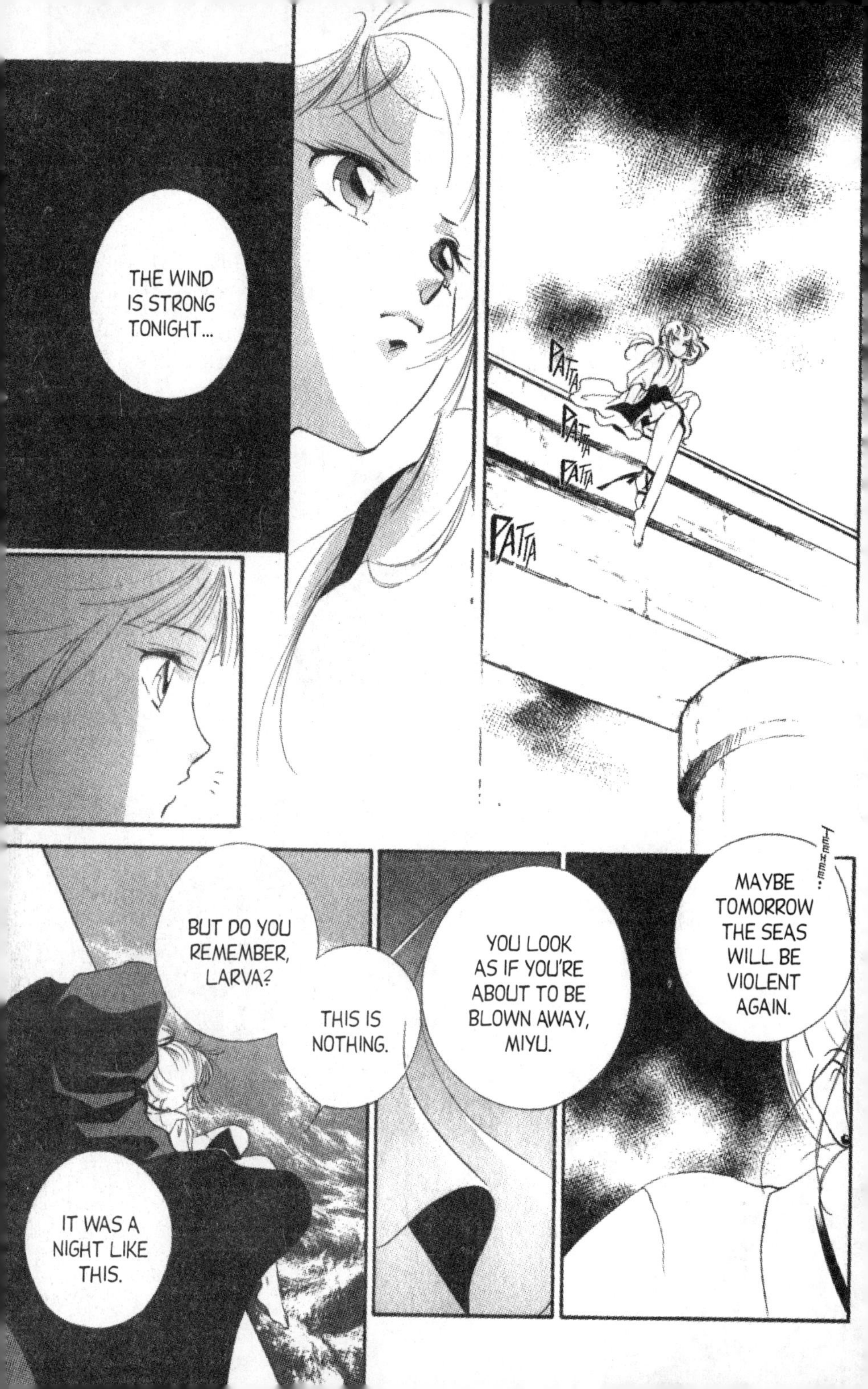
PATTA
PATTA
PATTA
PATTA
THE WIND IS STRONG TONIGHT...
MAYBE TOMORROW THE SEAS WILL BE VIOLENT AGAIN.
YOU LOOK AS IF YOU'RE ABOUT TO BE BLOWN AWAY, MIYU.
THIS IS NOTHING.
BUT DO YOU REMEMBER, LARVA?
IT WAS A NIGHT LIKE THIS.

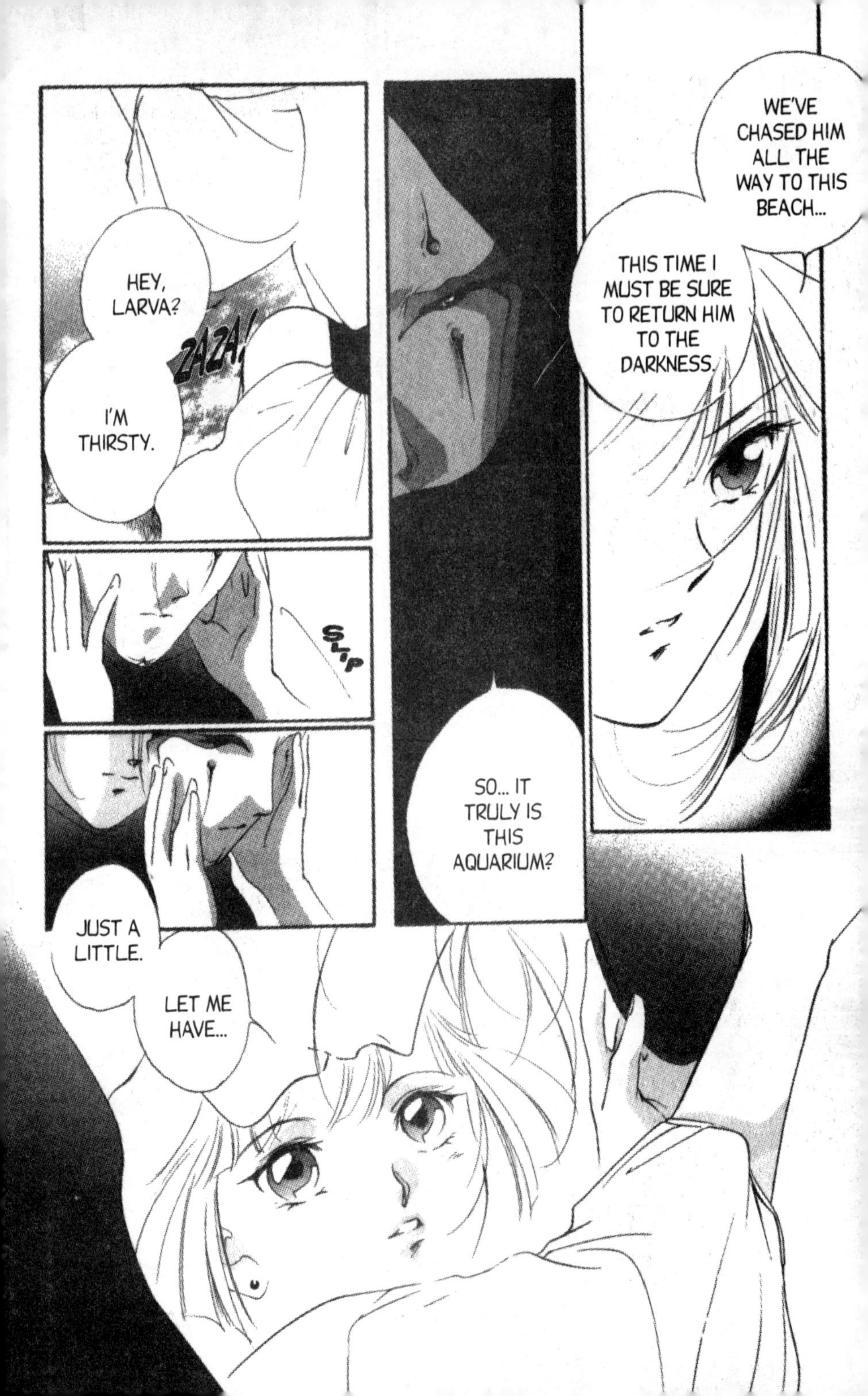
WE'VE CHASED HIM ALL THE WAY TO THIS BEACH...
THIS TIME I MUST BE SURE TO RETURN HIM TO THE DARKNESS.
SO... IT TRULY IS THIS AQUARIUM?
HEY, LARVA?
ZAZA!
I'M THIRSTY.
SLIP
JUST A LITTLE.
LET ME HAVE...

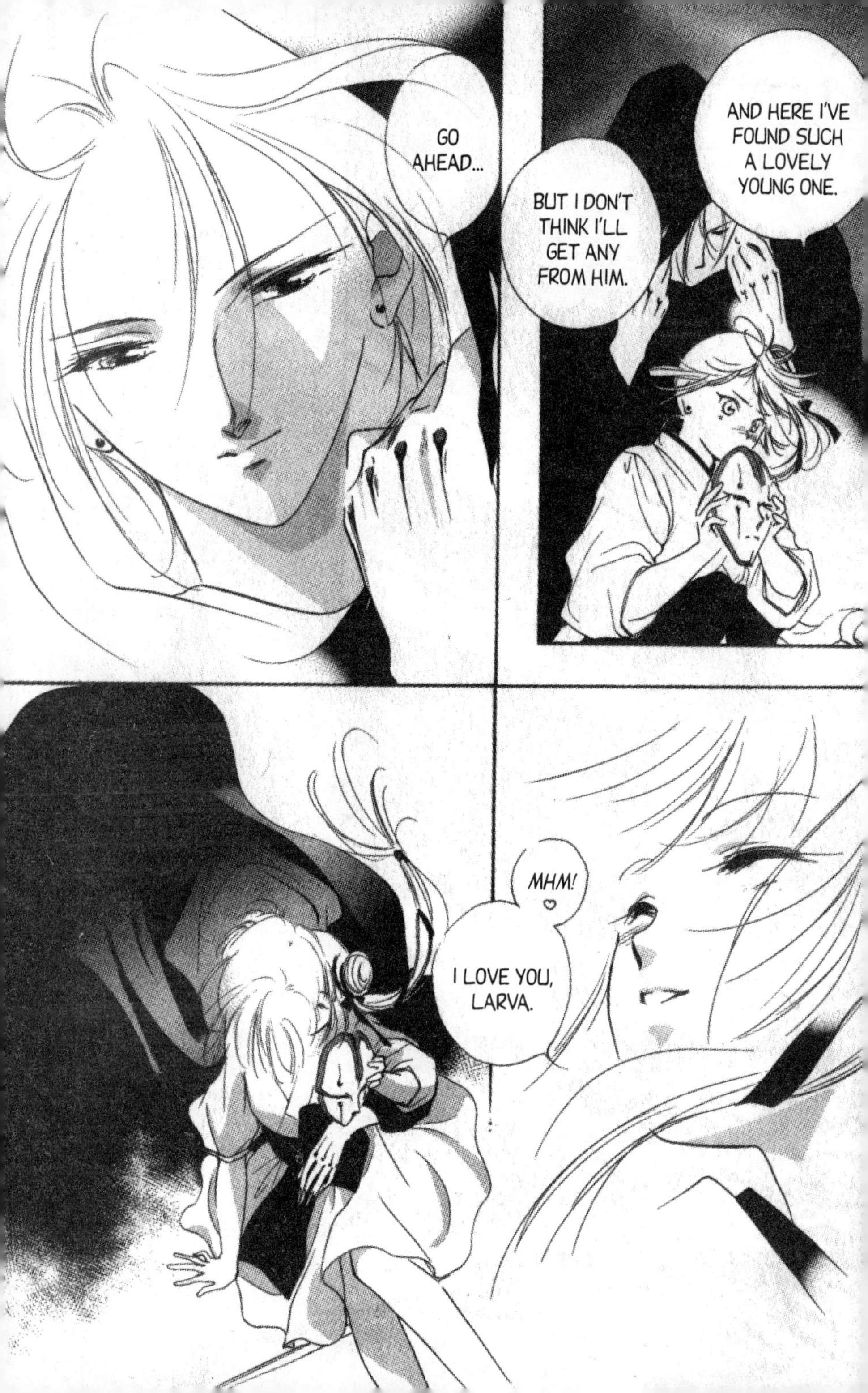
AND HERE I'VE FOUND SUCH A LOVELY YOUNG ONE.
BUT I DON'T THINK I'LL GET ANY FROM HIM.
GO AHEAD...
I LOVE YOU, LARVA.
MHM! ♡

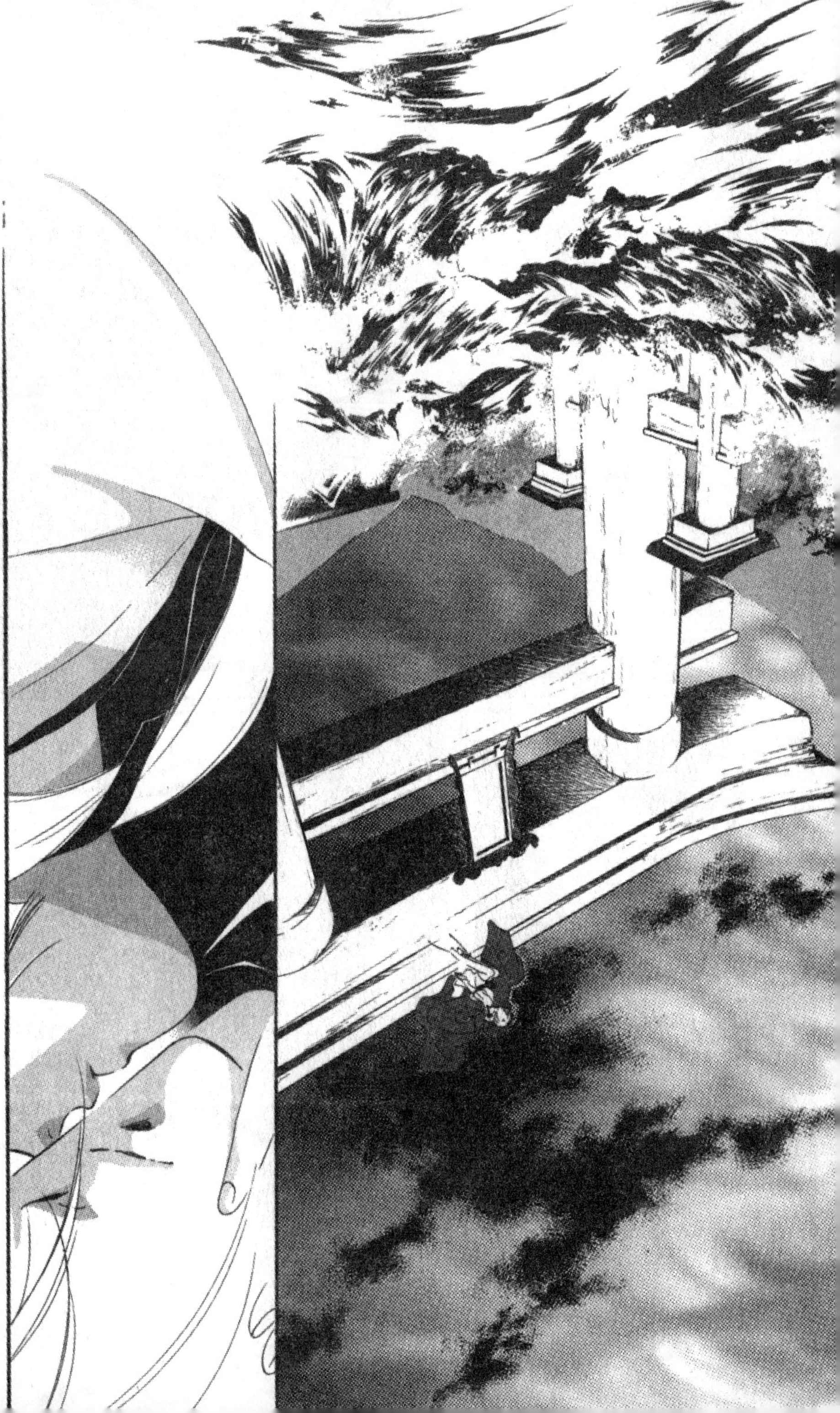

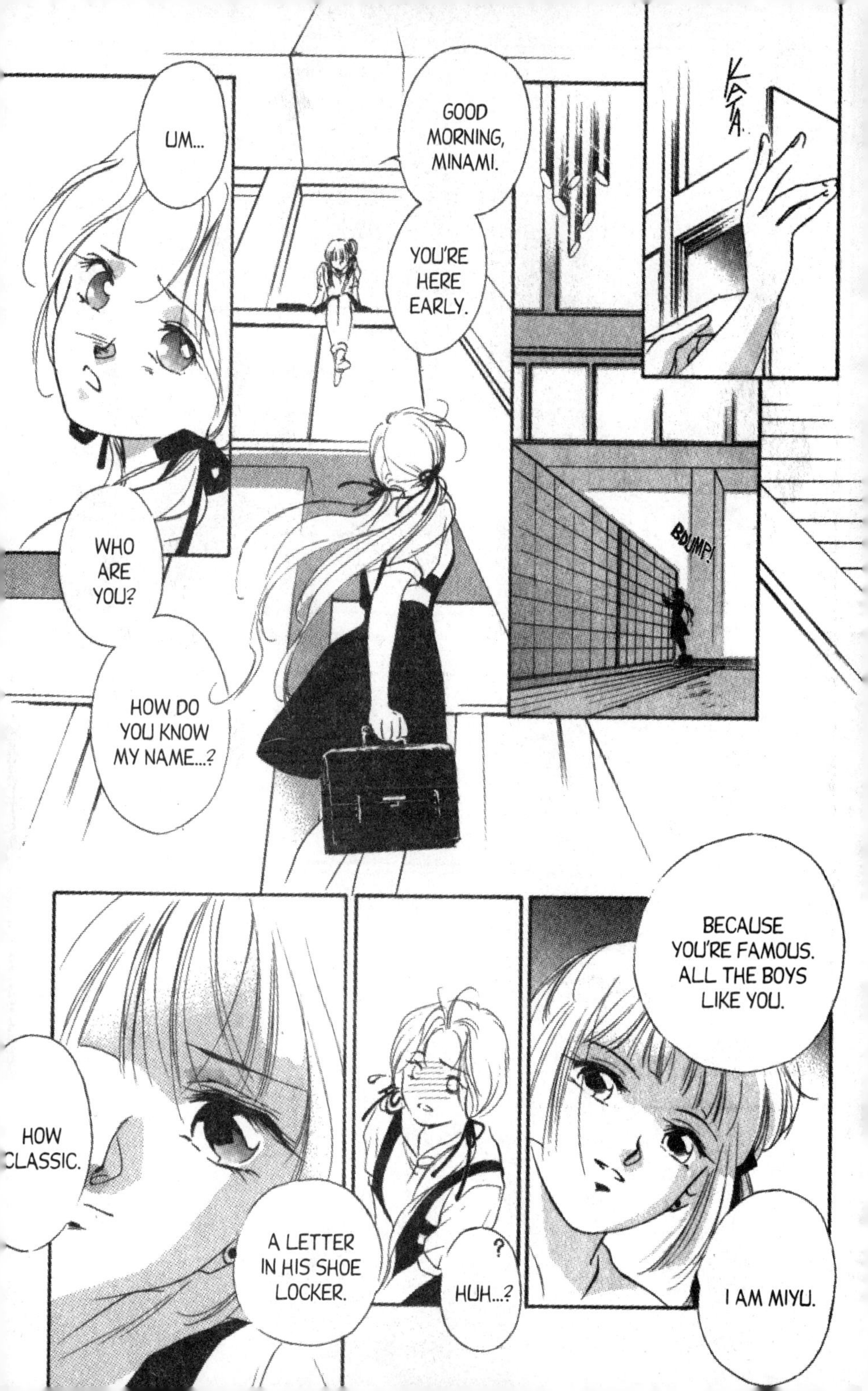
KATA
BDUMP!
GOOD MORNING, MINAMI.
YOU'RE HERE EARLY.
UM...
WHO ARE YOU?
HOW DO YOU KNOW MY NAME...?
BECAUSE YOU'RE FAMOUS. ALL THE BOYS LIKE YOU.
I AM MIYU.
?
HUH...?
A LETTER IN HIS SHOE LOCKER.
HOW CLASSIC.

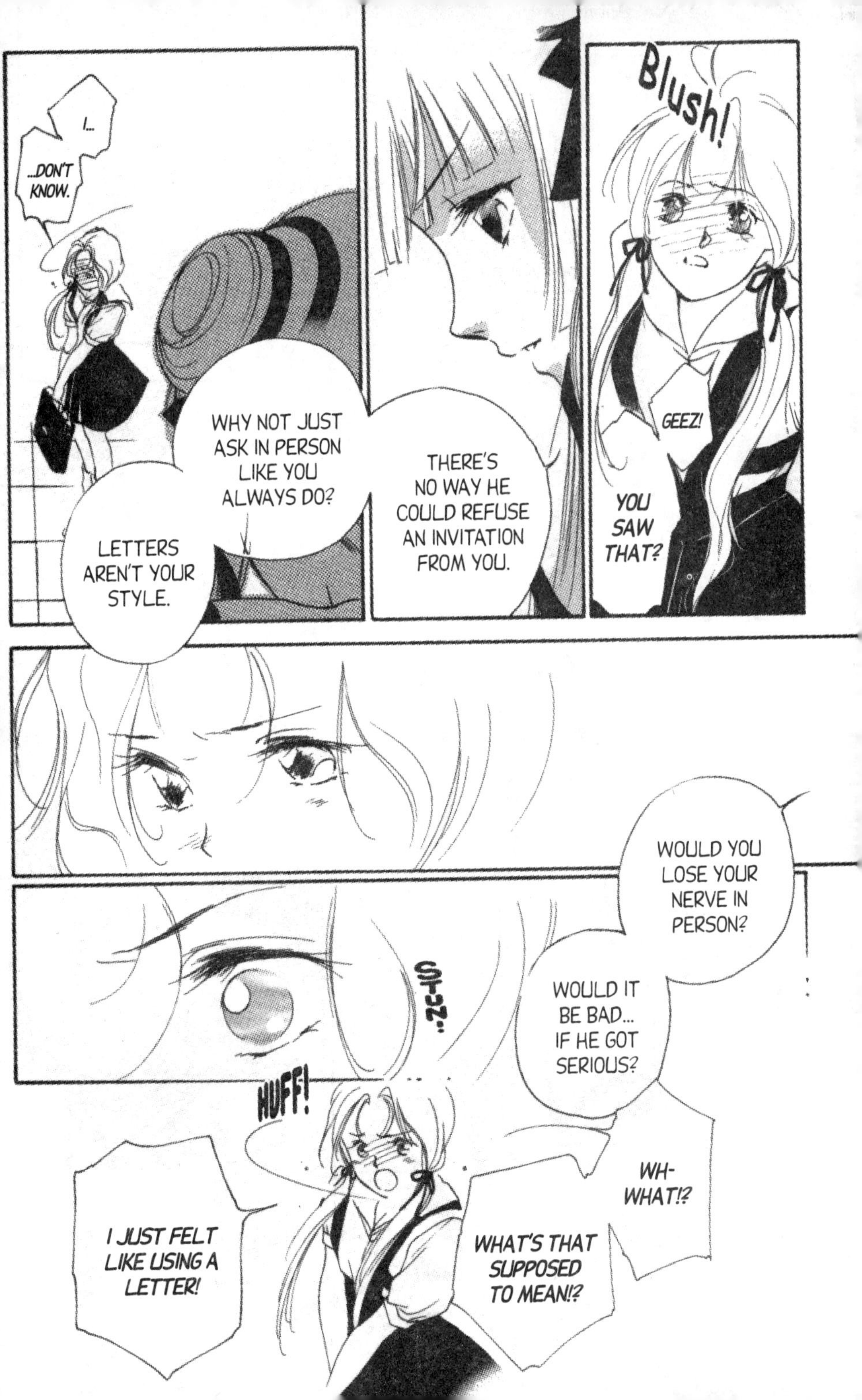
Blush!
GEEZ!
YOU SAW THAT?
THERE'S NO WAY HE COULD REFUSE AN INVITATION FROM YOU.
LETTERS AREN'T YOUR STYLE.
WHY NOT JUST ASK IN PERSON LIKE YOU ALWAYS DO?
I...
...DON'T KNOW.
WOULD YOU LOSE YOUR NERVE IN PERSON?
WOULD IT BE BAD... IF HE GOT SERIOUS?
STUN..
HUFF!
WH- WHAT!?
WHAT'S THAT SUPPOSED TO MEAN!?
I JUST FELT LIKE USING A LETTER!

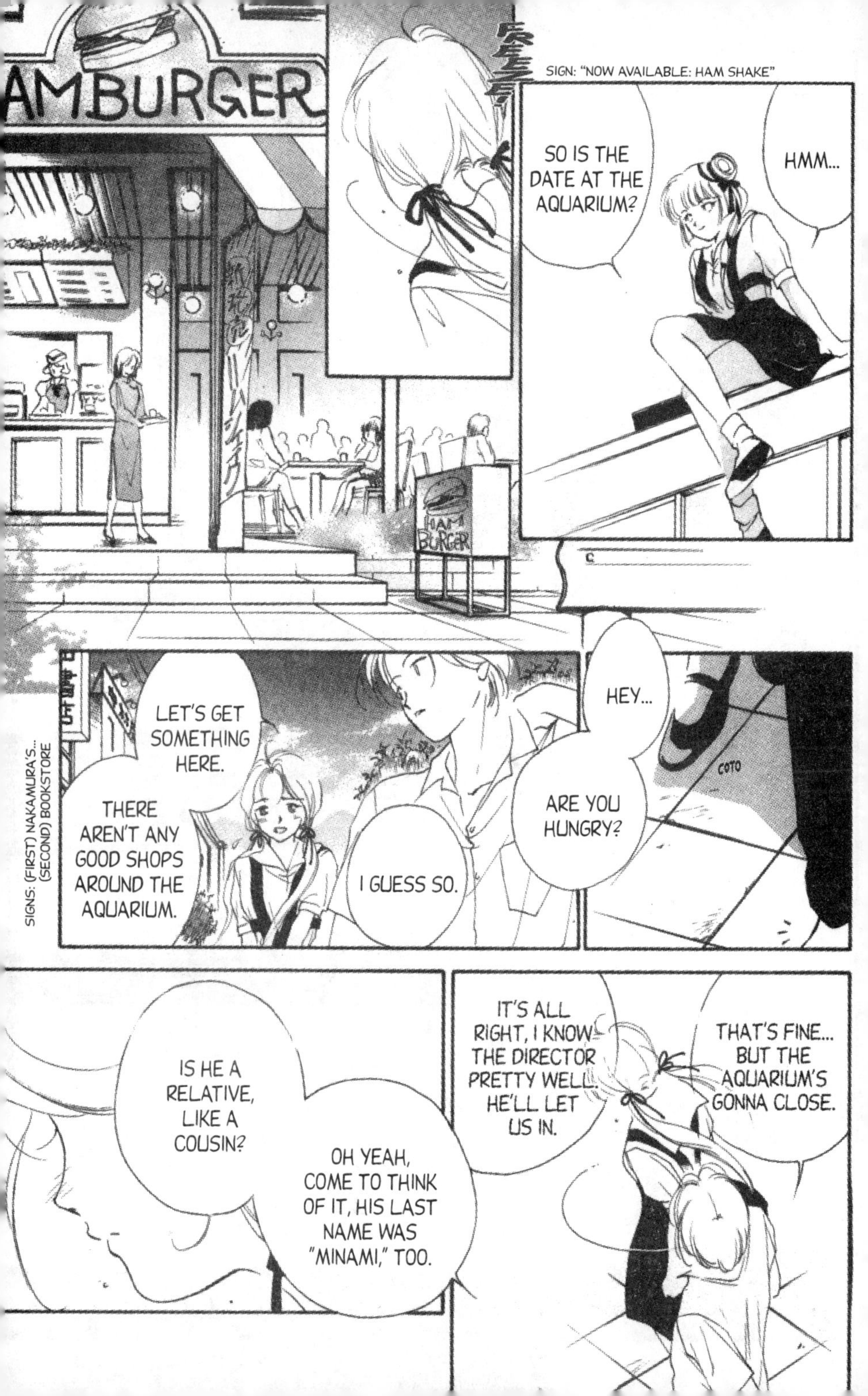
HMM...
SO IS THE DATE AT THE AQUARIUM?
AMBURGER
HAM BURGER
SIGN: "NOW AVAILABLE: HAM SHAKE"
COTO
HEY...
ARE YOU HUNGRY?
I GUESS SO.
LET'S GET SOMETHING HERE.
THERE AREN'T ANY GOOD SHOPS AROUND THE AQUARIUM.
SIGNS: (FIRST) NAKAMURA'S... (SECOND) BOOKSTORE
THAT'S FINE... BUT THE AQUARIUM'S GONNA CLOSE.
IT'S ALL RIGHT, I KNOW THE DIRECTOR PRETTY WELL. HE'LL LET US IN.
IS HE A RELATIVE, LIKE A COUSIN?
OH YEAH, COME TO THINK OF IT, HIS LAST NAME WAS "MINAMI," TOO.

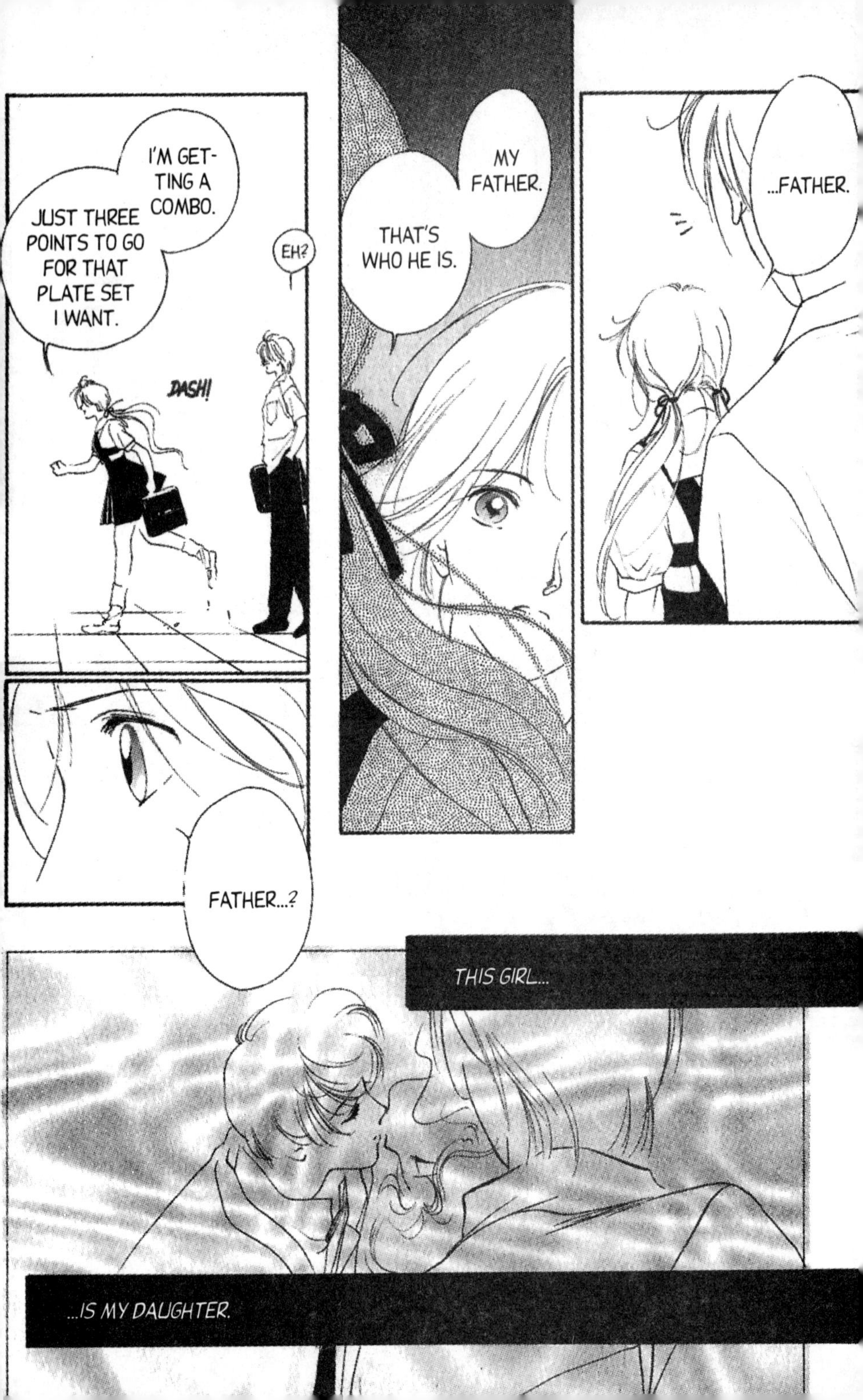
...FATHER.
MY FATHER.
THAT'S WHO HE IS.
I'M GETTING A COMBO.
JUST THREE POINTS TO GO FOR THAT PLATE SET I WANT.
EH?
DASH!
FATHER...?
THIS GIRL...
...IS MY DAUGHTER.

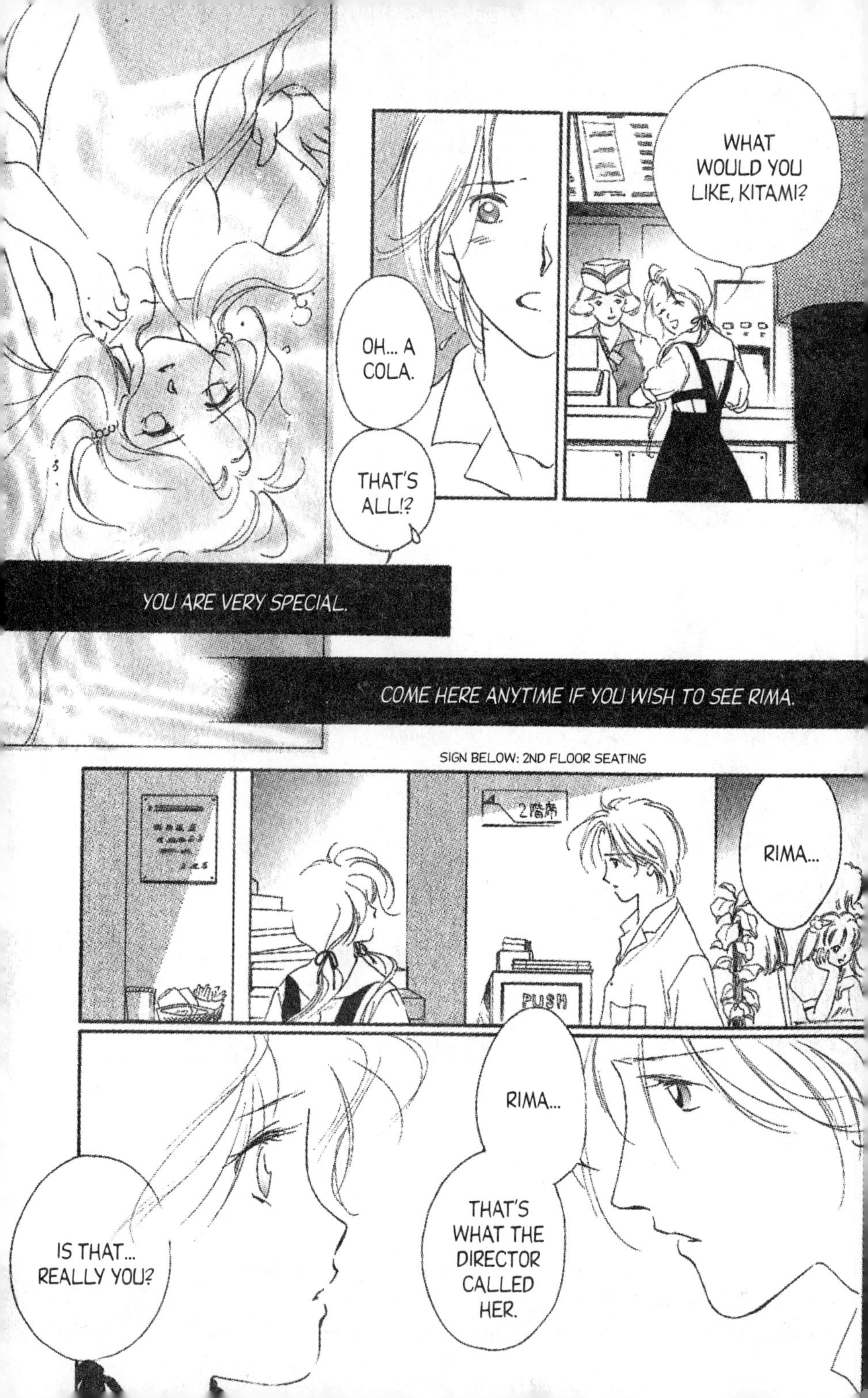
WHAT WOULD YOU LIKE, KITAMI?
OH... A COLA.
THAT'S ALL!?
YOU ARE VERY SPECIAL.
COME HERE ANYTIME IF YOU WISH TO SEE RIMA.
SIGN BELOW: 2ND FLOOR SEATING
2階席
RIMA...
PUSH
RIMA...
THAT'S WHAT THE DIRECTOR CALLED HER.
IS THAT... REALLY YOU?

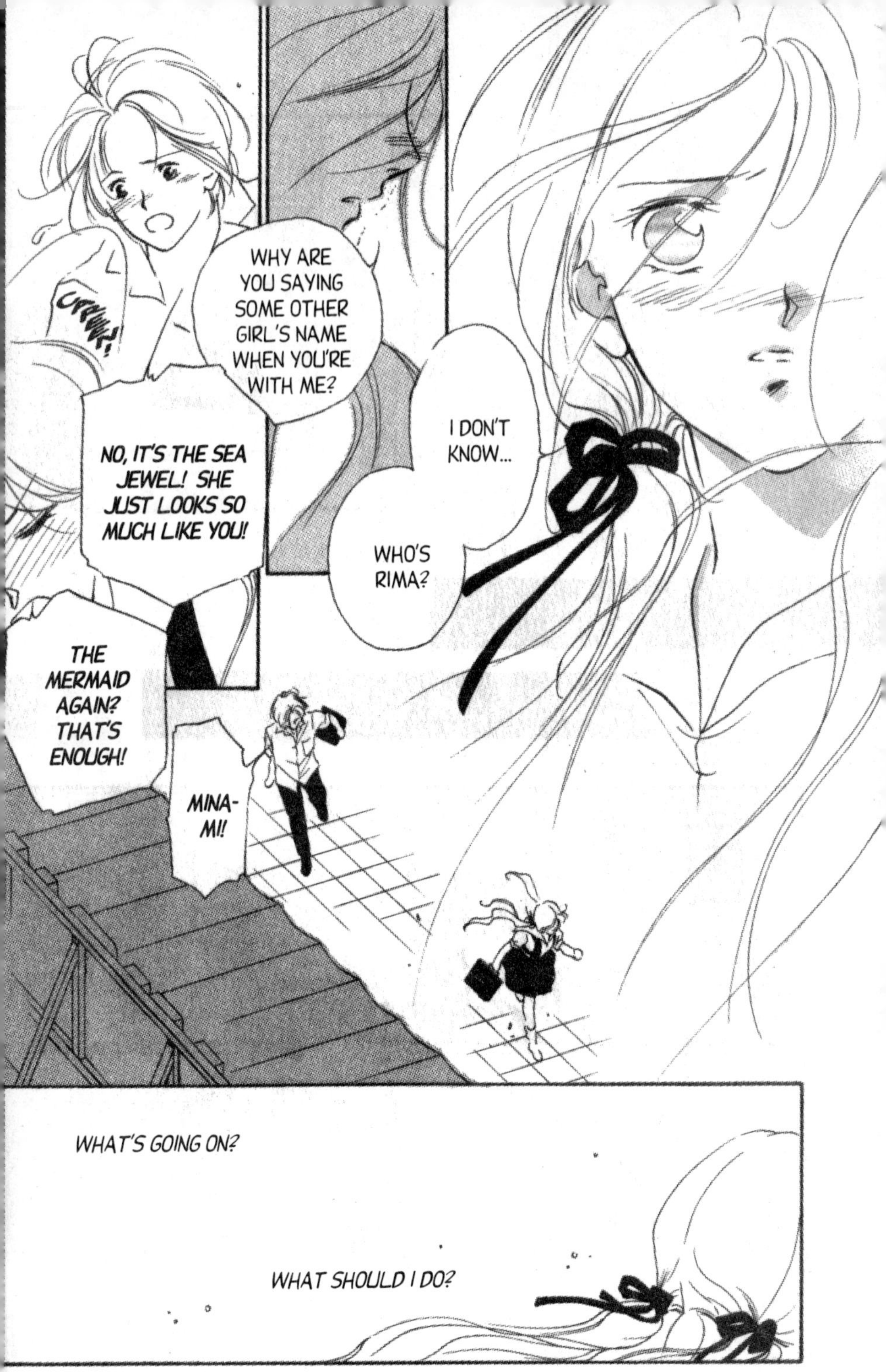
I DON'T KNOW...
WHO'S RIMA?
WHY ARE YOU SAYING SOME OTHER GIRL'S NAME WHEN YOU'RE WITH ME?
NO, IT'S THE SEA JEWEL! SHE JUST LOOKS SO MUCH LIKE YOU!
THE MERMAID AGAIN? THAT'S ENOUGH!
MINA-MI!
WHAT'S GOING ON?
WHAT SHOULD I DO?

I FEEL SO STRANGE.
WOULD YOU LOSE YOUR NERVE IN PERSON?
WOULD IT BE BAD... IF HE GOT SERIOUS?
YES, IT WOULD BE BAD.
...IT HURTS.
BEING ON THE OUTSIDE HURTS.... JUST LIKE IT WOULD FOR RIMA...
SCREE!
SIGN: "TODAY WE ARE OPENING A NEW HALL. WE LOOK FORWARD TO YOUR NEXT VISIT."

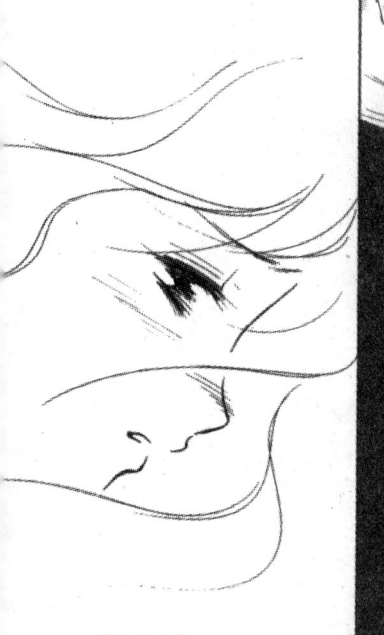

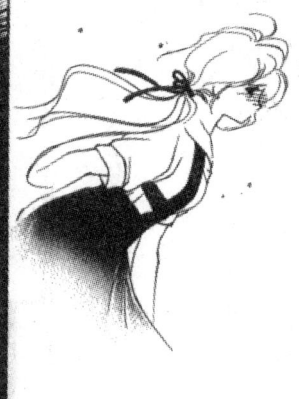

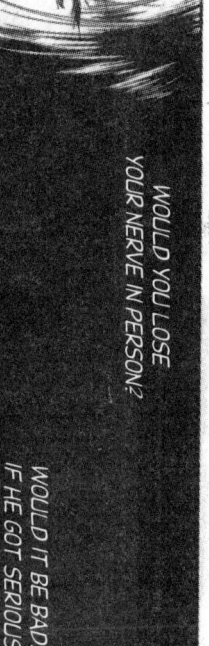

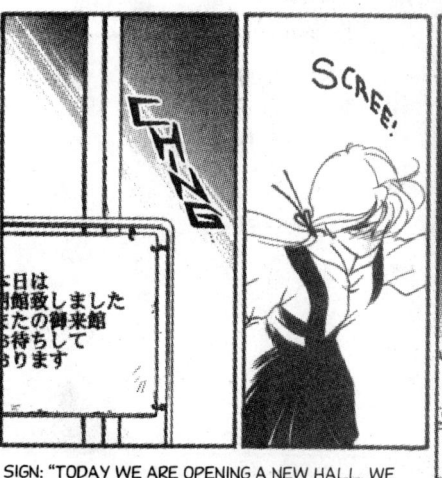

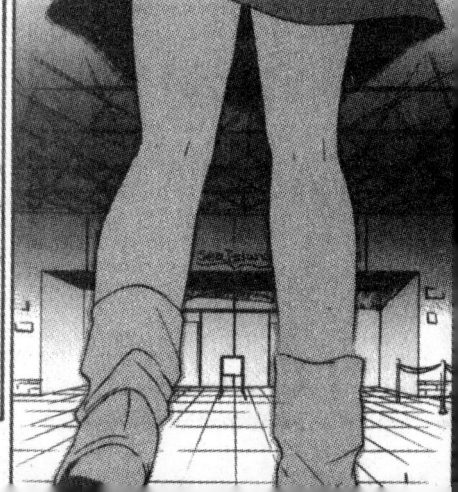

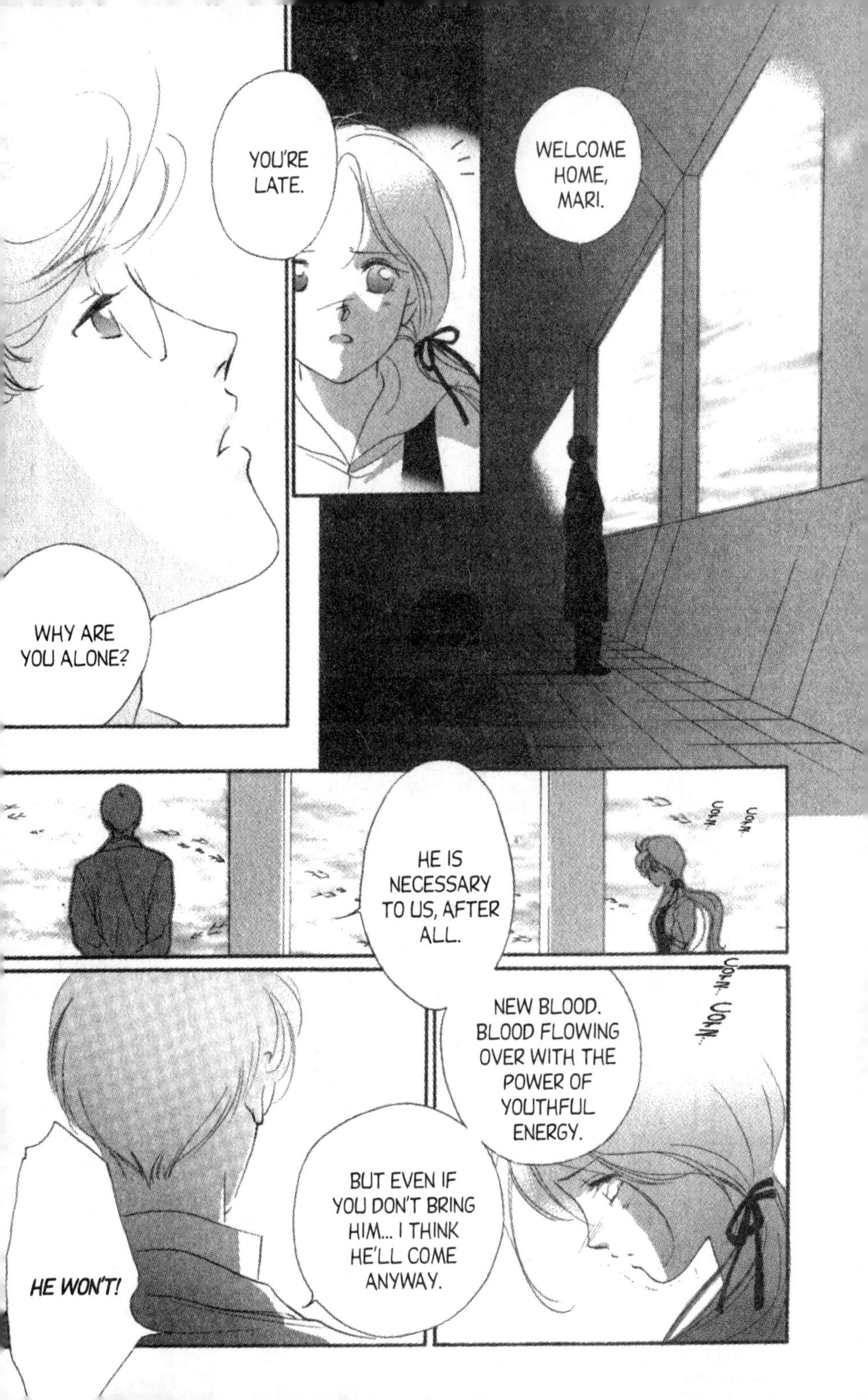
WELCOME HOME, MARI.
YOU'RE LATE.
WHY ARE YOU ALONE?
HE IS NECESSARY TO US, AFTER ALL.
NEW BLOOD. BLOOD FLOWING OVER WITH THE POWER OF YOUTHFUL ENERGY.
BUT EVEN IF YOU DON'T BRING HIM... I THINK HE'LL COME ANYWAY.
HE WON'T!

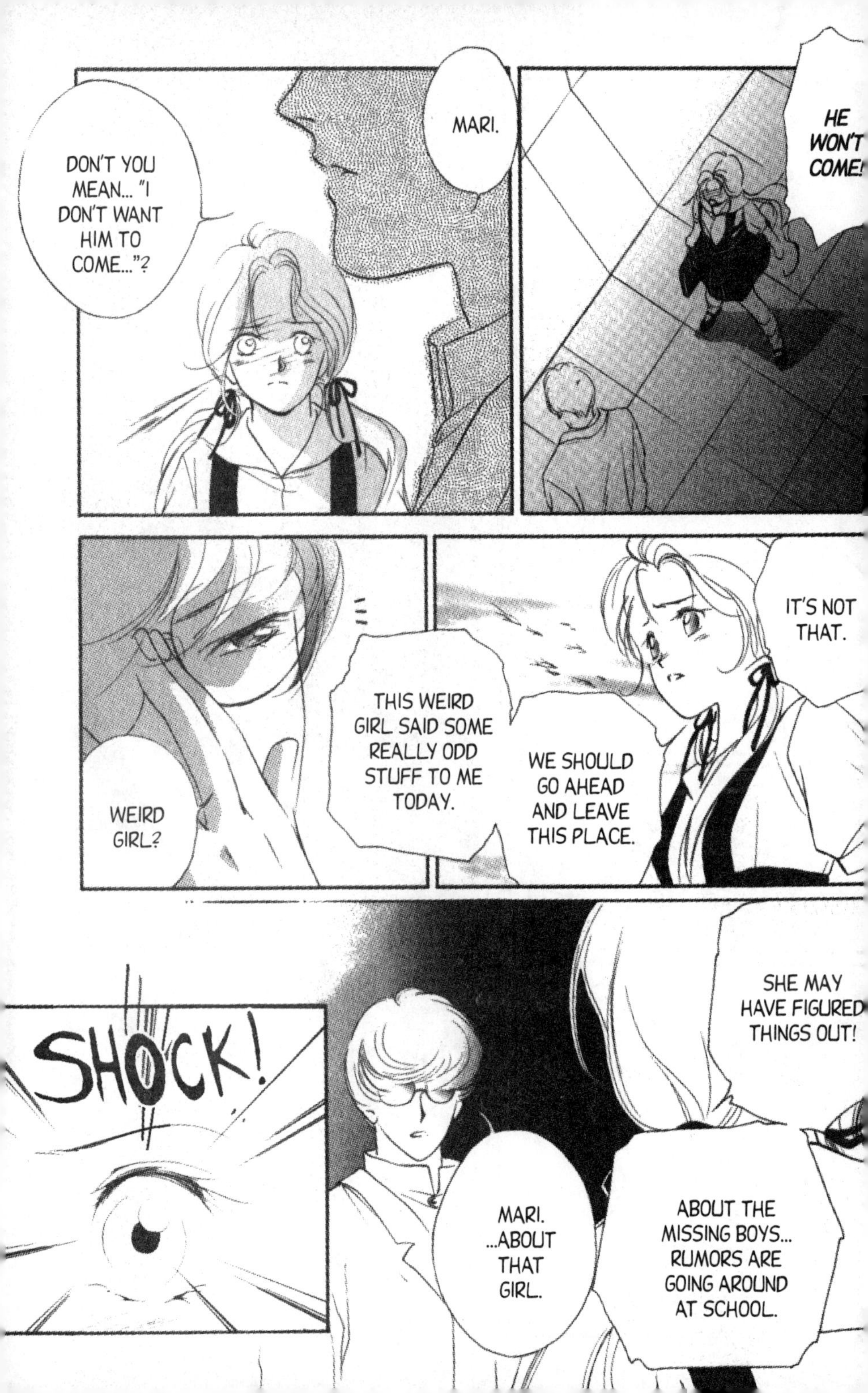
HE WON'T COME!
MARI.
DON'T YOU MEAN... "I DON'T WANT HIM TO COME..."?
IT'S NOT THAT.
WE SHOULD GO AHEAD AND LEAVE THIS PLACE.
THIS WEIRD GIRL SAID SOME REALLY ODD STUFF TO ME TODAY.
WEIRD GIRL?
SHE MAY HAVE FIGURED THINGS OUT!
ABOUT THE MISSING BOYS... RUMORS ARE GOING AROUND AT SCHOOL.
MARI. ...ABOUT THAT GIRL.
SHOCK!

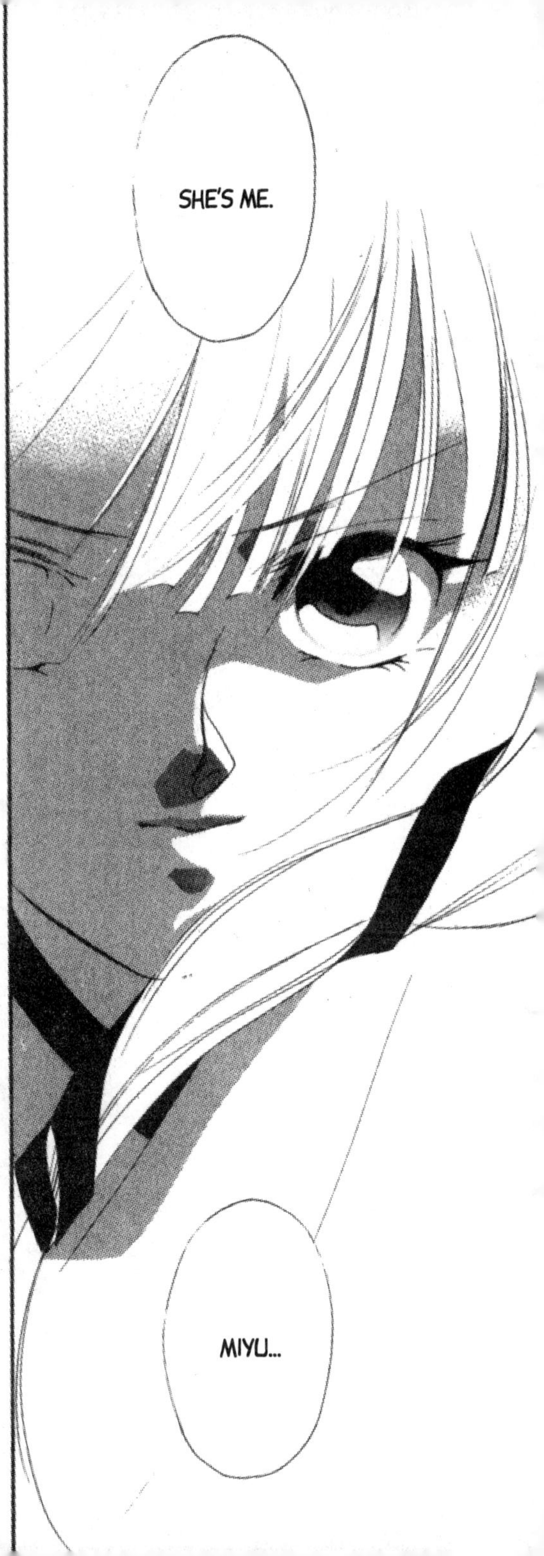
SHE'S ME.
MIYU...

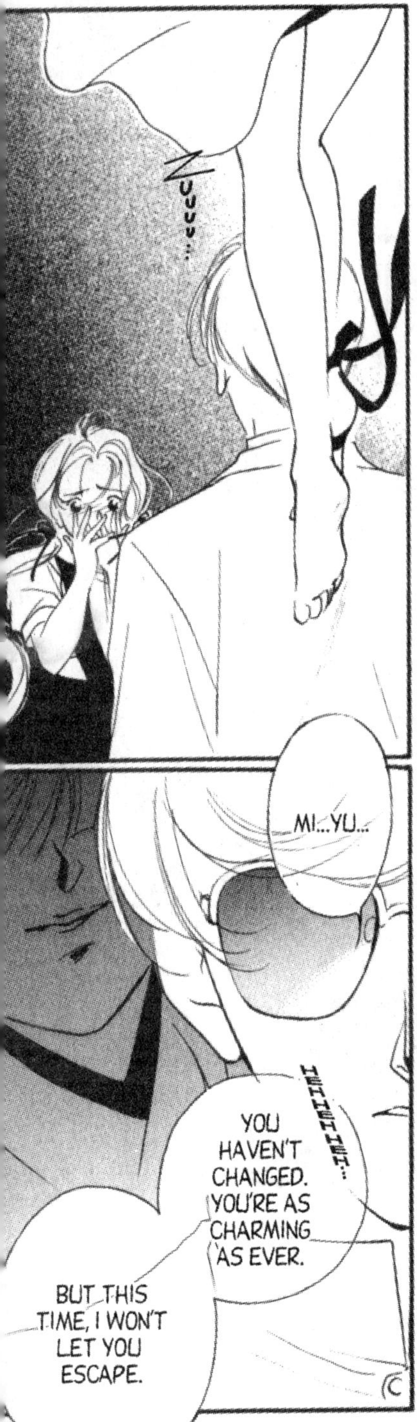
NUUUU...
MI...YU...
HEHHEHHEH...
YOU HAVEN'T CHANGED. YOU'RE AS CHARMING AS EVER.
BUT THIS TIME, I WON'T LET YOU ESCAPE.

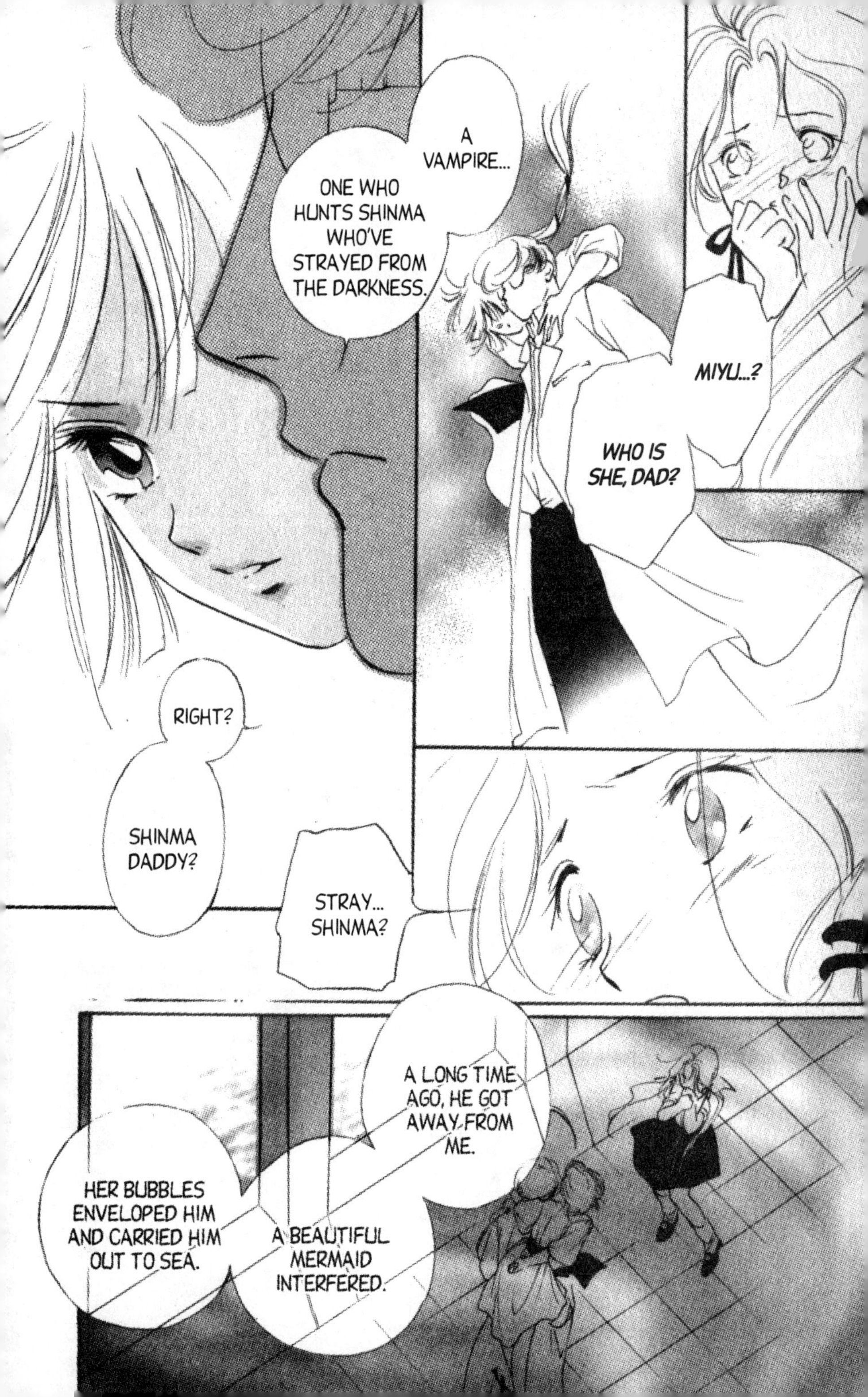
MIYU...?
WHO IS SHE, DAD?
A VAMPIRE...
ONE WHO HUNTS SHINMA WHO'VE STRAYED FROM THE DARKNESS.
STRAY... SHINMA?
SHINMA DADDY?
RIGHT?
A LONG TIME AGO, HE GOT AWAY FROM ME.
A BEAUTIFUL MERMAID INTERFERED.
HER BUBBLES ENVELOPED HIM AND CARRIED HIM OUT TO SEA.

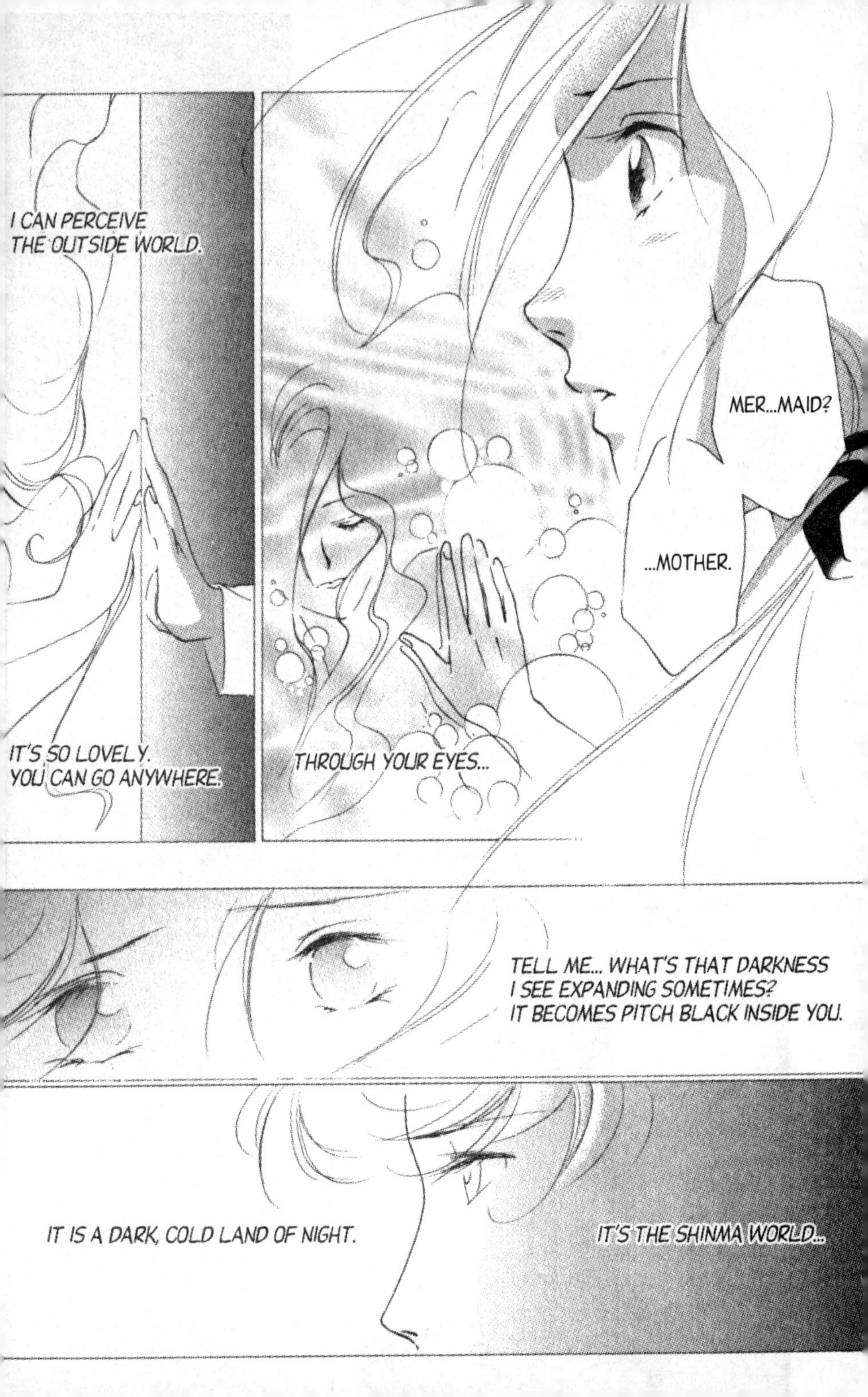
MER...MAID?
...MOTHER.
THROUGH YOUR EYES...
I CAN PERCEIVE THE OUTSIDE WORLD.
IT'S SO LOVELY. YOU CAN GO ANYWHERE.
TELL ME... WHAT'S THAT DARKNESS I SEE EXPANDING SOMETIMES? IT BECOMES PITCH BLACK INSIDE YOU.
IT'S THE SHINMA WORLD...
IT IS A DARK, COLD LAND OF NIGHT.

THE DARKNESS IS FRIGHTENING...

FWSHA!...

YES... THE SEA IS TEMPESTUOUS TONIGHT.

STOP!

THUNK.

I'M SORRY, BOY.

MIYU HAS SAID... THAT YOU MUST REST FOR A WHILE.

SHUU...

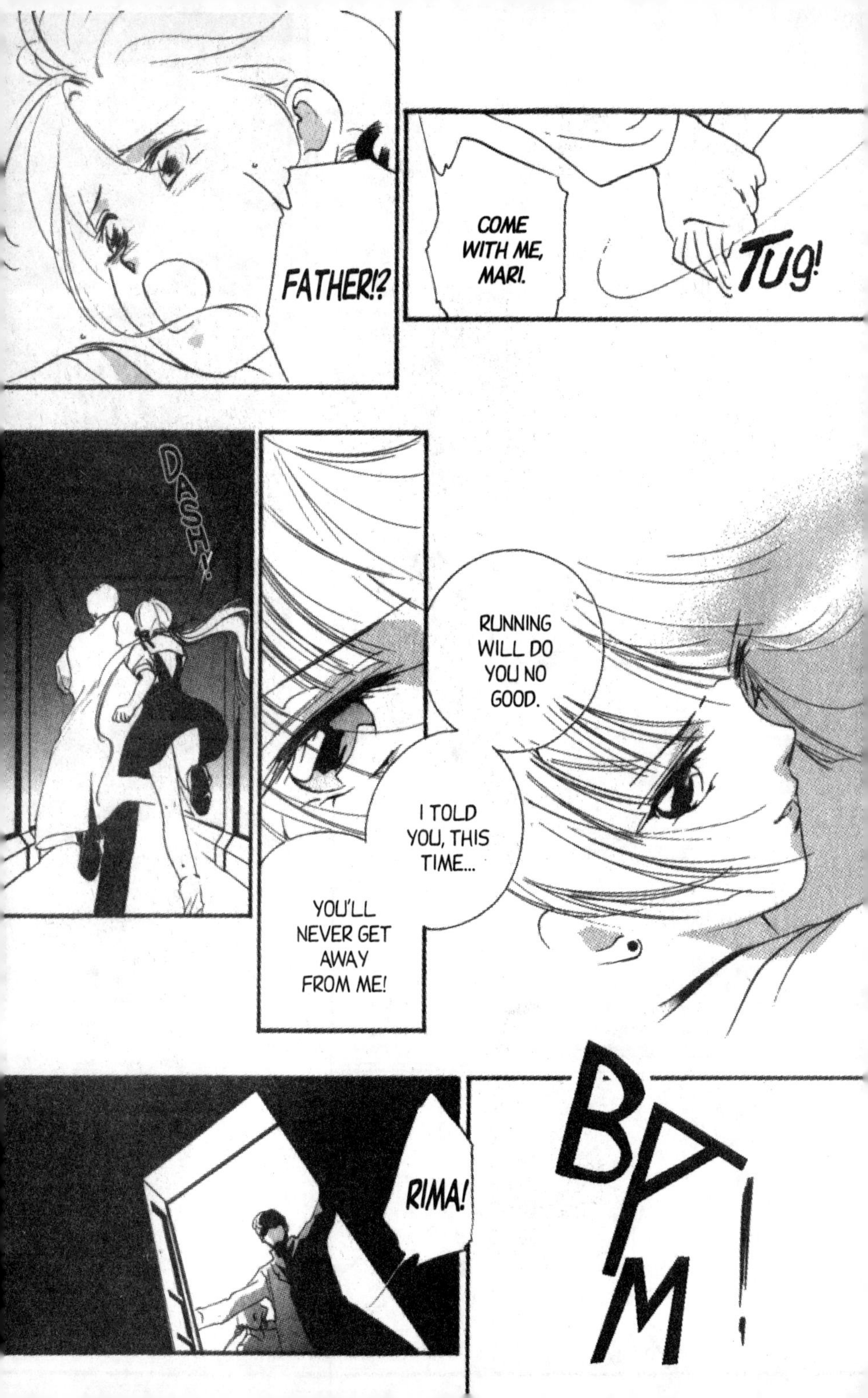
TUG!
COME WITH ME, MARI.
FATHER!?
RUNNING WILL DO YOU NO GOOD.
I TOLD YOU, THIS TIME...
YOU'LL NEVER GET AWAY FROM ME!
DASH!
BAM!
RIMA!

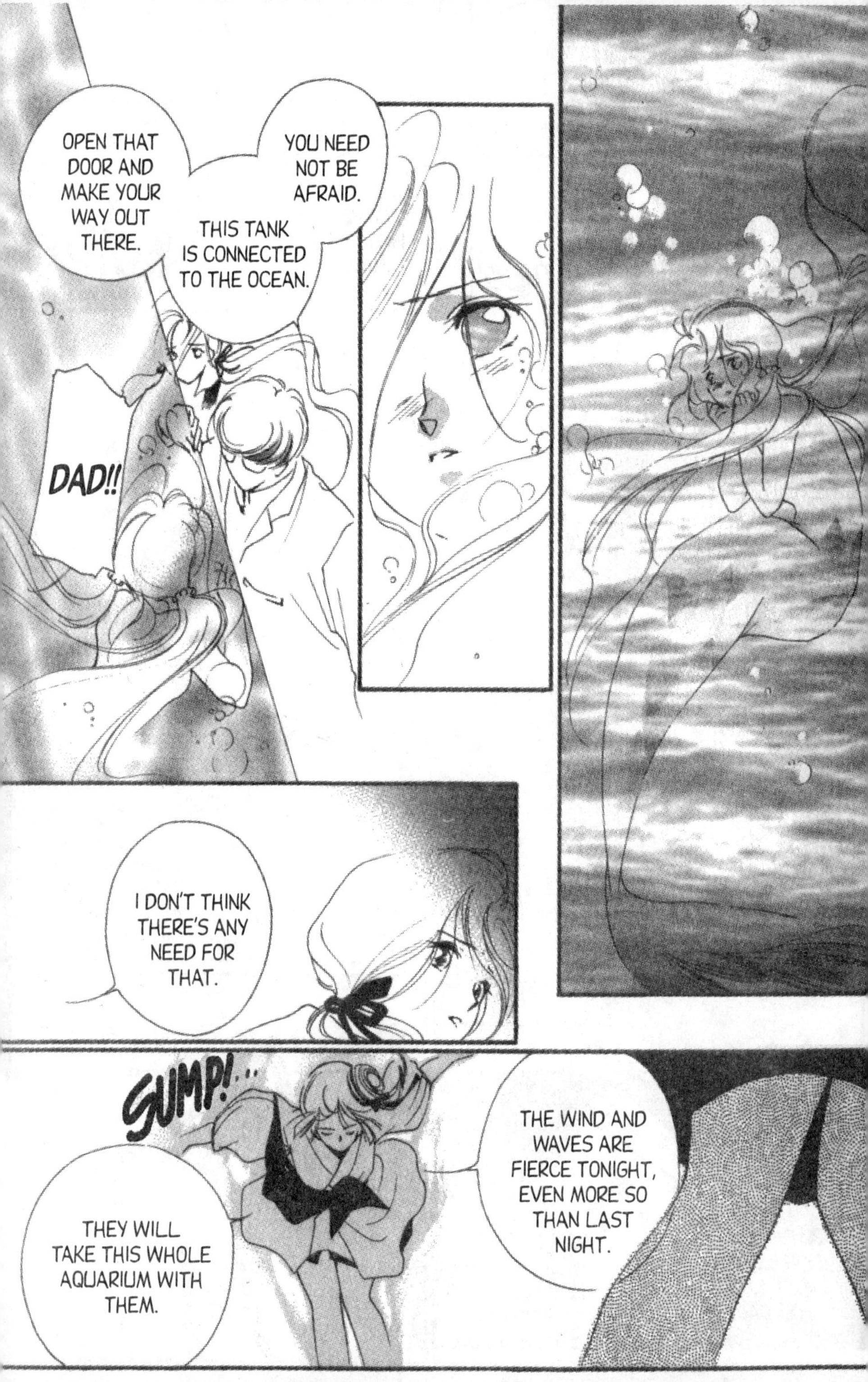
YOU NEED NOT BE AFRAID.
THIS TANK IS CONNECTED TO THE OCEAN.
OPEN THAT DOOR AND MAKE YOUR WAY OUT THERE.
DAD!!
I DON'T THINK THERE'S ANY NEED FOR THAT.
THE WIND AND WAVES ARE FIERCE TONIGHT, EVEN MORE SO THAN LAST NIGHT.
SUMP!...
THEY WILL TAKE THIS WHOLE AQUARIUM WITH THEM.

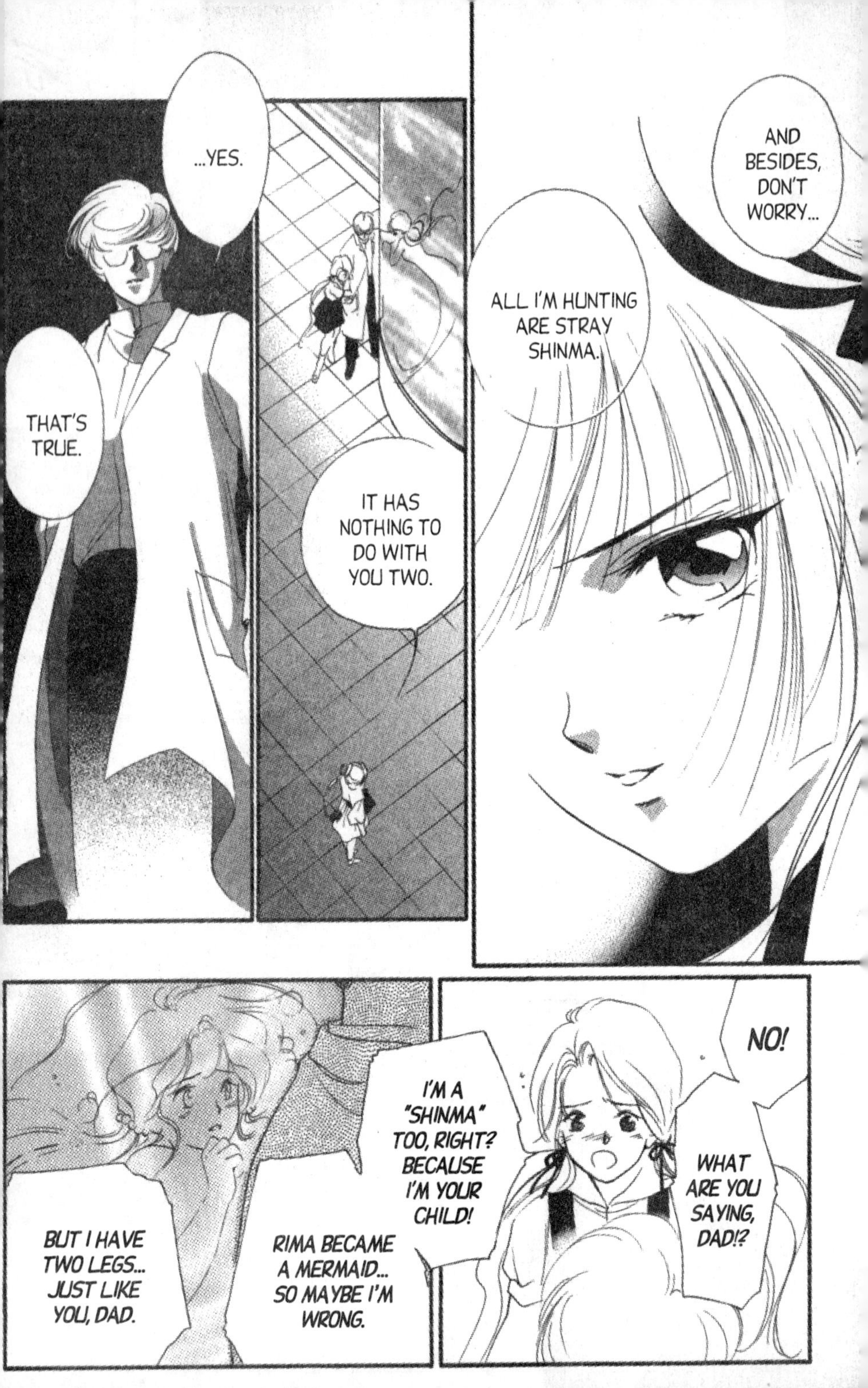
AND BESIDES, DON'T WORRY...
ALL I'M HUNTING ARE STRAY SHINMA.
...YES.
IT HAS NOTHING TO DO WITH YOU TWO.
THAT'S TRUE.
NO!
WHAT ARE YOU SAYING, DAD!?
I'M A "SHINMA" TOO, RIGHT? BECAUSE I'M YOUR CHILD!
RIMA BECAME A MERMAID... SO MAYBE I'M WRONG.
BUT I HAVE TWO LEGS... JUST LIKE YOU, DAD.

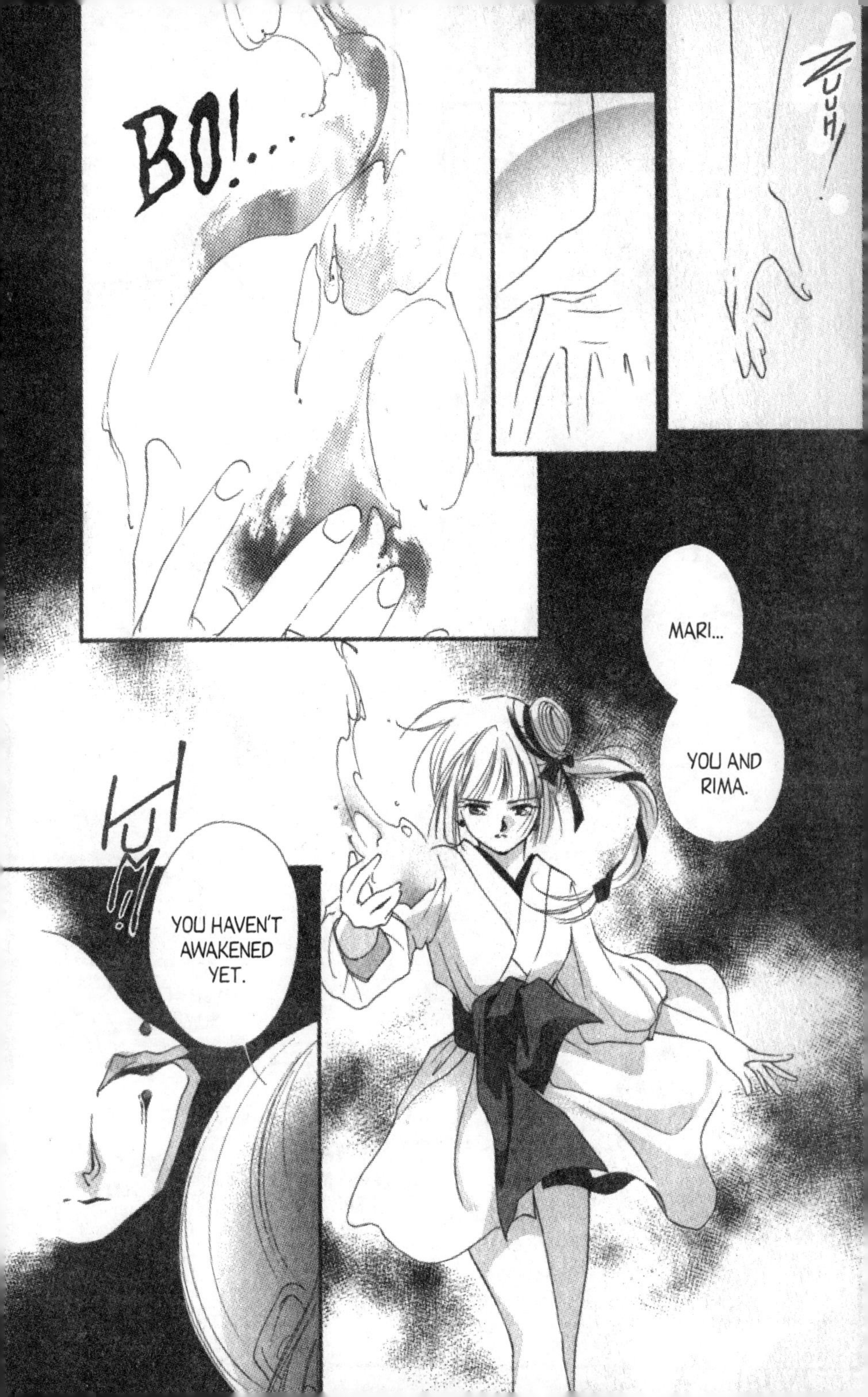
ZUUH!
BO!...
MARI...
YOU AND RIMA.
HUM!!
YOU HAVEN'T AWAKENED YET.

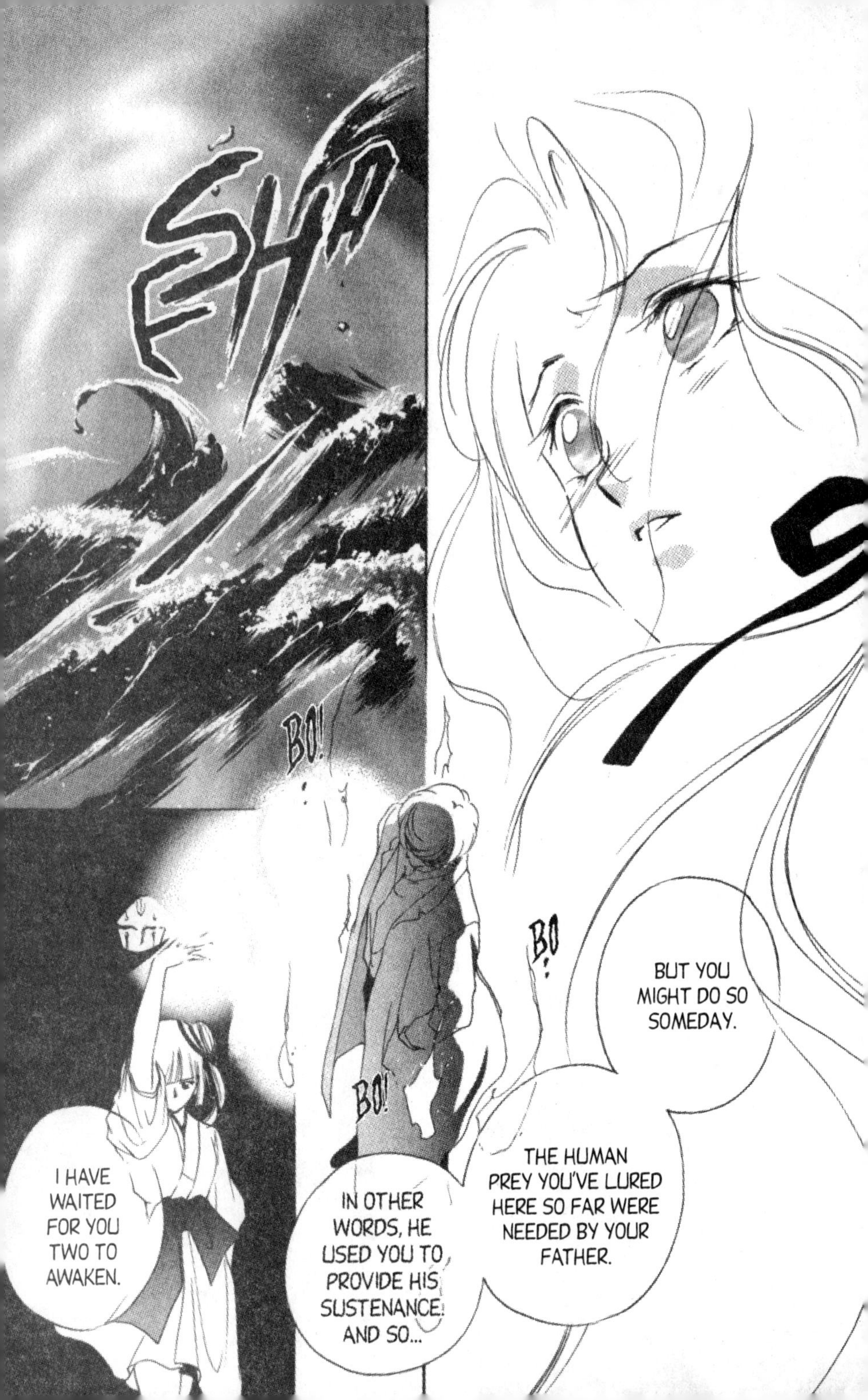
BUT YOU MIGHT DO SO SOMEDAY.
BO
THE HUMAN PREY YOU'VE LURED HERE SO FAR WERE NEEDED BY YOUR FATHER.
IN OTHER WORDS, HE USED YOU TO PROVIDE HIS SUSTENANCE. AND SO...
SHA
BO!
BO!
I HAVE WAITED FOR YOU TWO TO AWAKEN.

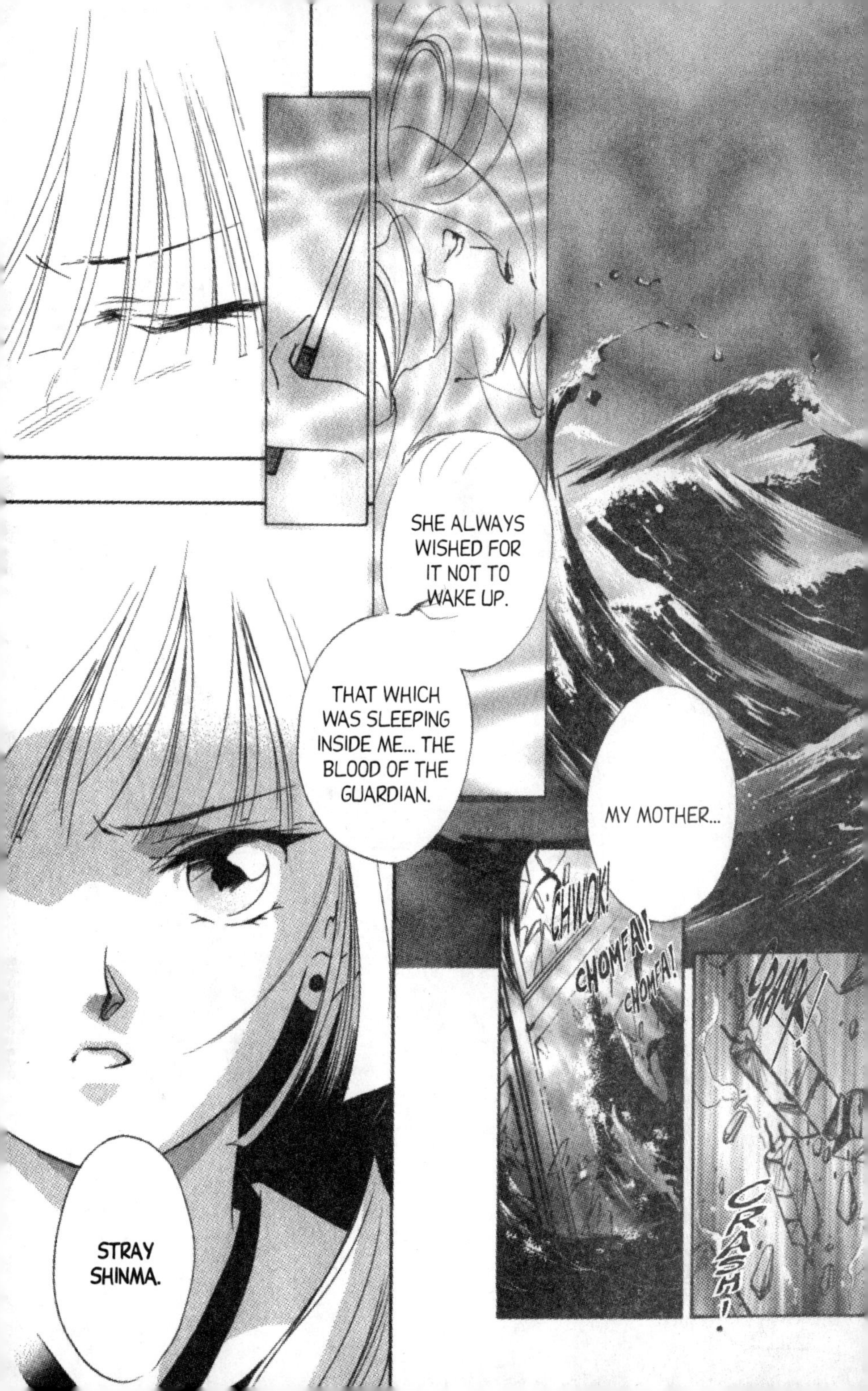
MY MOTHER...
SHE ALWAYS WISHED FOR IT NOT TO WAKE UP.
THAT WHICH WAS SLEEPING INSIDE ME... THE BLOOD OF THE GUARDIAN.
CHWOK!
CHOMFA!
CHOMFA!
CRANK!
CRASH!
STRAY SHINMA.

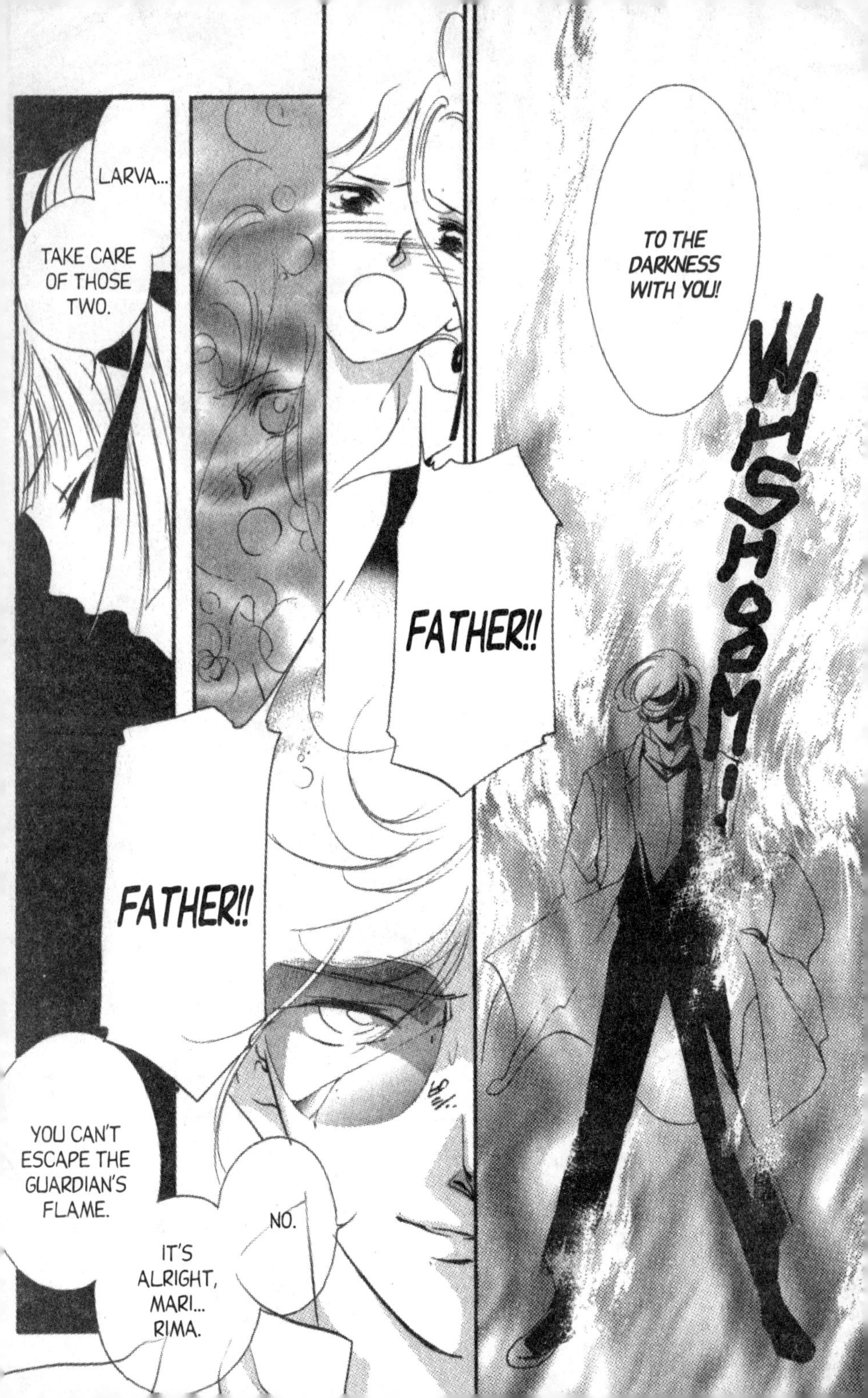
TO THE DARKNESS WITH YOU!
WHSHOOM!!
FATHER!!
LARVA...
TAKE CARE OF THOSE TWO.
FATHER!!
YOU CAN'T ESCAPE THE GUARDIAN'S FLAME.
NO.
IT'S ALRIGHT, MARI... RIMA.

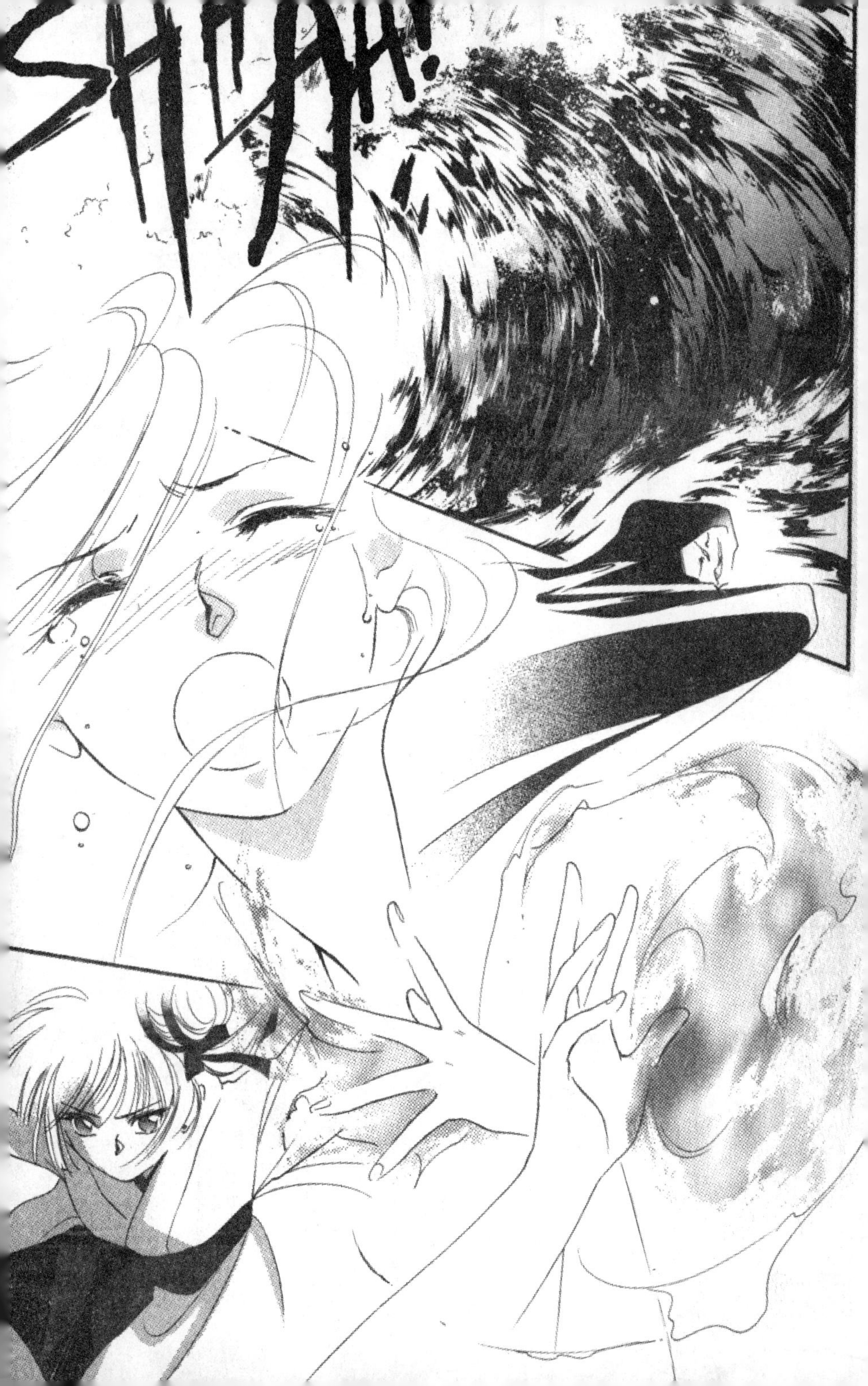
SHOAH!

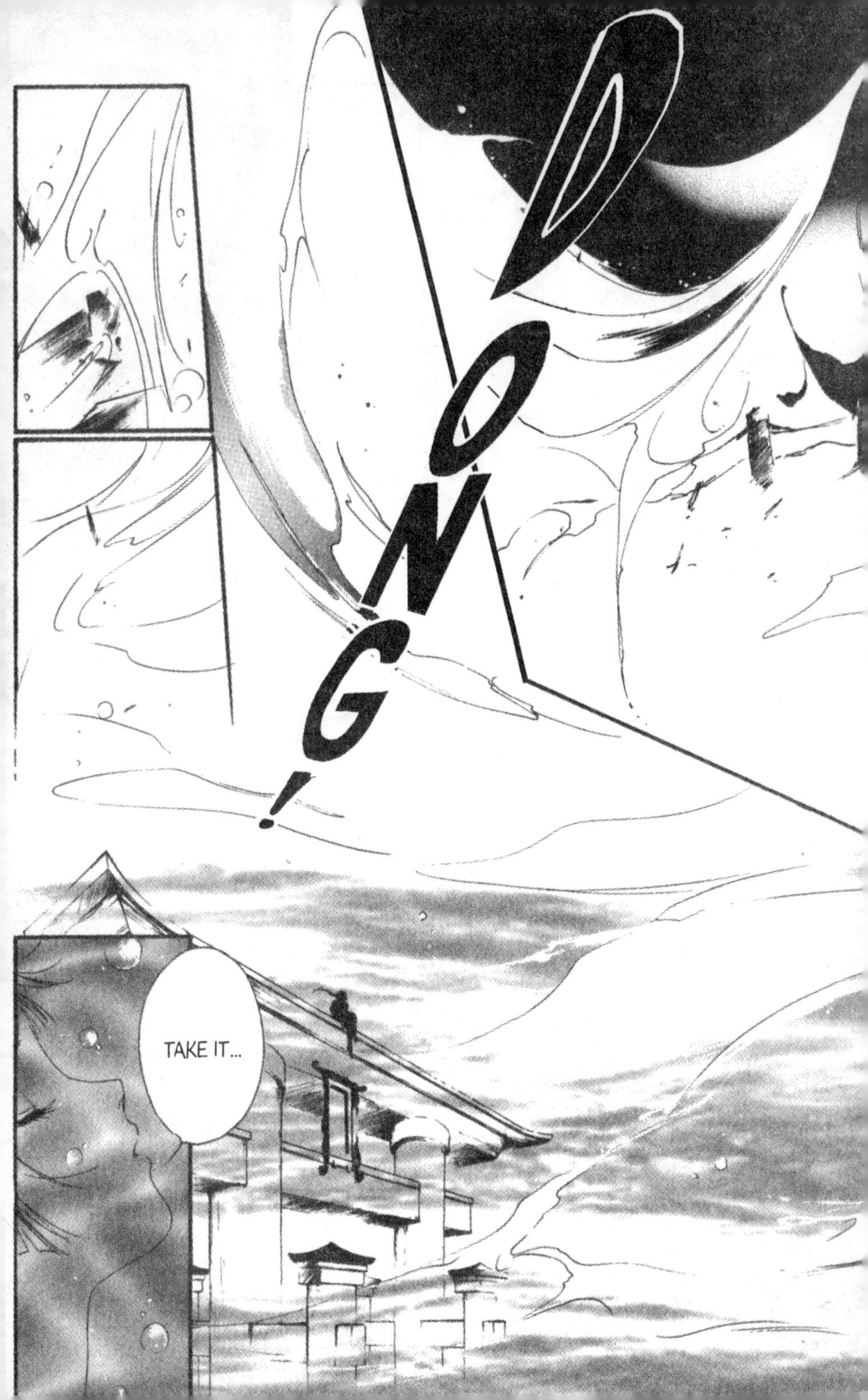
DOONG!
TAKE IT...

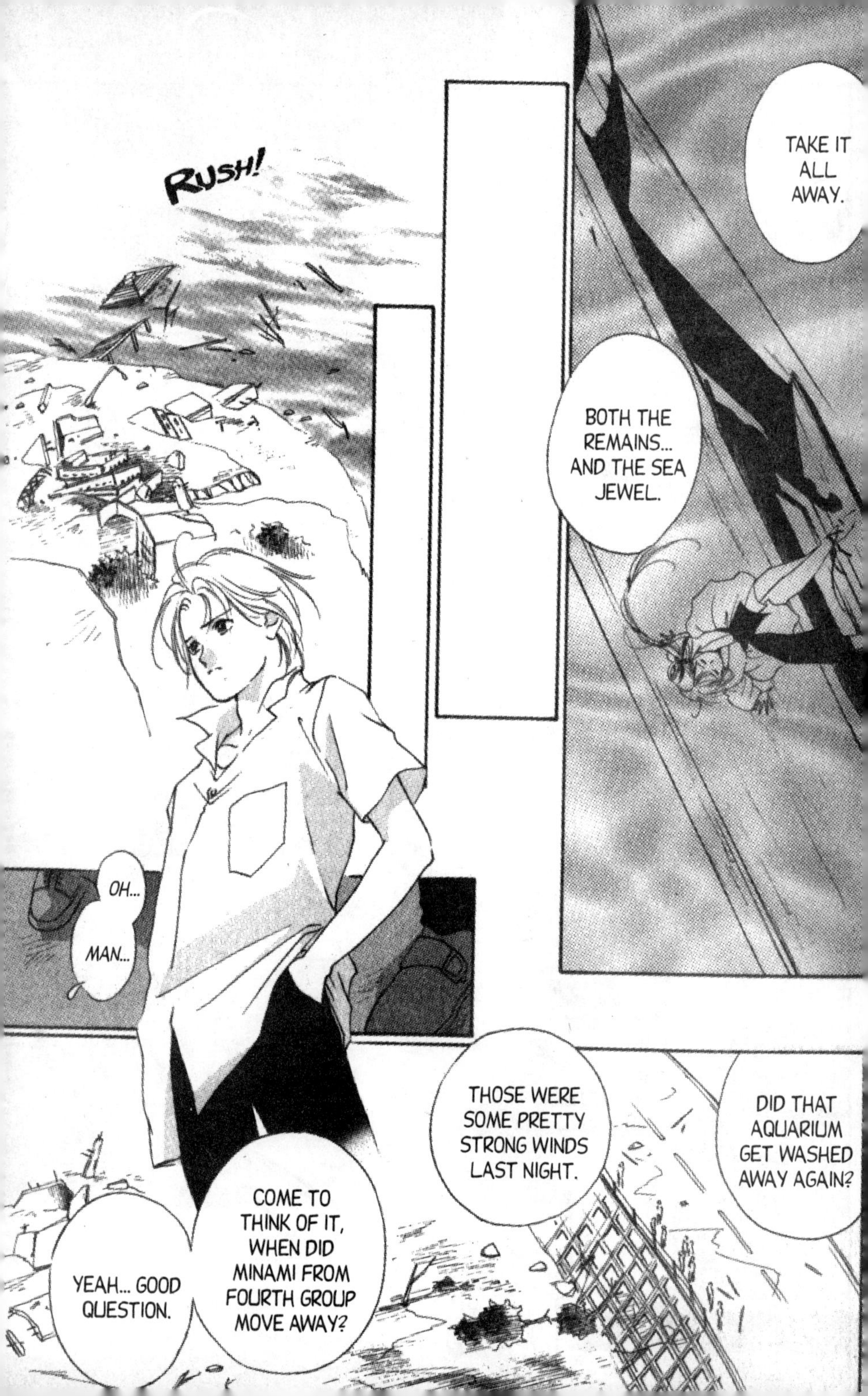
TAKE IT ALL AWAY.
BOTH THE REMAINS... AND THE SEA JEWEL.
RUSH!
OH...
MAN...
DID THAT AQUARIUM GET WASHED AWAY AGAIN?
THOSE WERE SOME PRETTY STRONG WINDS LAST NIGHT.
COME TO THINK OF IT, WHEN DID MINAMI FROM FOURTH GROUP MOVE AWAY?
YEAH... GOOD QUESTION.

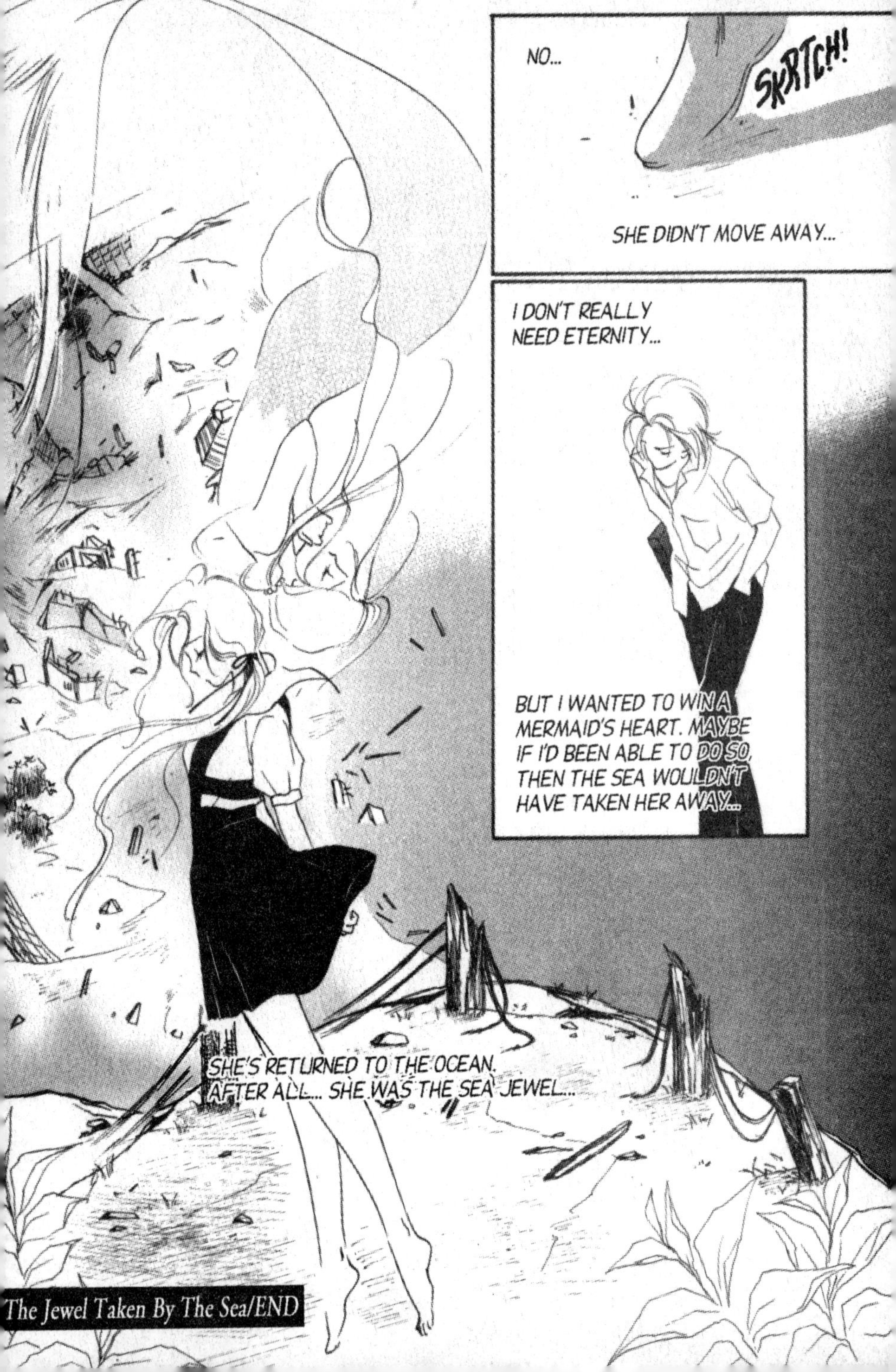
NO...
SKRTCH!
SHE DIDN'T MOVE AWAY...
I DON'T REALLY NEED ETERNITY...
BUT I WANTED TO WIN A MERMAID'S HEART. MAYBE IF I'D BEEN ABLE TO DO SO, THEN THE SEA WOULDN'T HAVE TAKEN HER AWAY...
SHE'S RETURNED TO THE OCEAN. AFTER ALL... SHE WAS THE SEA JEWEL...
The Jewel Taken By The Sea/END

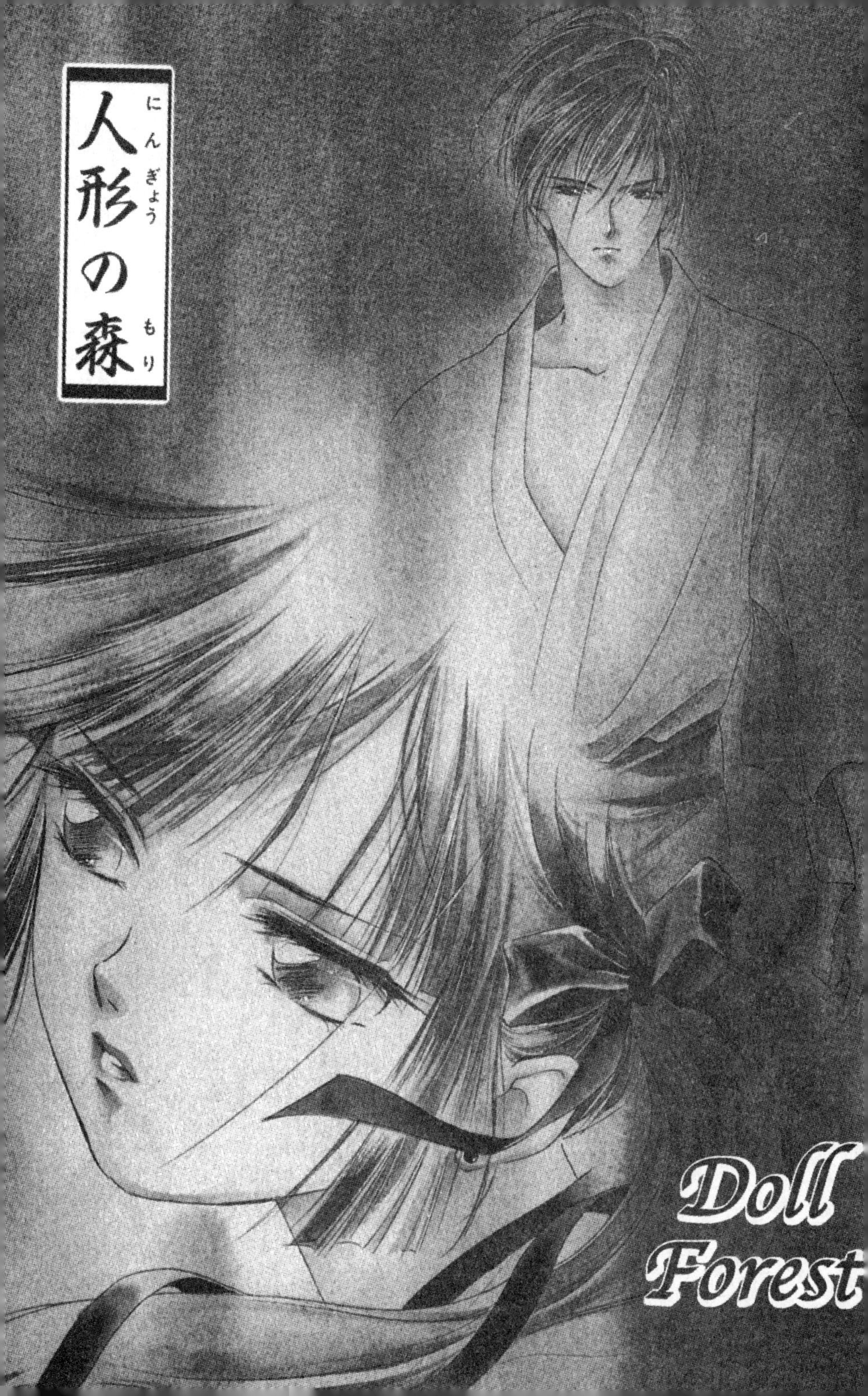
人形の森
にんぎょう もり
Doll Forest

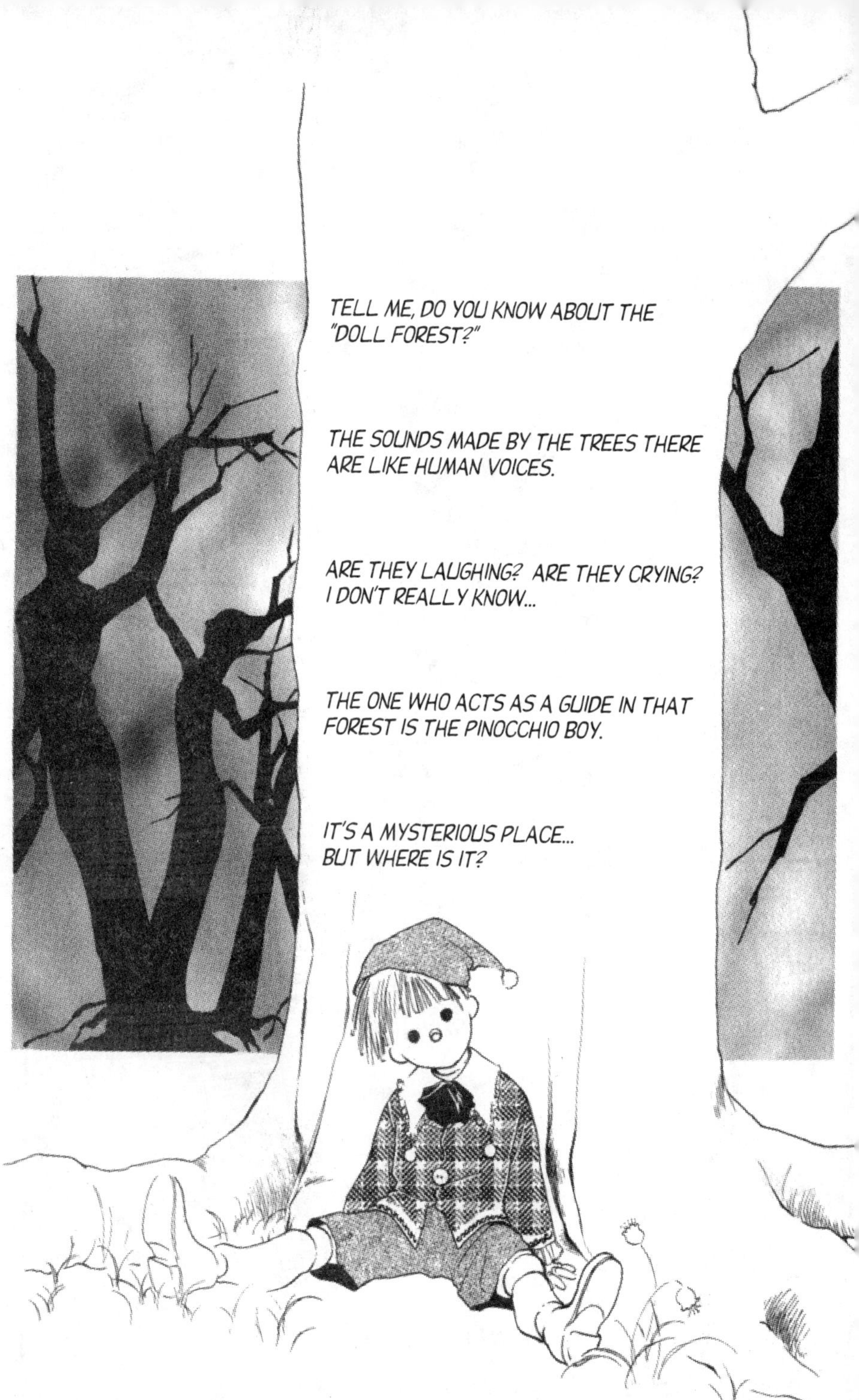
TELL ME, DO YOU KNOW ABOUT THE "DOLL FOREST?"
THE SOUNDS MADE BY THE TREES THERE ARE LIKE HUMAN VOICES.
ARE THEY LAUGHING? ARE THEY CRYING? I DON'T REALLY KNOW...
THE ONE WHO ACTS AS A GUIDE IN THAT FOREST IS THE PINOCCHIO BOY.
IT'S A MYSTERIOUS PLACE... BUT WHERE IS IT?

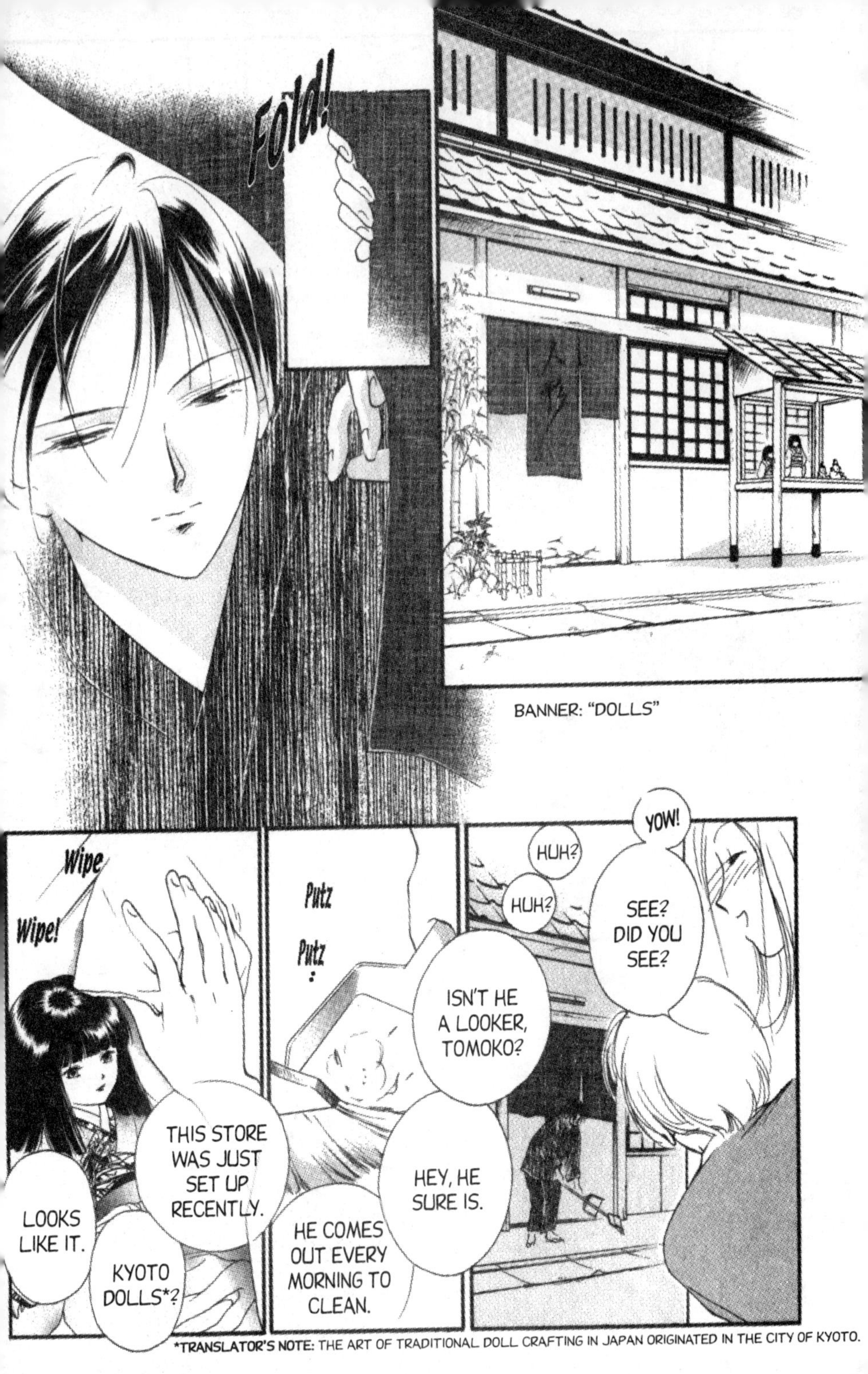
BANNER: "DOLLS"
Fold!
YOW!
HUH?
HUH?
SEE? DID YOU SEE?
Putz
Putz
ISN'T HE A LOOKER, TOMOKO?
HEY, HE SURE IS.
HE COMES OUT EVERY MORNING TO CLEAN.
Wipe
Wipe!
THIS STORE WAS JUST SET UP RECENTLY.
LOOKS LIKE IT.
KYOTO DOLLS*?

***TRANSLATOR'S NOTE:** THE ART OF TRADITIONAL DOLL CRAFTING IN JAPAN ORIGINATED IN THE CITY OF KYOTO.

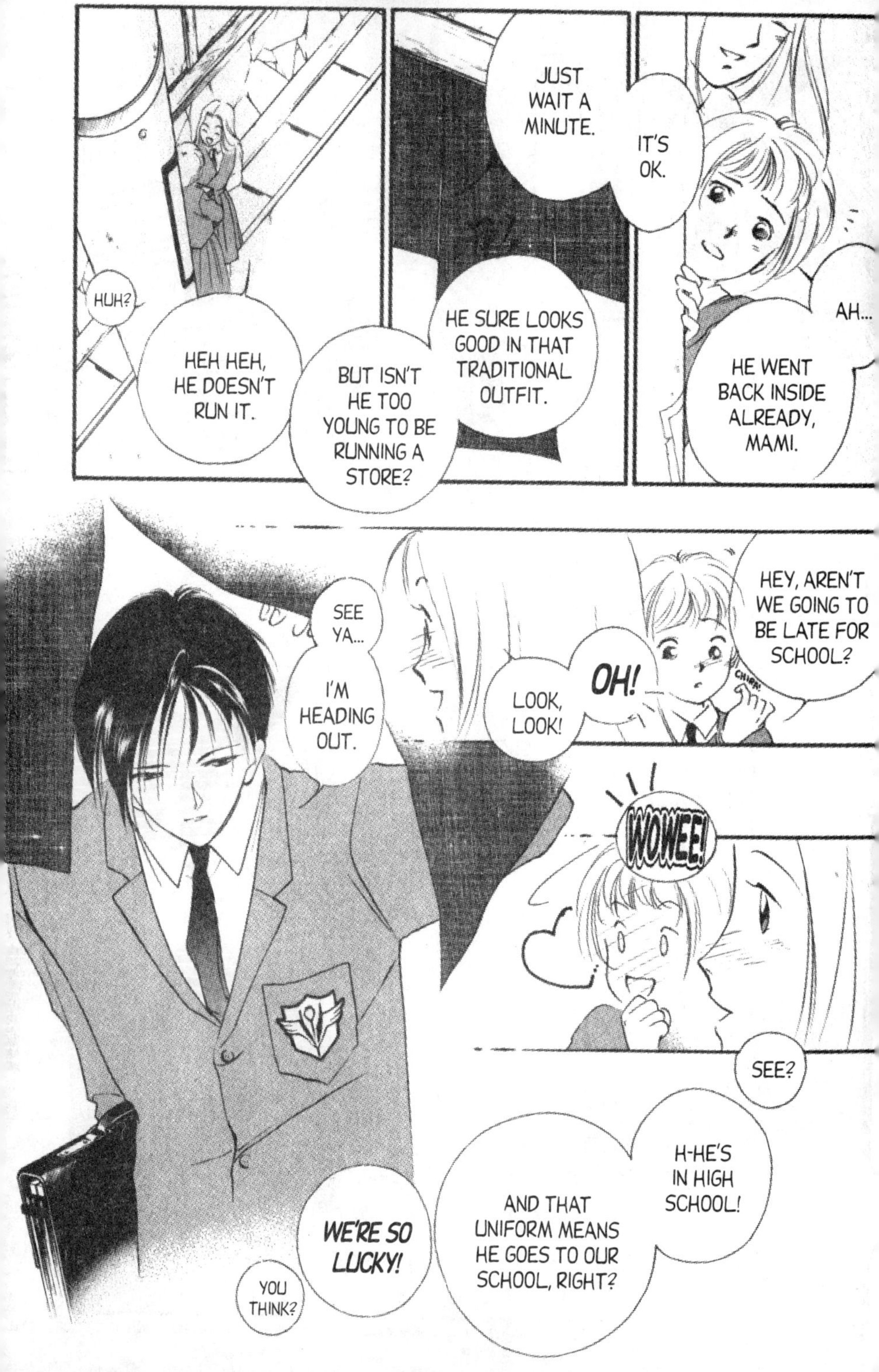
AH...
HE WENT BACK INSIDE ALREADY, MAMI.
IT'S OK.
JUST WAIT A MINUTE.
HE SURE LOOKS GOOD IN THAT TRADITIONAL OUTFIT.
BUT ISN'T HE TOO YOUNG TO BE RUNNING A STORE?
HUH?
HEH HEH, HE DOESN'T RUN IT.
HEY, AREN'T WE GOING TO BE LATE FOR SCHOOL?
CHIRP!
OH!
LOOK, LOOK!
WOWEE!
SEE?
H-HE'S IN HIGH SCHOOL!
AND THAT UNIFORM MEANS HE GOES TO OUR SCHOOL, RIGHT?
WE'RE SO LUCKY!
YOU THINK?
SEE YA...
I'M HEADING OUT.

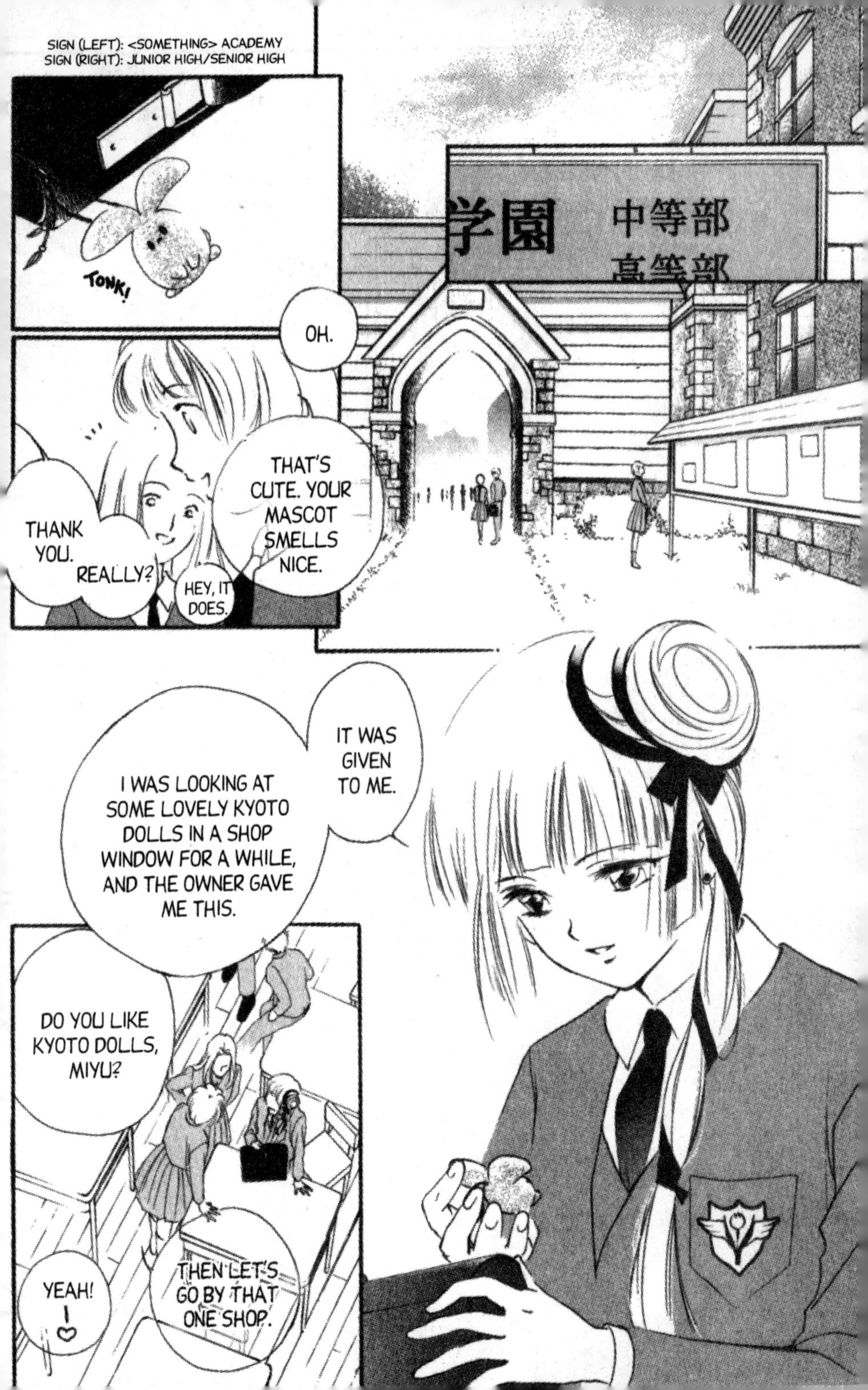
学園 中等部
高等部
SIGN (LEFT): <SOMETHING> ACADEMY
SIGN (RIGHT): JUNIOR HIGH/SENIOR HIGH
TONK!
OH.
THAT'S CUTE. YOUR MASCOT SMELLS NICE.
HEY, IT DOES.
REALLY?
THANK YOU.
IT WAS GIVEN TO ME.
I WAS LOOKING AT SOME LOVELY KYOTO DOLLS IN A SHOP WINDOW FOR A WHILE, AND THE OWNER GAVE ME THIS.
DO YOU LIKE KYOTO DOLLS, MIYU?
THEN LET'S GO BY THAT ONE SHOP.
YEAH! ♡

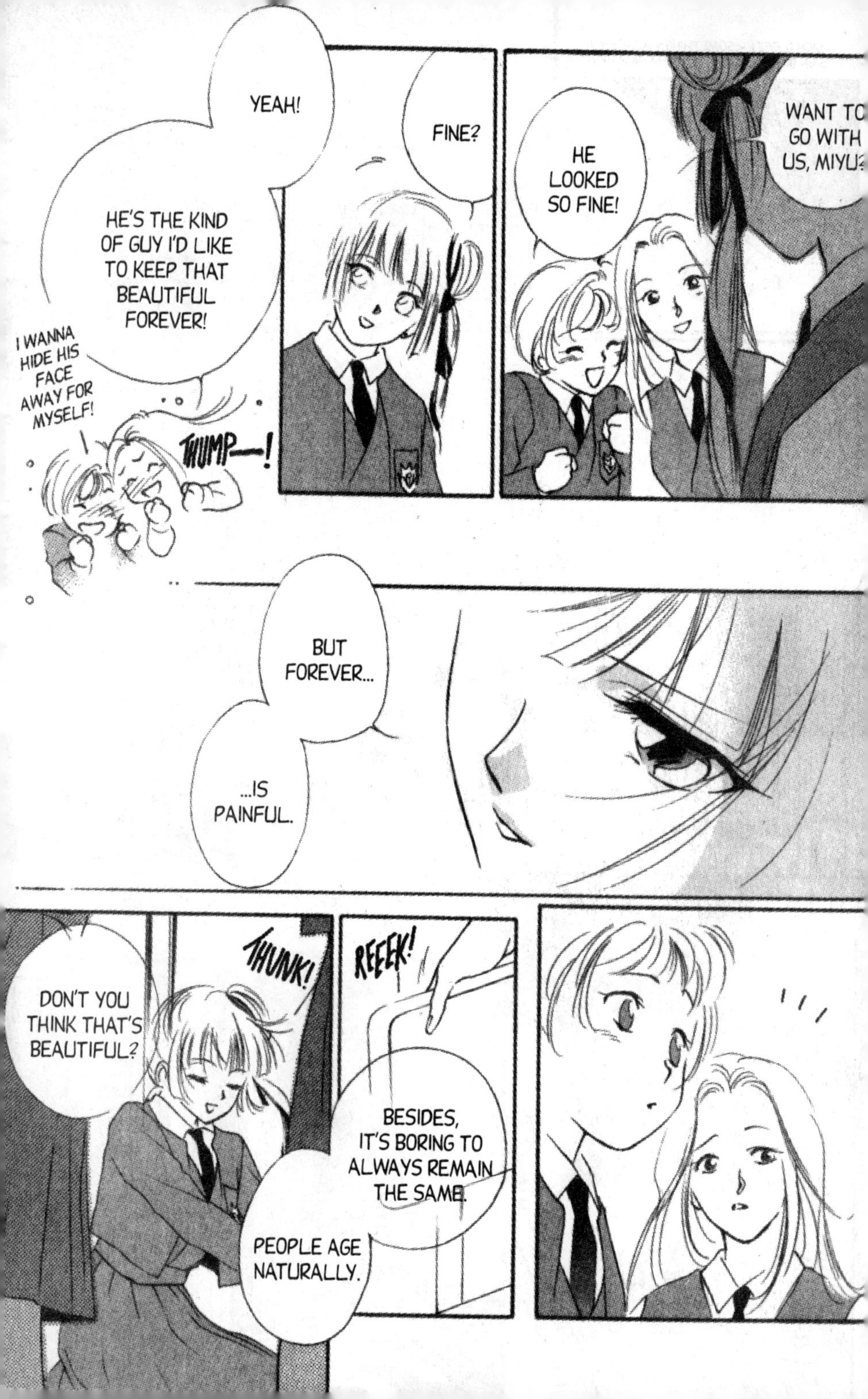
WANT TO GO WITH US, MIYU?
HE LOOKED SO FINE!
FINE?
YEAH!
HE'S THE KIND OF GUY I'D LIKE TO KEEP THAT BEAUTIFUL FOREVER!
I WANNA HIDE HIS FACE AWAY FOR MYSELF!
THUMP—!
BUT FOREVER...
...IS PAINFUL.
BESIDES, IT'S BORING TO ALWAYS REMAIN THE SAME.
PEOPLE AGE NATURALLY.
REEEK!
THUNK!
DON'T YOU THINK THAT'S BEAUTIFUL?

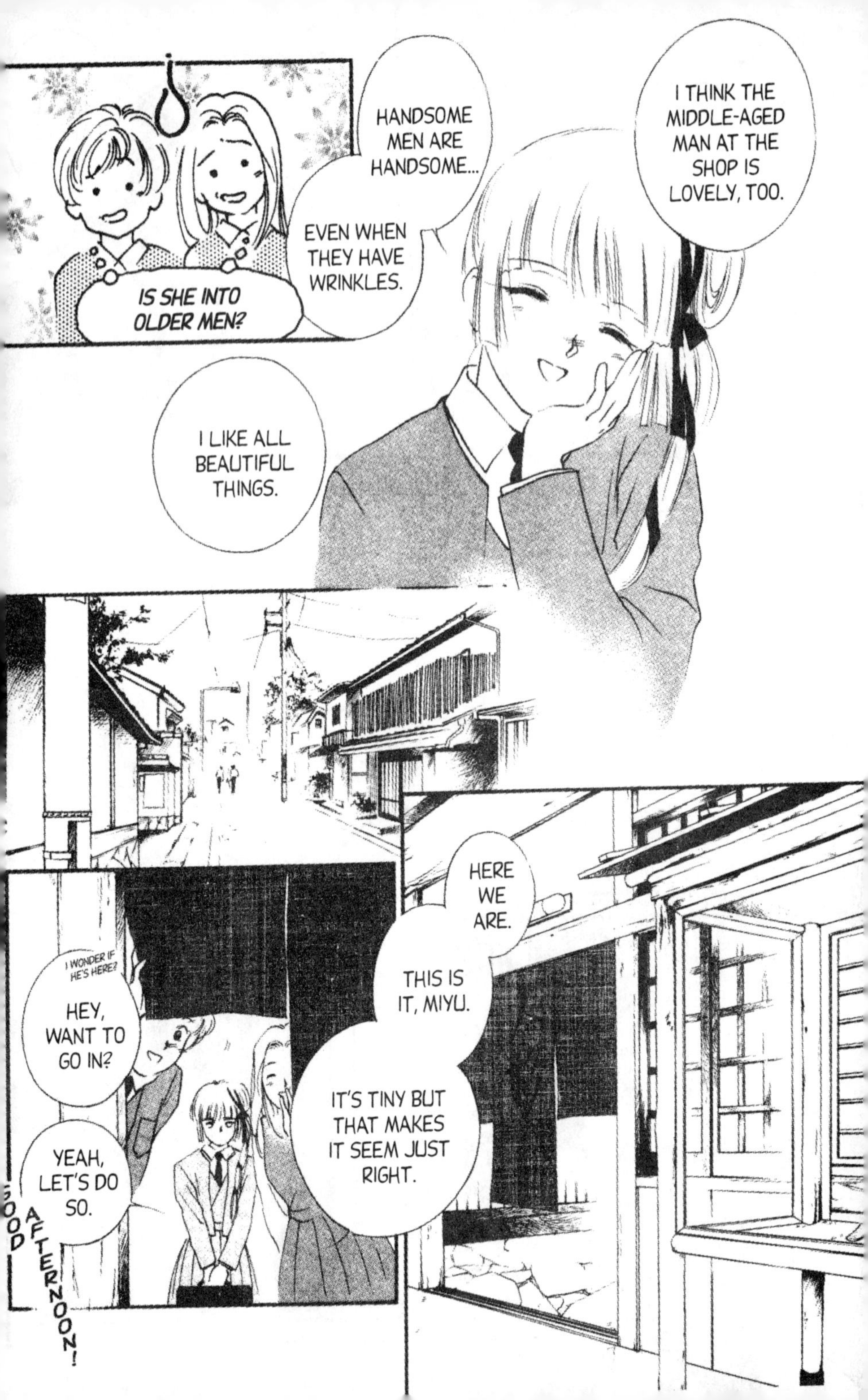
I THINK THE MIDDLE-AGED MAN AT THE SHOP IS LOVELY, TOO.
HANDSOME MEN ARE HANDSOME...
EVEN WHEN THEY HAVE WRINKLES.
?
IS SHE INTO OLDER MEN?
I LIKE ALL BEAUTIFUL THINGS.
HERE WE ARE.
THIS IS IT, MIYU.
IT'S TINY BUT THAT MAKES IT SEEM JUST RIGHT.
HEY, WANT TO GO IN?
I WONDER IF HE'S HERE?
YEAH, LET'S DO SO.
GOOD AFTERNOON!

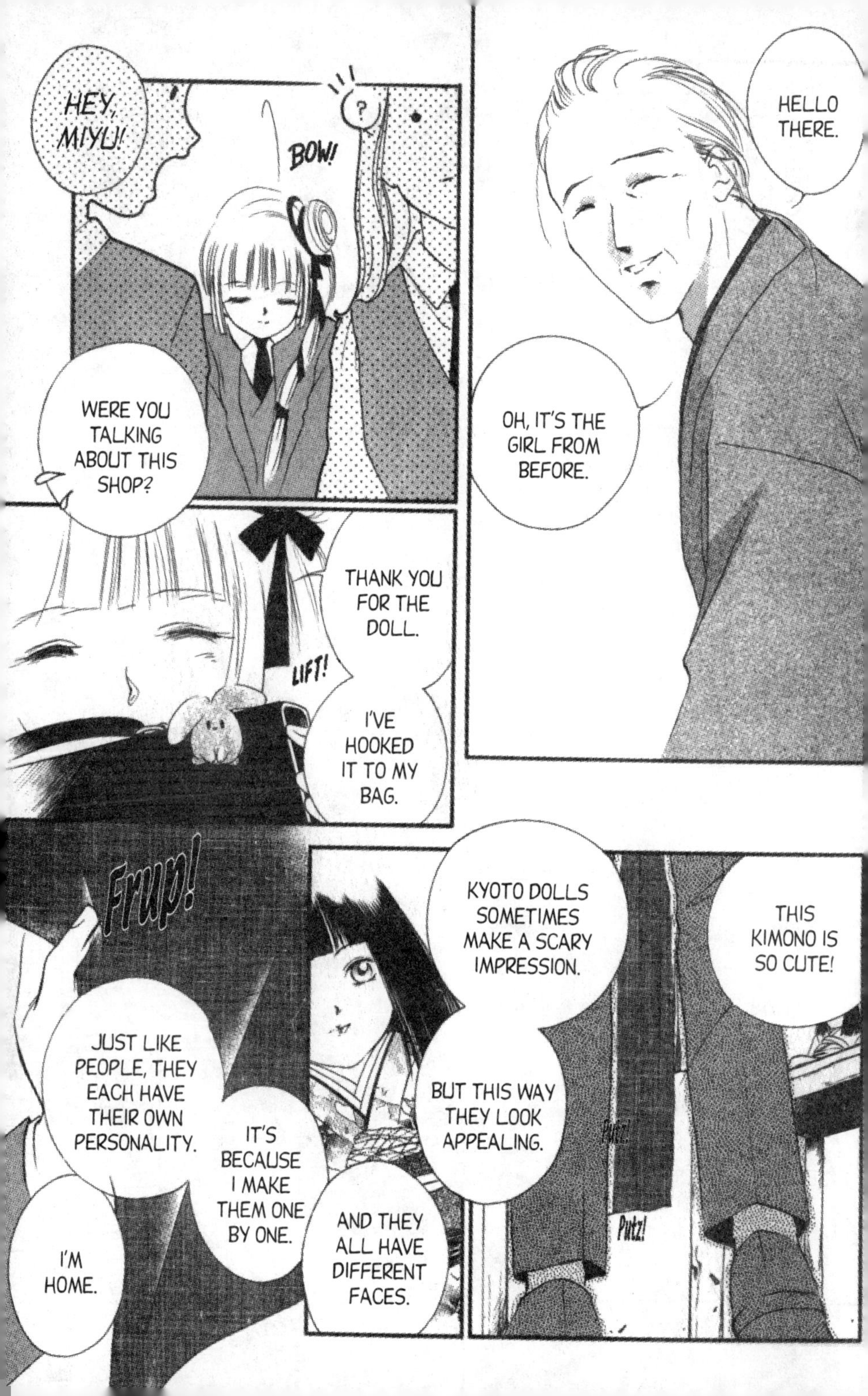
HELLO THERE.
OH, IT'S THE GIRL FROM BEFORE.
HEY, MIYU!
BOW!
WERE YOU TALKING ABOUT THIS SHOP?
THANK YOU FOR THE DOLL.
LIFT!
I'VE HOOKED IT TO MY BAG.
THIS KIMONO IS SO CUTE!
Putz!
Putz!
KYOTO DOLLS SOMETIMES MAKE A SCARY IMPRESSION.
BUT THIS WAY THEY LOOK APPEALING.
Frup!
JUST LIKE PEOPLE, THEY EACH HAVE THEIR OWN PERSONALITY.
IT'S BECAUSE I MAKE THEM ONE BY ONE.
AND THEY ALL HAVE DIFFERENT FACES.
I'M HOME.

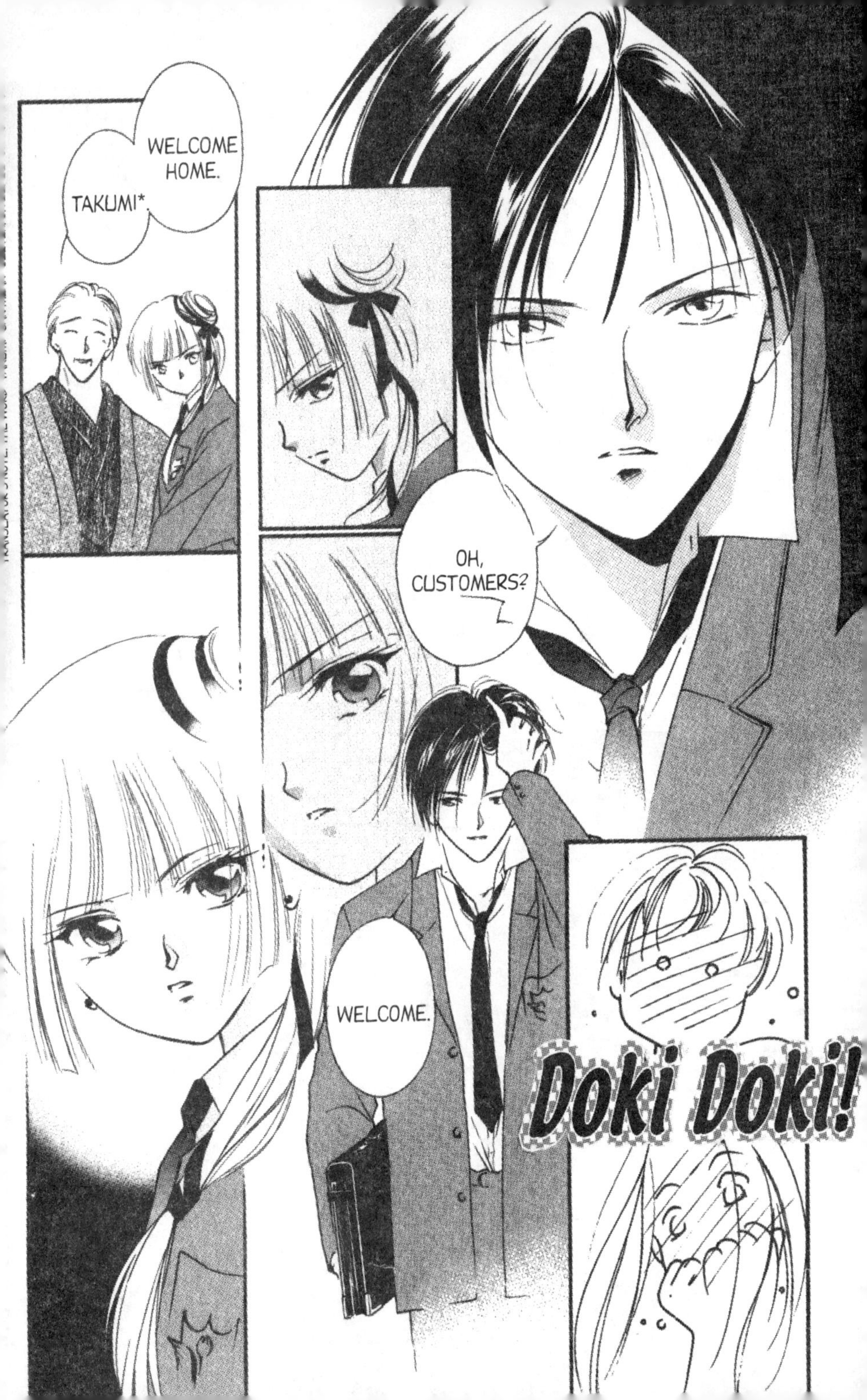
WELCOME HOME.
TAKUMI*.
OH, CUSTOMERS?
WELCOME.
Doki Doki!

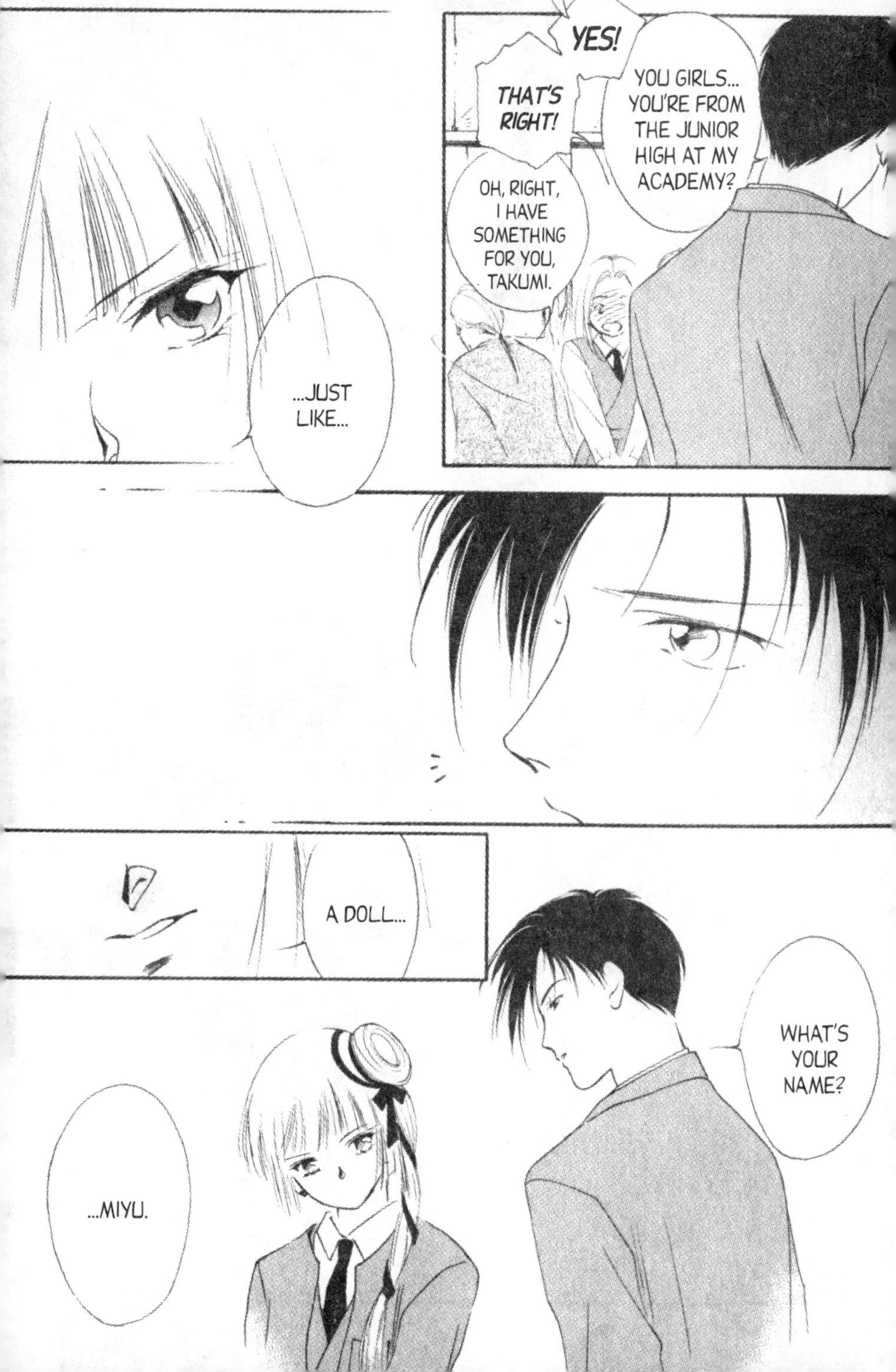
YOU GIRLS... YOU'RE FROM THE JUNIOR HIGH AT MY ACADEMY?
YES!
THAT'S RIGHT!
OH, RIGHT, I HAVE SOMETHING FOR YOU, TAKUMI.
...JUST LIKE...
A DOLL...
WHAT'S YOUR NAME?
...MIYU.

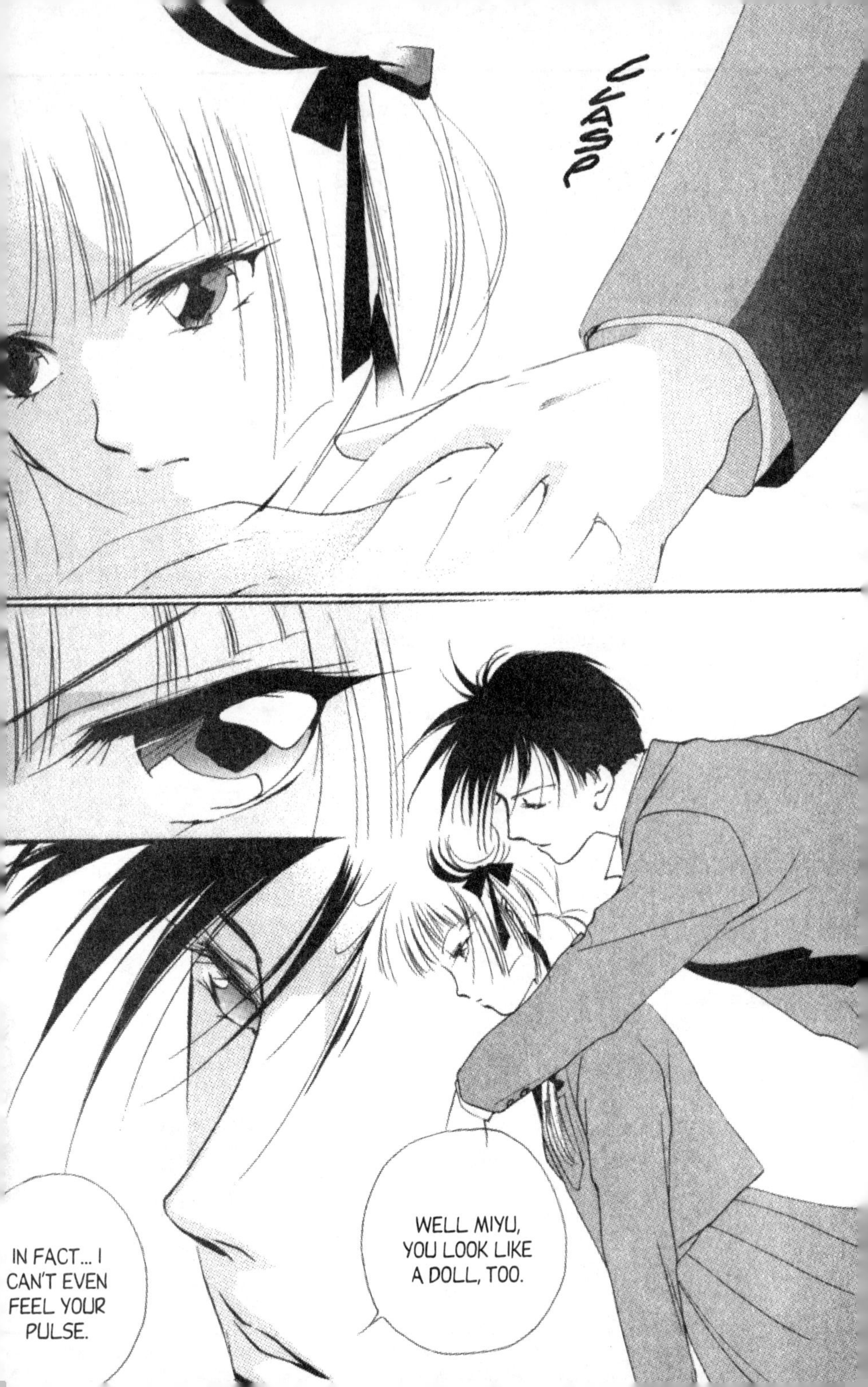
WELL MIYU, YOU LOOK LIKE A DOLL, TOO.
IN FACT... I CAN'T EVEN FEEL YOUR PULSE.

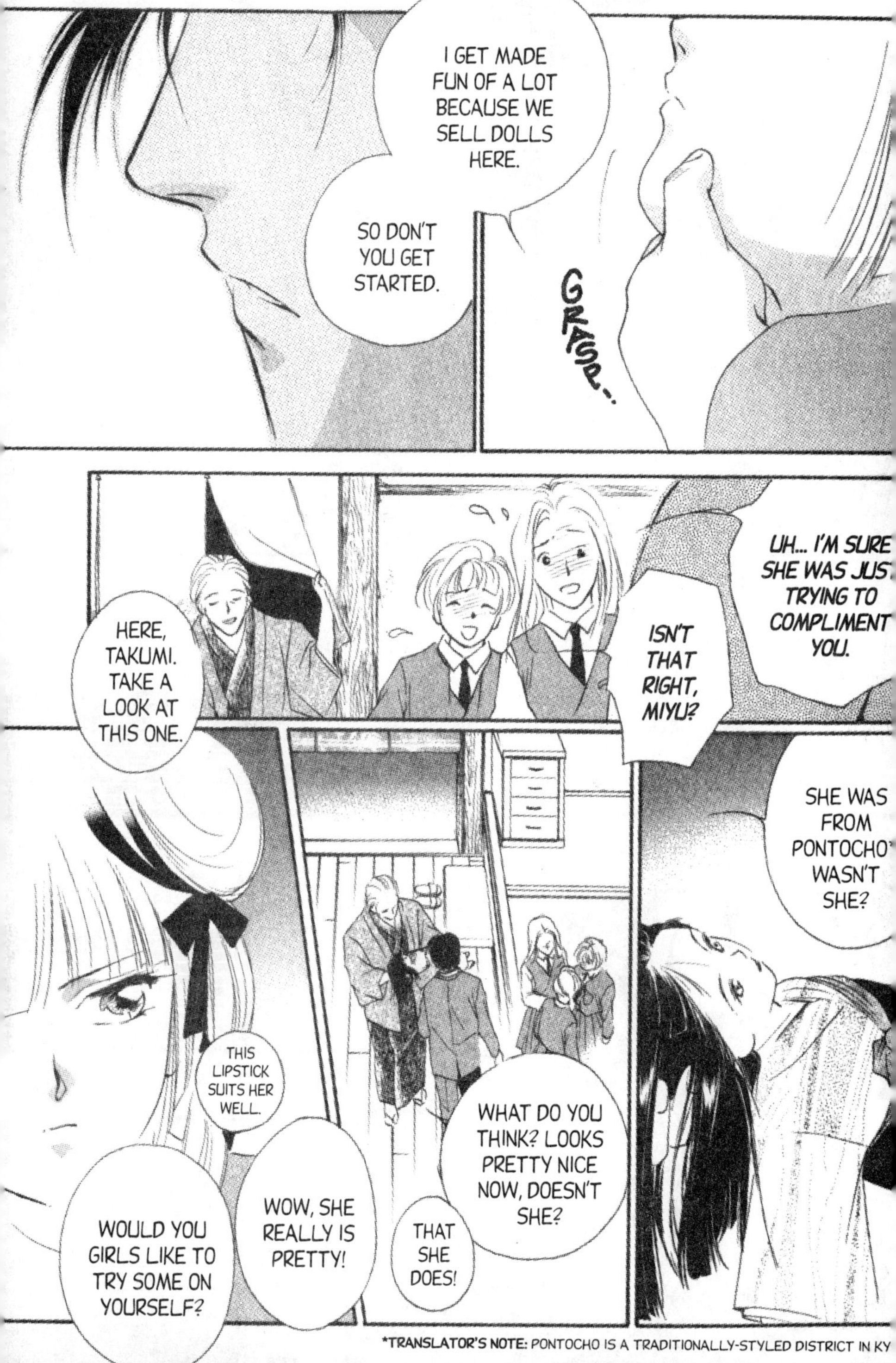
GRASP...
I GET MADE FUN OF A LOT BECAUSE WE SELL DOLLS HERE.
SO DON'T YOU GET STARTED.
UH... I'M SURE SHE WAS JUST TRYING TO COMPLIMENT YOU.
ISN'T THAT RIGHT, MIYU?
HERE, TAKUMI. TAKE A LOOK AT THIS ONE.
SHE WAS FROM PONTOCHO* WASN'T SHE?
WHAT DO YOU THINK? LOOKS PRETTY NICE NOW, DOESN'T SHE?
THAT SHE DOES!
WOW, SHE REALLY IS PRETTY!
THIS LIPSTICK SUITS HER WELL.
WOULD YOU GIRLS LIKE TO TRY SOME ON YOURSELF?

*TRANSLATOR'S NOTE: PONTOCHO IS A TRADITIONALLY-STYLED DISTRICT IN KY

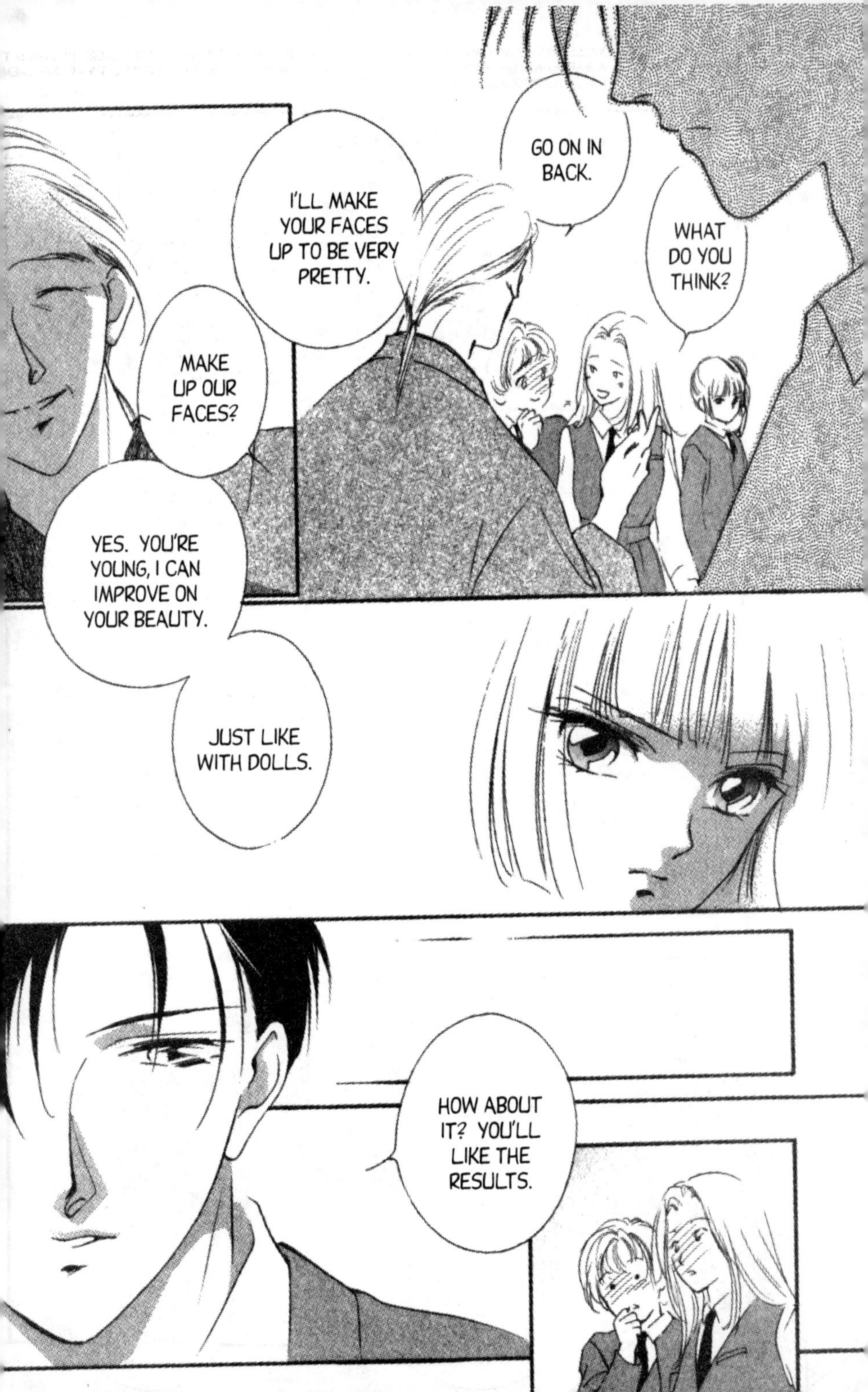
GO ON IN BACK.
WHAT DO YOU THINK?
I'LL MAKE YOUR FACES UP TO BE VERY PRETTY.
MAKE UP OUR FACES?
YES. YOU'RE YOUNG, I CAN IMPROVE ON YOUR BEAUTY.
JUST LIKE WITH DOLLS.
HOW ABOUT IT? YOU'LL LIKE THE RESULTS.

*TRANSLATOR'S NOTE: ICHIMATSU DOLLS WERE FIRST MADE IN THE KANPO AND HOREKI ERAS (1741-1764). FACES WERE DESIGNED T RESEMBLE SANOGAWA ICHIMATSU, A KABUKI ACTOR FAMOUS FOR PORTRAYING YOUNG MEN. THE DOLLS COULD WEAR DIFFEREN COSTUMES AND THE HIGH QUALITY ONES HAD POSEABLE JOINTS.

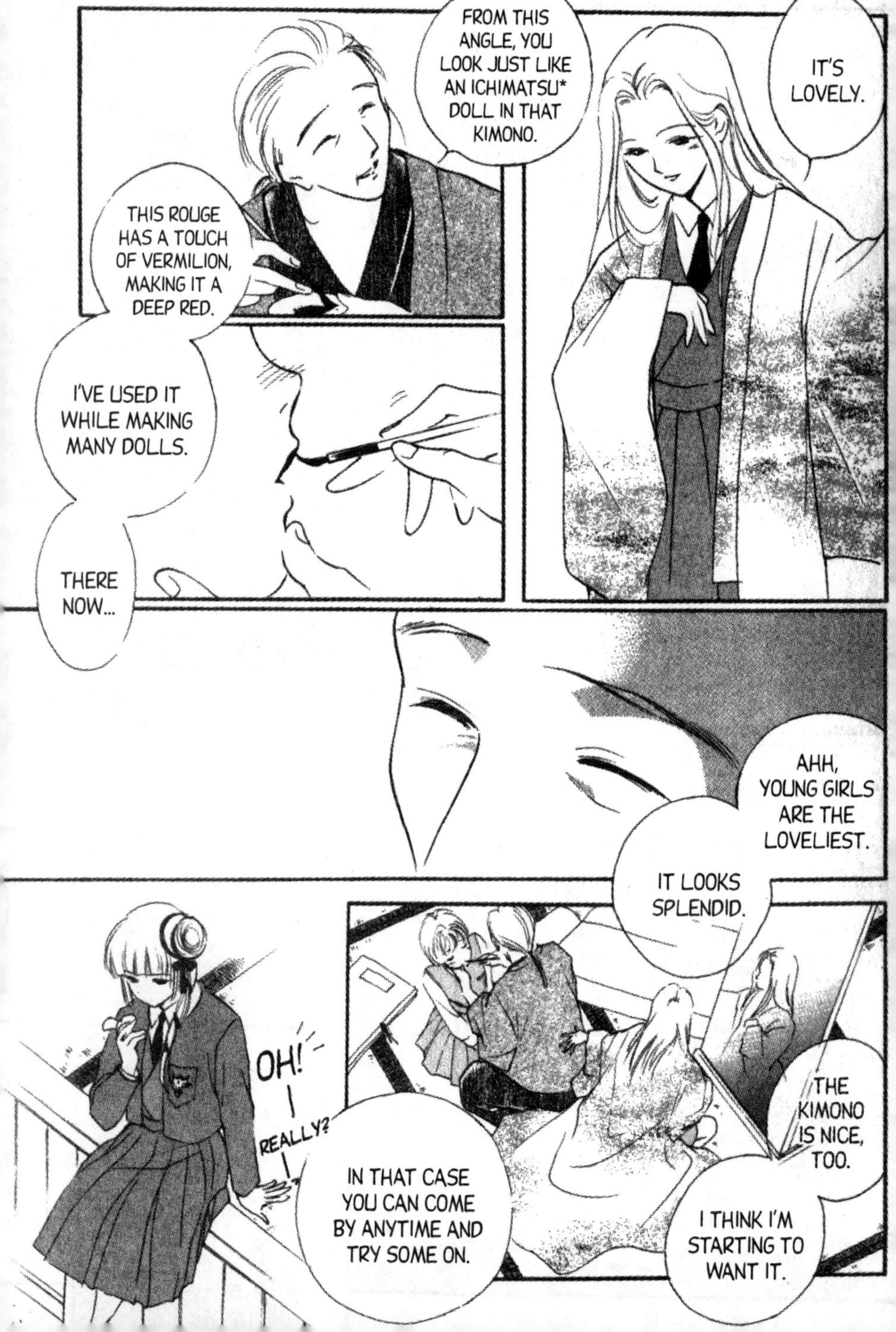
IT'S LOVELY.
FROM THIS ANGLE, YOU LOOK JUST LIKE AN ICHIMATSU* DOLL IN THAT KIMONO.
THIS ROUGE HAS A TOUCH OF VERMILION, MAKING IT A DEEP RED.
I'VE USED IT WHILE MAKING MANY DOLLS.
THERE NOW...
AHH, YOUNG GIRLS ARE THE LOVELIEST.
IT LOOKS SPLENDID.
THE KIMONO IS NICE, TOO.
I THINK I'M STARTING TO WANT IT.
IN THAT CASE YOU CAN COME BY ANYTIME AND TRY SOME ON.
OH!
REALLY?

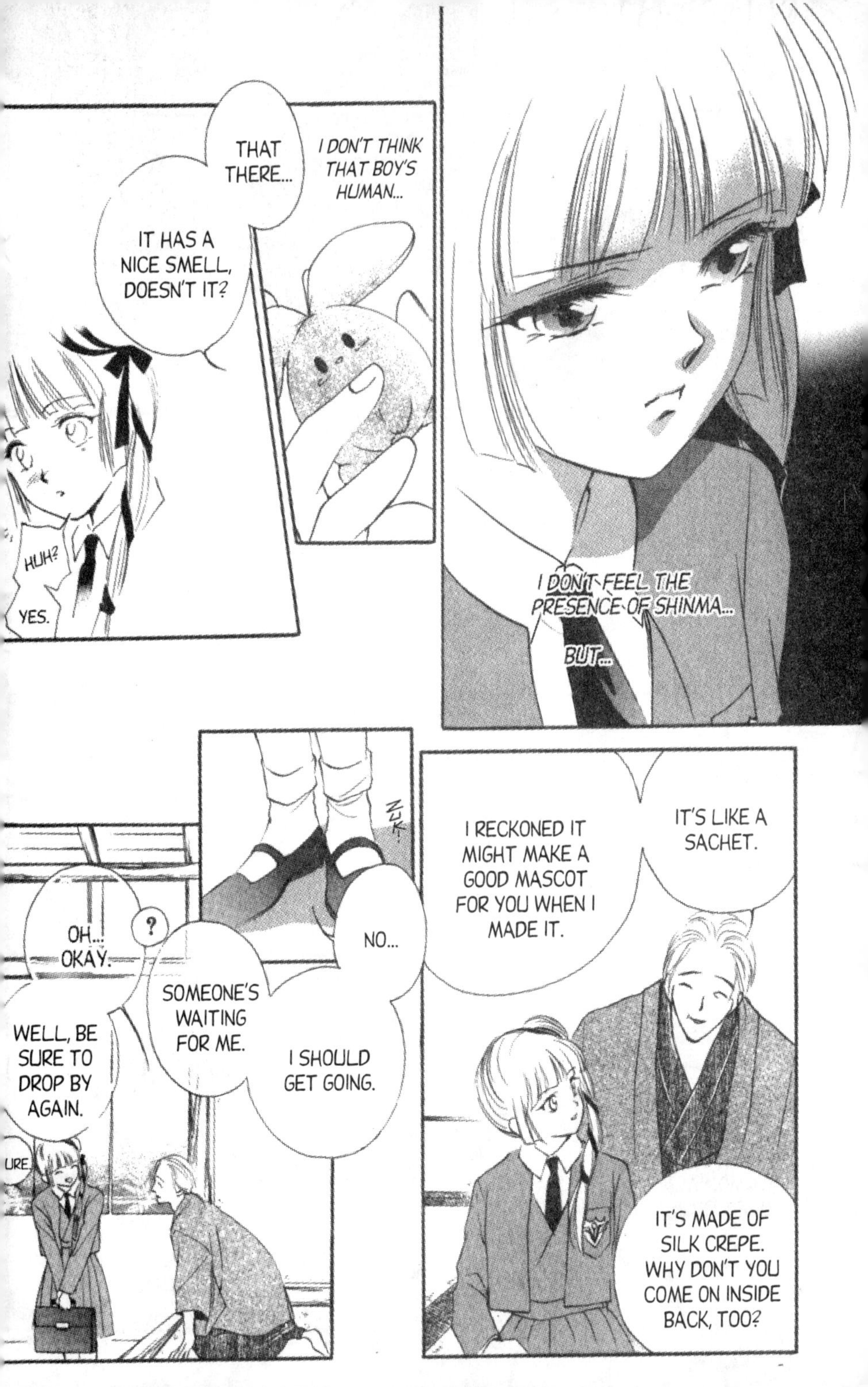
I DON'T FEEL THE PRESENCE OF SHINMA...
BUT...
I DON'T THINK THAT BOY'S HUMAN...
THAT THERE...
IT HAS A NICE SMELL, DOESN'T IT?
HUH?
YES.
IT'S LIKE A SACHET.
I RECKONED IT MIGHT MAKE A GOOD MASCOT FOR YOU WHEN I MADE IT.
IT'S MADE OF SILK CREPE. WHY DON'T YOU COME ON INSIDE BACK, TOO?
ZUK
NO...
I SHOULD GET GOING.
SOMEONE'S WAITING FOR ME.
?
OH... OKAY.
WELL, BE SURE TO DROP BY AGAIN.
URE.

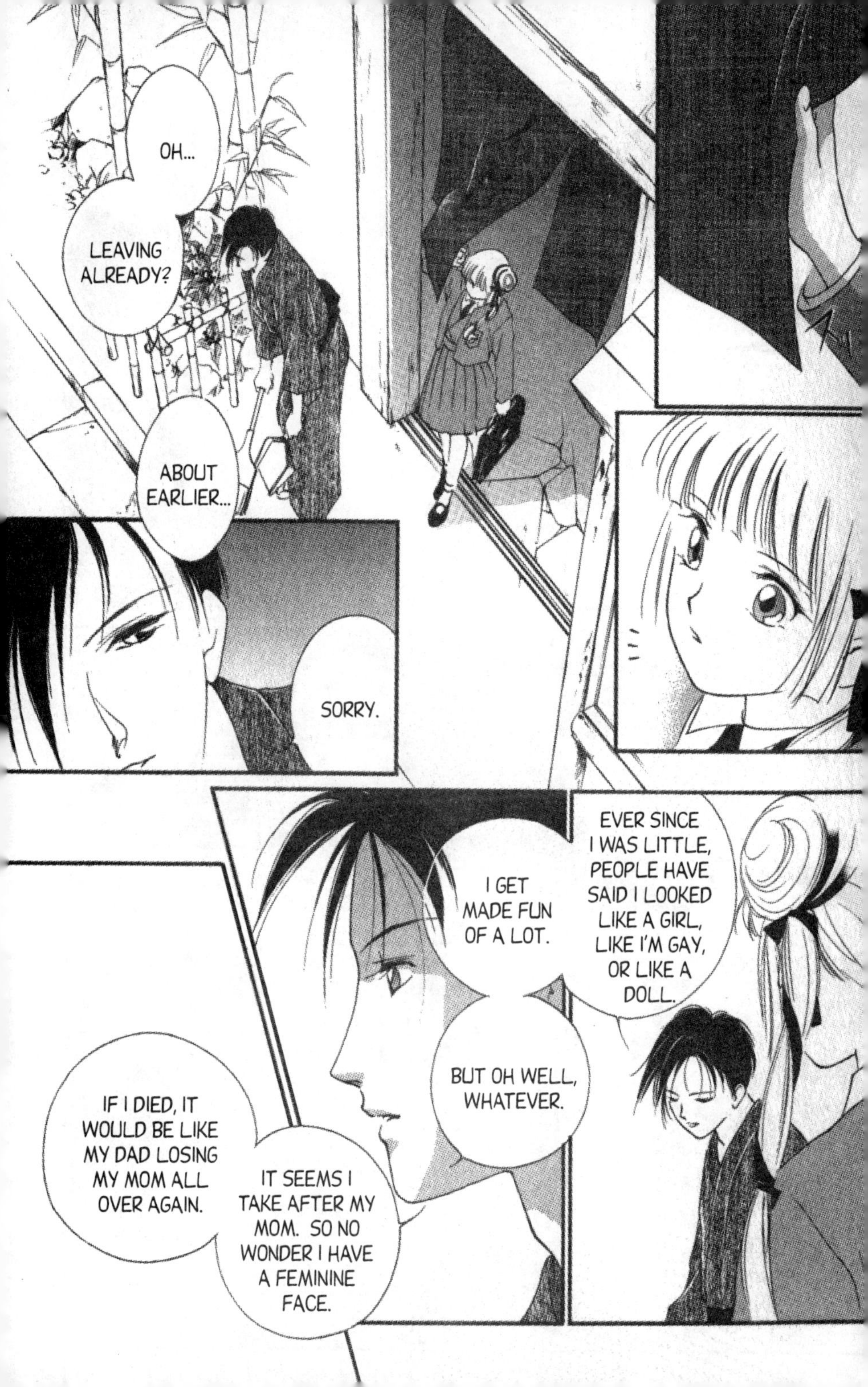
OH...
LEAVING ALREADY?
ABOUT EARLIER...
SORRY.
EVER SINCE I WAS LITTLE, PEOPLE HAVE SAID I LOOKED LIKE A GIRL, LIKE I'M GAY, OR LIKE A DOLL.
I GET MADE FUN OF A LOT.
BUT OH WELL, WHATEVER.
IT SEEMS I TAKE AFTER MY MOM. SO NO WONDER I HAVE A FEMININE FACE.
IF I DIED, IT WOULD BE LIKE MY DAD LOSING MY MOM ALL OVER AGAIN.

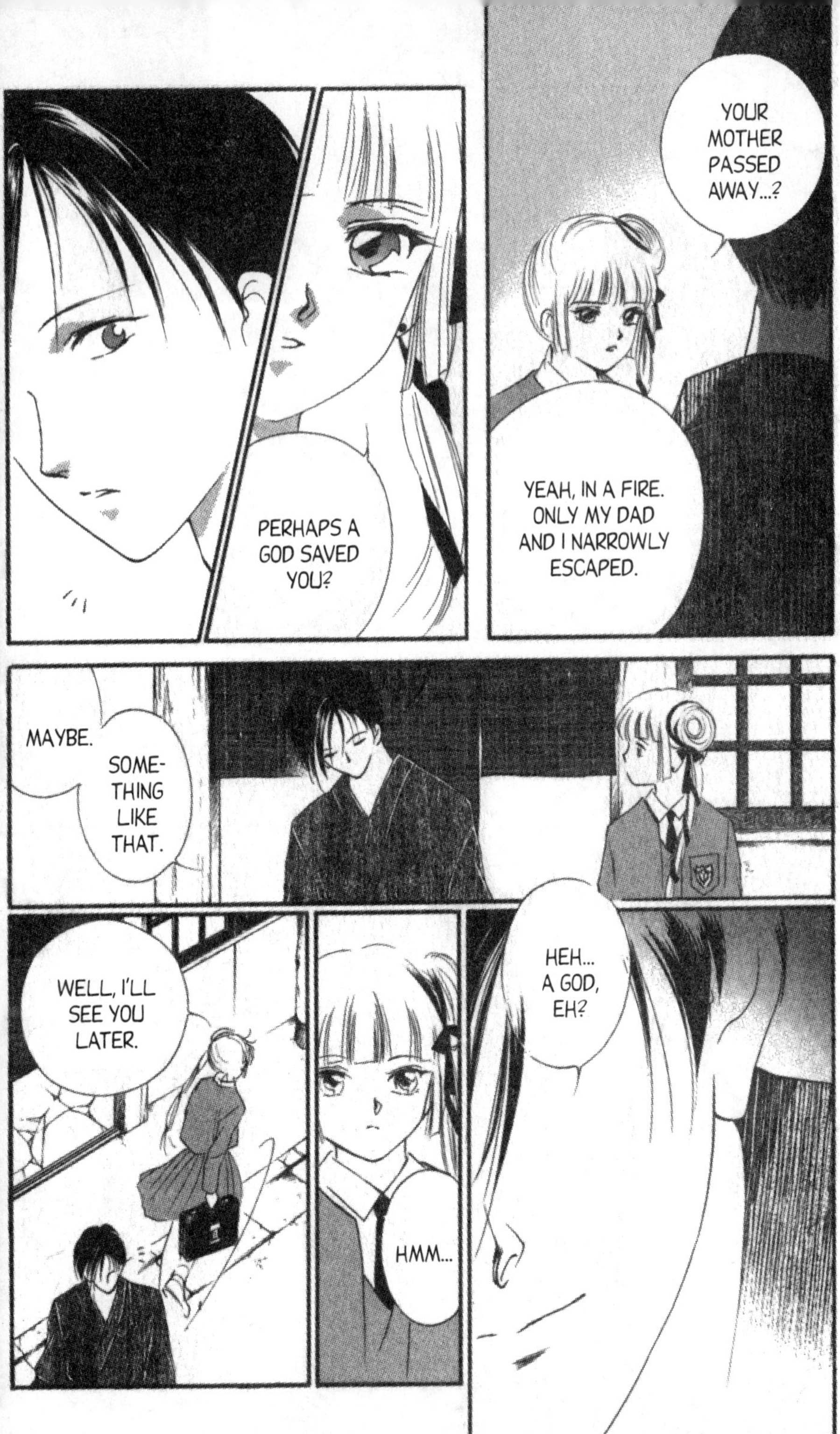
YOUR MOTHER PASSED AWAY...?
YEAH, IN A FIRE. ONLY MY DAD AND I NARROWLY ESCAPED.
PERHAPS A GOD SAVED YOU?
MAYBE.
SOME-THING LIKE THAT.
HEH... A GOD, EH?
HMM...
WELL, I'LL SEE YOU LATER.

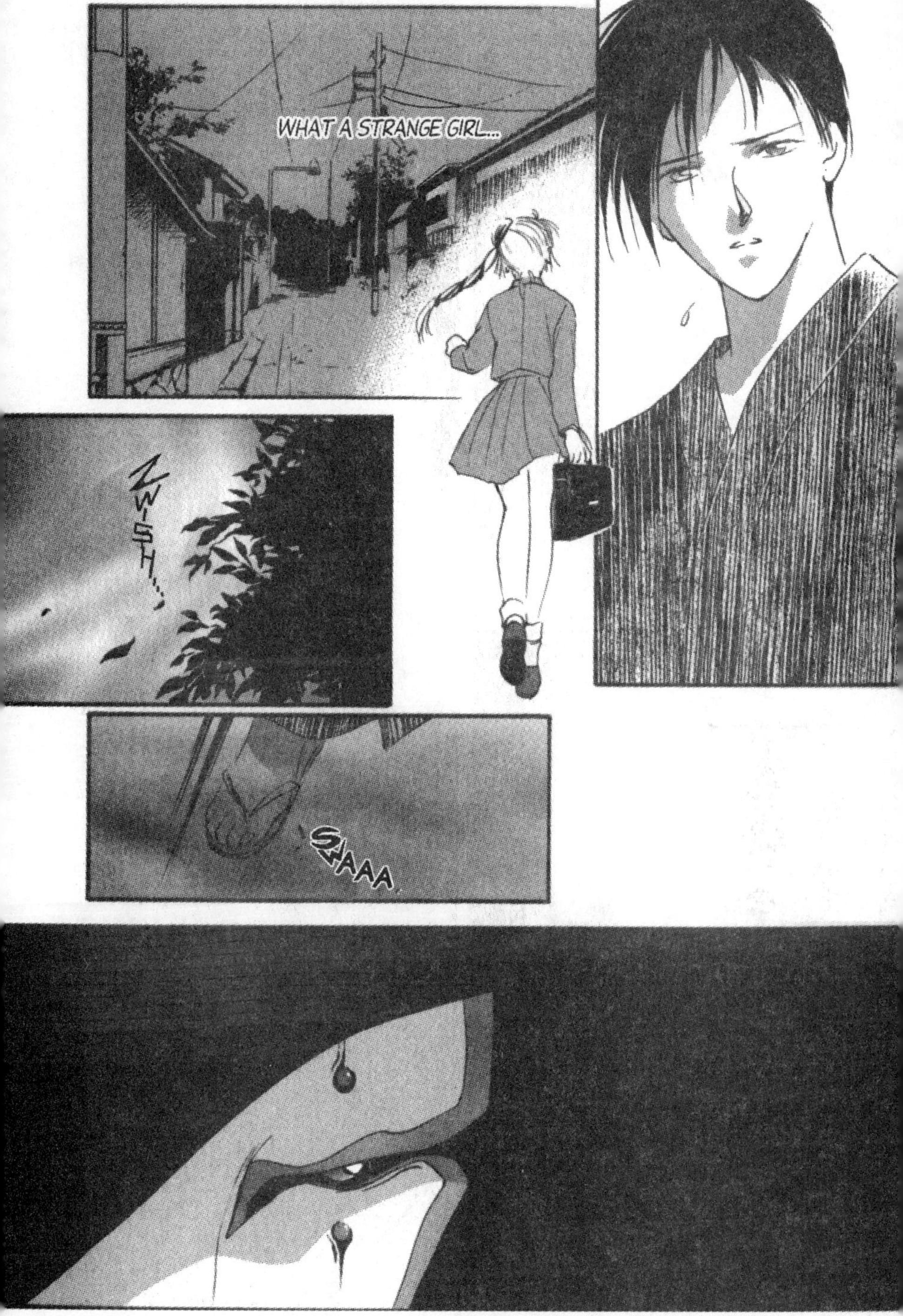
WHAT A STRANGE GIRL...
ZWISH...
SWAAA

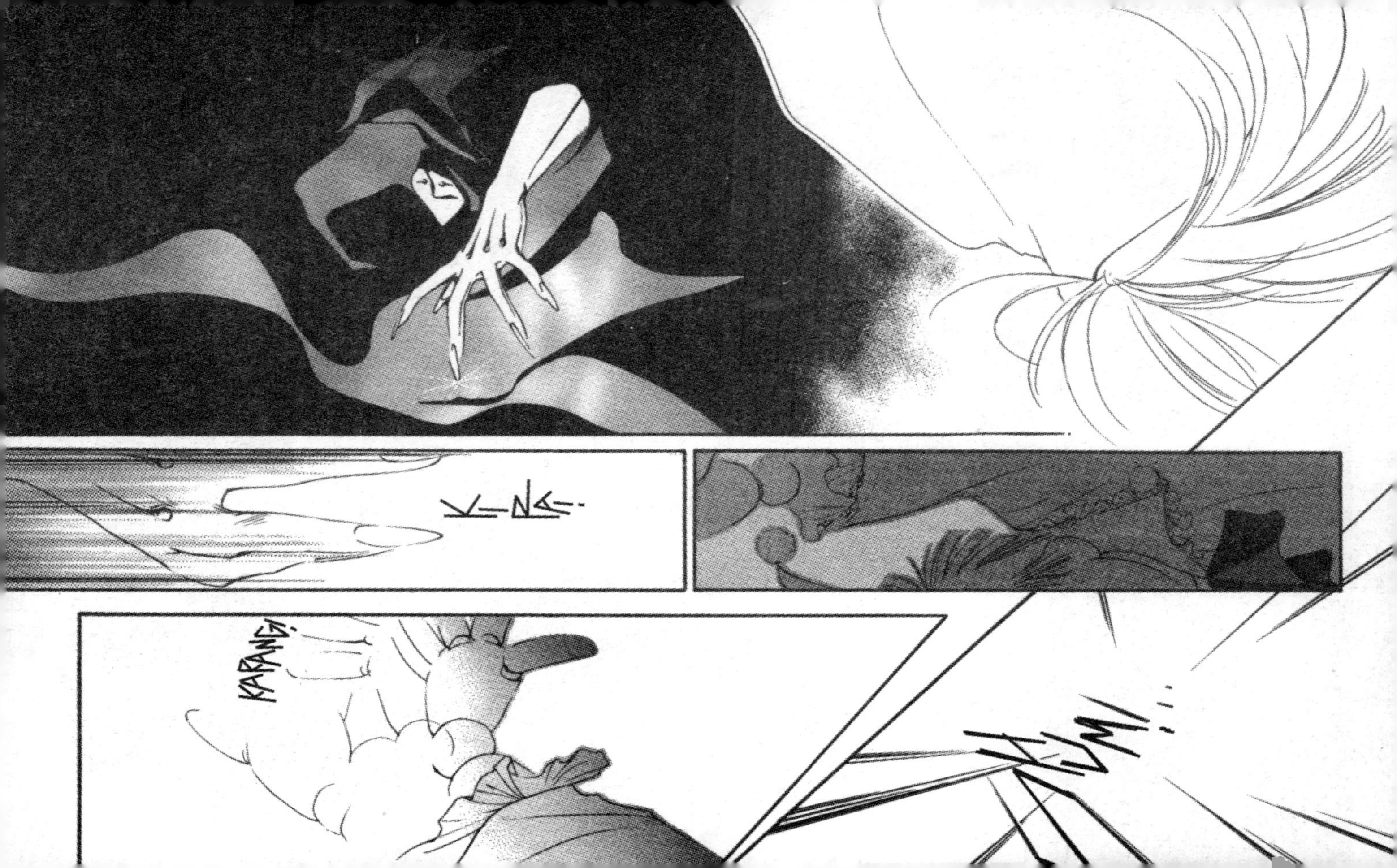
WHUM!!...
KARANG!

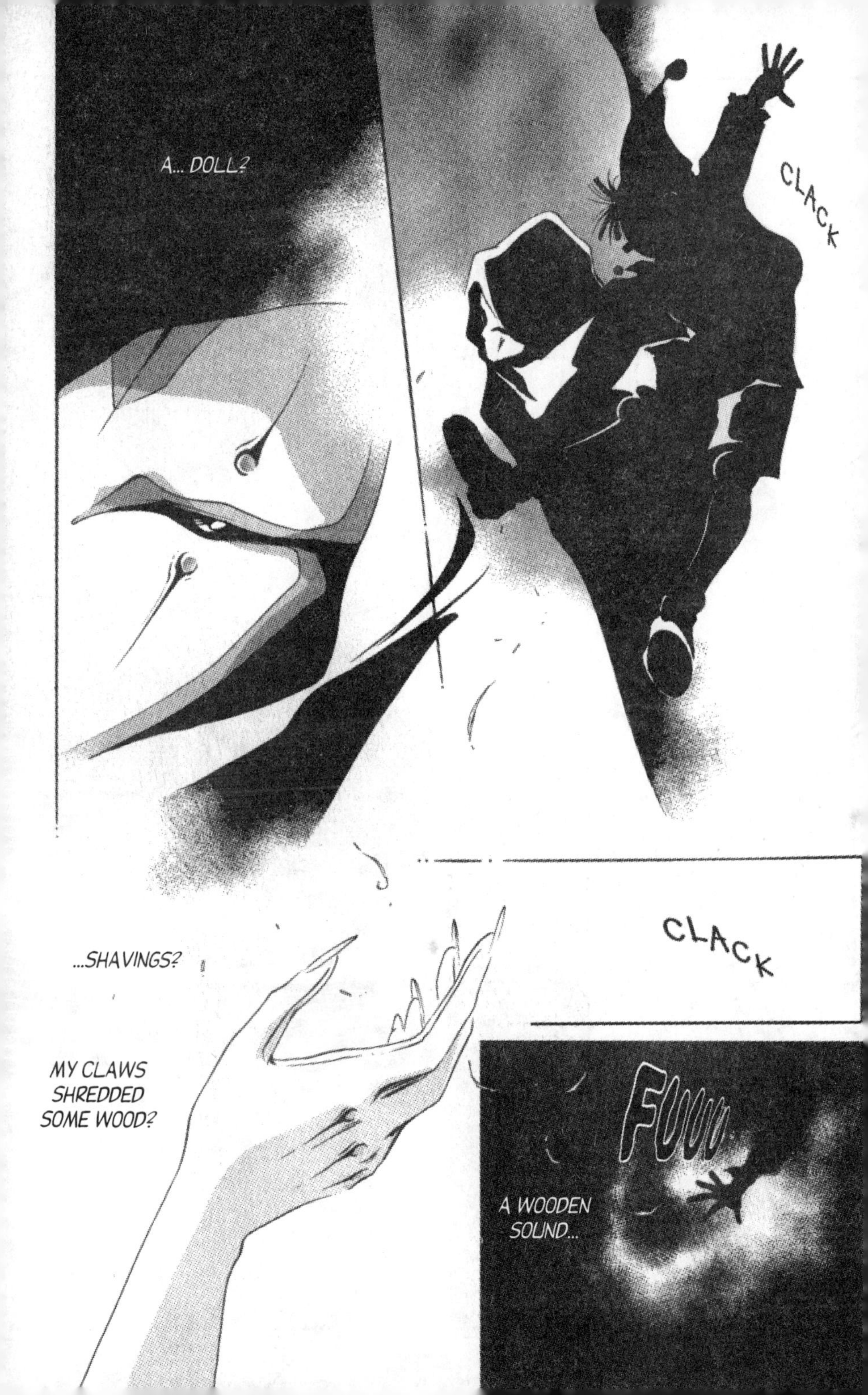
CLACK
A... DOLL?
CLACK
FUUU
A WOODEN SOUND...
...SHAVINGS?
MY CLAWS SHREDDED SOME WOOD?

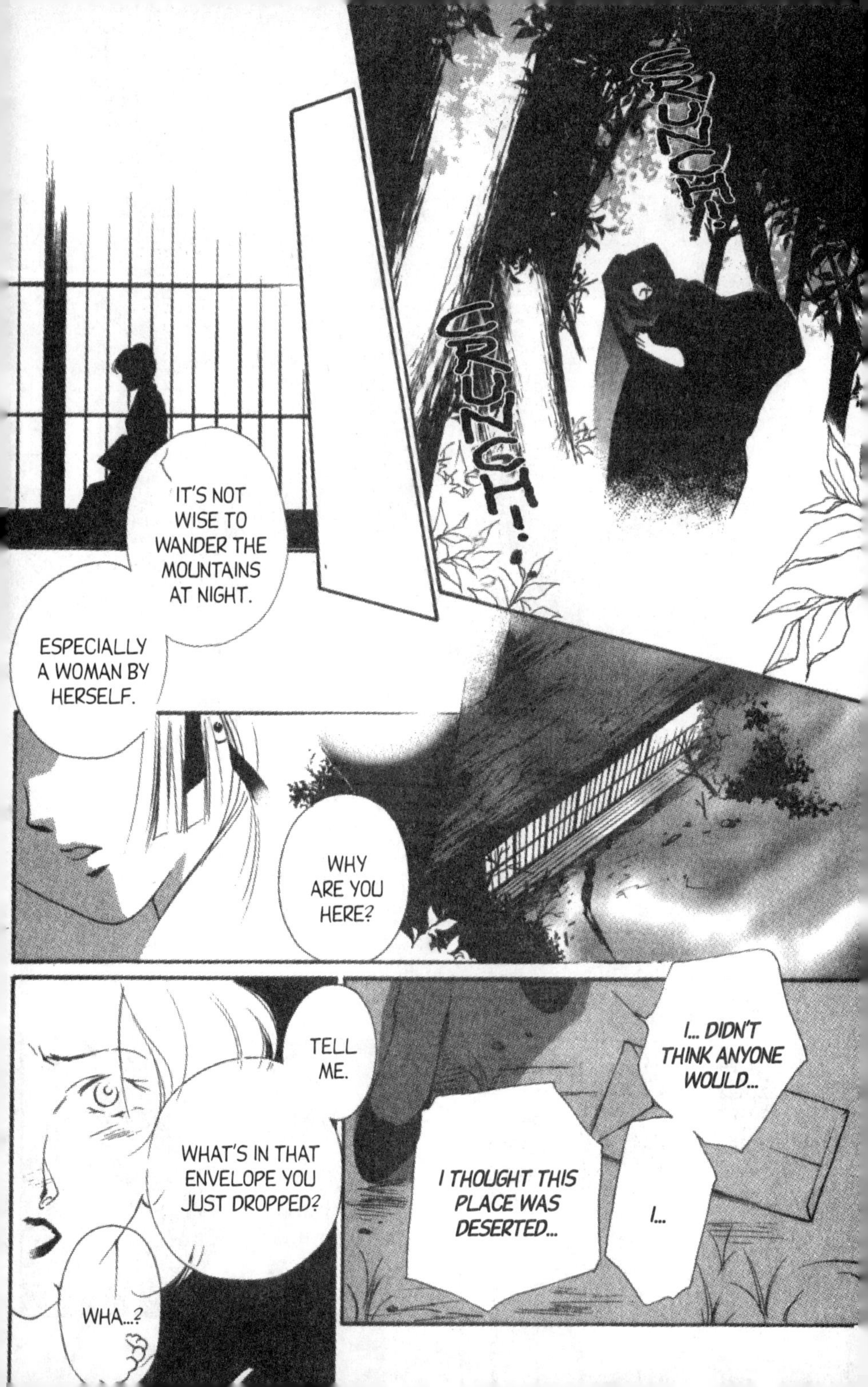
CRUNCH!
CRUNCH!!
IT'S NOT WISE TO WANDER THE MOUNTAINS AT NIGHT.
ESPECIALLY A WOMAN BY HERSELF.
WHY ARE YOU HERE?
I... DIDN'T THINK ANYONE WOULD...
I THOUGHT THIS PLACE WAS DESERTED...
I...
TELL ME.
WHAT'S IN THAT ENVELOPE YOU JUST DROPPED?
WHA...?

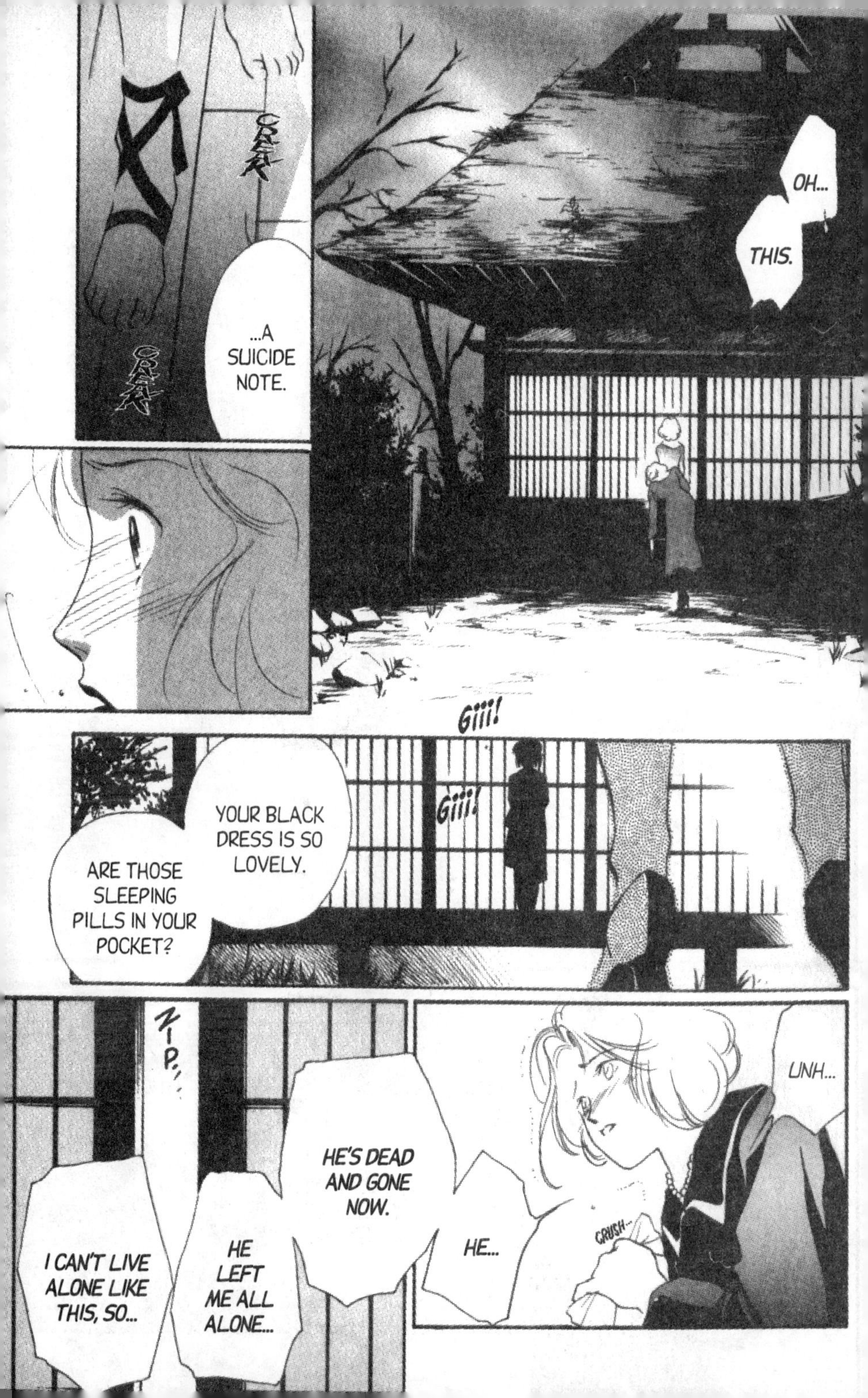
OH...
THIS.
CREAK
...A SUICIDE NOTE.
CREAK
Giii!
Giii!
YOUR BLACK DRESS IS SO LOVELY.
ARE THOSE SLEEPING PILLS IN YOUR POCKET?
UNH...
CRUSH...
HE...
HE'S DEAD AND GONE NOW.
HE LEFT ME ALL ALONE...
ZIP...
I CAN'T LIVE ALONE LIKE THIS, SO...

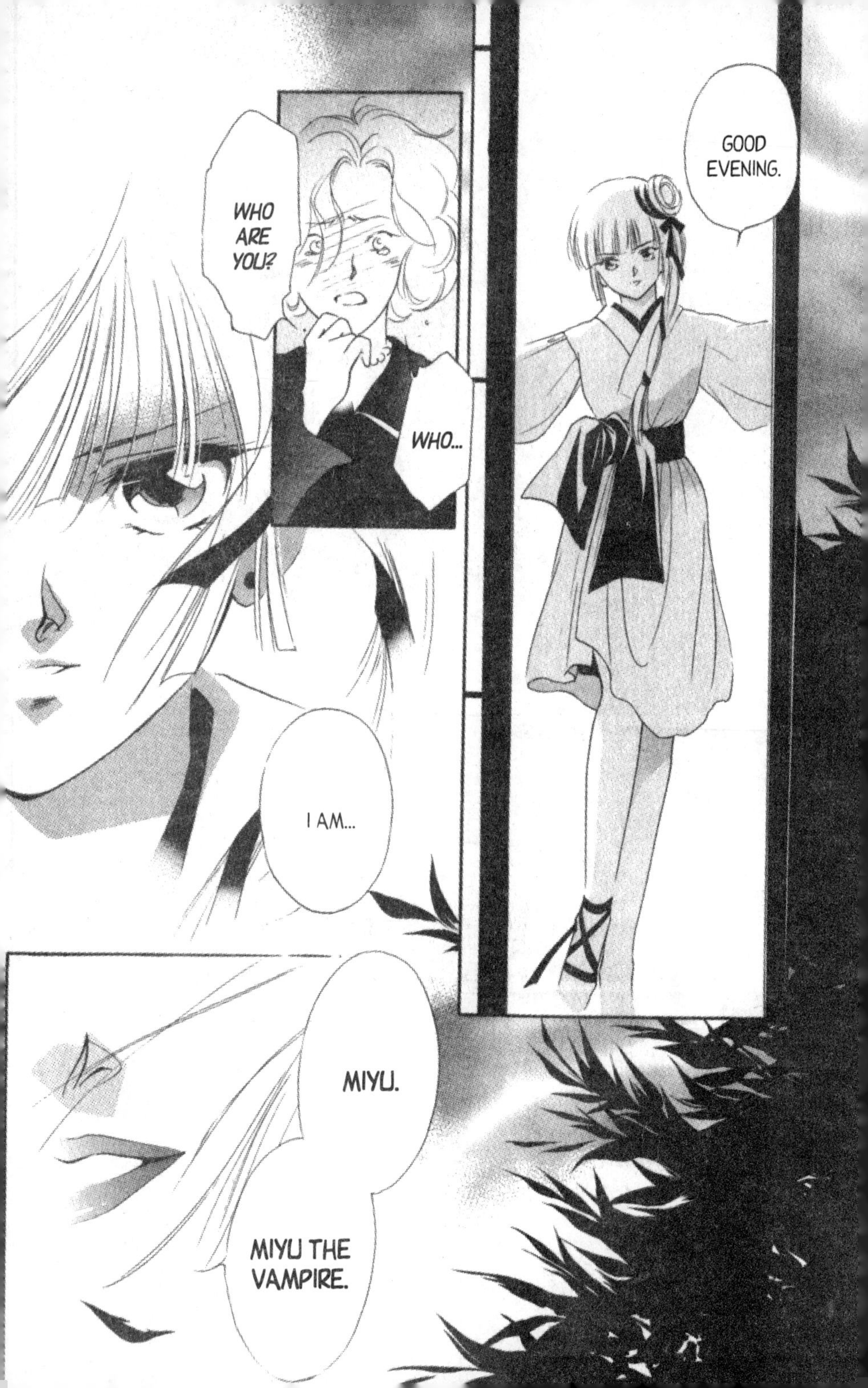
GOOD EVENING.
WHO ARE YOU?
WHO...
I AM...
MIYU.
MIYU THE VAMPIRE.

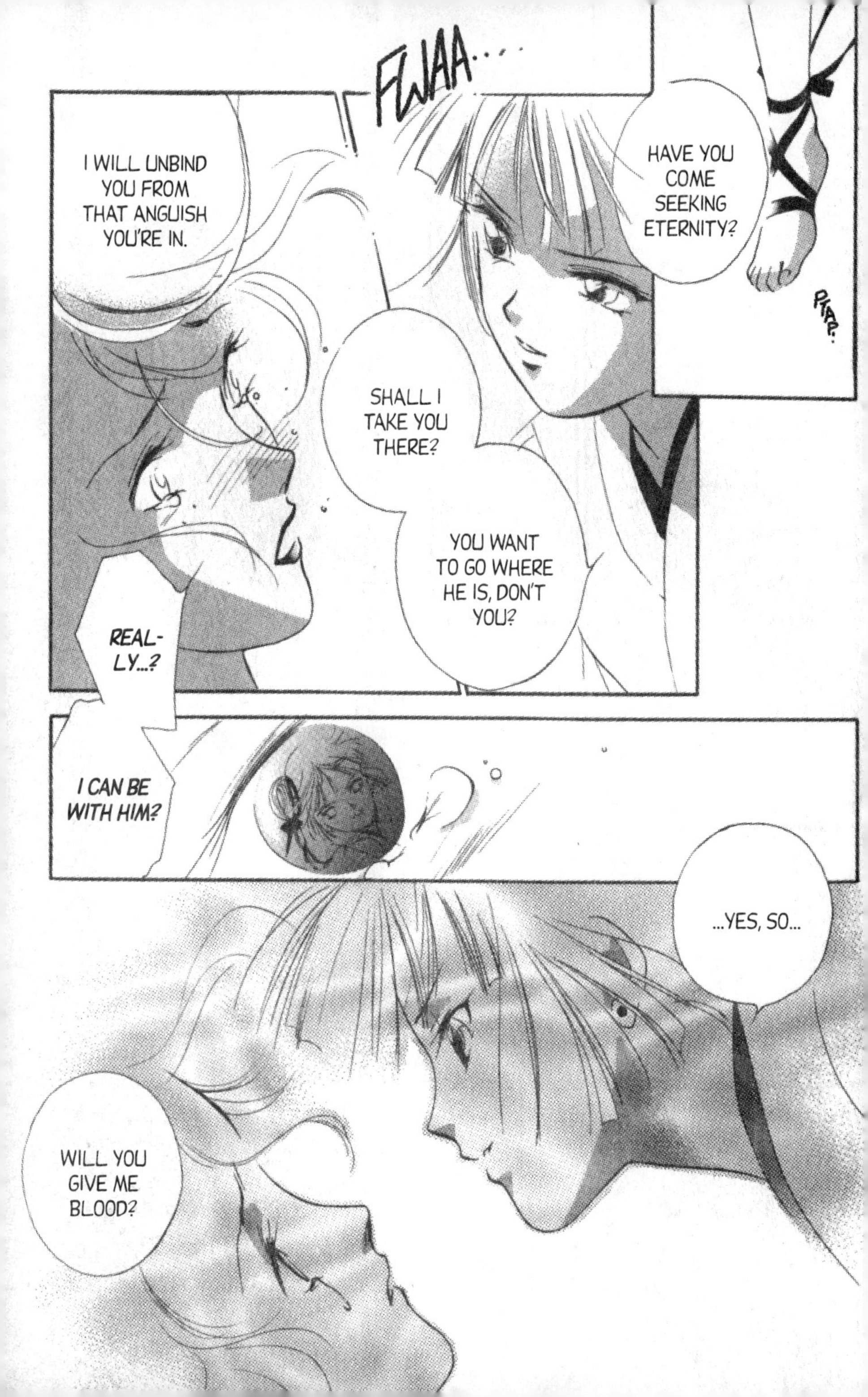
HAVE YOU COME SEEKING ETERNITY?
FWAA....
I WILL UNBIND YOU FROM THAT ANGUISH YOU'RE IN.
SHALL I TAKE YOU THERE?
YOU WANT TO GO WHERE HE IS, DON'T YOU?
REAL-LY...?
I CAN BE WITH HIM?
...YES, SO...
WILL YOU GIVE ME BLOOD?

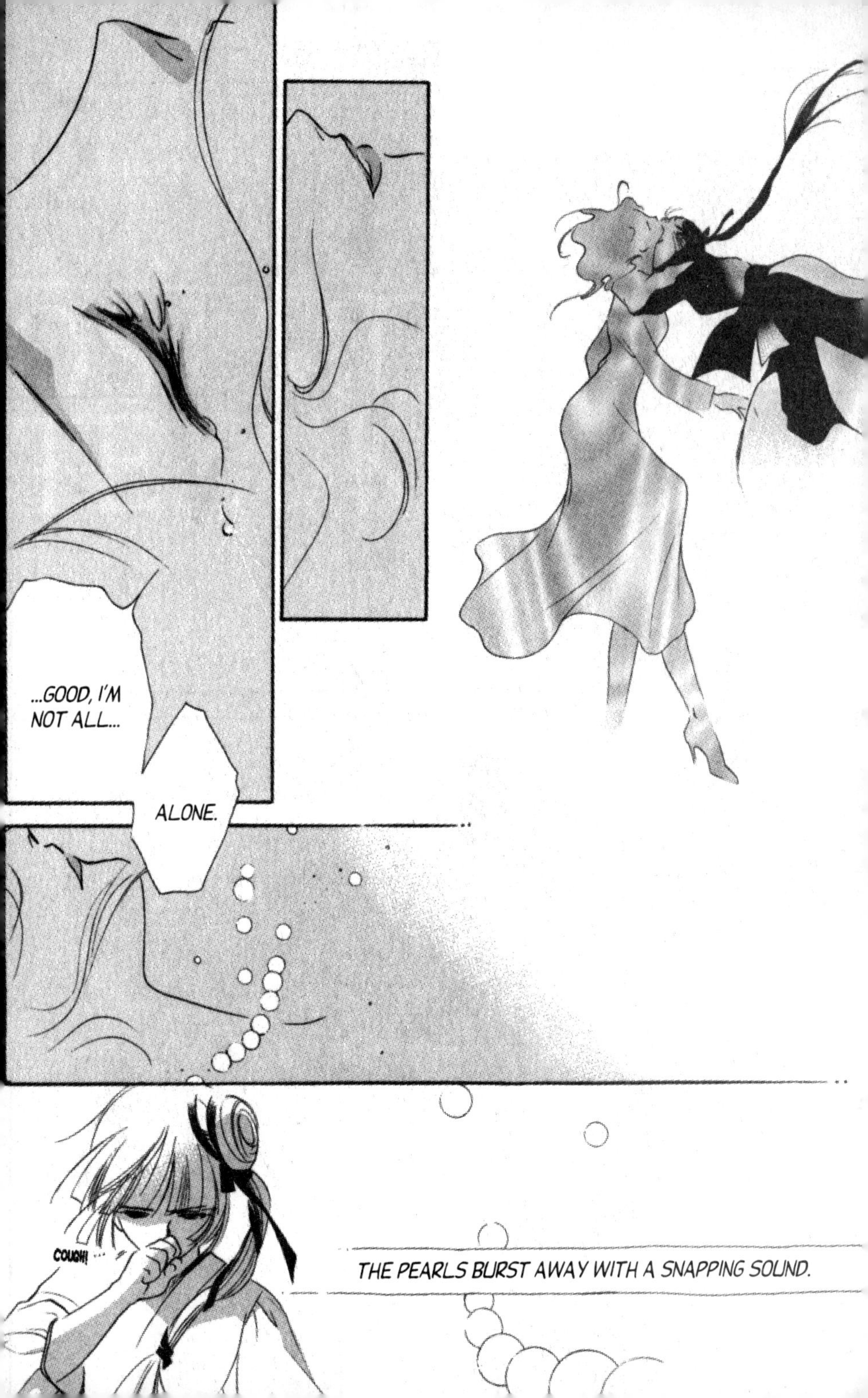
...GOOD, I'M NOT ALL...
ALONE.
THE PEARLS BURST AWAY WITH A SNAPPING SOUND.
COUGH! ...

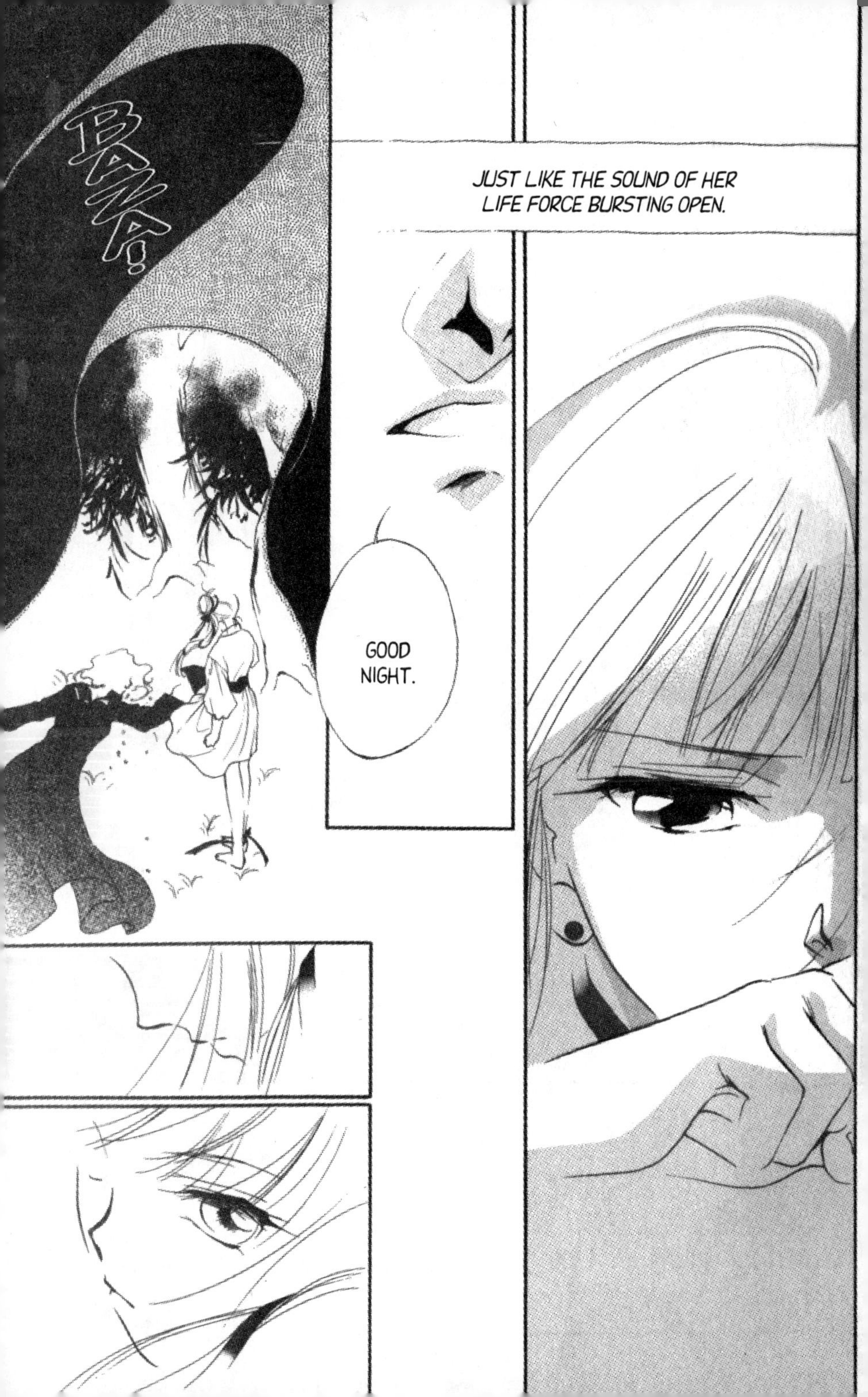
JUST LIKE THE SOUND OF HER LIFE FORCE BURSTING OPEN.
GOOD NIGHT.
BANG!

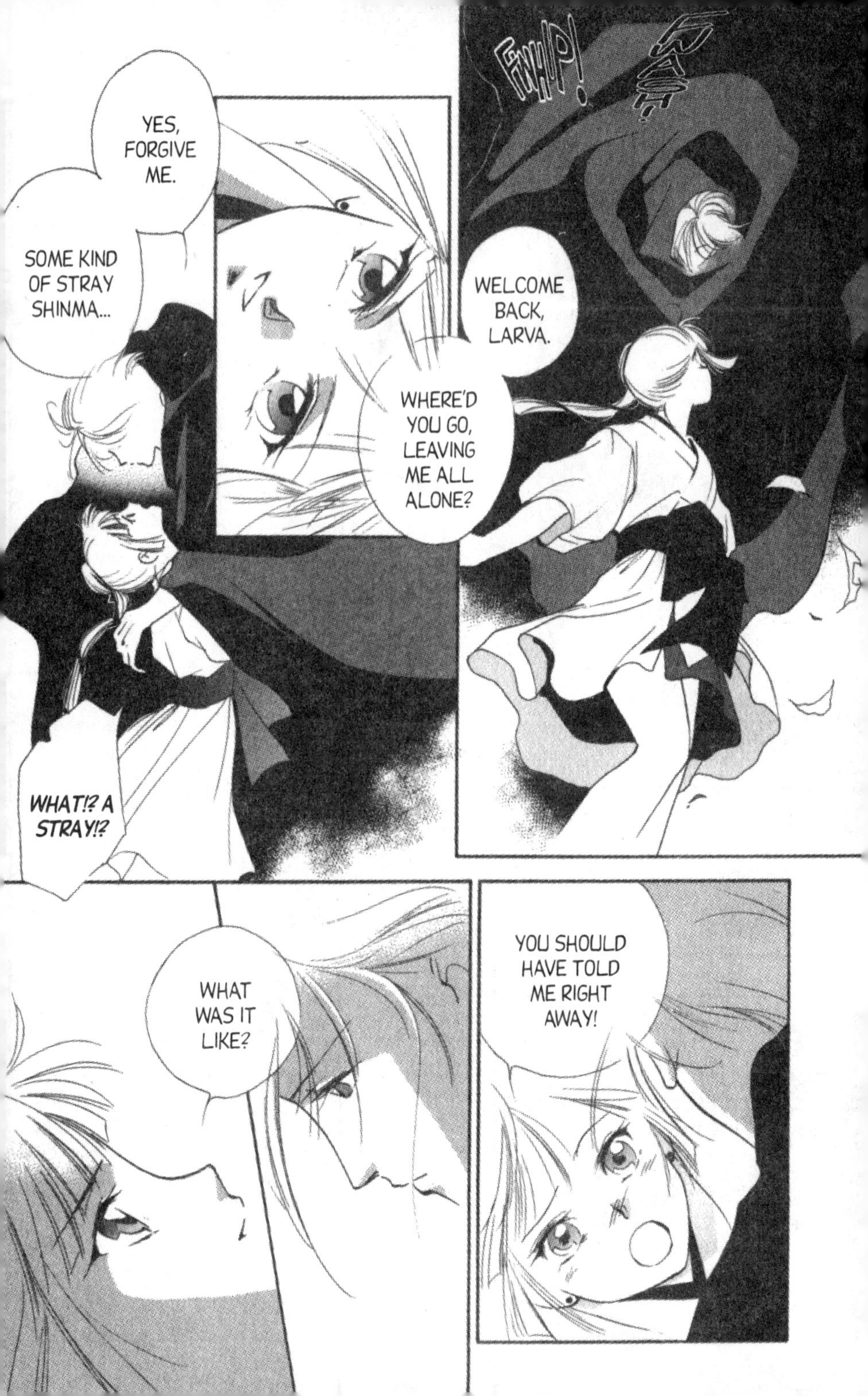
FWHUP!
FWOOH!
WELCOME BACK, LARVA.
WHERE'D YOU GO, LEAVING ME ALL ALONE?
YES, FORGIVE ME.
SOME KIND OF STRAY SHINMA...
WHAT!? A STRAY!?
YOU SHOULD HAVE TOLD ME RIGHT AWAY!
WHAT WAS IT LIKE?

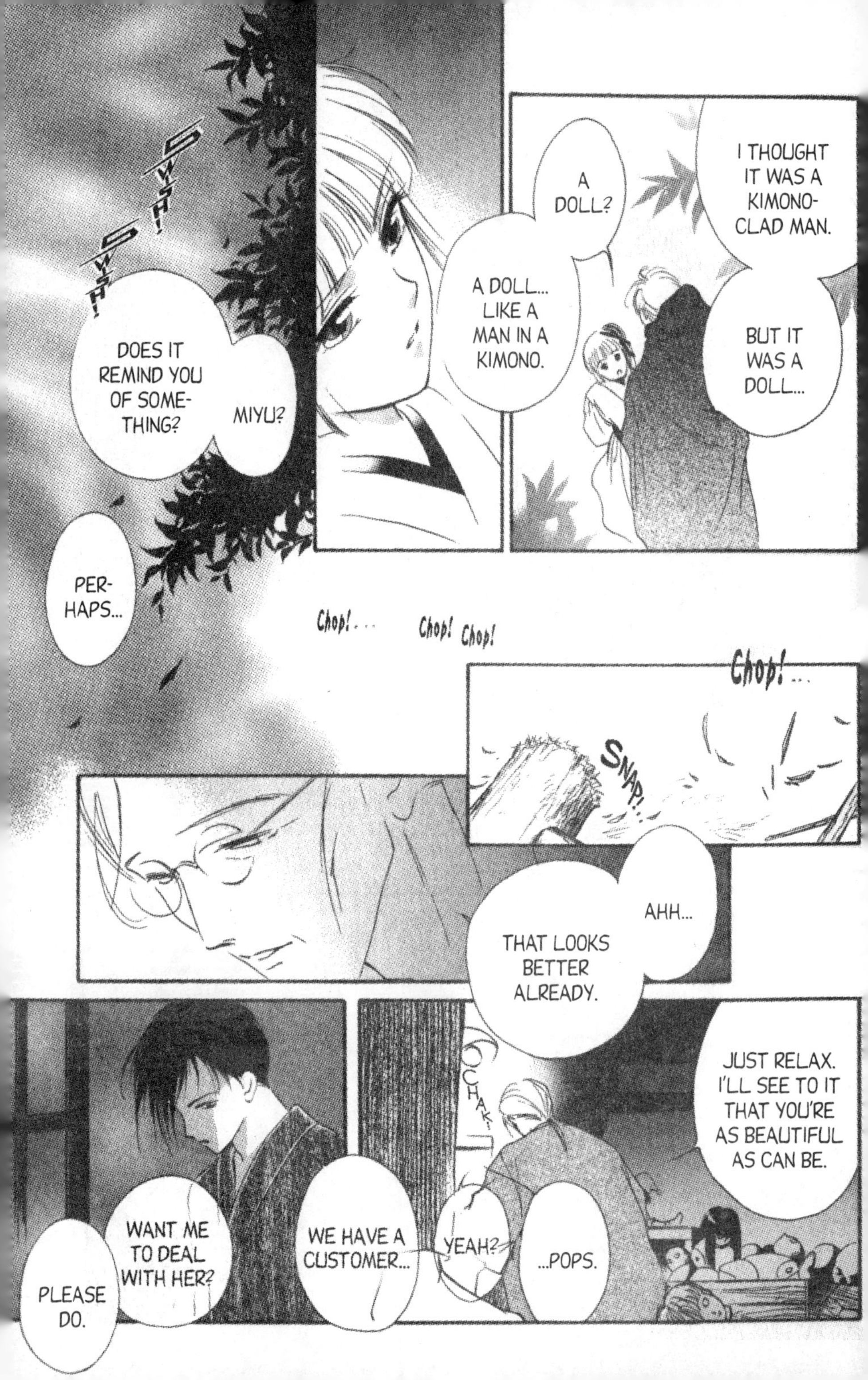
I THOUGHT IT WAS A KIMONO-CLAD MAN.
BUT IT WAS A DOLL...
A DOLL?
A DOLL... LIKE A MAN IN A KIMONO.
SWISH! SWISH!
DOES IT REMIND YOU OF SOME-THING?
MIYU?
PER-HAPS...
Chop!... Chop! Chop!
Chop!...
SNAP!!
AHH...
THAT LOOKS BETTER ALREADY.
JUST RELAX. I'LL SEE TO IT THAT YOU'RE AS BEAUTIFUL AS CAN BE.
CHAK!
...POPS.
YEAH?
WE HAVE A CUSTOMER...
WANT ME TO DEAL WITH HER?
PLEASE DO.

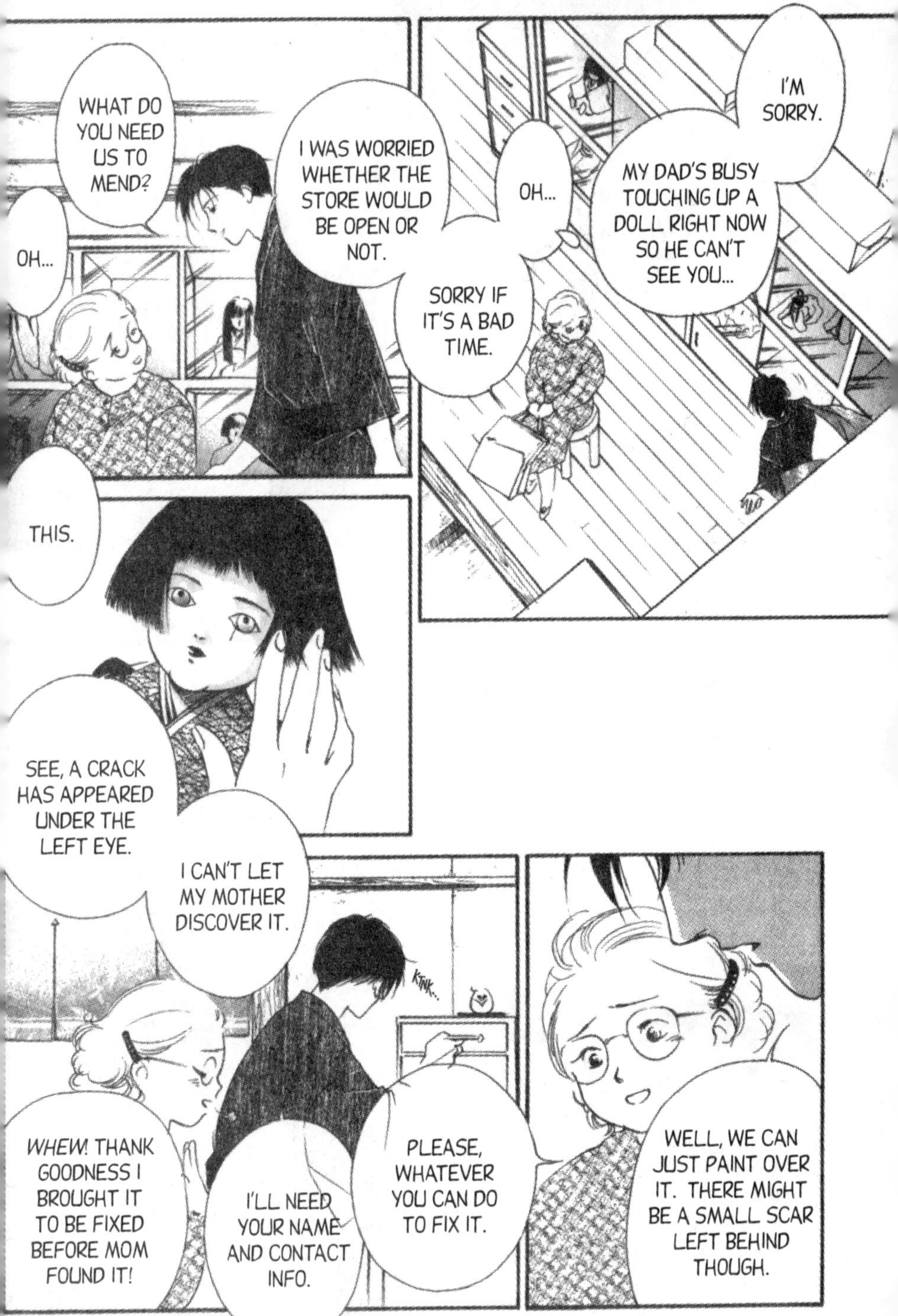
I'M SORRY.
MY DAD'S BUSY TOUCHING UP A DOLL RIGHT NOW SO HE CAN'T SEE YOU...
OH...
SORRY IF IT'S A BAD TIME.
I WAS WORRIED WHETHER THE STORE WOULD BE OPEN OR NOT.
WHAT DO YOU NEED US TO MEND?
OH...
THIS.
SEE, A CRACK HAS APPEARED UNDER THE LEFT EYE.
I CAN'T LET MY MOTHER DISCOVER IT.
WELL, WE CAN JUST PAINT OVER IT. THERE MIGHT BE A SMALL SCAR LEFT BEHIND THOUGH.
PLEASE, WHATEVER YOU CAN DO TO FIX IT.
KTINK..
I'LL NEED YOUR NAME AND CONTACT INFO.
WHEW! THANK GOODNESS I BROUGHT IT TO BE FIXED BEFORE MOM FOUND IT!

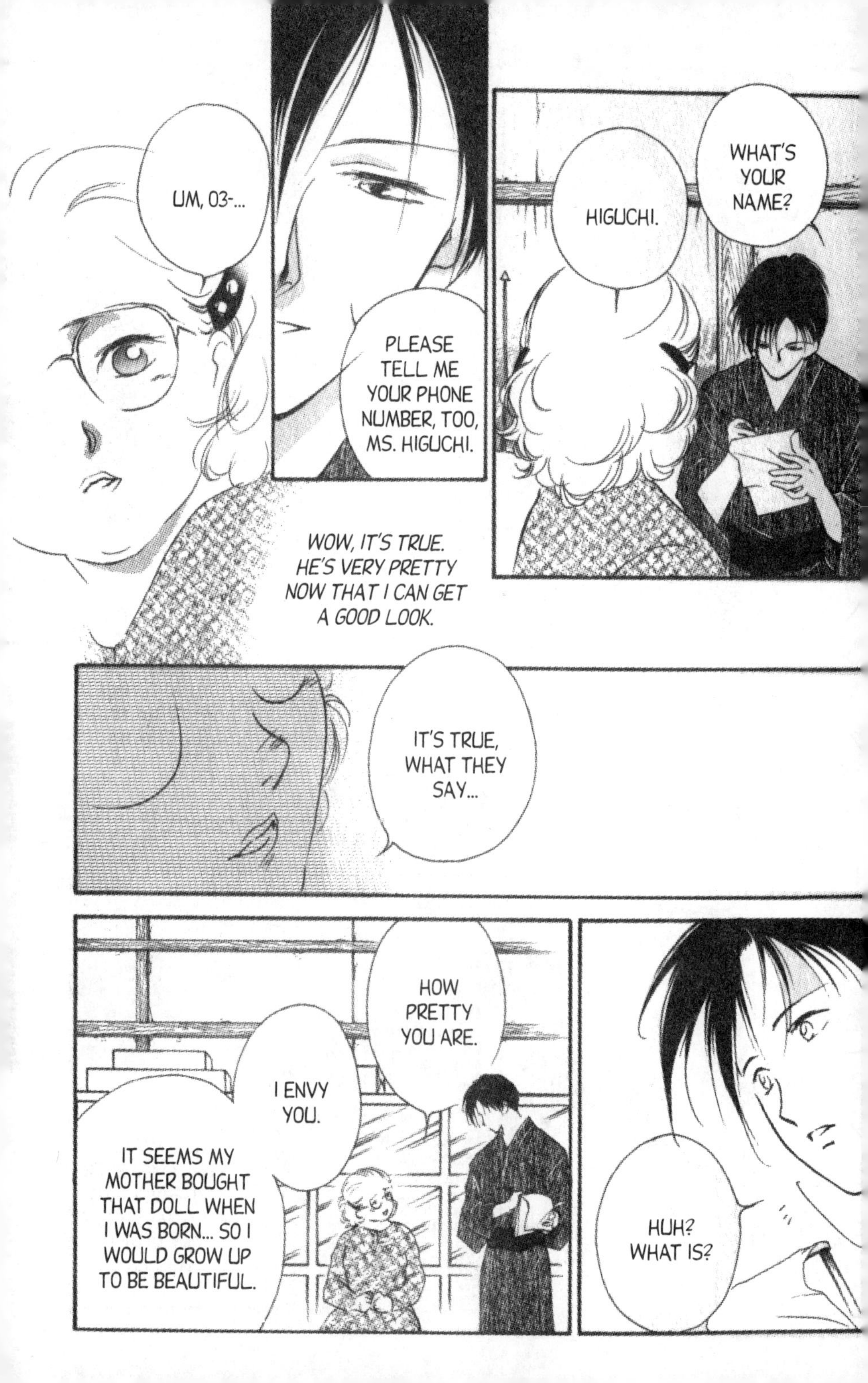
WHAT'S YOUR NAME?
HIGUCHI.
PLEASE TELL ME YOUR PHONE NUMBER, TOO, MS. HIGUCHI.
UM, 03-...
WOW, IT'S TRUE. HE'S VERY PRETTY NOW THAT I CAN GET A GOOD LOOK.
IT'S TRUE, WHAT THEY SAY...
HUH? WHAT IS?
HOW PRETTY YOU ARE.
I ENVY YOU.
IT SEEMS MY MOTHER BOUGHT THAT DOLL WHEN I WAS BORN... SO I WOULD GROW UP TO BE BEAUTIFUL.

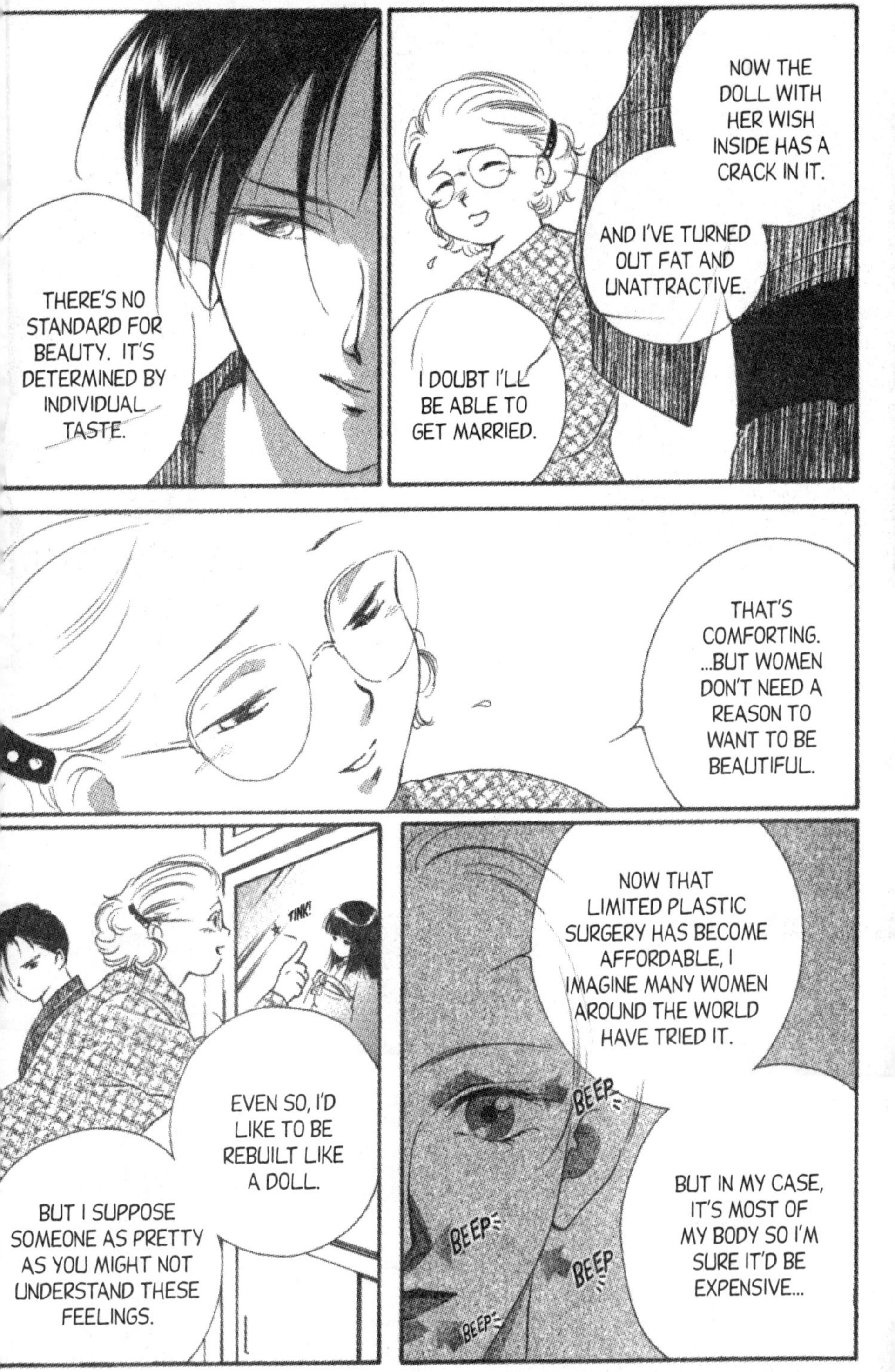
NOW THE DOLL WITH HER WISH INSIDE HAS A CRACK IN IT.
AND I'VE TURNED OUT FAT AND UNATTRACTIVE.
I DOUBT I'LL BE ABLE TO GET MARRIED.
THERE'S NO STANDARD FOR BEAUTY. IT'S DETERMINED BY INDIVIDUAL TASTE.
THAT'S COMFORTING. ...BUT WOMEN DON'T NEED A REASON TO WANT TO BE BEAUTIFUL.
NOW THAT LIMITED PLASTIC SURGERY HAS BECOME AFFORDABLE, I IMAGINE MANY WOMEN AROUND THE WORLD HAVE TRIED IT.
BEEP
BUT IN MY CASE, IT'S MOST OF MY BODY SO I'M SURE IT'D BE EXPENSIVE...
BEEP
BEEP
BEEP
TINK!
EVEN SO, I'D LIKE TO BE REBUILT LIKE A DOLL.
BUT I SUPPOSE SOMEONE AS PRETTY AS YOU MIGHT NOT UNDERSTAND THESE FEELINGS.

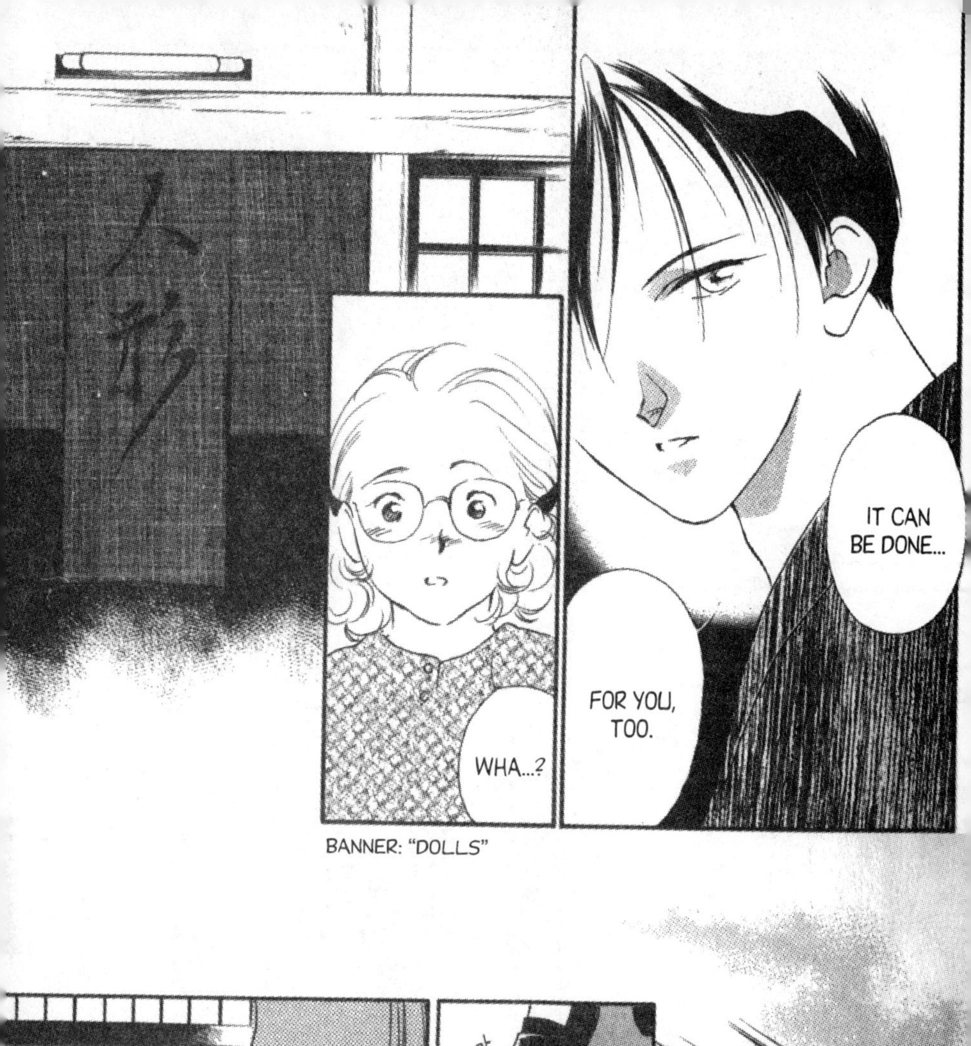
IT CAN BE DONE...
FOR YOU, TOO.
WHA...?

BANNER: "DOLLS"

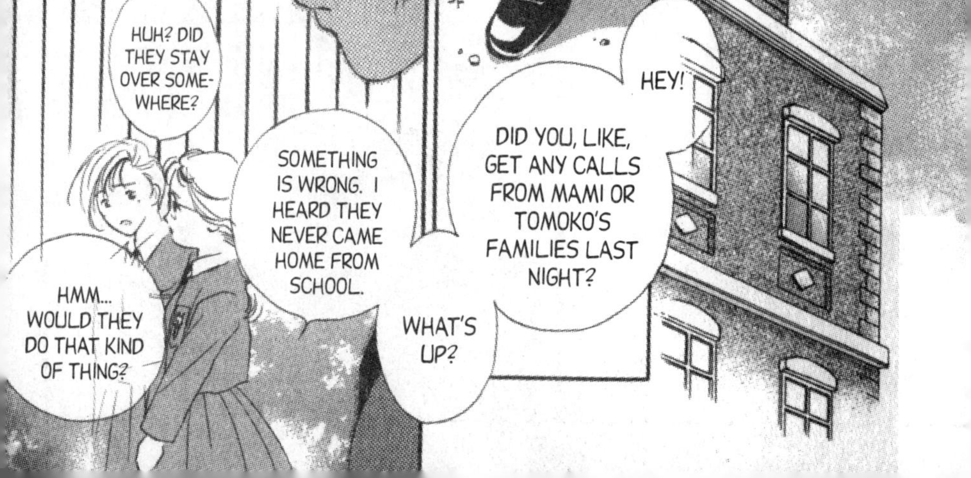
HEY!
DID YOU, LIKE, GET ANY CALLS FROM MAMI OR TOMOKO'S FAMILIES LAST NIGHT?
WHAT'S UP?
SOMETHING IS WRONG. I HEARD THEY NEVER CAME HOME FROM SCHOOL.
HUH? DID THEY STAY OVER SOME-WHERE?
HMM... WOULD THEY DO THAT KIND OF THING?

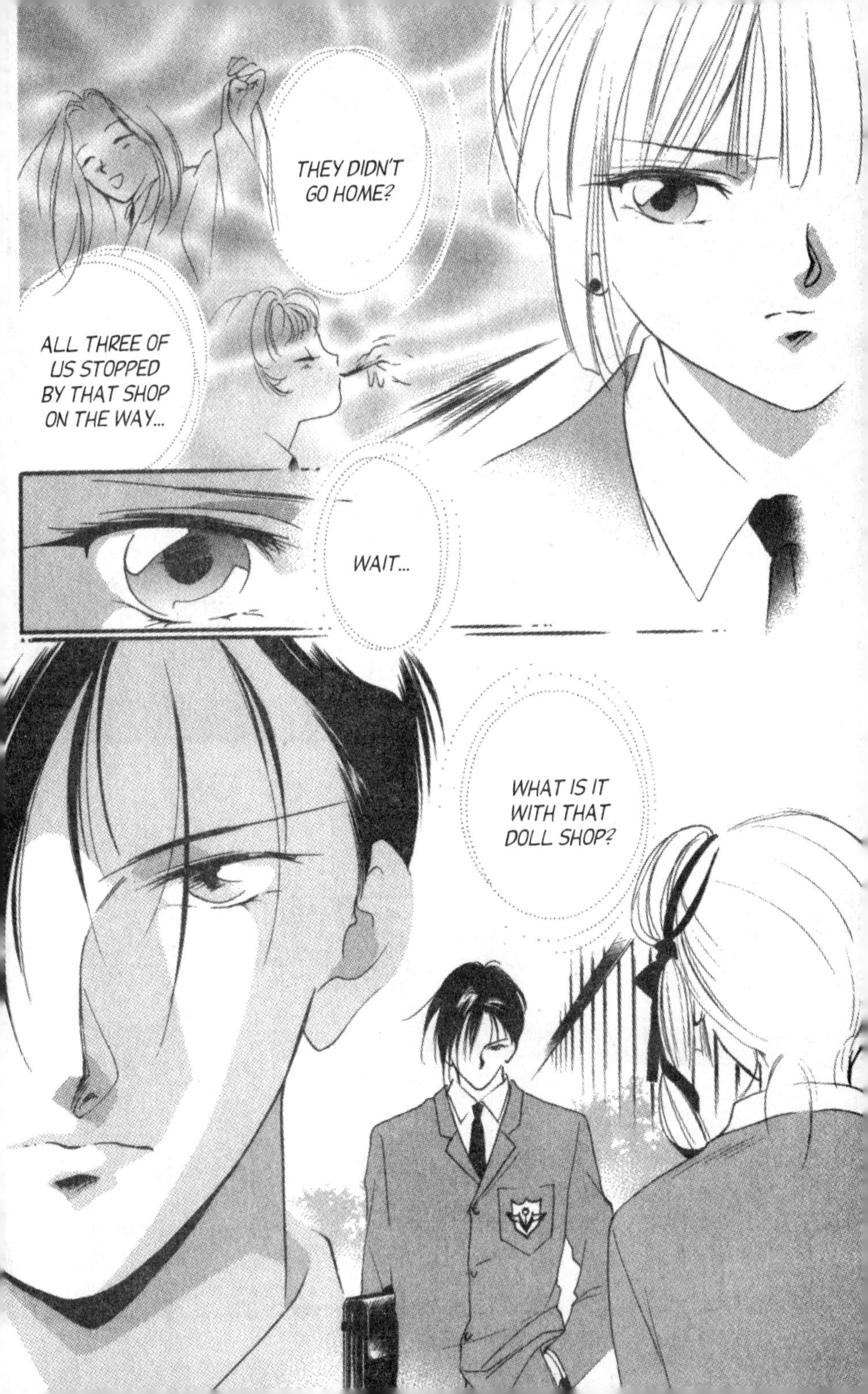
THEY DIDN'T GO HOME?
ALL THREE OF US STOPPED BY THAT SHOP ON THE WAY...
WAIT...
WHAT IS IT WITH THAT DOLL SHOP?

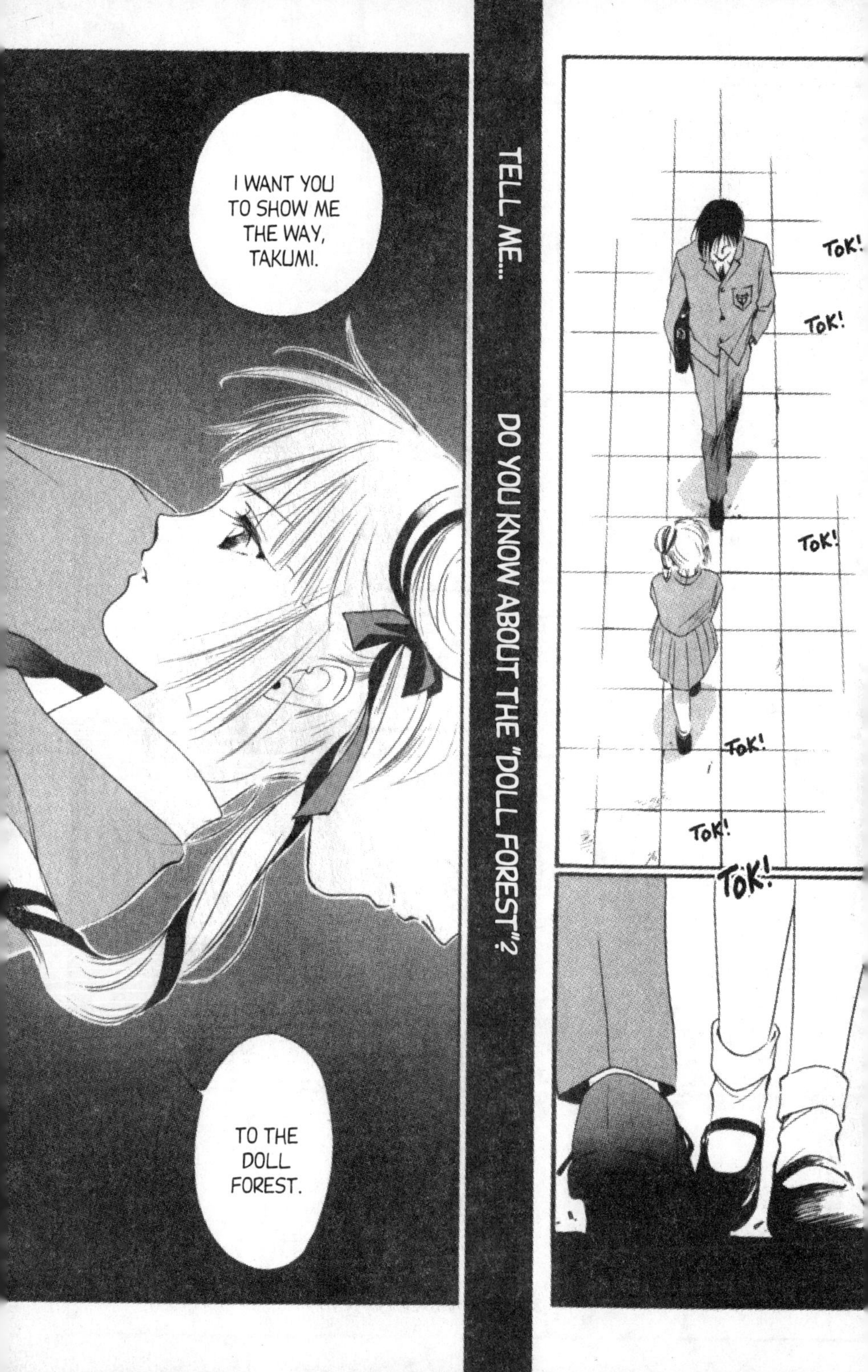
TOK!
TOK!
TOK!
TOK!
TOK!
TOK!
TELL ME... DO YOU KNOW ABOUT THE "DOLL FOREST"?
I WANT YOU TO SHOW ME THE WAY, TAKUMI.
TO THE DOLL FOREST.

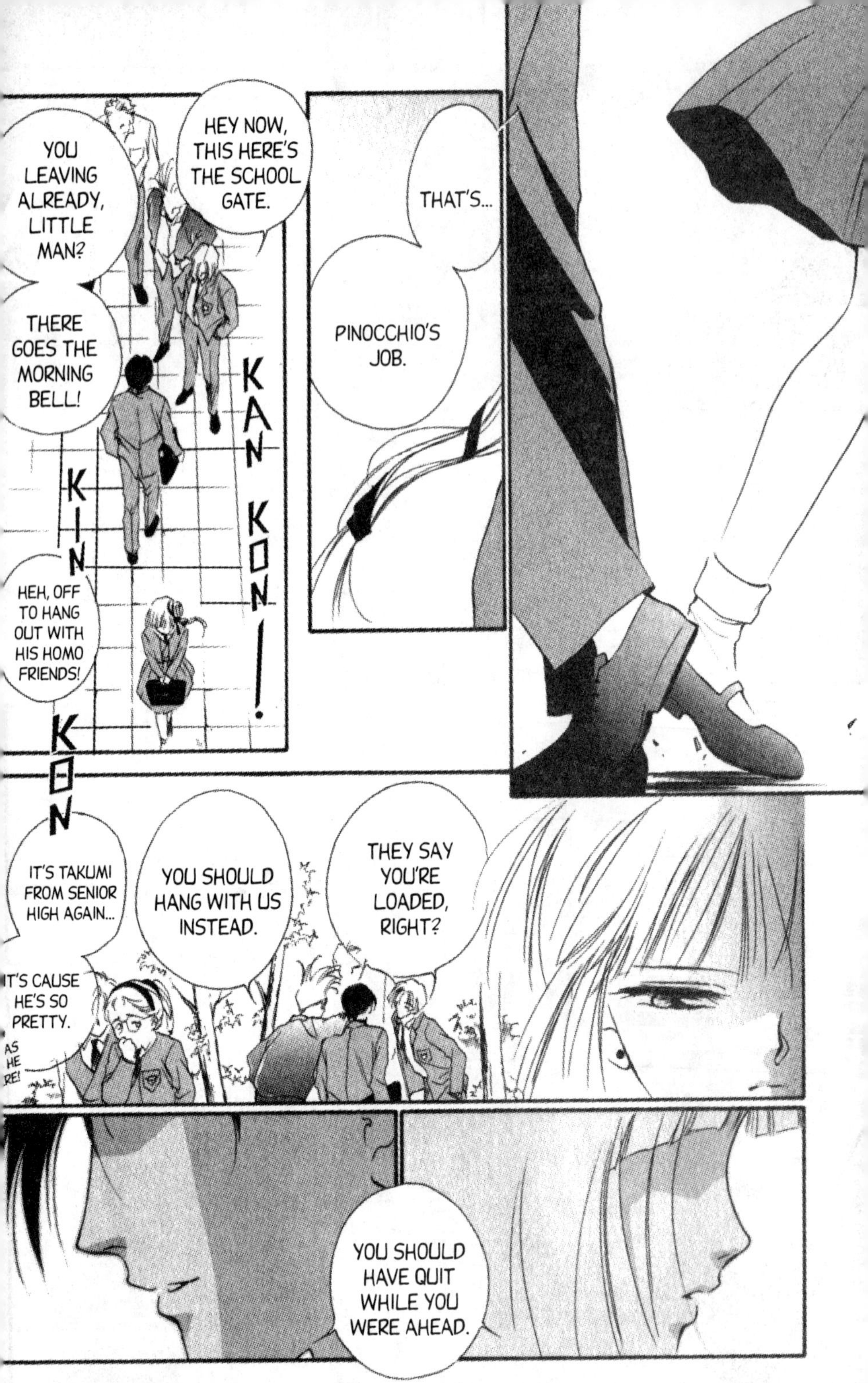
THAT'S...
PINOCCHIO'S JOB.
HEY NOW, THIS HERE'S THE SCHOOL GATE.
YOU LEAVING ALREADY, LITTLE MAN?
THERE GOES THE MORNING BELL!
KAN KON!
KIN
HEH, OFF TO HANG OUT WITH HIS HOMO FRIENDS!
KON
THEY SAY YOU'RE LOADED, RIGHT?
YOU SHOULD HANG WITH US INSTEAD.
IT'S TAKUMI FROM SENIOR HIGH AGAIN...
IT'S CAUSE HE'S SO PRETTY.
YOU SHOULD HAVE QUIT WHILE YOU WERE AHEAD.

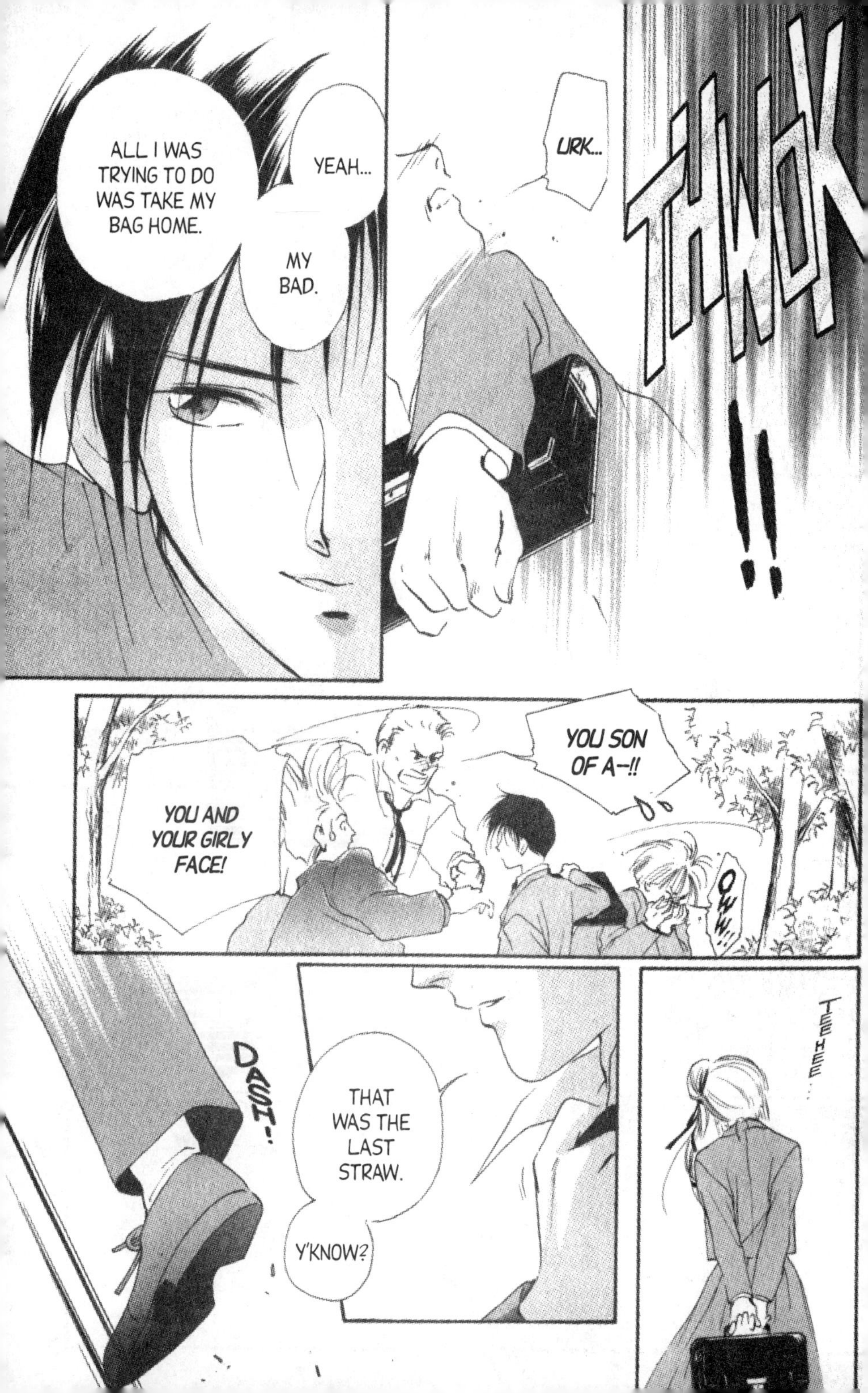
THWOK!!
URK...
ALL I WAS TRYING TO DO WAS TAKE MY BAG HOME.
YEAH...
MY BAD.
YOU SON OF A--!!
OWW!!
YOU AND YOUR GIRLY FACE!
TEE HEE...
THAT WAS THE LAST STRAW.
Y'KNOW?
DASH!

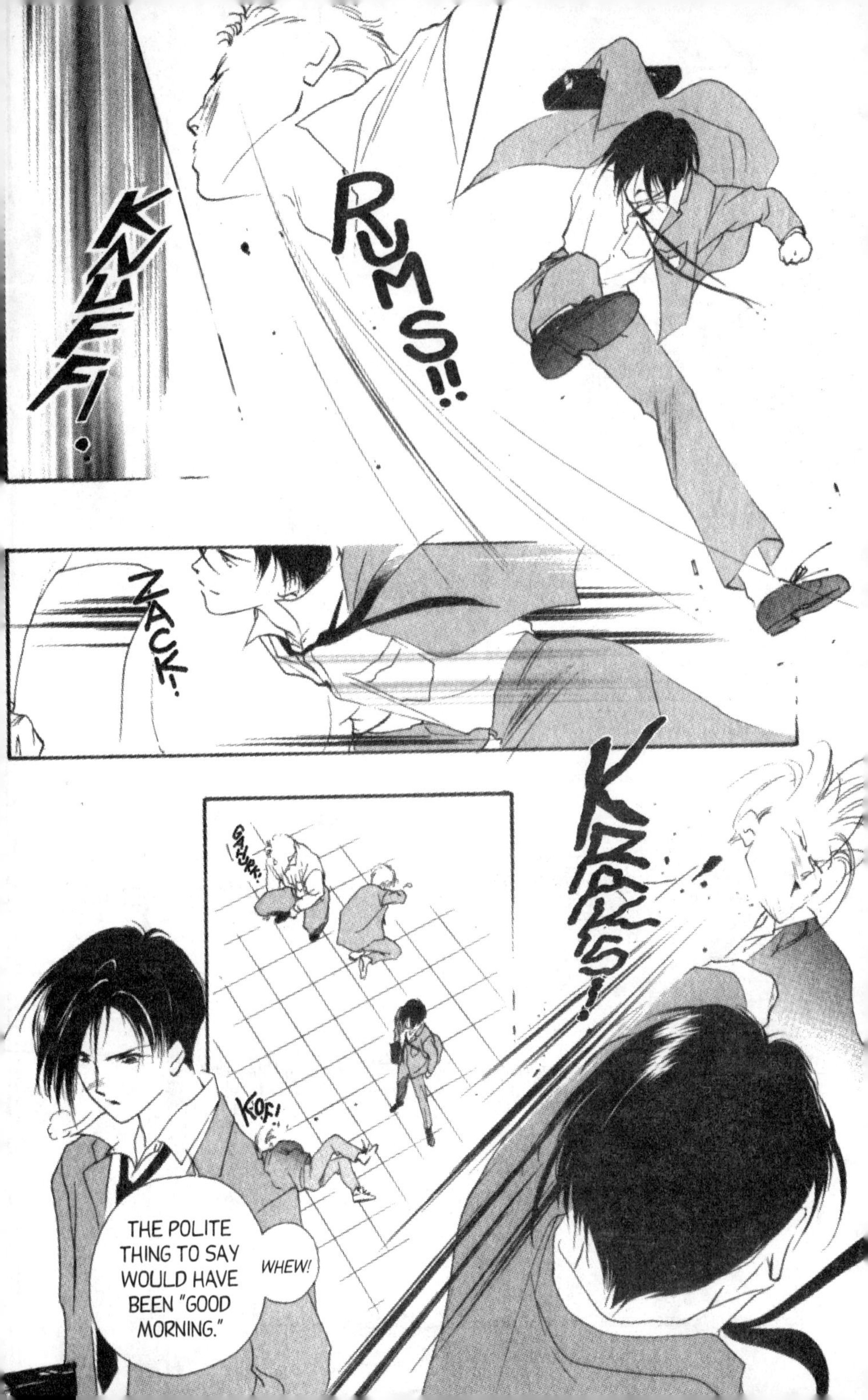
RUMS!!
KNUFF!
ZACK!
KRACKS!
GAHURK!
KOF!
THE POLITE THING TO SAY WOULD HAVE BEEN "GOOD MORNING."
WHEW!

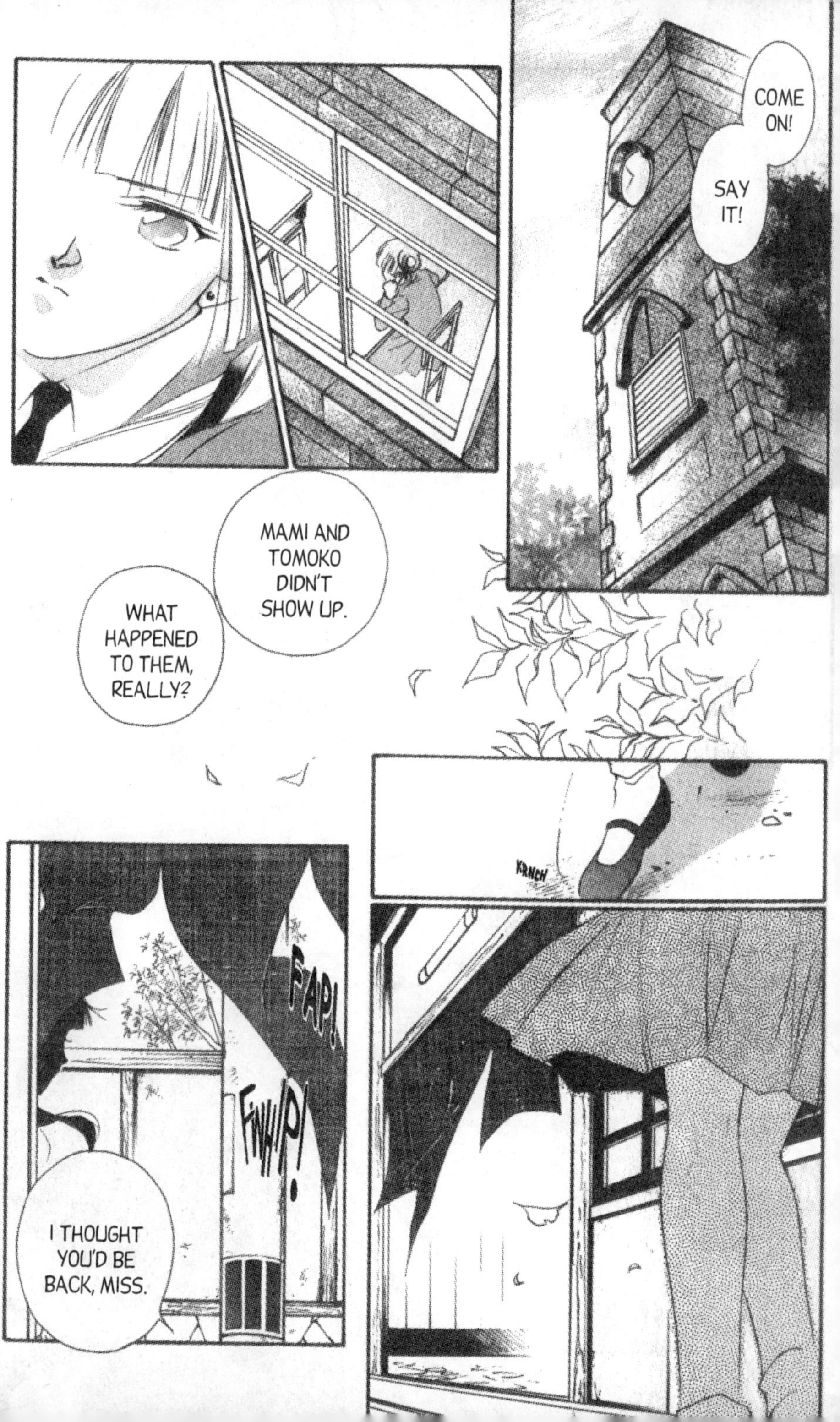
COME ON!
SAY IT!
MAMI AND TOMOKO DIDN'T SHOW UP.
WHAT HAPPENED TO THEM, REALLY?
KRNCH
FAP!
FWHIP!
I THOUGHT YOU'D BE BACK, MISS.

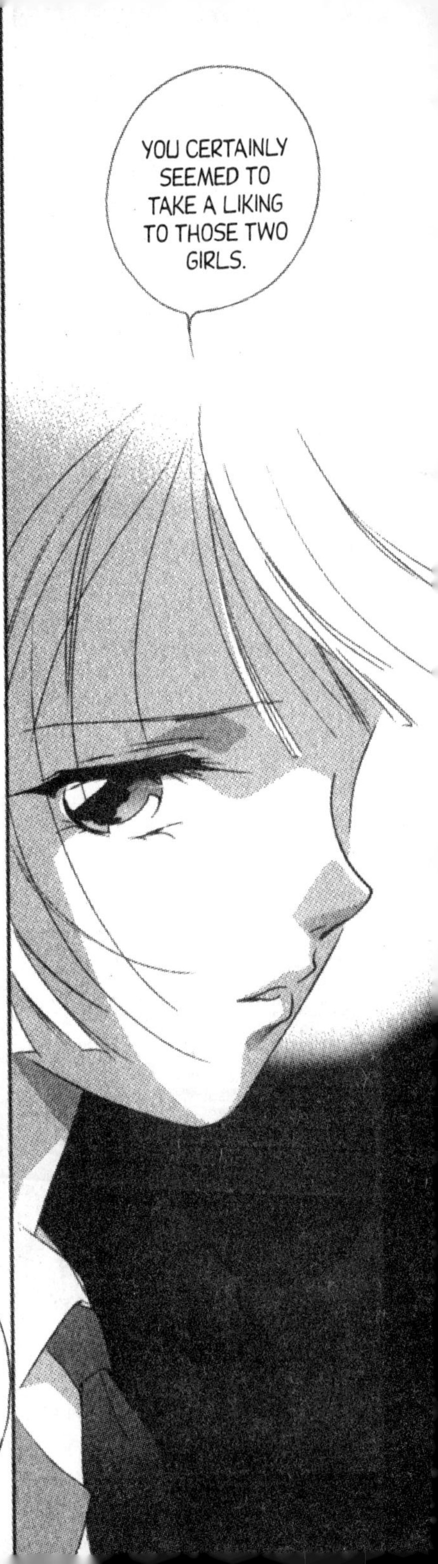
YOU CERTAINLY SEEMED TO TAKE A LIKING TO THOSE TWO GIRLS.

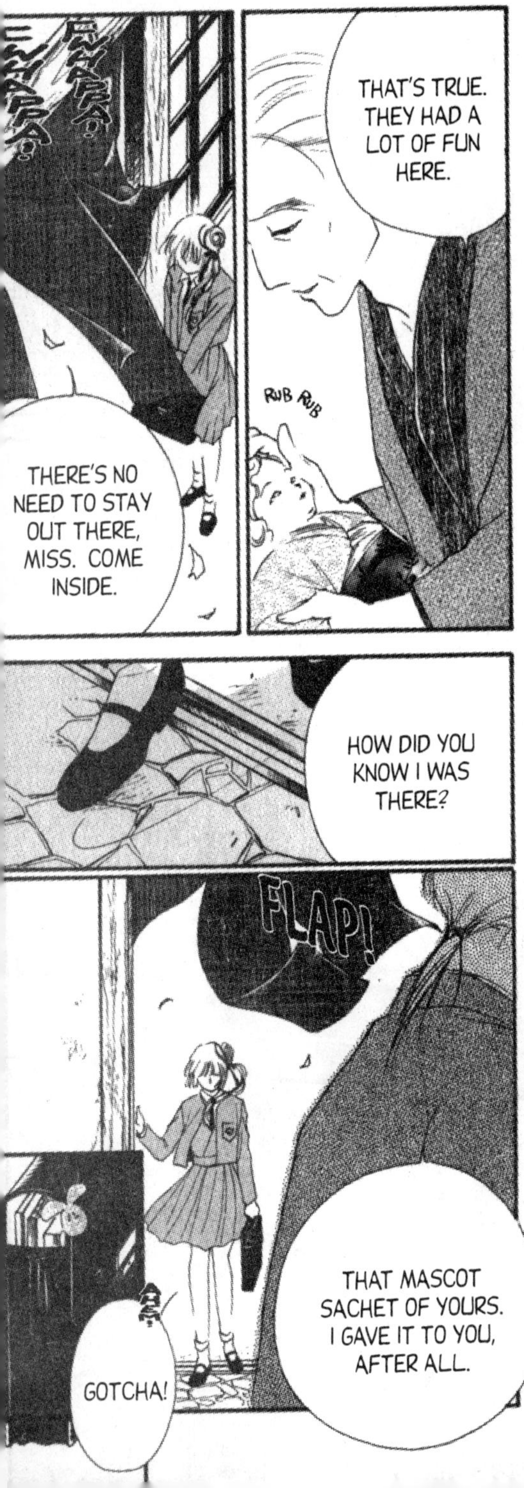
THAT'S TRUE. THEY HAD A LOT OF FUN HERE.
RUB RUB
FWAPPA!
WAPPA!
THERE'S NO NEED TO STAY OUT THERE, MISS. COME INSIDE.
HOW DID YOU KNOW I WAS THERE?
FLAP!
THAT MASCOT SACHET OF YOURS. I GAVE IT TO YOU, AFTER ALL.
GOTCHA!

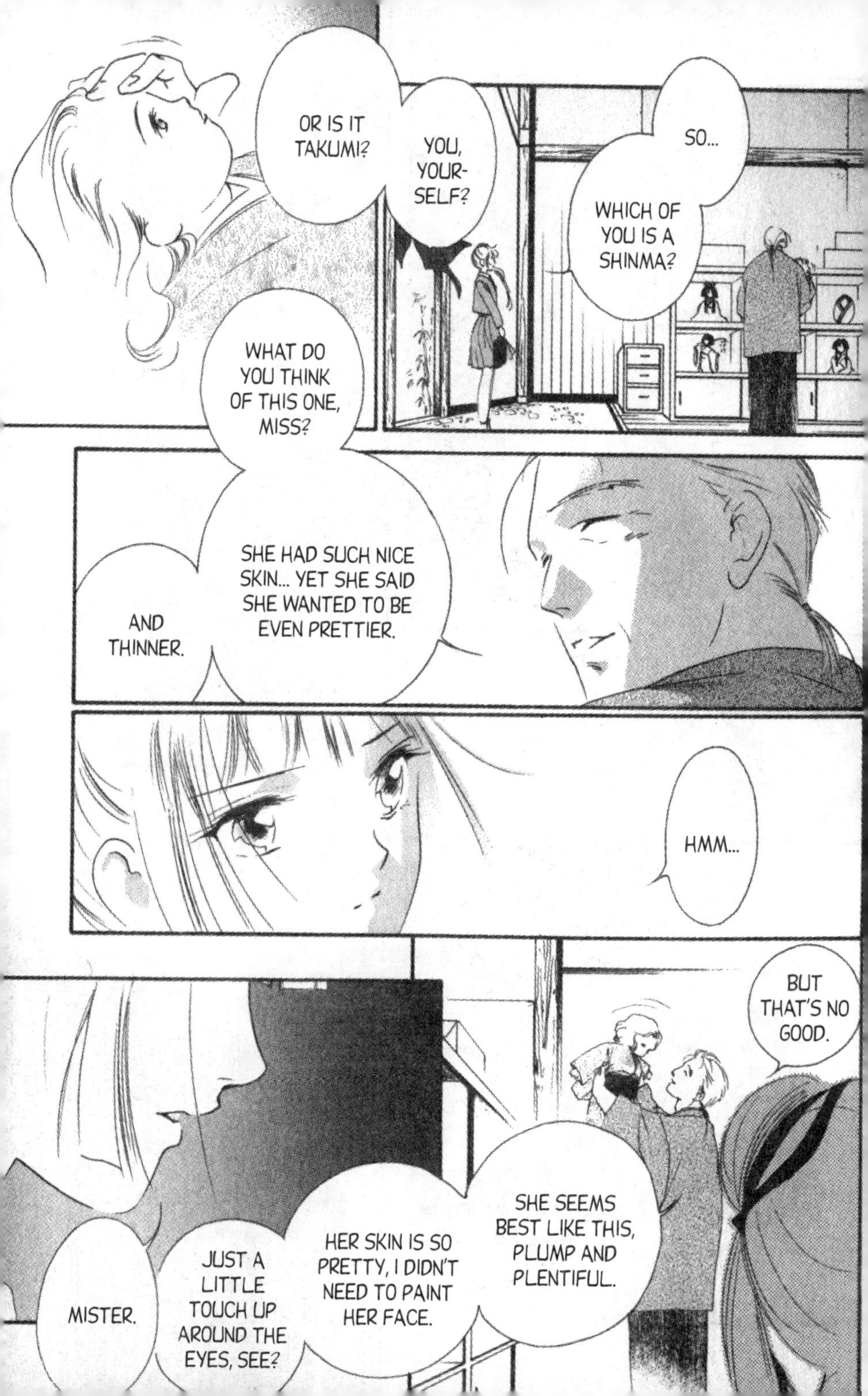
SO...
WHICH OF YOU IS A SHINMA?
YOU, YOURSELF?
OR IS IT TAKUMI?
WHAT DO YOU THINK OF THIS ONE, MISS?
SHE HAD SUCH NICE SKIN... YET SHE SAID SHE WANTED TO BE EVEN PRETTIER.
AND THINNER.
HMM...
BUT THAT'S NO GOOD.
SHE SEEMS BEST LIKE THIS, PLUMP AND PLENTIFUL.
HER SKIN IS SO PRETTY, I DIDN'T NEED TO PAINT HER FACE.
JUST A LITTLE TOUCH UP AROUND THE EYES, SEE?
MISTER.

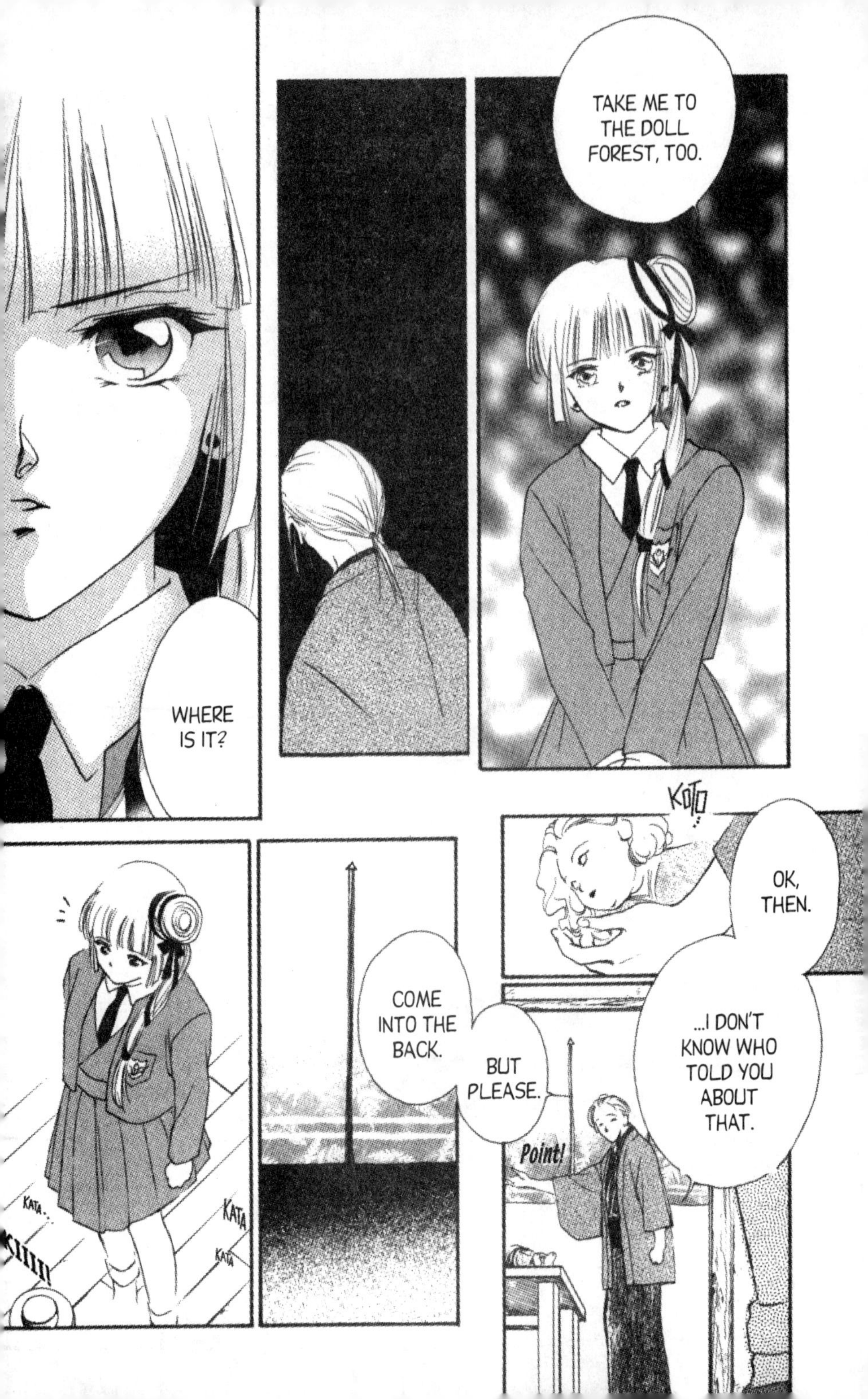
TAKE ME TO THE DOLL FOREST, TOO.
WHERE IS IT?
KOTO...
OK, THEN.
...I DON'T KNOW WHO TOLD YOU ABOUT THAT.
BUT PLEASE.
Point!
COME INTO THE BACK.
KATA
KATA
KATA...
KIIII

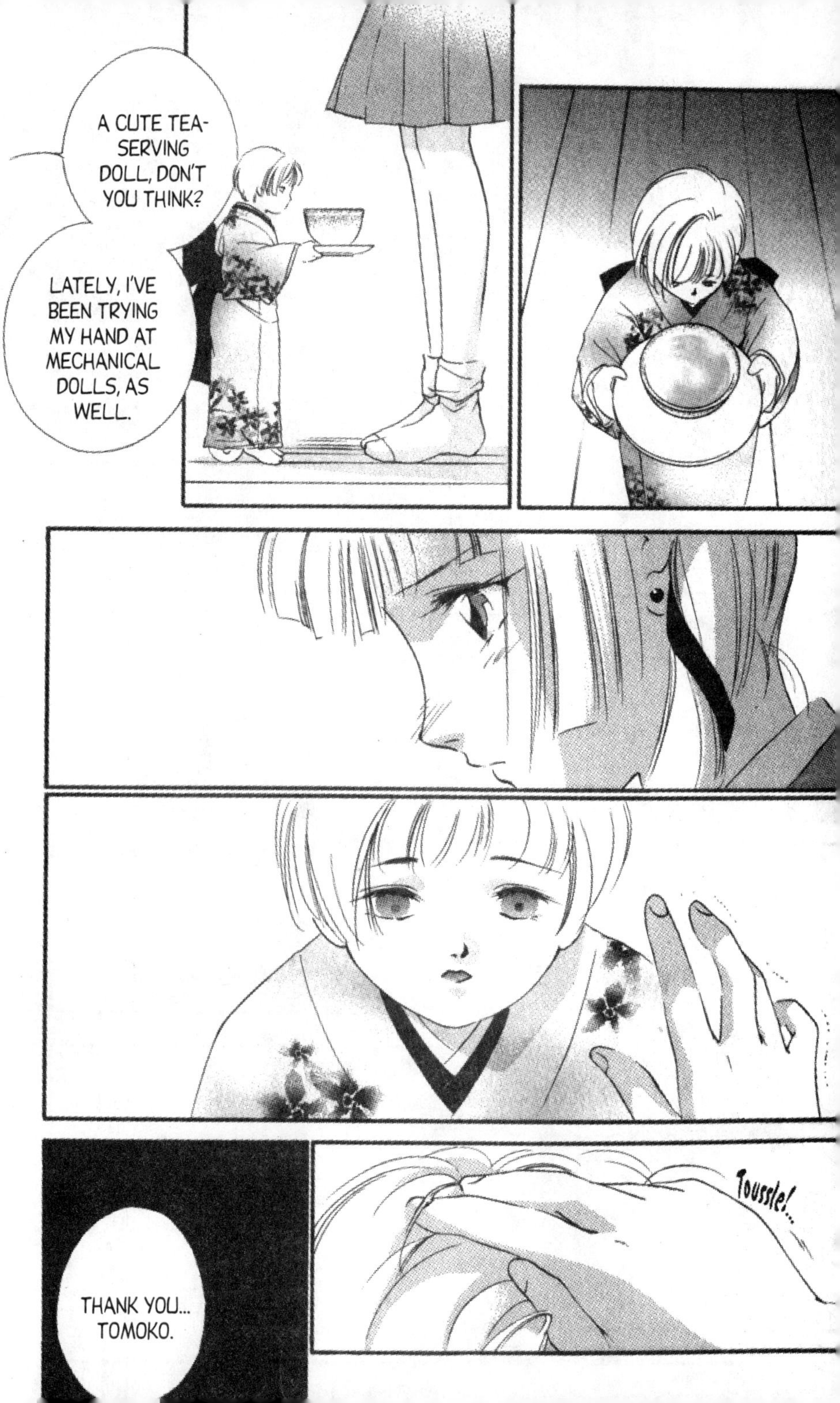
A CUTE TEA-SERVING DOLL, DON'T YOU THINK?
LATELY, I'VE BEEN TRYING MY HAND AT MECHANICAL DOLLS, AS WELL.
Toussle!...
THANK YOU... TOMOKO.

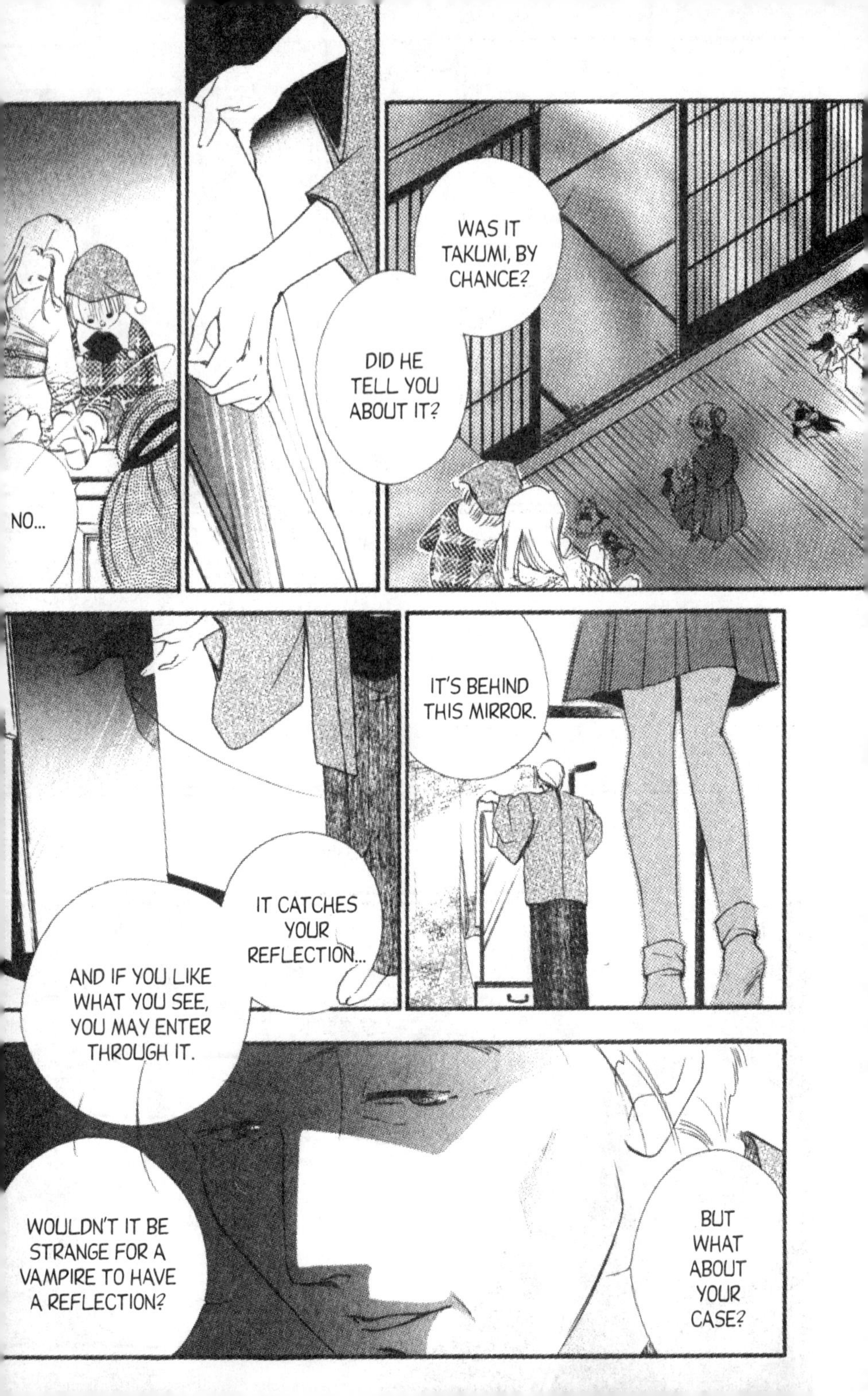
WAS IT TAKUMI, BY CHANCE?
DID HE TELL YOU ABOUT IT?
NO...
IT'S BEHIND THIS MIRROR.
IT CATCHES YOUR REFLECTION...
AND IF YOU LIKE WHAT YOU SEE, YOU MAY ENTER THROUGH IT.
BUT WHAT ABOUT YOUR CASE?
WOULDN'T IT BE STRANGE FOR A VAMPIRE TO HAVE A REFLECTION?

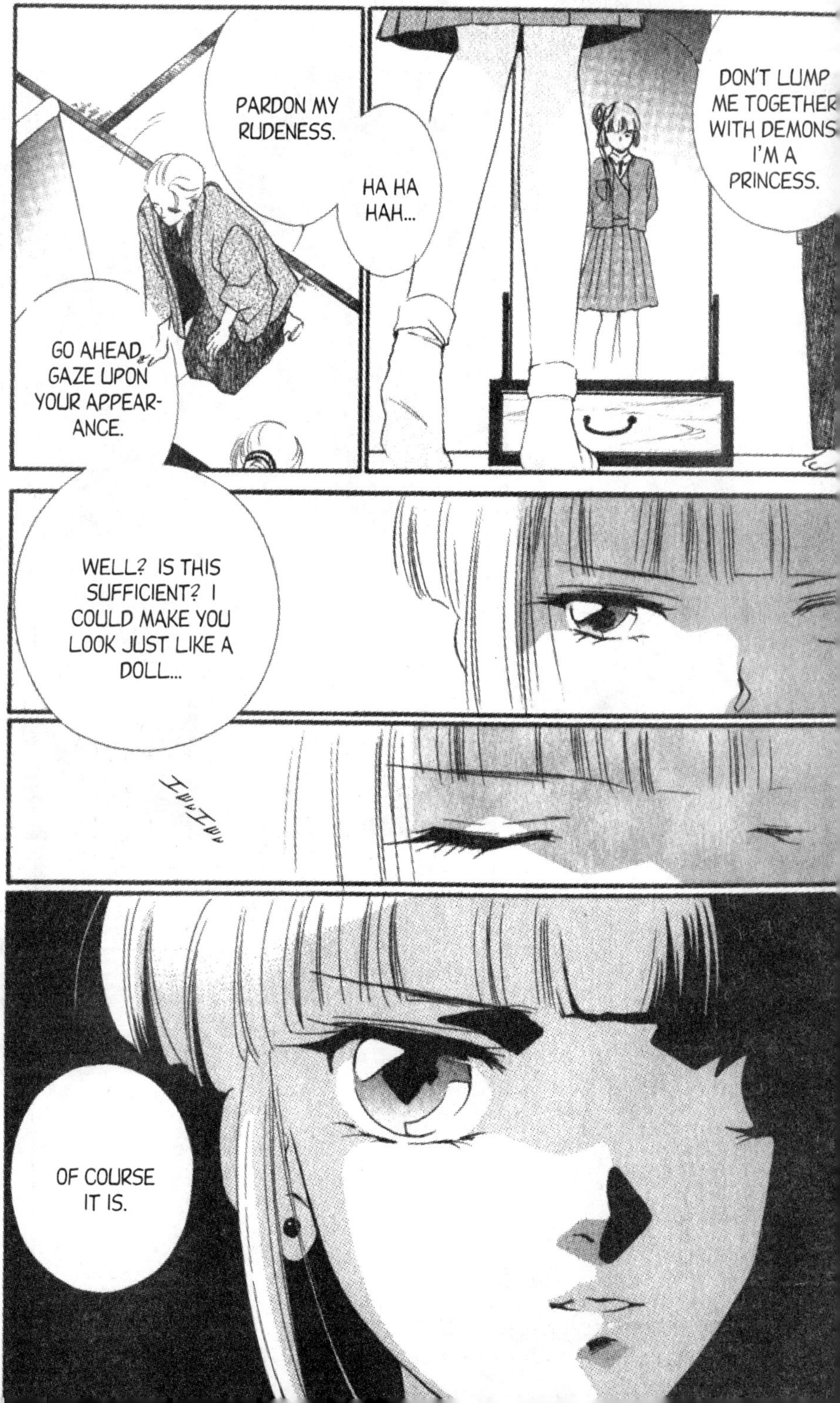
DON'T LUMP ME TOGETHER WITH DEMONS. I'M A PRINCESS.
HA HA HAH...
PARDON MY RUDENESS.
GO AHEAD. GAZE UPON YOUR APPEAR-ANCE.
WELL? IS THIS SUFFICIENT? I COULD MAKE YOU LOOK JUST LIKE A DOLL...
OF COURSE IT IS.

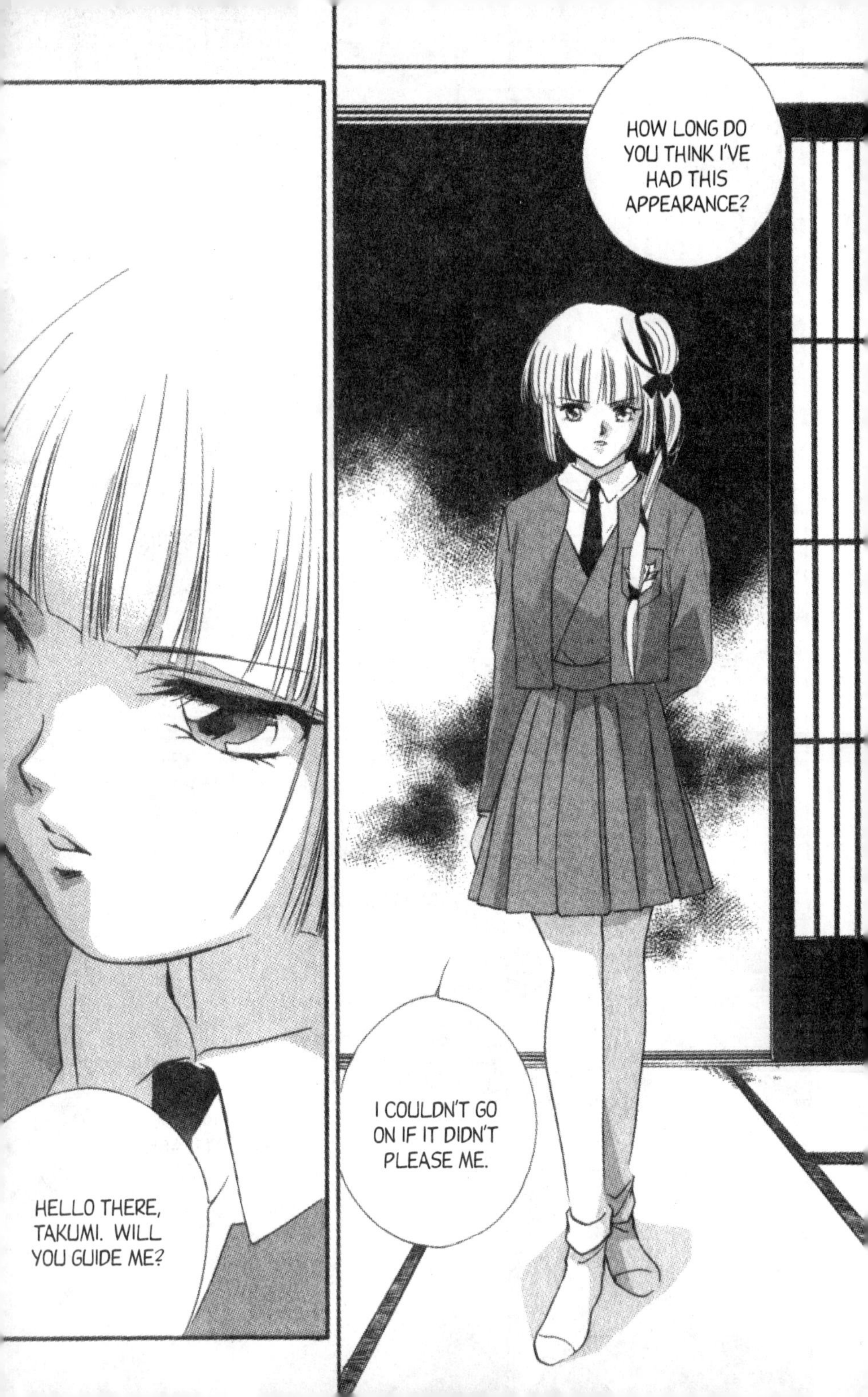
HOW LONG DO YOU THINK I'VE HAD THIS APPEARANCE?
I COULDN'T GO ON IF IT DIDN'T PLEASE ME.
HELLO THERE, TAKUMI. WILL YOU GUIDE ME?

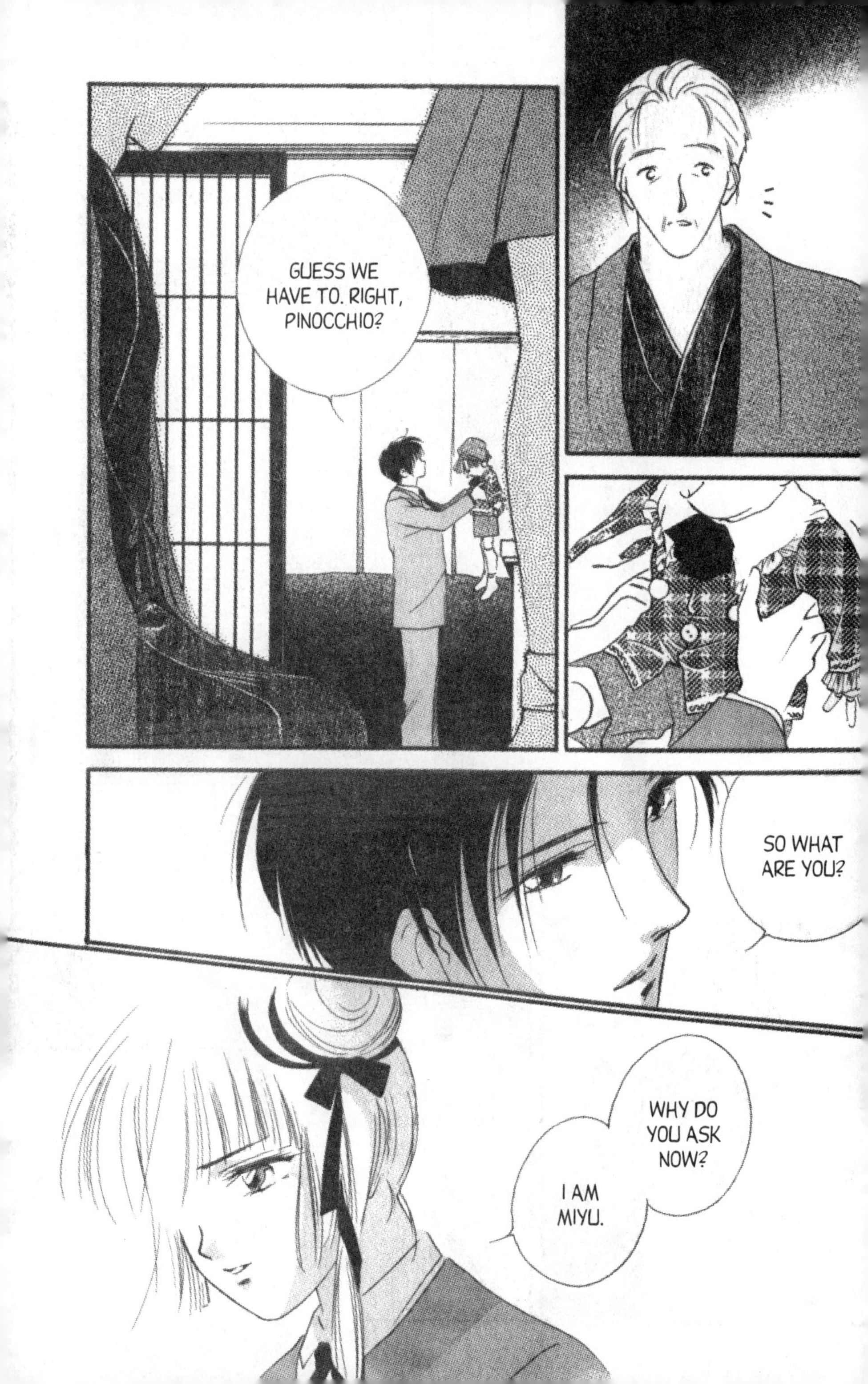
GUESS WE HAVE TO. RIGHT, PINOCCHIO?
SO WHAT ARE YOU?
WHY DO YOU ASK NOW?
I AM MIYU.

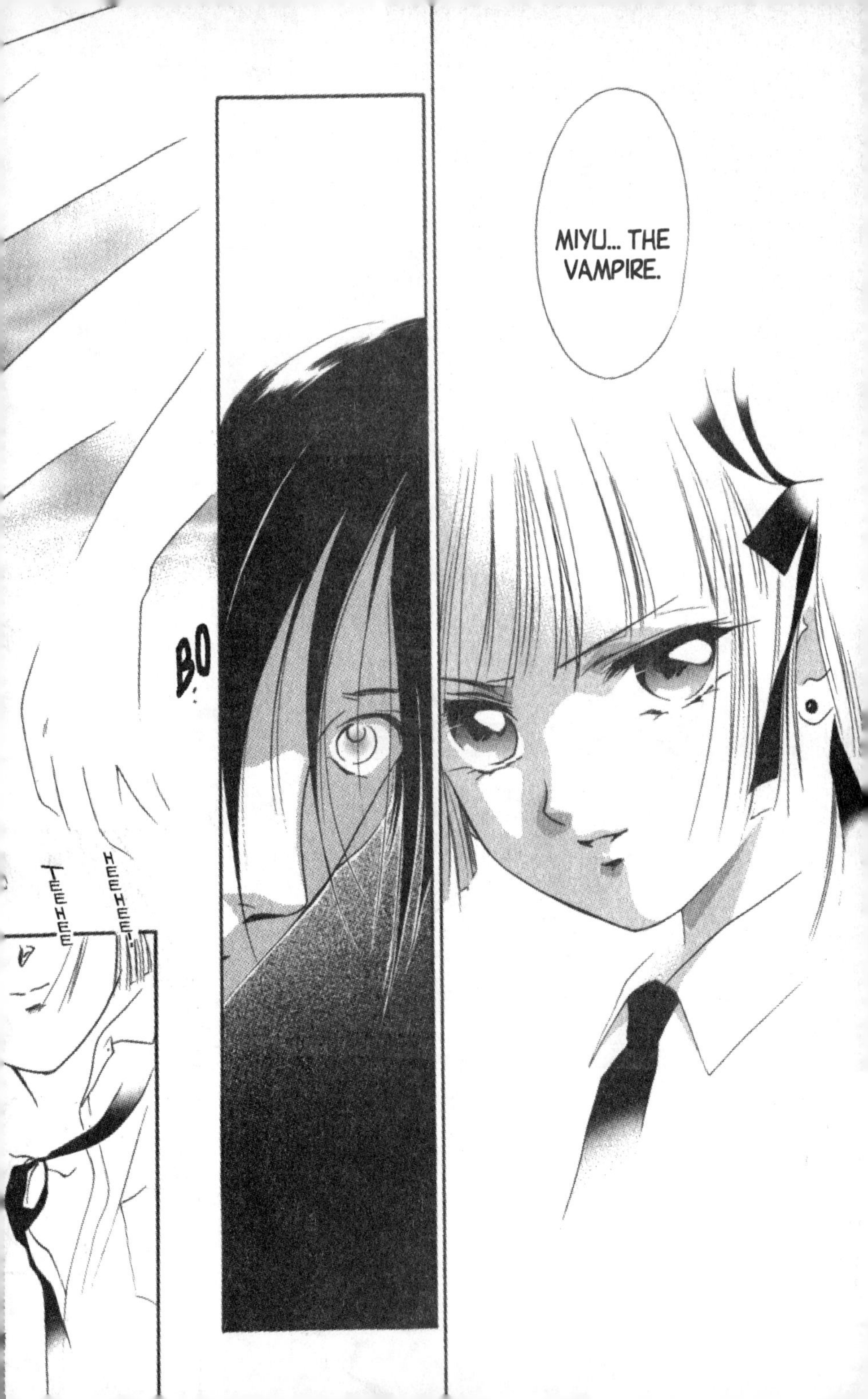
MIYU... THE VAMPIRE.
BO
HEEHEE!
TEEHEE

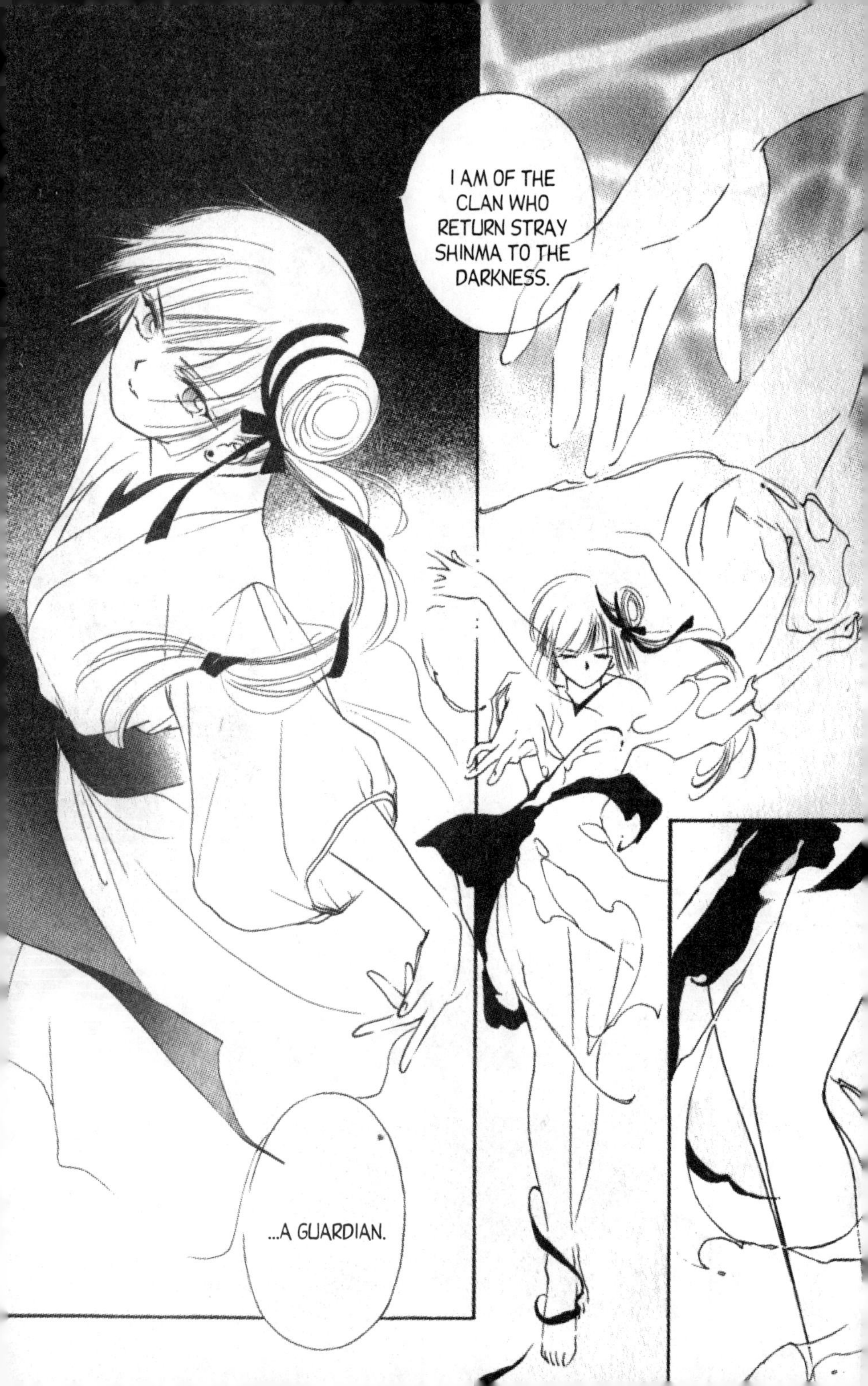
I AM OF THE CLAN WHO RETURN STRAY SHINMA TO THE DARKNESS.
...A GUARDIAN.

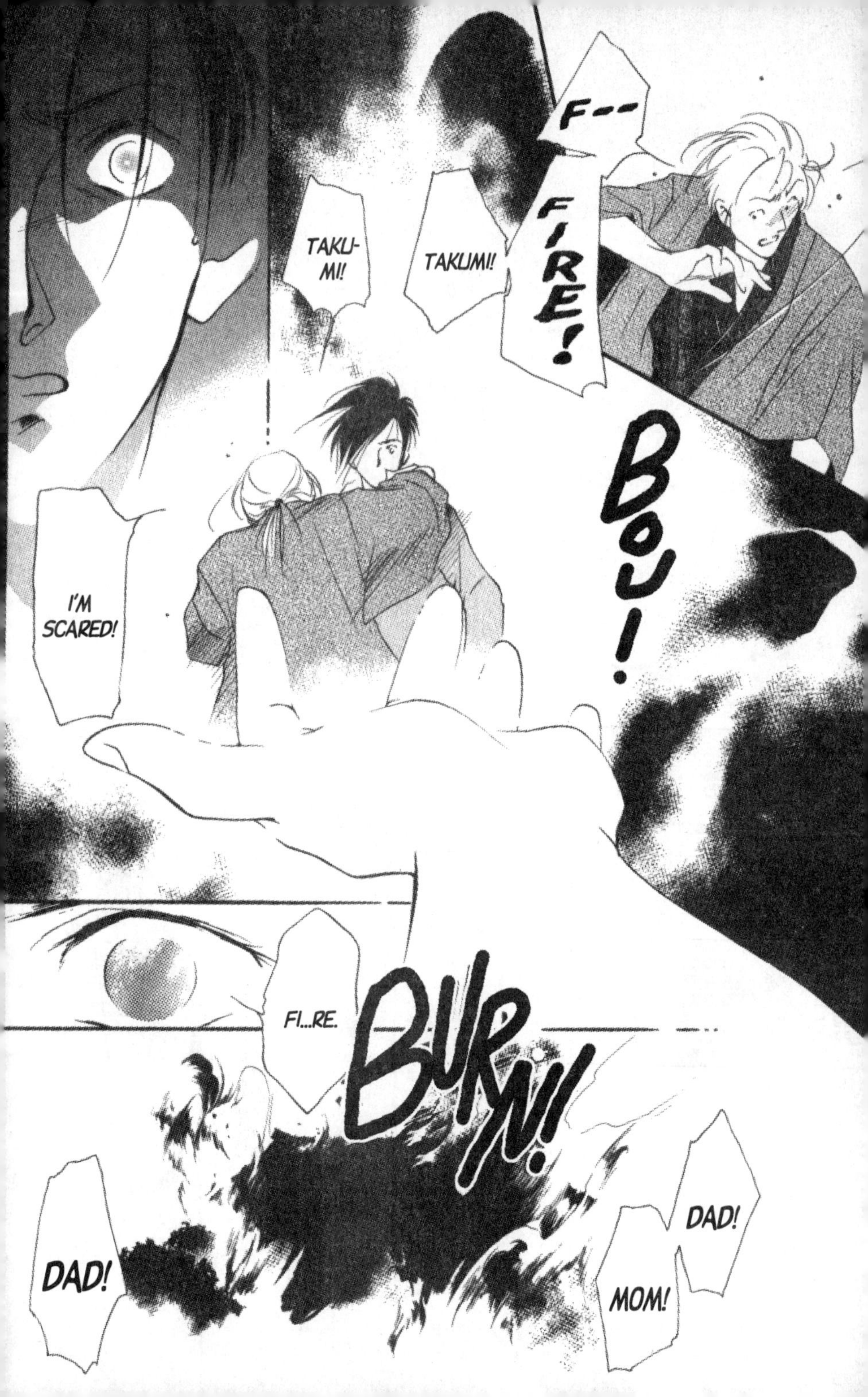
F--
FIRE!
TAKUMI!
TAKU-MI!
BOU!
I'M SCARED!
FI...RE.
BURN!
DAD!
MOM!
DAD!

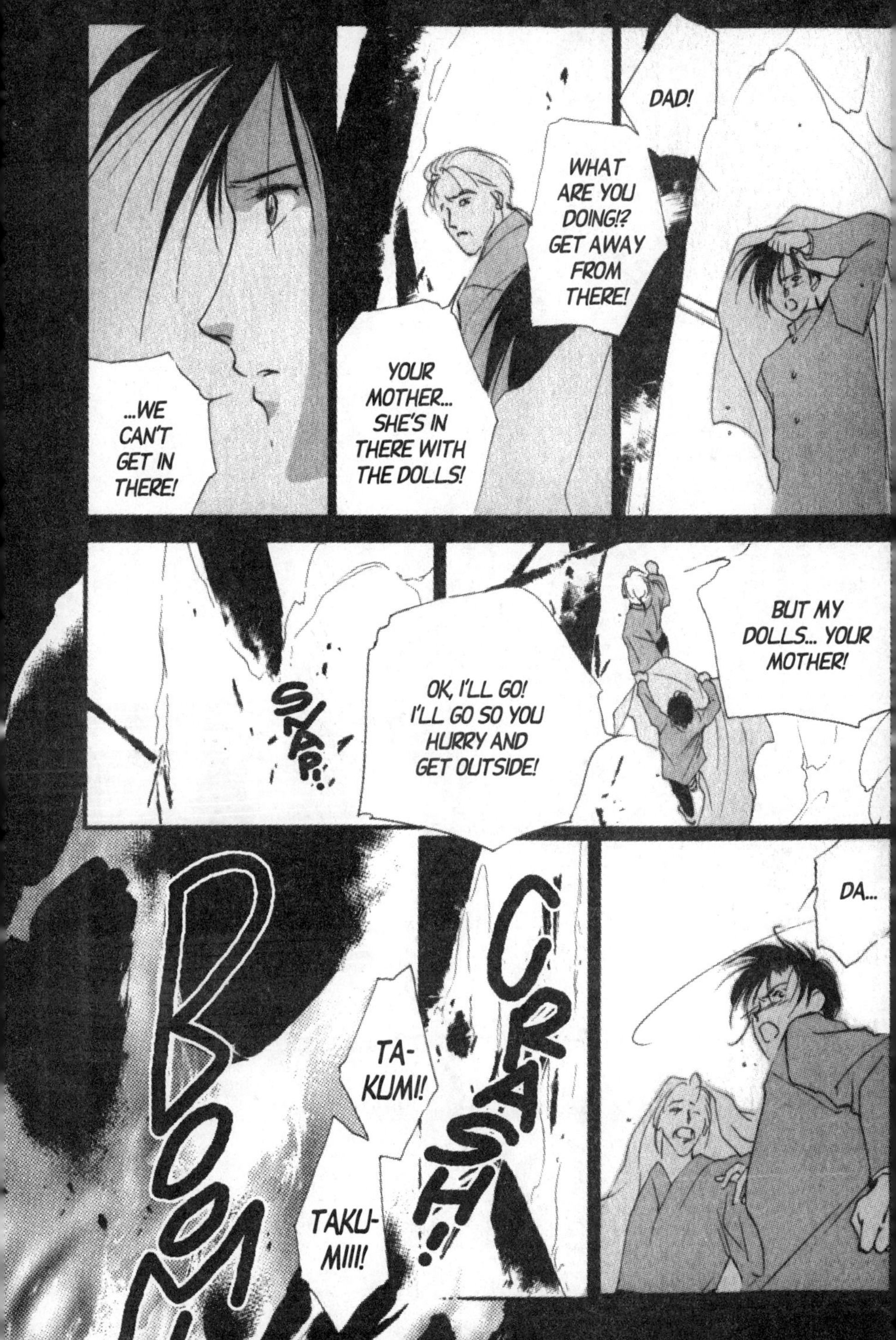
DAD!
WHAT ARE YOU DOING!? GET AWAY FROM THERE!
YOUR MOTHER... SHE'S IN THERE WITH THE DOLLS!
...WE CAN'T GET IN THERE!
BUT MY DOLLS... YOUR MOTHER!
OK, I'LL GO! I'LL GO SO YOU HURRY AND GET OUTSIDE!
SNAP!
DA...
CRASH!!
TA-KUMI!!
TAKU-MIII!
BOOM!!

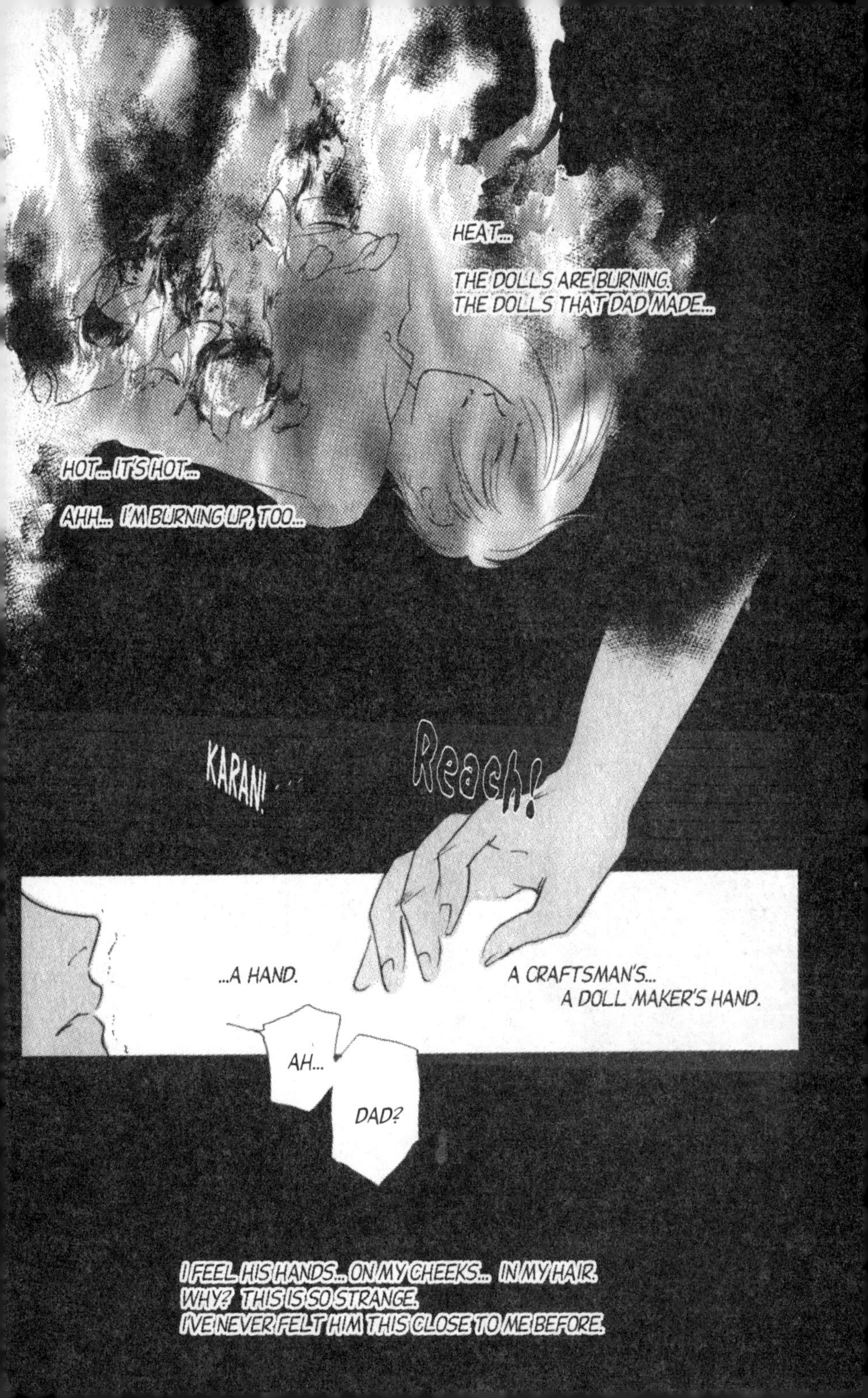
HEAT...
THE DOLLS ARE BURNING. THE DOLLS THAT DAD MADE...
HOT... IT'S HOT...
AHH... I'M BURNING UP, TOO...
KARAN!
Reach!
A CRAFTSMAN'S... A DOLL MAKER'S HAND.
...A HAND.
AH...
DAD?
I FEEL HIS HANDS... ON MY CHEEKS... IN MY HAIR. WHY? THIS IS SO STRANGE. I'VE NEVER FELT HIM THIS CLOSE TO ME BEFORE.

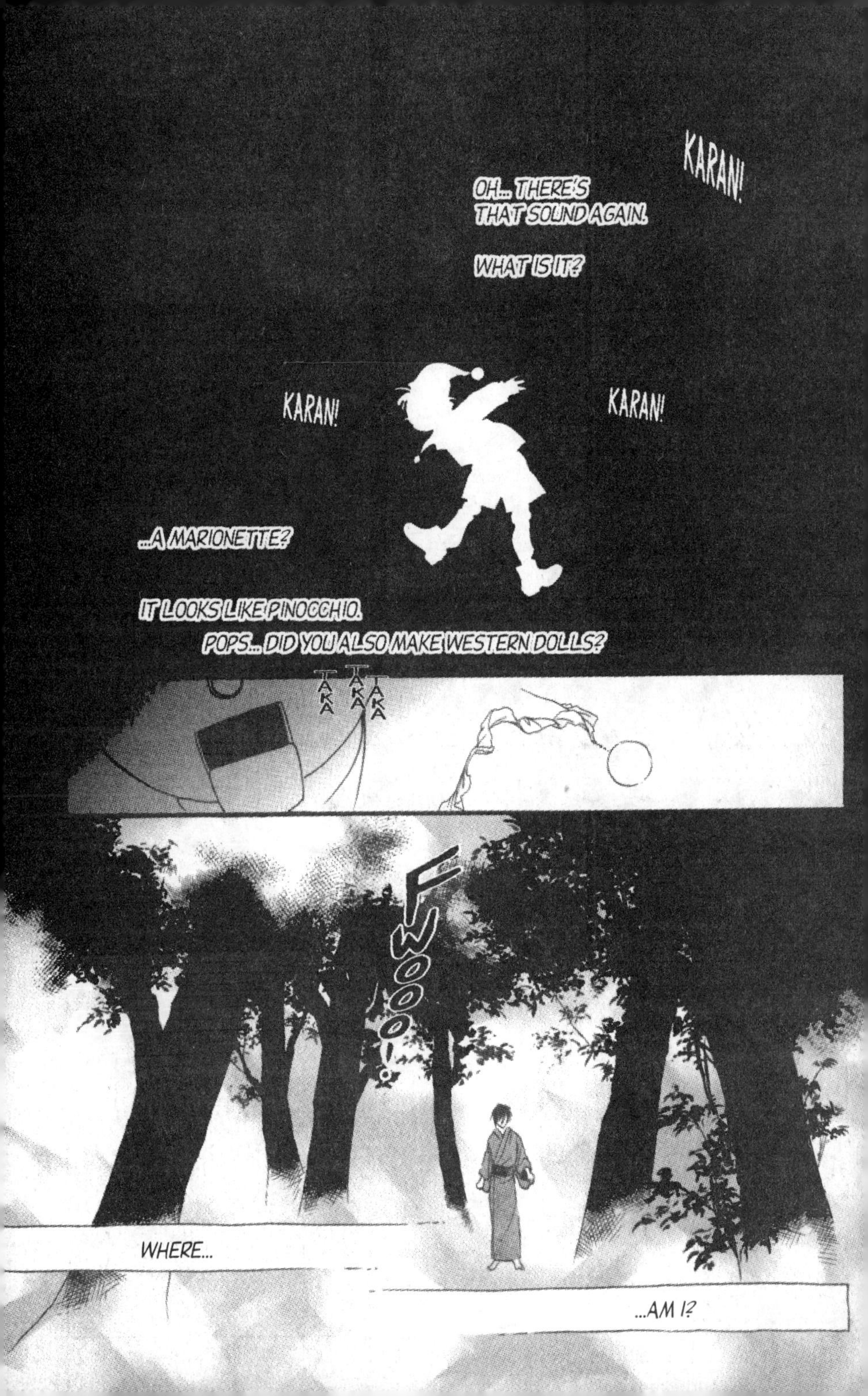
KARAN!
OH... THERE'S THAT SOUND AGAIN.
WHAT IS IT?
KARAN!
KARAN!
...A MARIONETTE?
IT LOOKS LIKE PINOCCHIO.
POPS... DID YOU ALSO MAKE WESTERN DOLLS?
TAKA TAKA TAKA
FWOOOO!
WHERE...
...AM I?

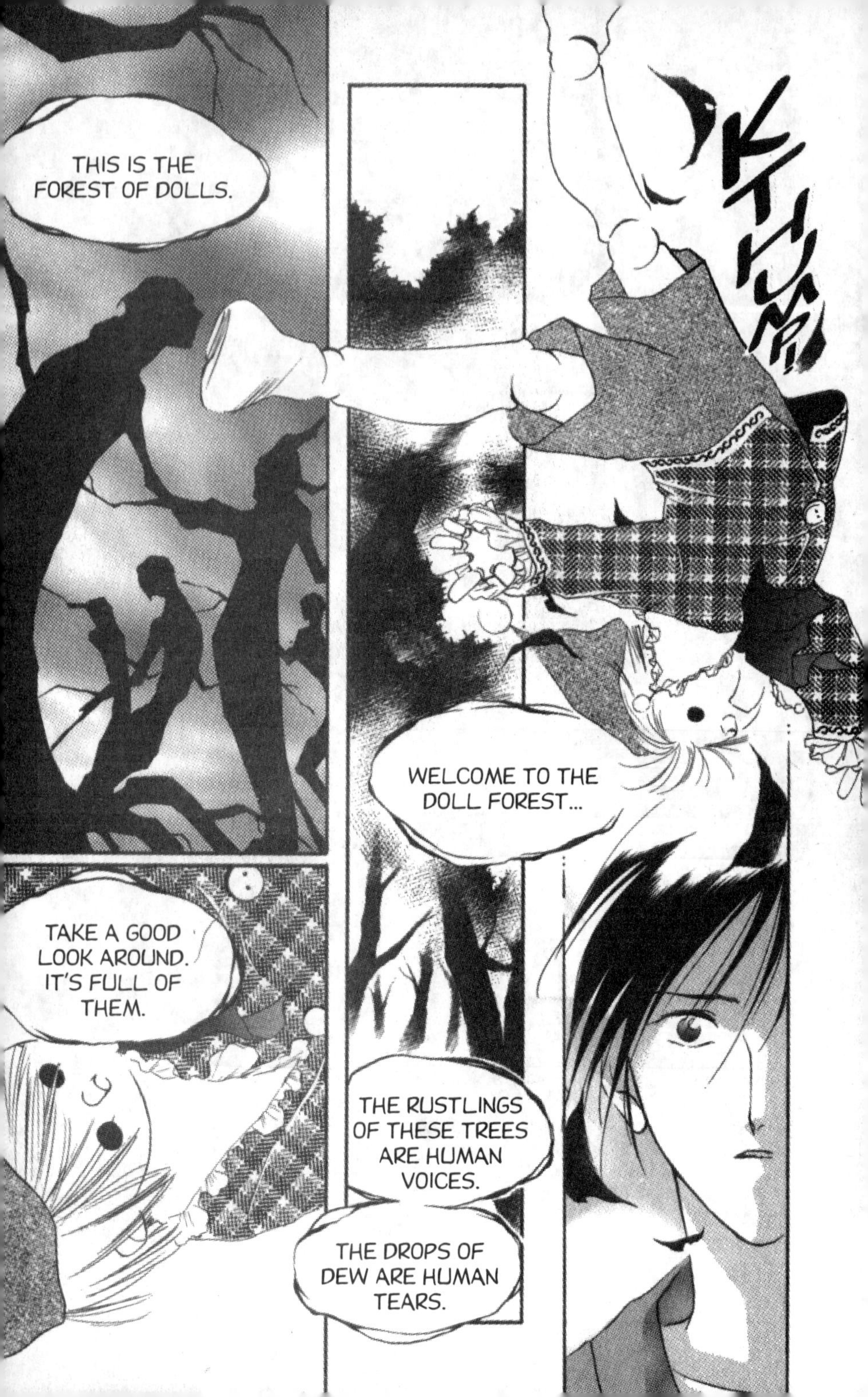
KTHUMP!
WELCOME TO THE DOLL FOREST...
THE RUSTLINGS OF THESE TREES ARE HUMAN VOICES.
THE DROPS OF DEW ARE HUMAN TEARS.
THIS IS THE FOREST OF DOLLS.
TAKE A GOOD LOOK AROUND. IT'S FULL OF THEM.

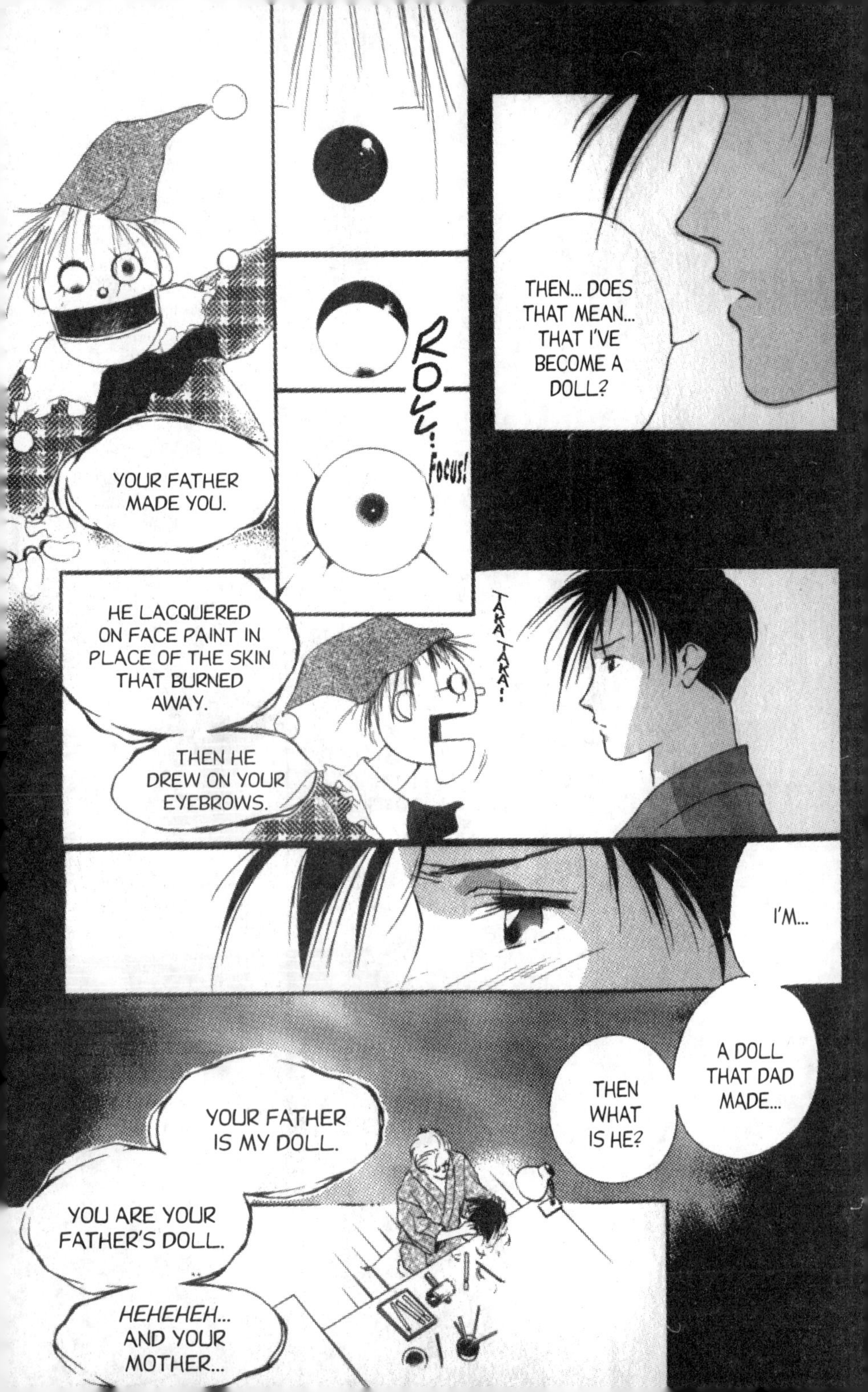
THEN... DOES THAT MEAN... THAT I'VE BECOME A DOLL?
ROLL... FOCUS!
YOUR FATHER MADE YOU.
TAKA TAKA...
HE LACQUERED ON FACE PAINT IN PLACE OF THE SKIN THAT BURNED AWAY.
THEN HE DREW ON YOUR EYEBROWS.
I'M...
A DOLL THAT DAD MADE...
THEN WHAT IS HE?
YOUR FATHER IS MY DOLL.
YOU ARE YOUR FATHER'S DOLL.
HEHEHEH... AND YOUR MOTHER...

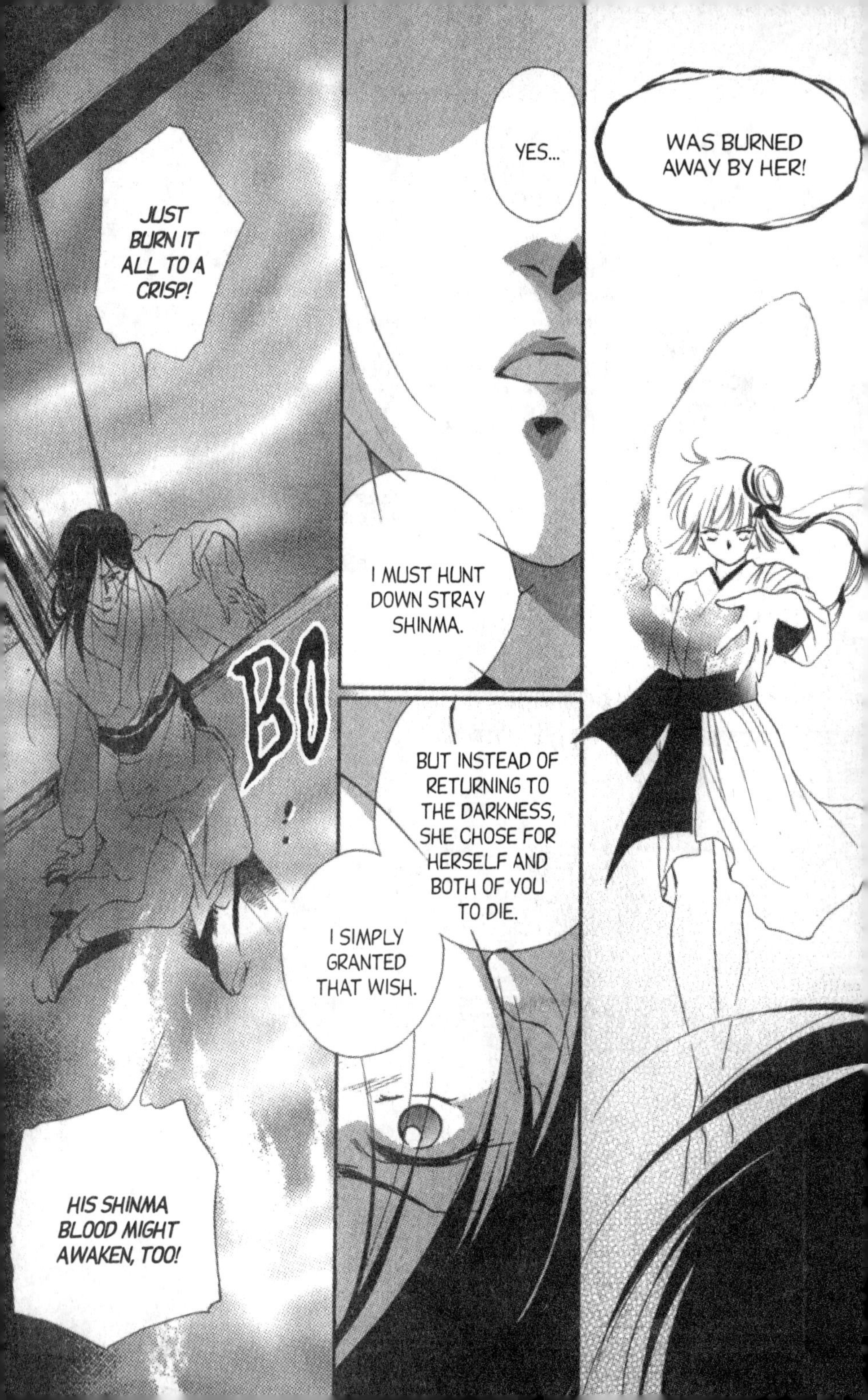
WAS BURNED AWAY BY HER!
YES...
I MUST HUNT DOWN STRAY SHINMA.
BUT INSTEAD OF RETURNING TO THE DARKNESS, SHE CHOSE FOR HERSELF AND BOTH OF YOU TO DIE.
I SIMPLY GRANTED THAT WISH.
JUST BURN IT ALL TO A CRISP!
BO
!
HIS SHINMA BLOOD MIGHT AWAKEN, TOO!

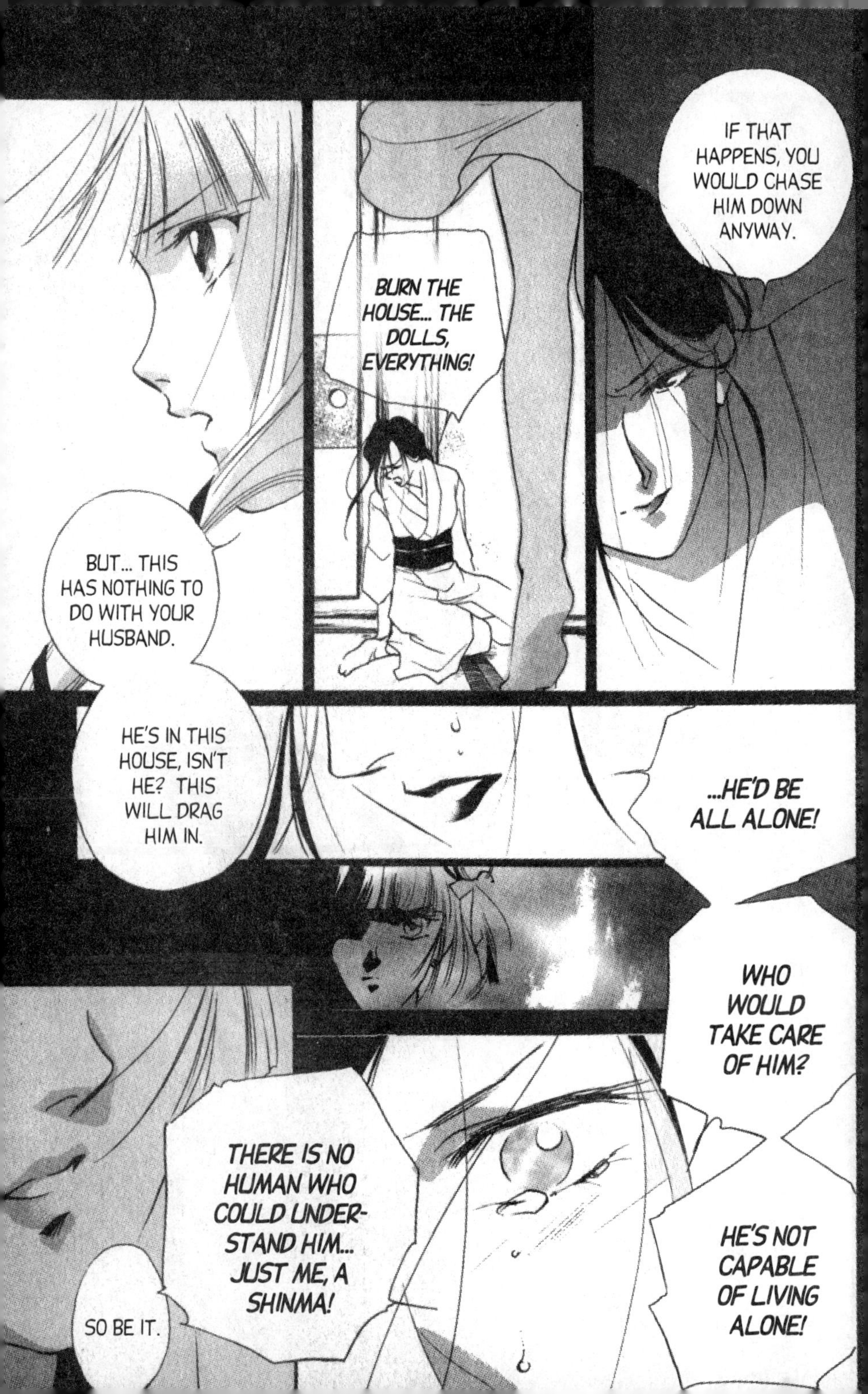
IF THAT HAPPENS, YOU WOULD CHASE HIM DOWN ANYWAY.
BURN THE HOUSE... THE DOLLS, EVERYTHING!
BUT... THIS HAS NOTHING TO DO WITH YOUR HUSBAND.
...HE'D BE ALL ALONE!
HE'S IN THIS HOUSE, ISN'T HE? THIS WILL DRAG HIM IN.
WHO WOULD TAKE CARE OF HIM?
HE'S NOT CAPABLE OF LIVING ALONE!
THERE IS NO HUMAN WHO COULD UNDER-STAND HIM... JUST ME, A SHINMA!
SO BE IT.

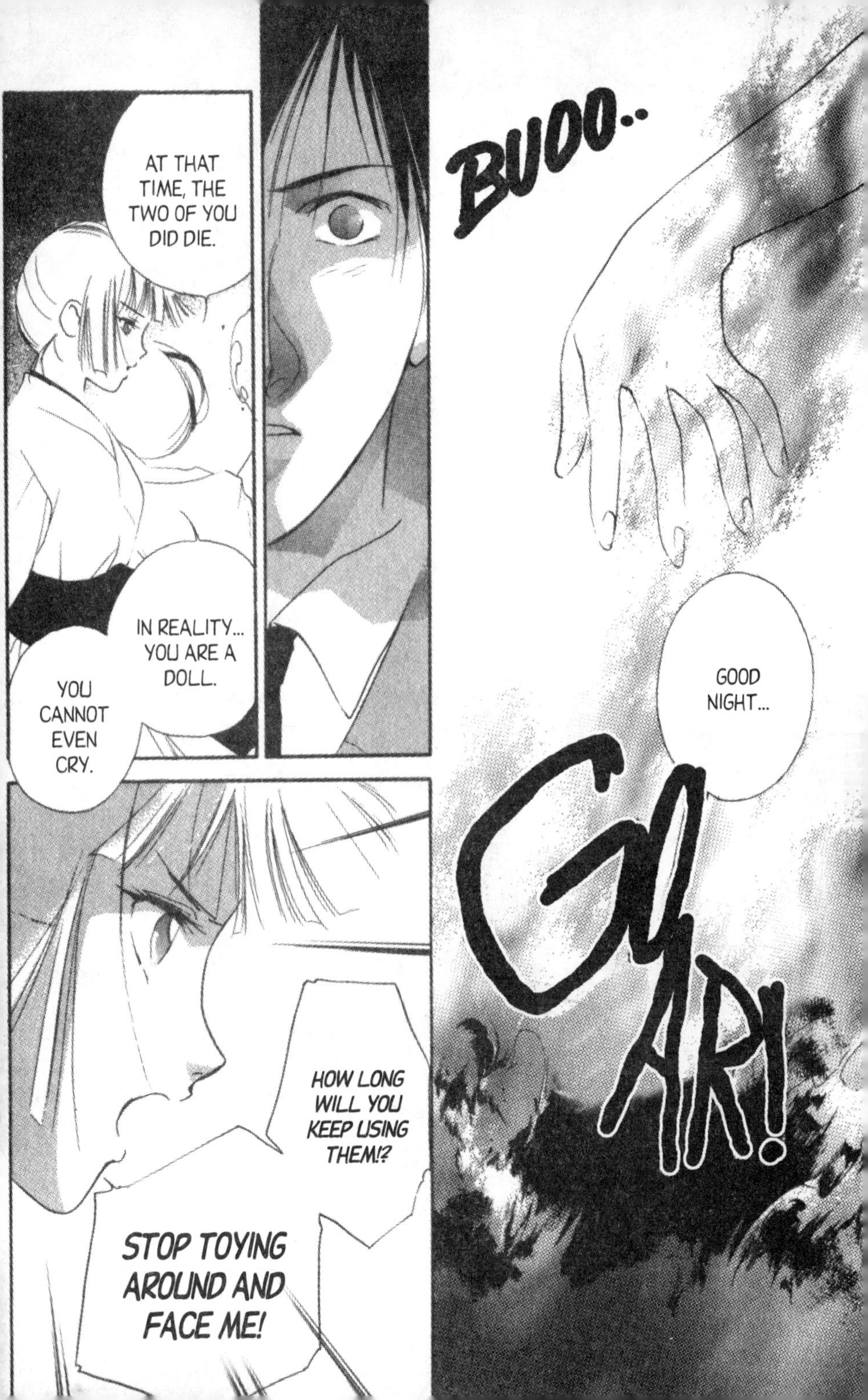
BUOO..
GOOD NIGHT...
GYAR!
AT THAT TIME, THE TWO OF YOU DID DIE.
IN REALITY... YOU ARE A DOLL.
YOU CANNOT EVEN CRY.
HOW LONG WILL YOU KEEP USING THEM!?
STOP TOYING AROUND AND FACE ME!

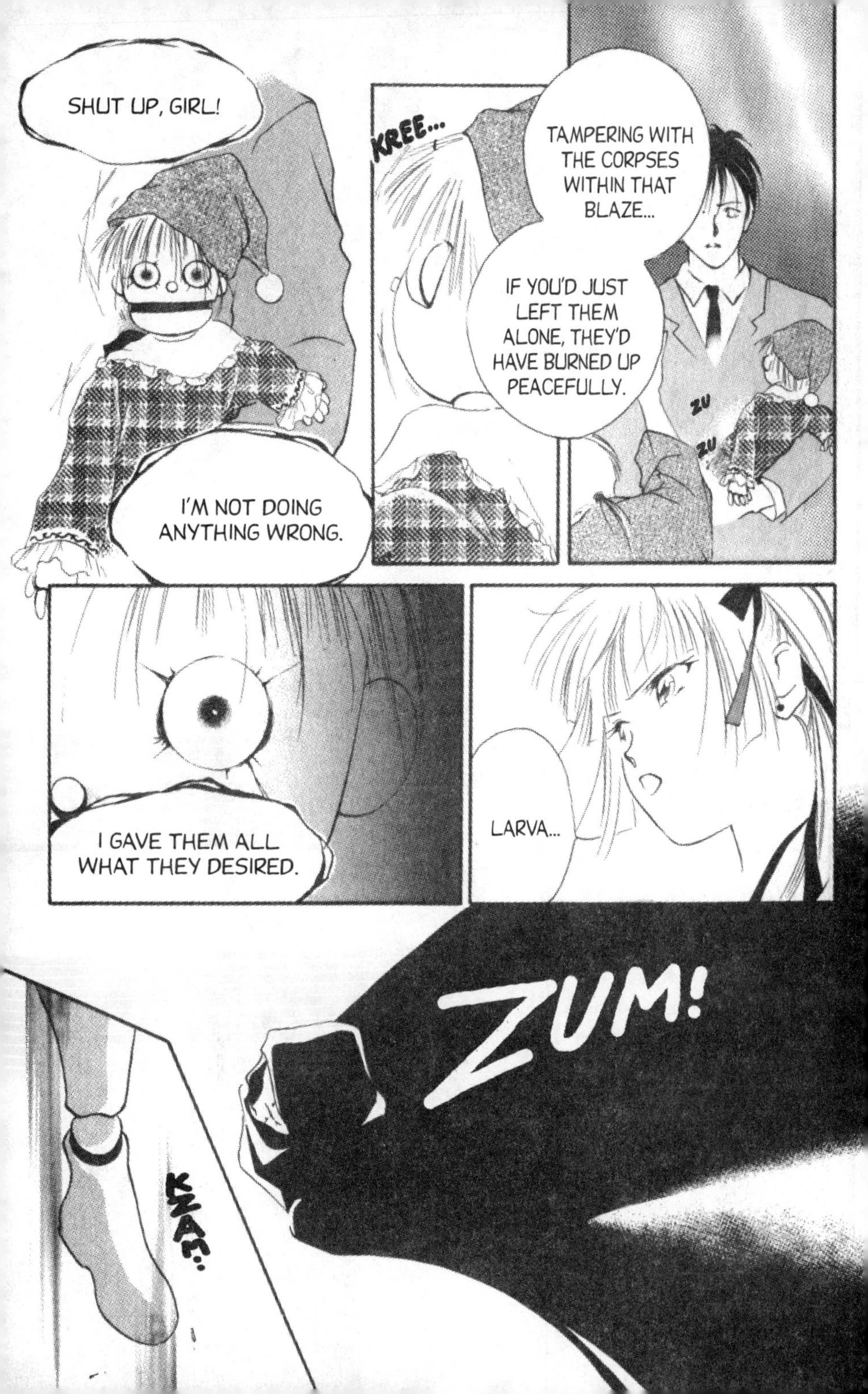
TAMPERING WITH THE CORPSES WITHIN THAT BLAZE...
IF YOU'D JUST LEFT THEM ALONE, THEY'D HAVE BURNED UP PEACEFULLY.
ZU
ZU
KREE...
SHUT UP, GIRL!
I'M NOT DOING ANYTHING WRONG.
LARVA...
I GAVE THEM ALL WHAT THEY DESIRED.
ZUM!
KLAM...

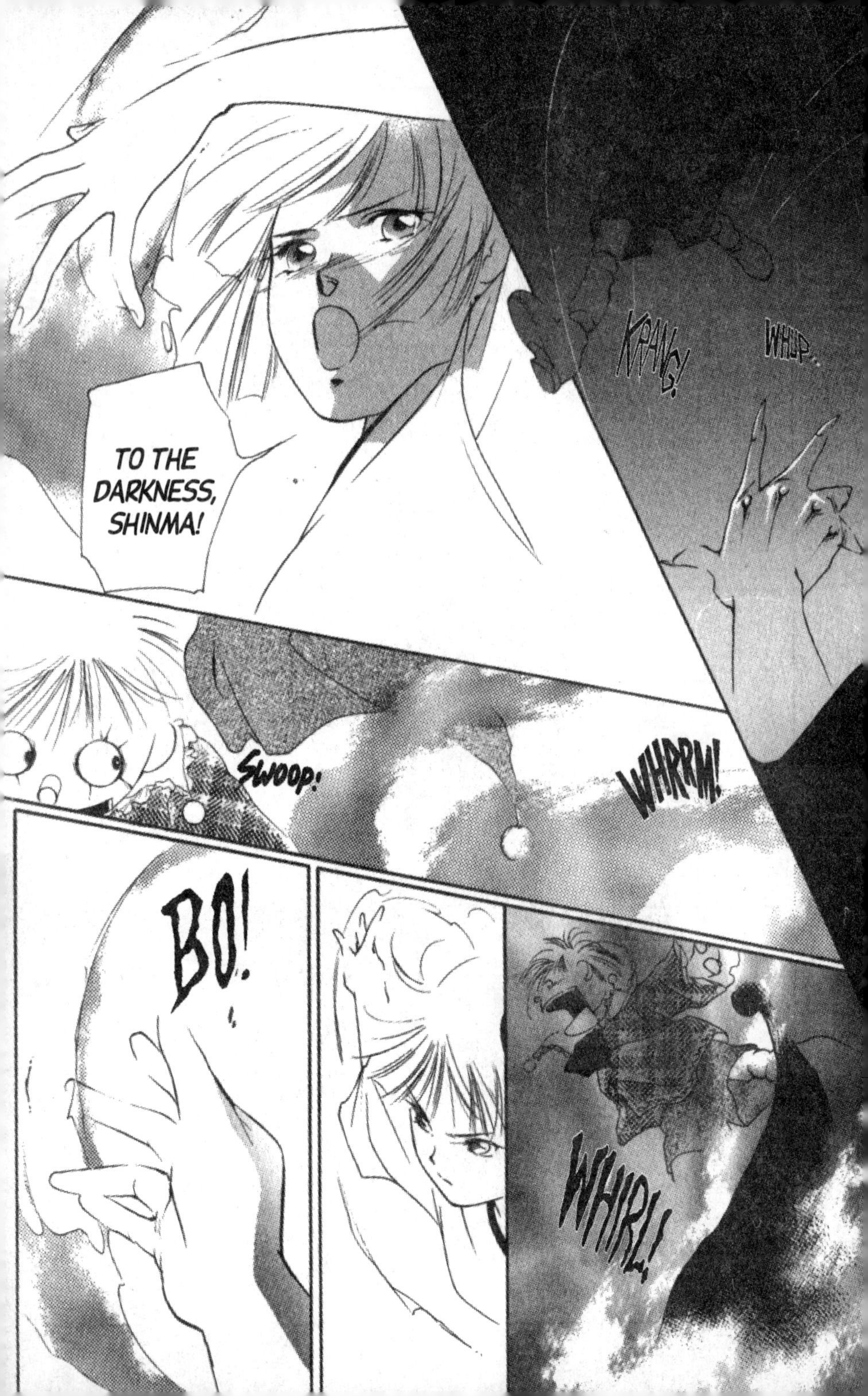
KRANG!
WHUP...
TO THE DARKNESS, SHINMA!
WHRRM!
SWOOP!
WHIRL!
BO!

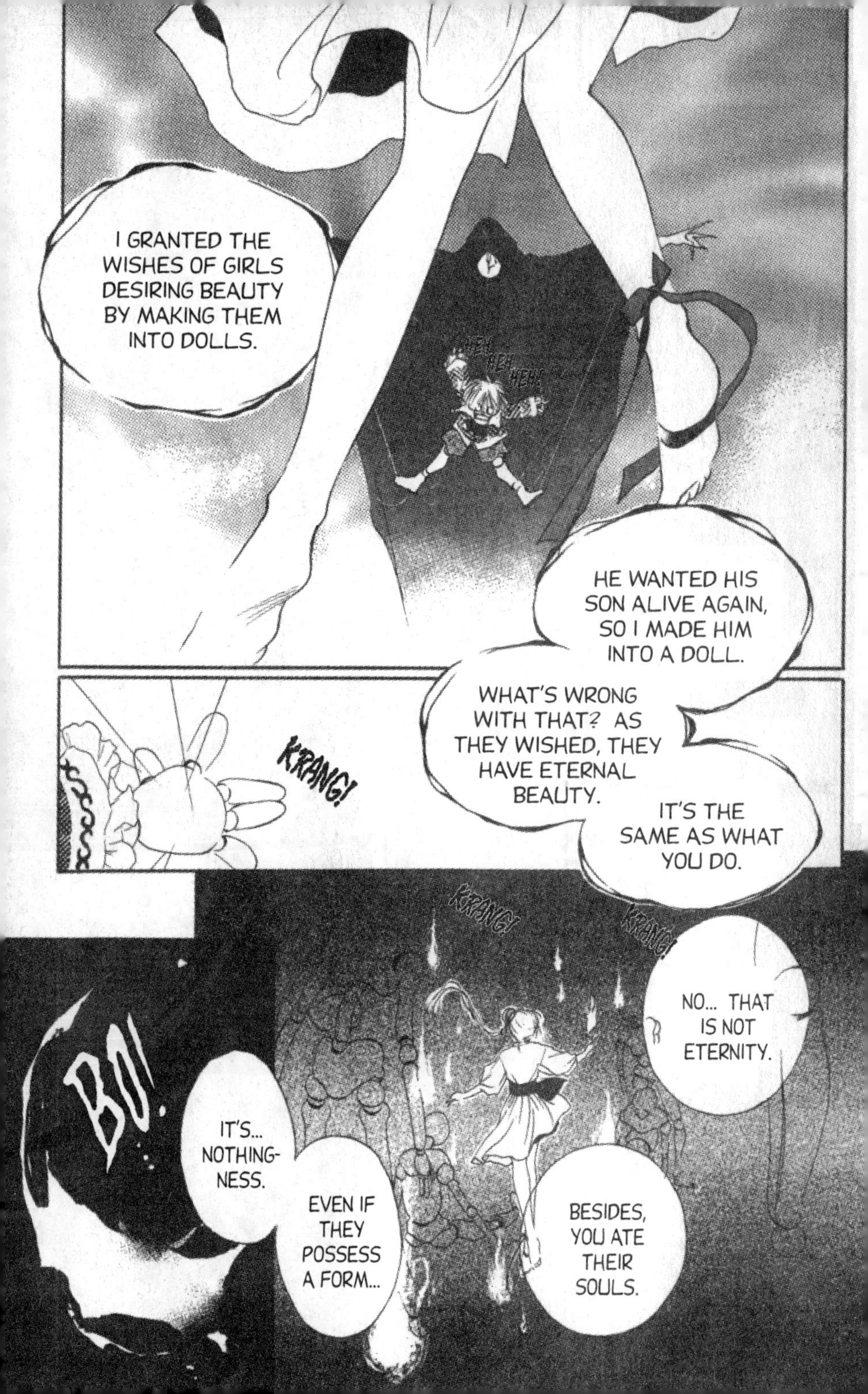
I GRANTED THE WISHES OF GIRLS DESIRING BEAUTY BY MAKING THEM INTO DOLLS.
HEH HEH HEH
HE WANTED HIS SON ALIVE AGAIN, SO I MADE HIM INTO A DOLL.
WHAT'S WRONG WITH THAT? AS THEY WISHED, THEY HAVE ETERNAL BEAUTY.
IT'S THE SAME AS WHAT YOU DO.
KRANG!
KRANG!
KRANG!
NO... THAT IS NOT ETERNITY.
BESIDES, YOU ATE THEIR SOULS.
EVEN IF THEY POSSESS A FORM...
IT'S... NOTHING-NESS.
BO!

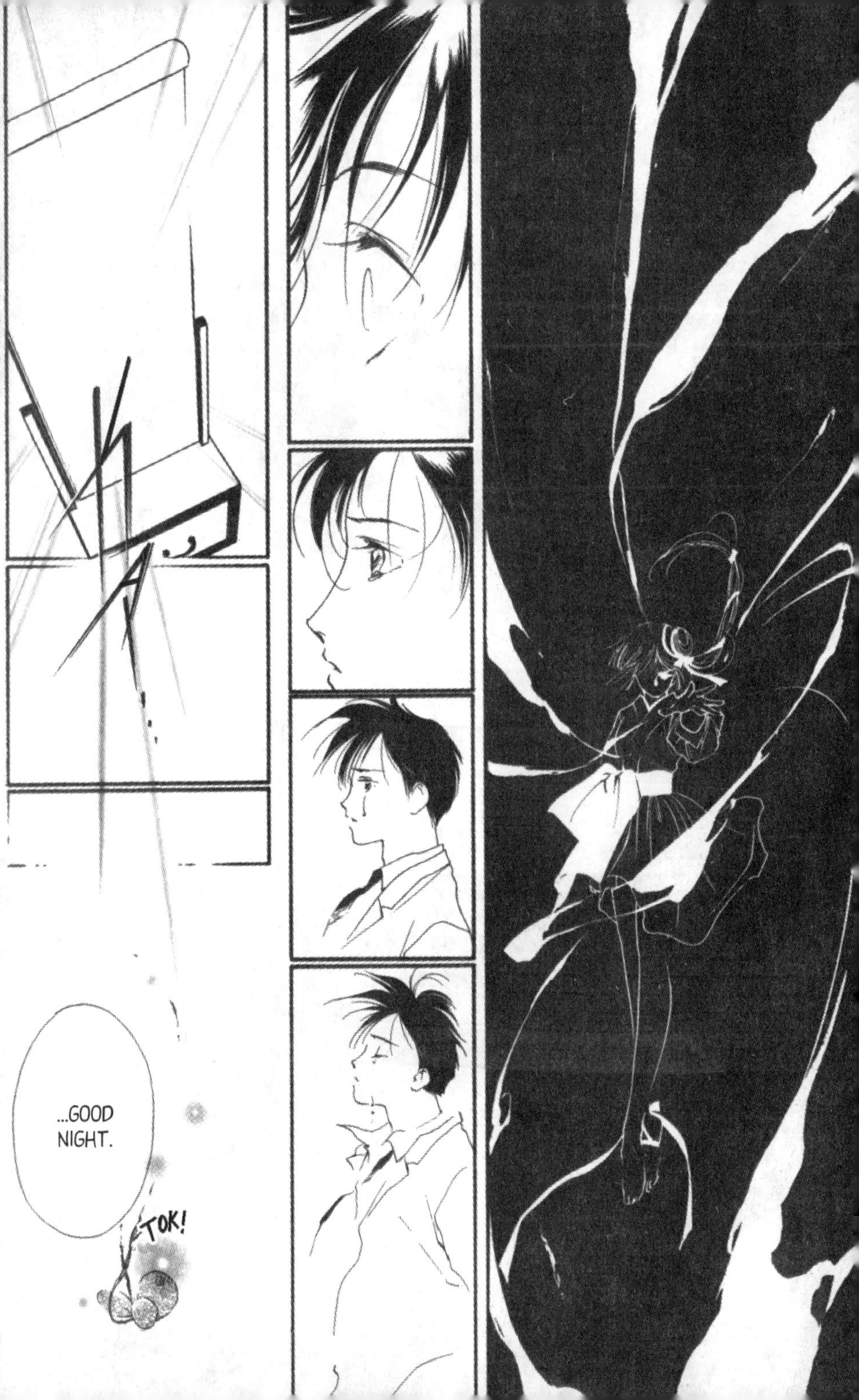
...GOOD NIGHT.
TOK!

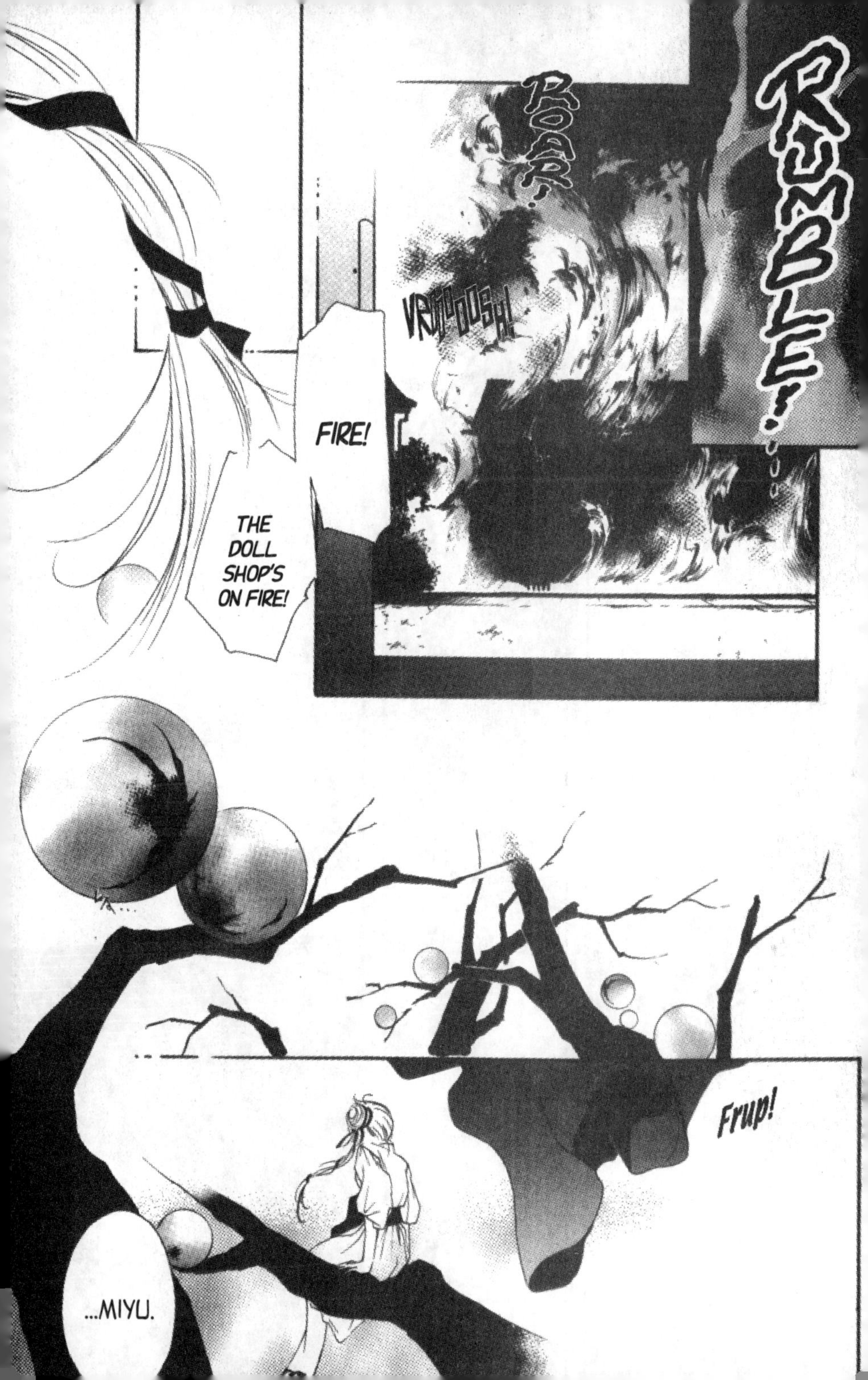
RUMBLE!......
ROAR!
VROOOOOSH!
FIRE!
THE DOLL SHOP'S ON FIRE!
Frup!
...MIYU.

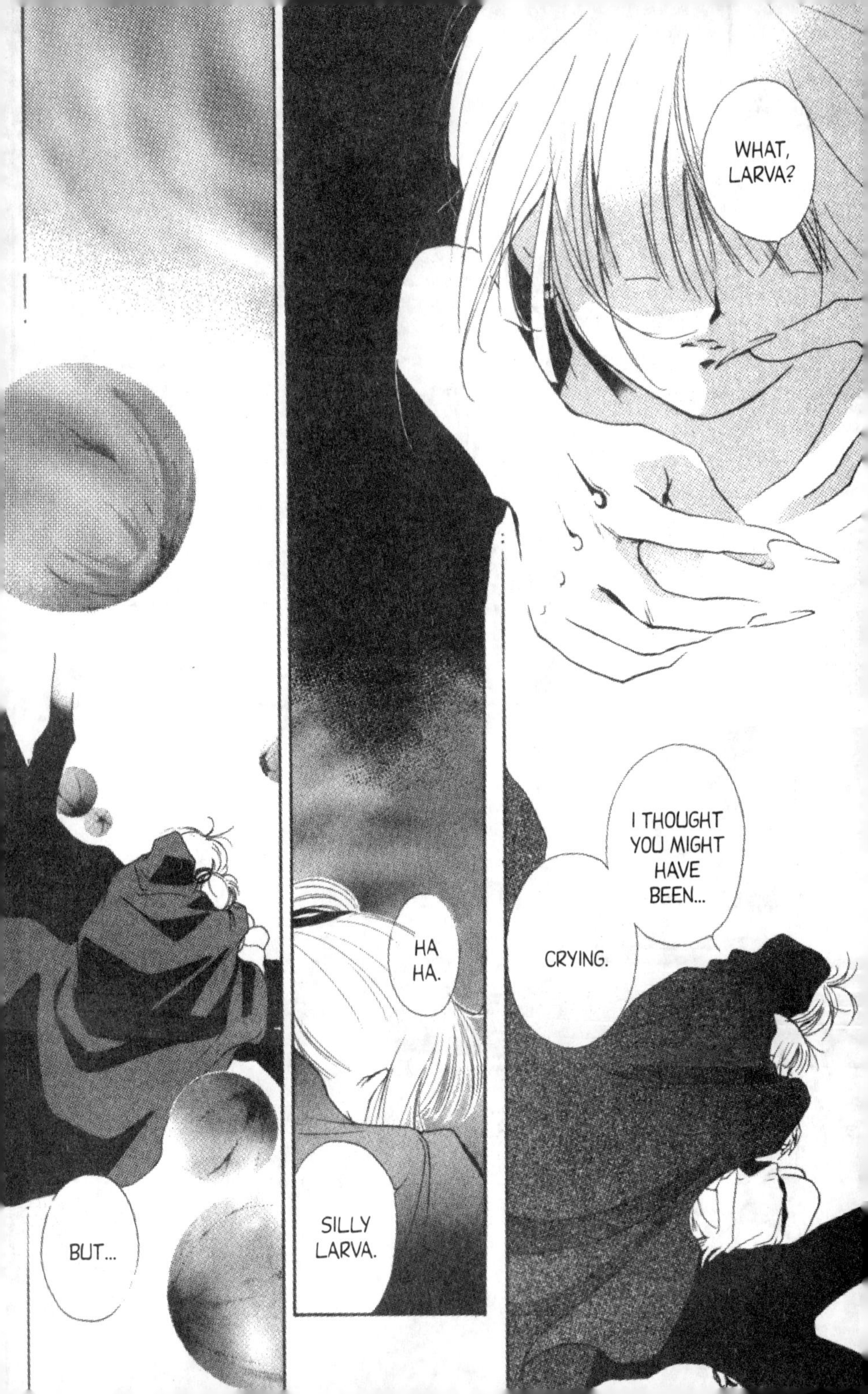
WHAT, LARVA?
I THOUGHT YOU MIGHT HAVE BEEN...
CRYING.
HA HA.
SILLY LARVA.
BUT...

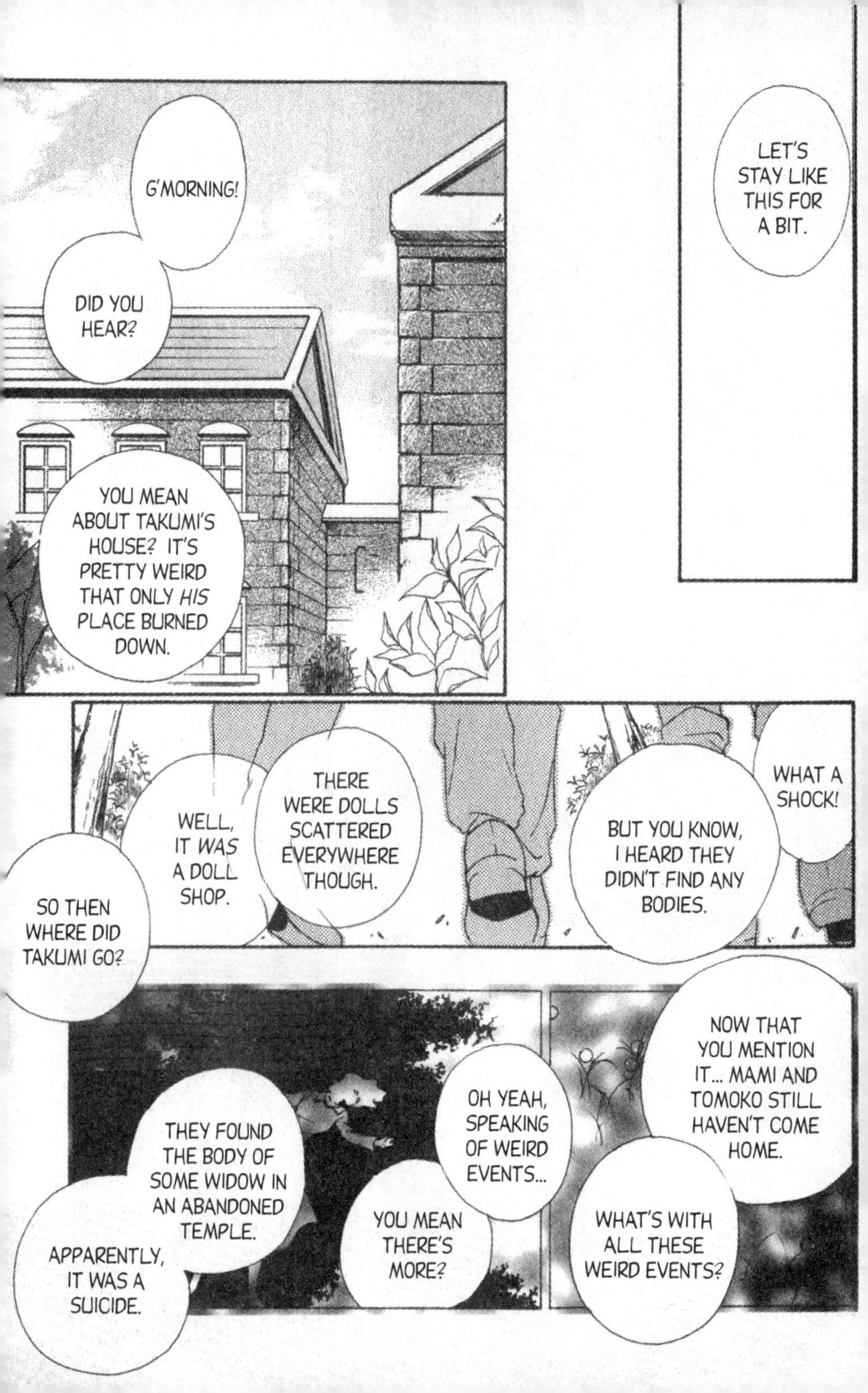
LET'S STAY LIKE THIS FOR A BIT.
G'MORNING!
DID YOU HEAR?
YOU MEAN ABOUT TAKUMI'S HOUSE? IT'S PRETTY WEIRD THAT ONLY *HIS* PLACE BURNED DOWN.
WHAT A SHOCK!
BUT YOU KNOW, I HEARD THEY DIDN'T FIND ANY BODIES.
THERE WERE DOLLS SCATTERED EVERYWHERE THOUGH.
WELL, IT *WAS* A DOLL SHOP.
SO THEN WHERE DID TAKUMI GO?
NOW THAT YOU MENTION IT... MAMI AND TOMOKO STILL HAVEN'T COME HOME.
WHAT'S WITH ALL THESE WEIRD EVENTS?
OH YEAH, SPEAKING OF WEIRD EVENTS...
YOU MEAN THERE'S MORE?
THEY FOUND THE BODY OF SOME WIDOW IN AN ABANDONED TEMPLE.
APPARENTLY, IT WAS A SUICIDE.

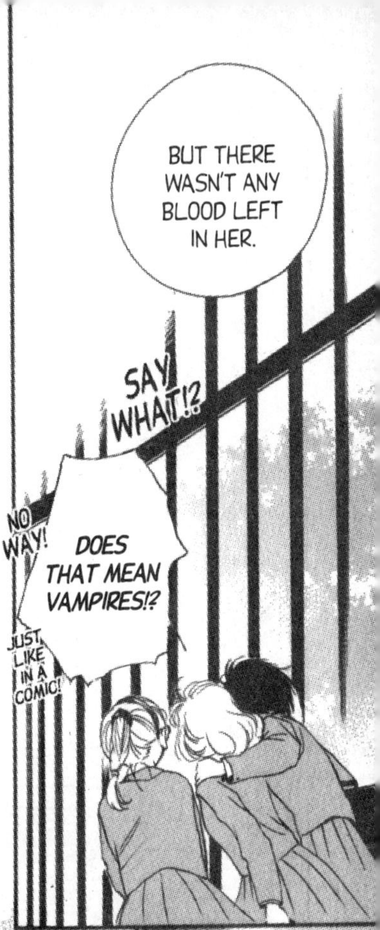
BUT THERE WASN'T ANY BLOOD LEFT IN HER.
SAY WHAT!?
DOES THAT MEAN VAMPIRES!?
NO WAY!
JUST LIKE IN A COMIC!
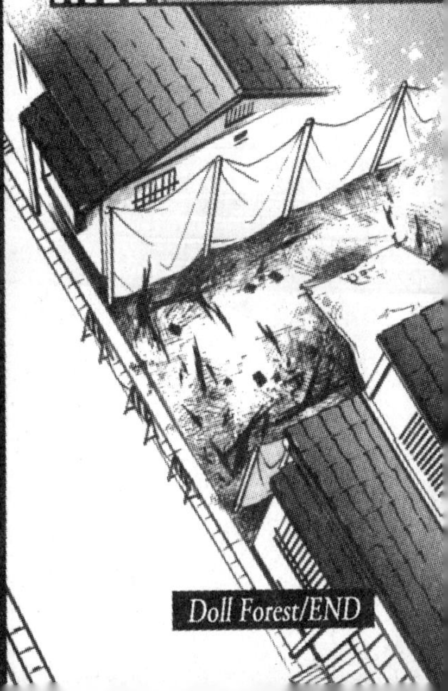
Doll Forest/END
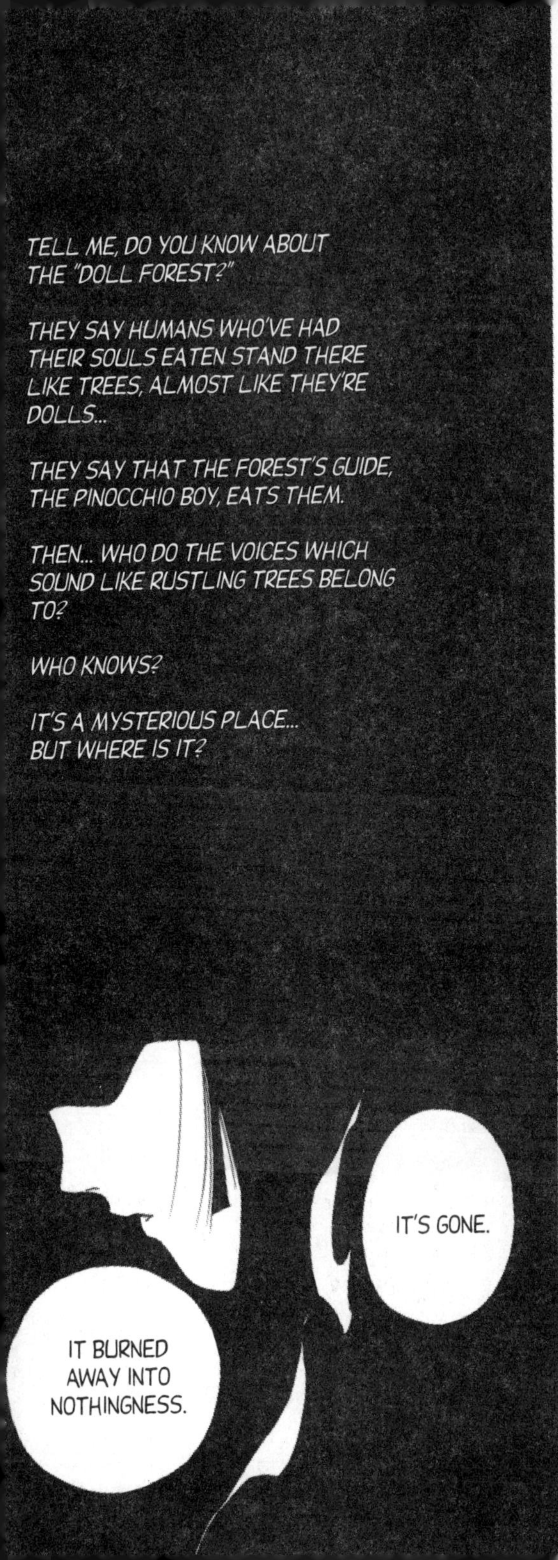
TELL ME, DO YOU KNOW ABOUT THE "DOLL FOREST?"
THEY SAY HUMANS WHO'VE HAD THEIR SOULS EATEN STAND THERE LIKE TREES, ALMOST LIKE THEY'RE DOLLS...
THEY SAY THAT THE FOREST'S GUIDE, THE PINOCCHIO BOY, EATS THEM.
THEN... WHO DO THE VOICES WHICH SOUND LIKE RUSTLING TREES BELONG TO?
WHO KNOWS?
IT'S A MYSTERIOUS PLACE... BUT WHERE IS IT?
IT'S GONE.
IT BURNED AWAY INTO NOTHINGNESS.

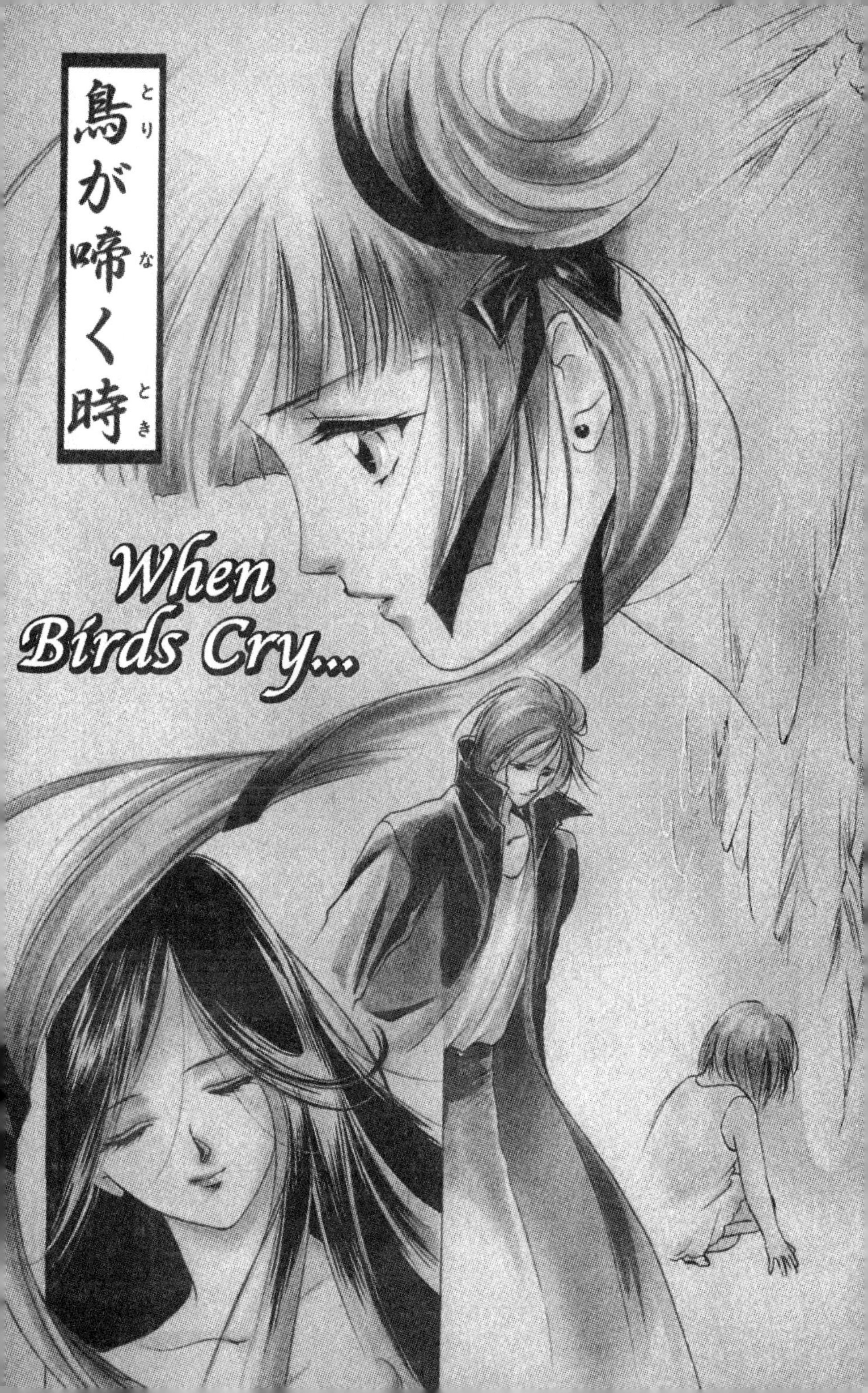

鳥が啼く時
When Birds Cry...

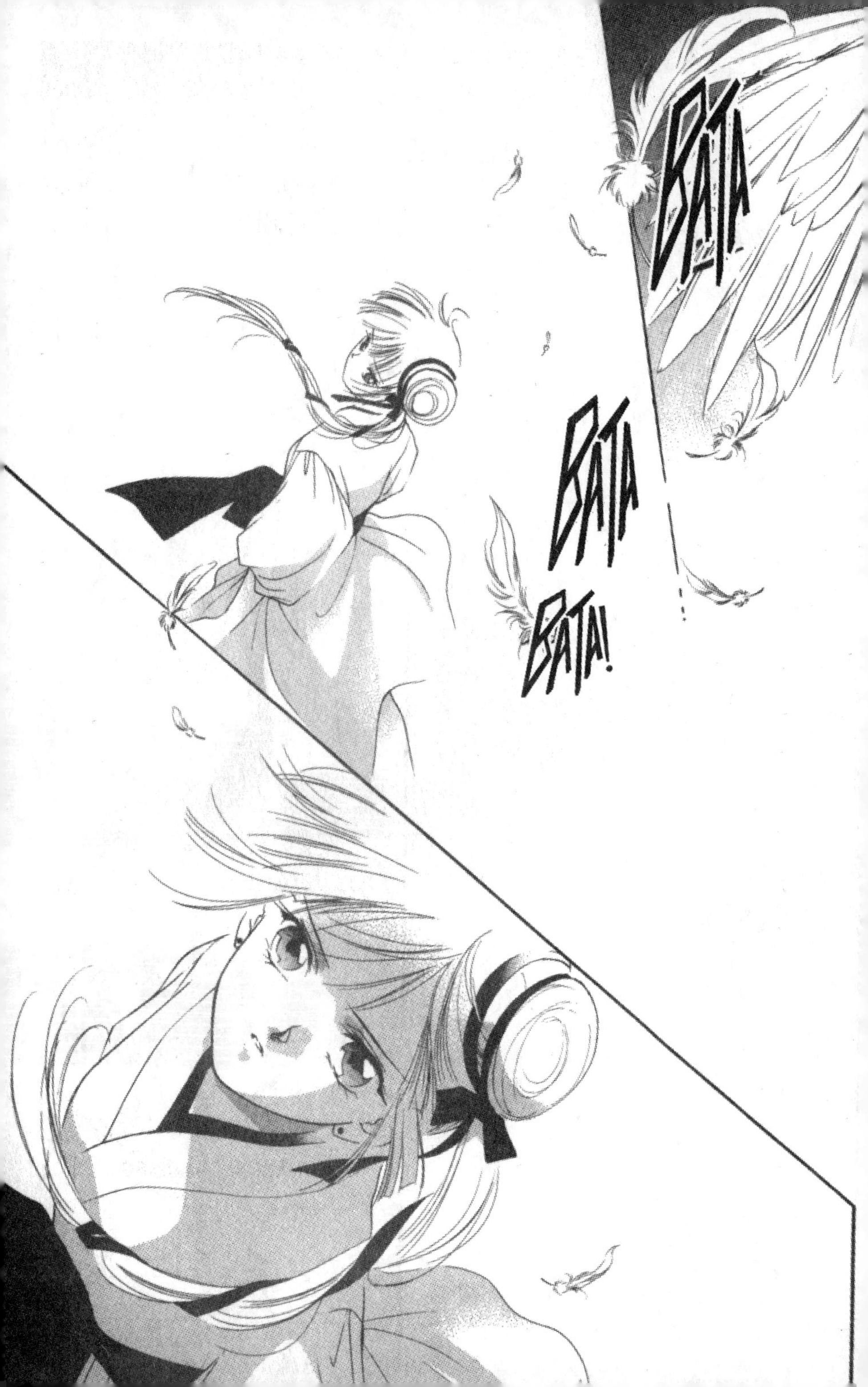
BATA
BATA
BATA!

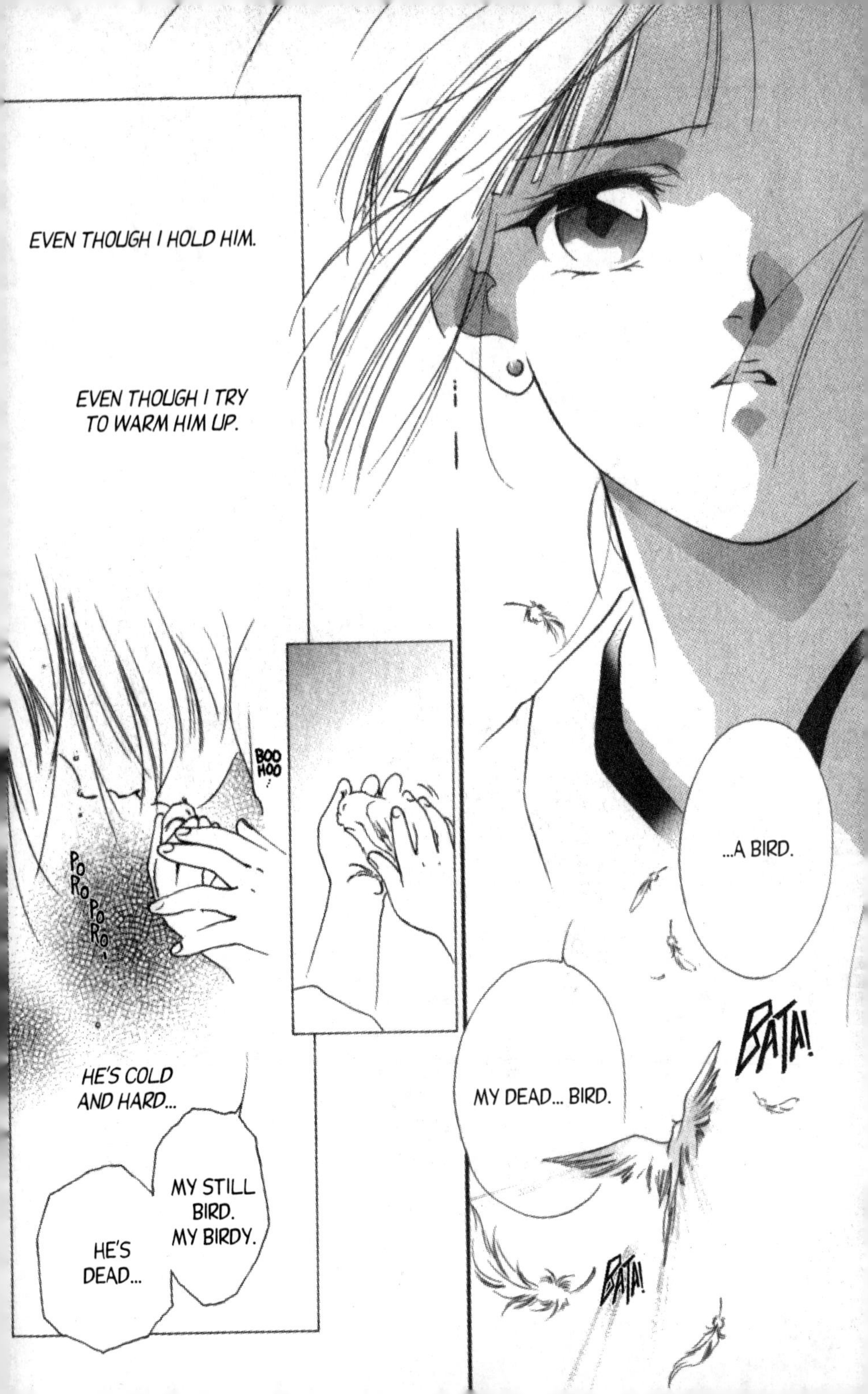
...A BIRD.
BATA!
MY DEAD... BIRD.
BATA!
EVEN THOUGH I HOLD HIM.
EVEN THOUGH I TRY TO WARM HIM UP.
BOO HOO...
PORO PORO...
HE'S COLD AND HARD...
MY STILL BIRD. MY BIRDY.
HE'S DEAD...

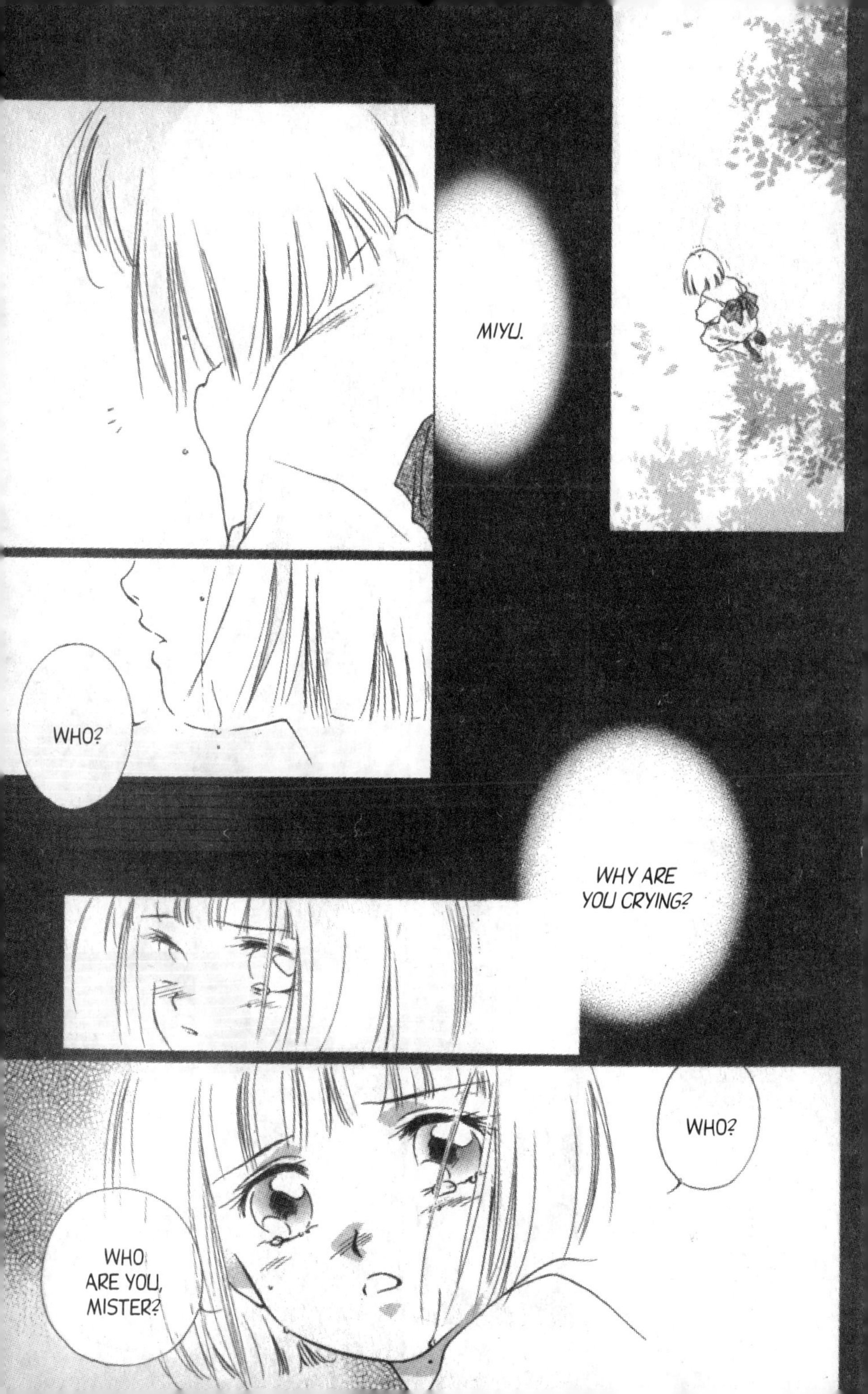
MIYU.
WHO?
WHY ARE YOU CRYING?
WHO?
WHO ARE YOU, MISTER?

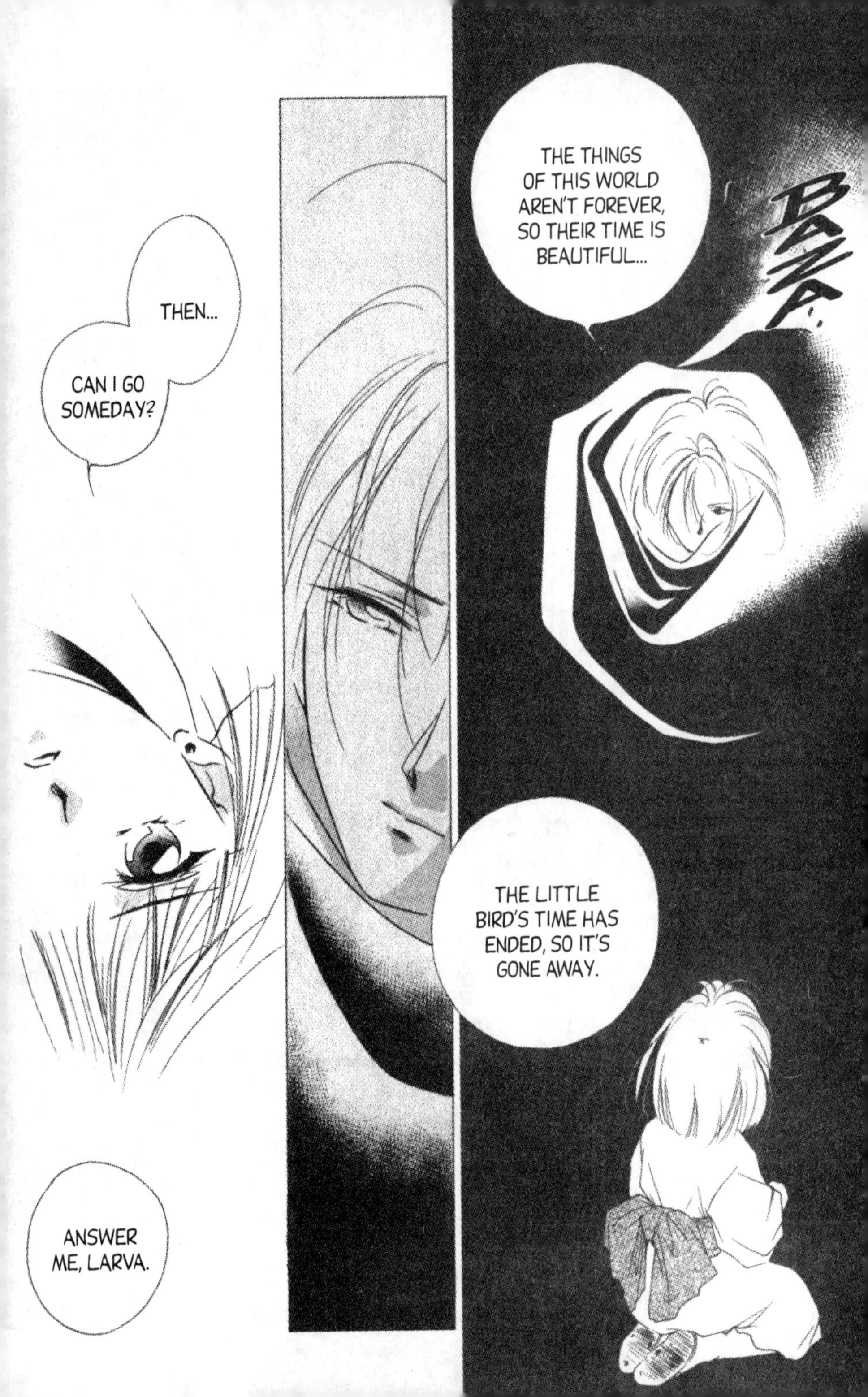
THE THINGS OF THIS WORLD AREN'T FOREVER, SO THEIR TIME IS BEAUTIFUL...
BAZA!
THE LITTLE BIRD'S TIME HAS ENDED, SO IT'S GONE AWAY.
THEN...
CAN I GO SOMEDAY?
ANSWER ME, LARVA.

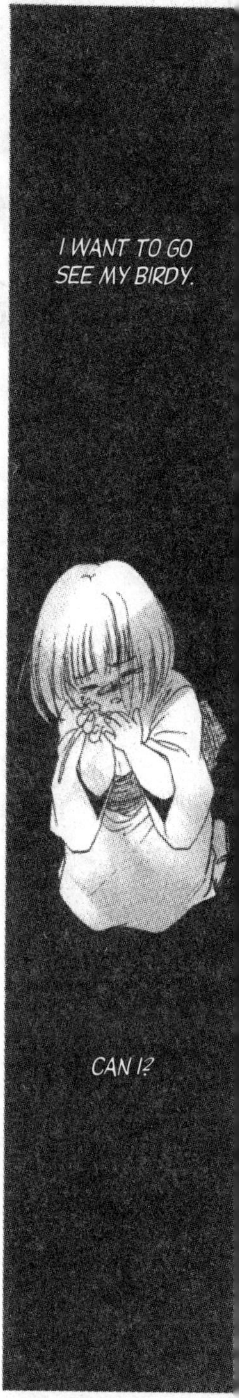
I WANT TO GO SEE MY BIRDY.
CAN I?
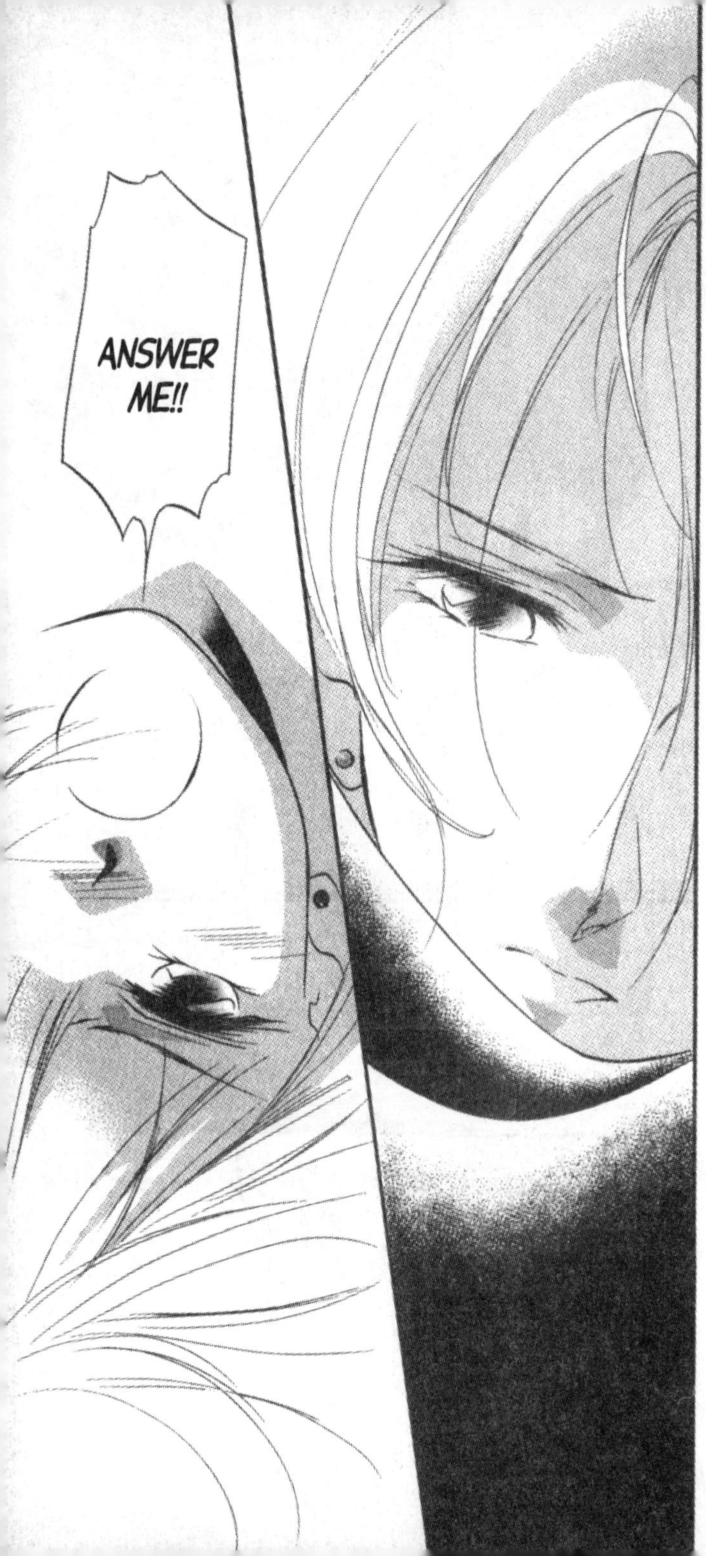
ANSWER ME!!

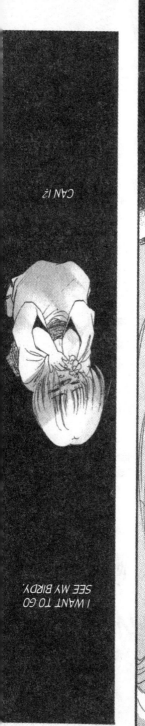

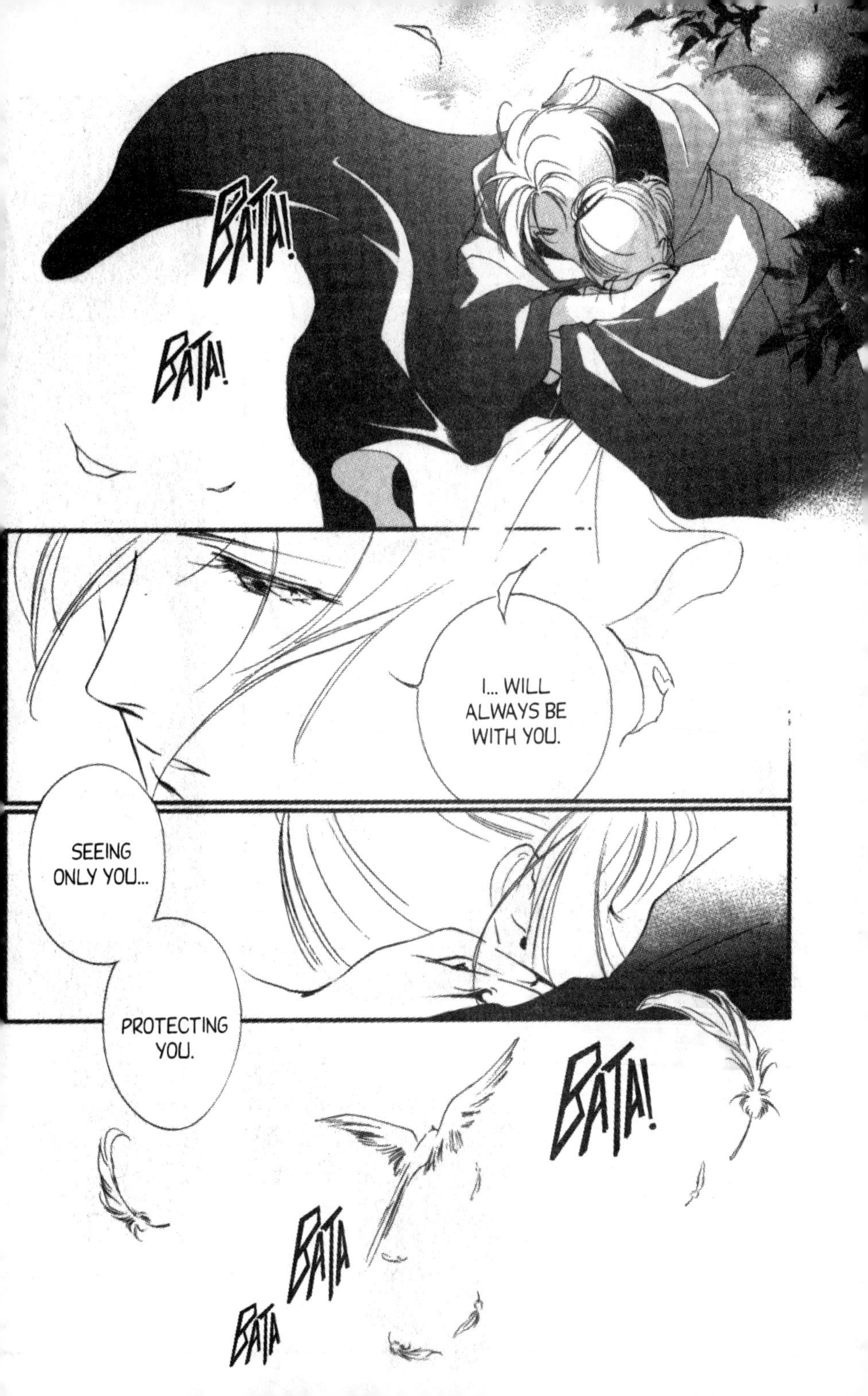
BATA!
BATA!
I... WILL ALWAYS BE WITH YOU.
SEEING ONLY YOU...
PROTECTING YOU.
BATA!
BATA
BATA

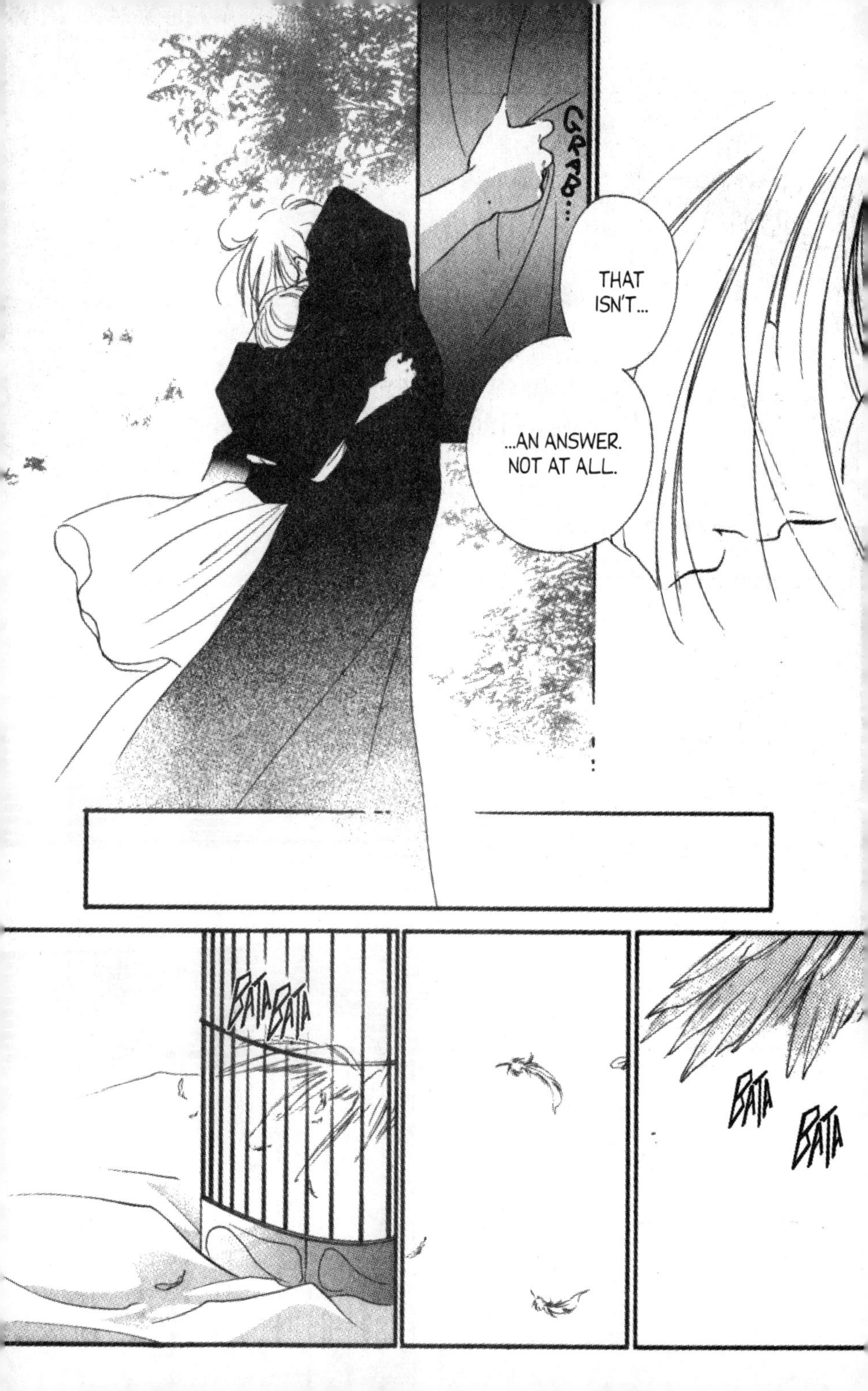
GRAB...
THAT ISN'T...
...AN ANSWER. NOT AT ALL.
BATA BATA
BATA BATA

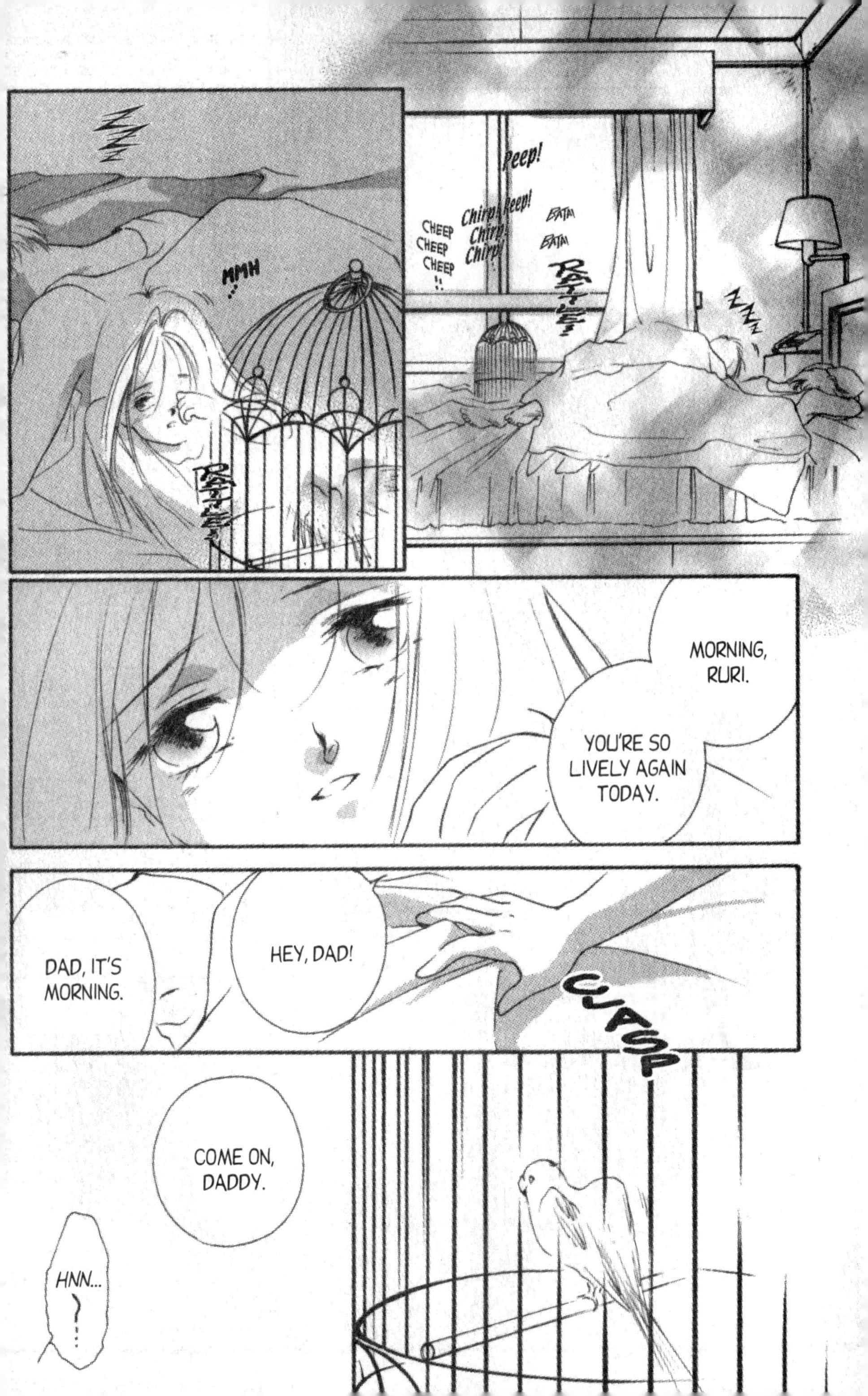
Reep!
Chirp! Reep!
Chirp!
Chirp!
CHEEP
CHEEP
CHEEP
BATA
BATA
ZZZ
ZZZ
MMH
MORNING, RURI.
YOU'RE SO LIVELY AGAIN TODAY.
HEY, DAD!
DAD, IT'S MORNING.
CLASP
COME ON, DADDY.
HNN...

*TRANSLATOR'S NOTE: BOTH THE LITTLE GIRL AND THE BIRD ARE NAMED RURI. IN JAPANE THE BIRD'S NAME IS WRITTEN IN KATAKANA AND THE GIRL'S NAME IS WRITTEN IN KANJI AND HIRAGANA. THE KANJI IN THE GIRL'S NAME MEAN "LAPIS LAZULI; AZURE; BRIGHT BLUE."

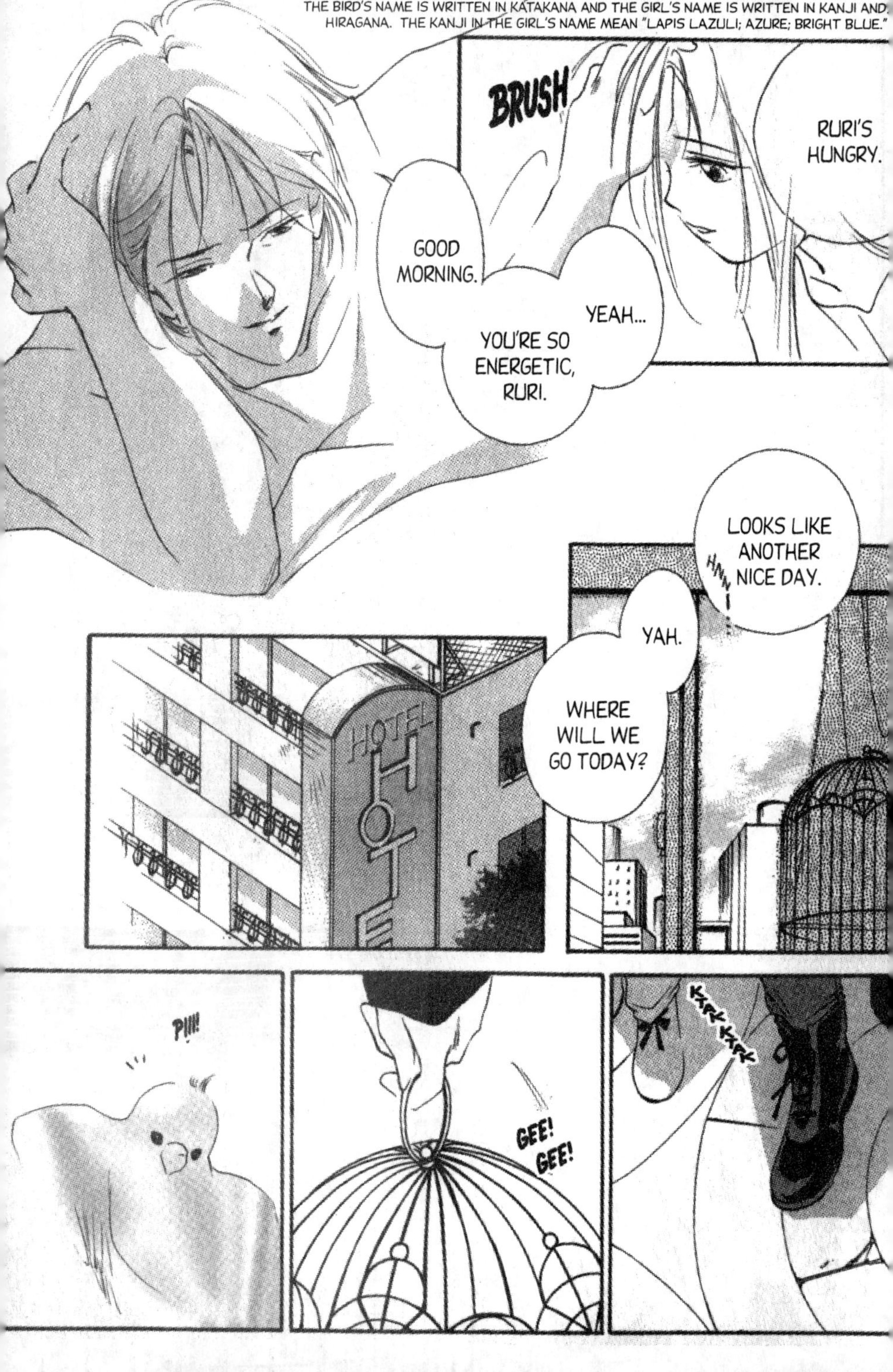
RURI'S HUNGRY.
BRUSH
GOOD MORNING.
YEAH...
YOU'RE SO ENERGETIC, RURI.
LOOKS LIKE ANOTHER NICE DAY.
HNN!
YAH.
WHERE WILL WE GO TODAY?
HOTEL
KAPK KAPK
GEE! GEE!
P!!!

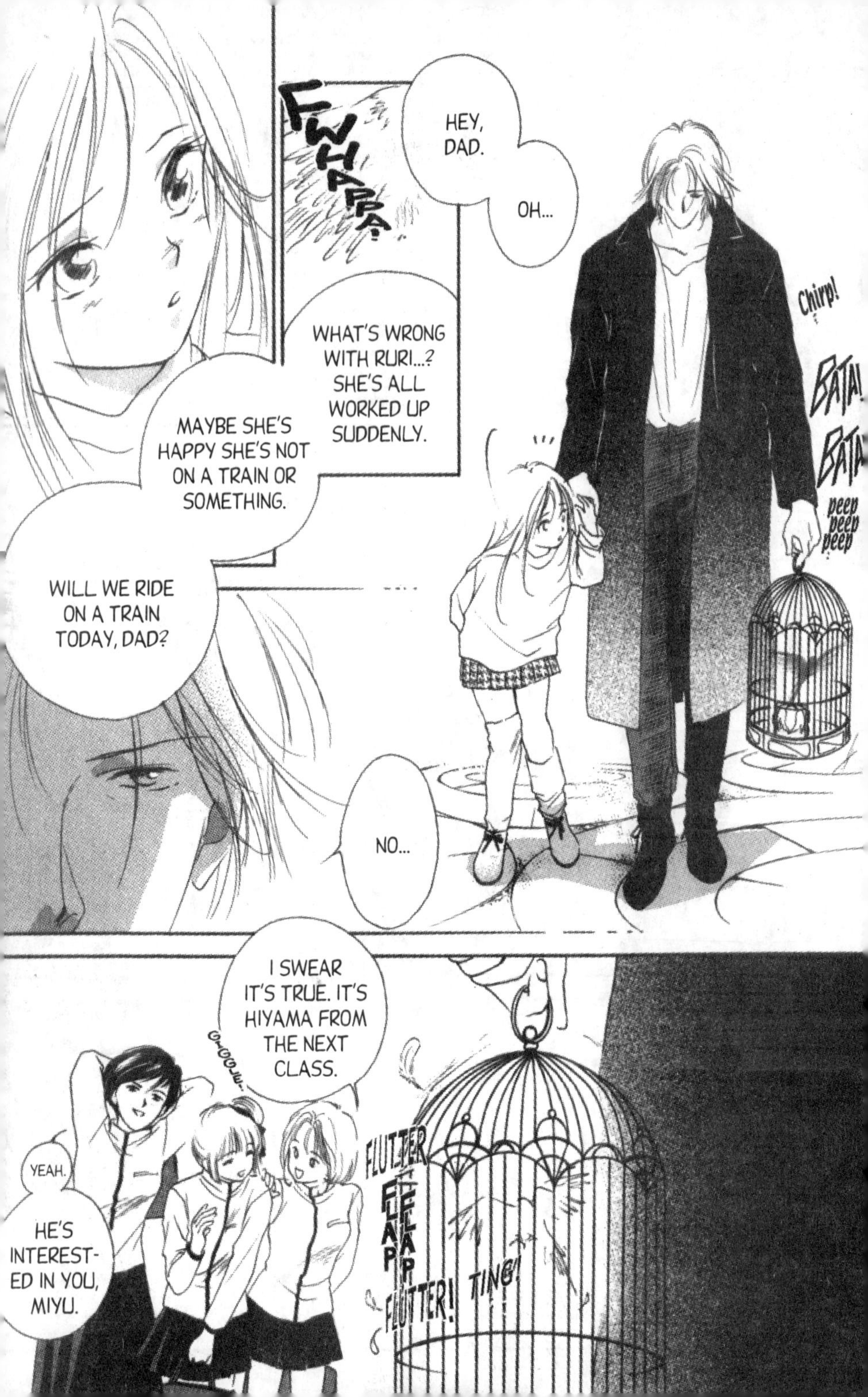
Chirp!
BATA! BATA!
peep peep peep
HEY, DAD.
OH...
FWHAPPA!
WHAT'S WRONG WITH RURI...? SHE'S ALL WORKED UP SUDDENLY.
MAYBE SHE'S HAPPY SHE'S NOT ON A TRAIN OR SOMETHING.
WILL WE RIDE ON A TRAIN TODAY, DAD?
NO...
FLUTTER FLAP FLAP FLUTTER! TING!
I SWEAR IT'S TRUE. IT'S HIYAMA FROM THE NEXT CLASS.
GIGGLE...
YEAH.
HE'S INTEREST-ED IN YOU, MIYU.

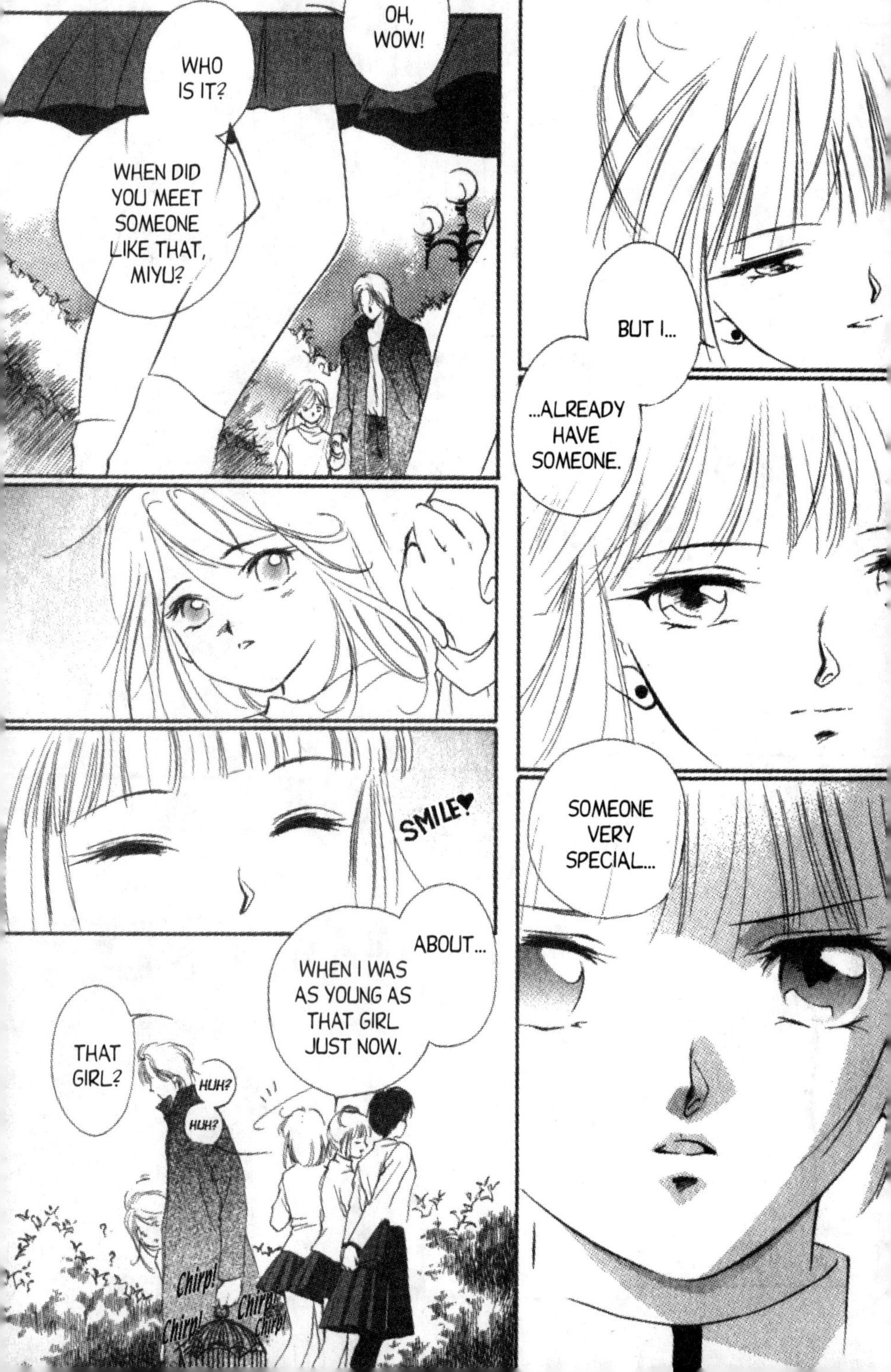
BUT I...
...ALREADY HAVE SOMEONE.
SOMEONE VERY SPECIAL...
OH, WOW!
WHO IS IT?
WHEN DID YOU MEET SOMEONE LIKE THAT, MIYU?
SMILE♥
ABOUT... WHEN I WAS AS YOUNG AS THAT GIRL JUST NOW.
THAT GIRL?
HUH?
HUH?
Chirp!
Chirp!
Chirp!
Chirp!

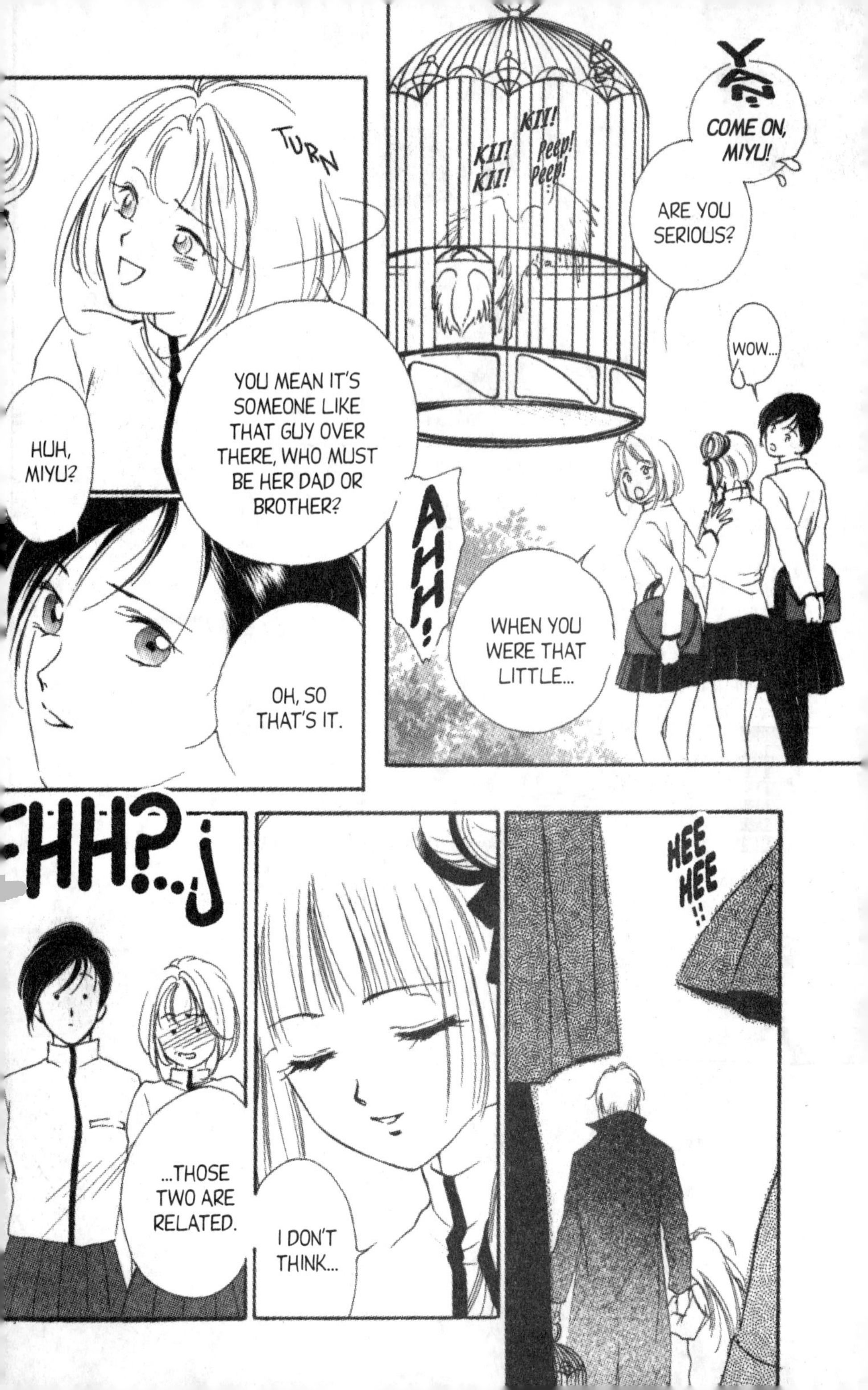
YAN
COME ON, MIYU!
ARE YOU SERIOUS?
KII! KII! KII!
Peep! Peep!
WOW...
WHEN YOU WERE THAT LITTLE...
AHH!
TURN
YOU MEAN IT'S SOMEONE LIKE THAT GUY OVER THERE, WHO MUST BE HER DAD OR BROTHER?
HUH, MIYU?
OH, SO THAT'S IT.
HEE HEE!!
I DON'T THINK...
...THOSE TWO ARE RELATED.
HH?...¿

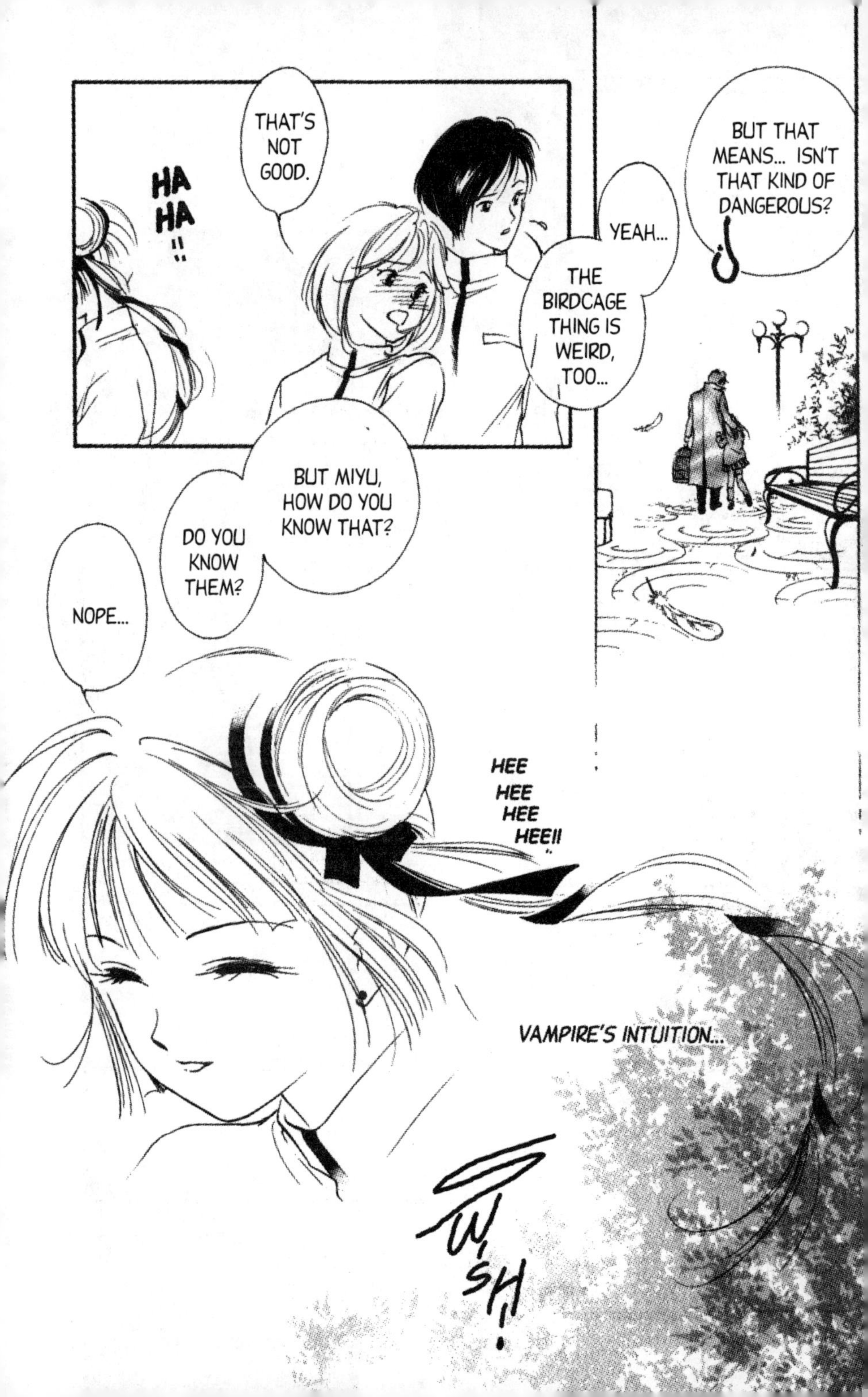
BUT THAT MEANS... ISN'T THAT KIND OF DANGEROUS?
YEAH...
THE BIRDCAGE THING IS WEIRD, TOO...
THAT'S NOT GOOD.
HA HA !!
BUT MIYU, HOW DO YOU KNOW THAT?
DO YOU KNOW THEM?
NOPE...
HEE HEE HEE HEE!!
VAMPIRE'S INTUITION...
WUSH!

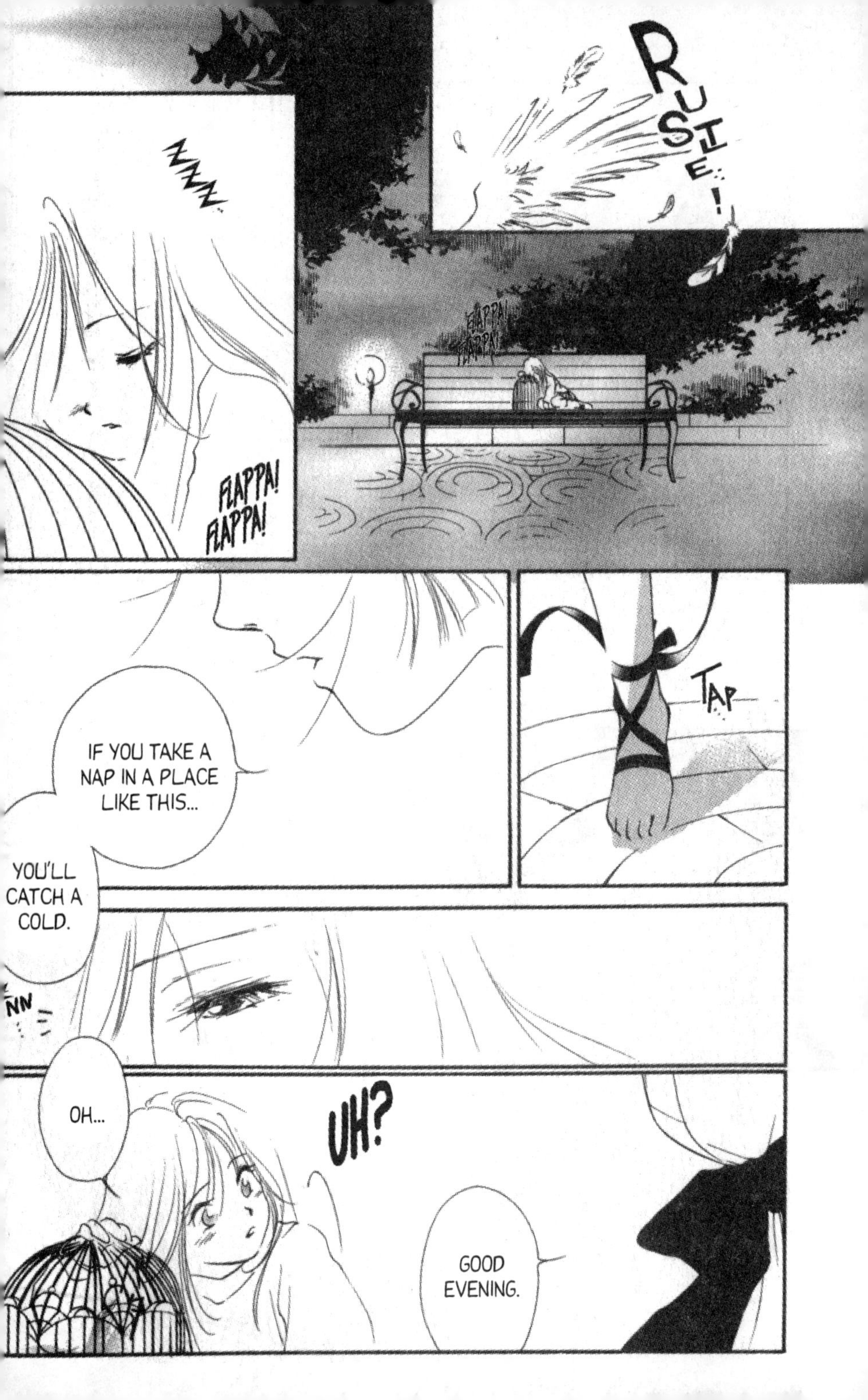
RUSTLE...!
FLAPPA! FLAPPA!
NNN
FLAPPA! FLAPPA!
TAP
IF YOU TAKE A NAP IN A PLACE LIKE THIS...
YOU'LL CATCH A COLD.
NN
GOOD EVENING.
UH?
OH...

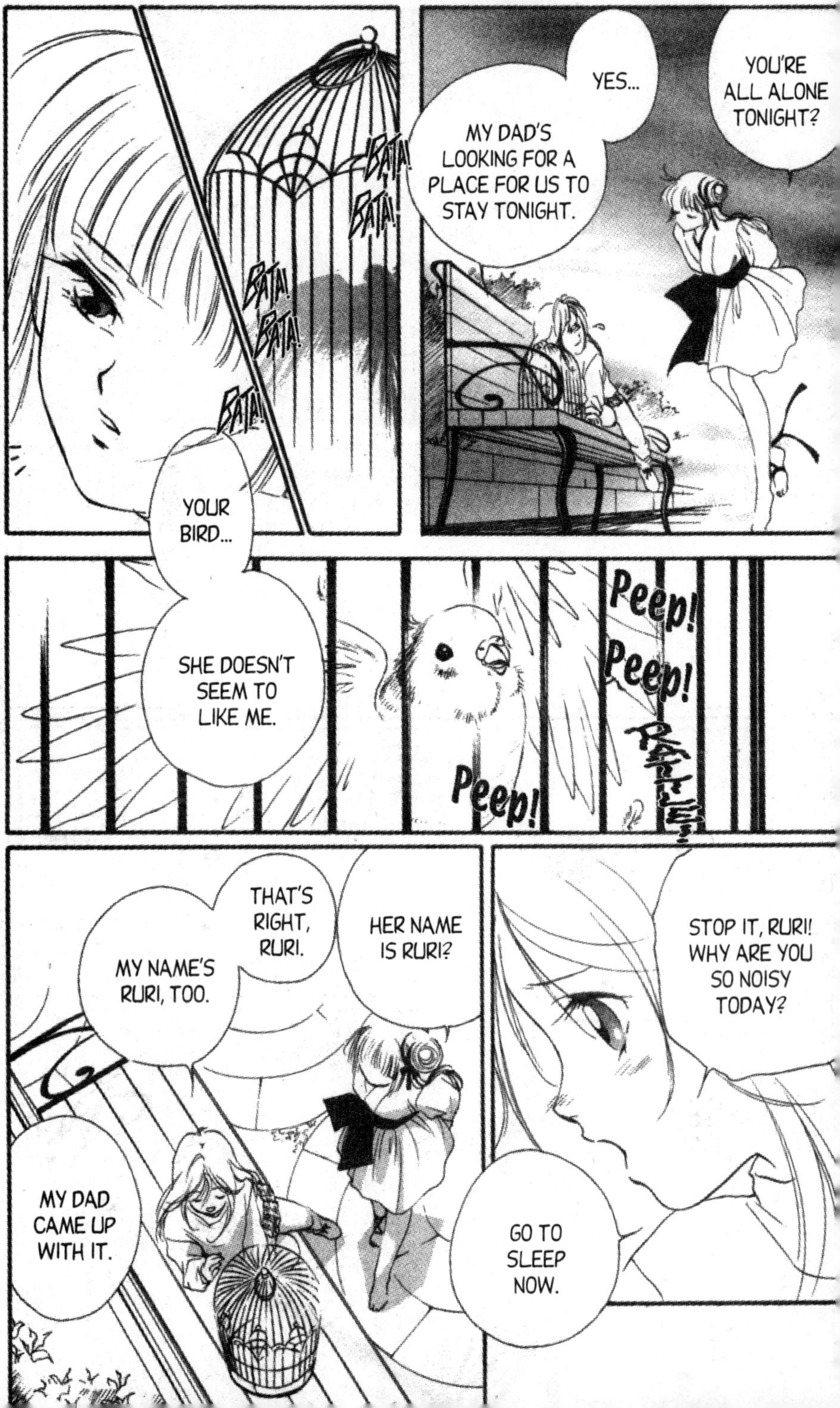
YOU'RE ALL ALONE TONIGHT?
YES...
MY DAD'S LOOKING FOR A PLACE FOR US TO STAY TONIGHT.
BATA! BATA!
BATA! BATA!
BATA!
YOUR BIRD...
Peep!
Peep!
Peep!
SHE DOESN'T SEEM TO LIKE ME.
STOP IT, RURI! WHY ARE YOU SO NOISY TODAY?
GO TO SLEEP NOW.
HER NAME IS RURI?
THAT'S RIGHT, RURI.
MY NAME'S RURI, TOO.
MY DAD CAME UP WITH IT.

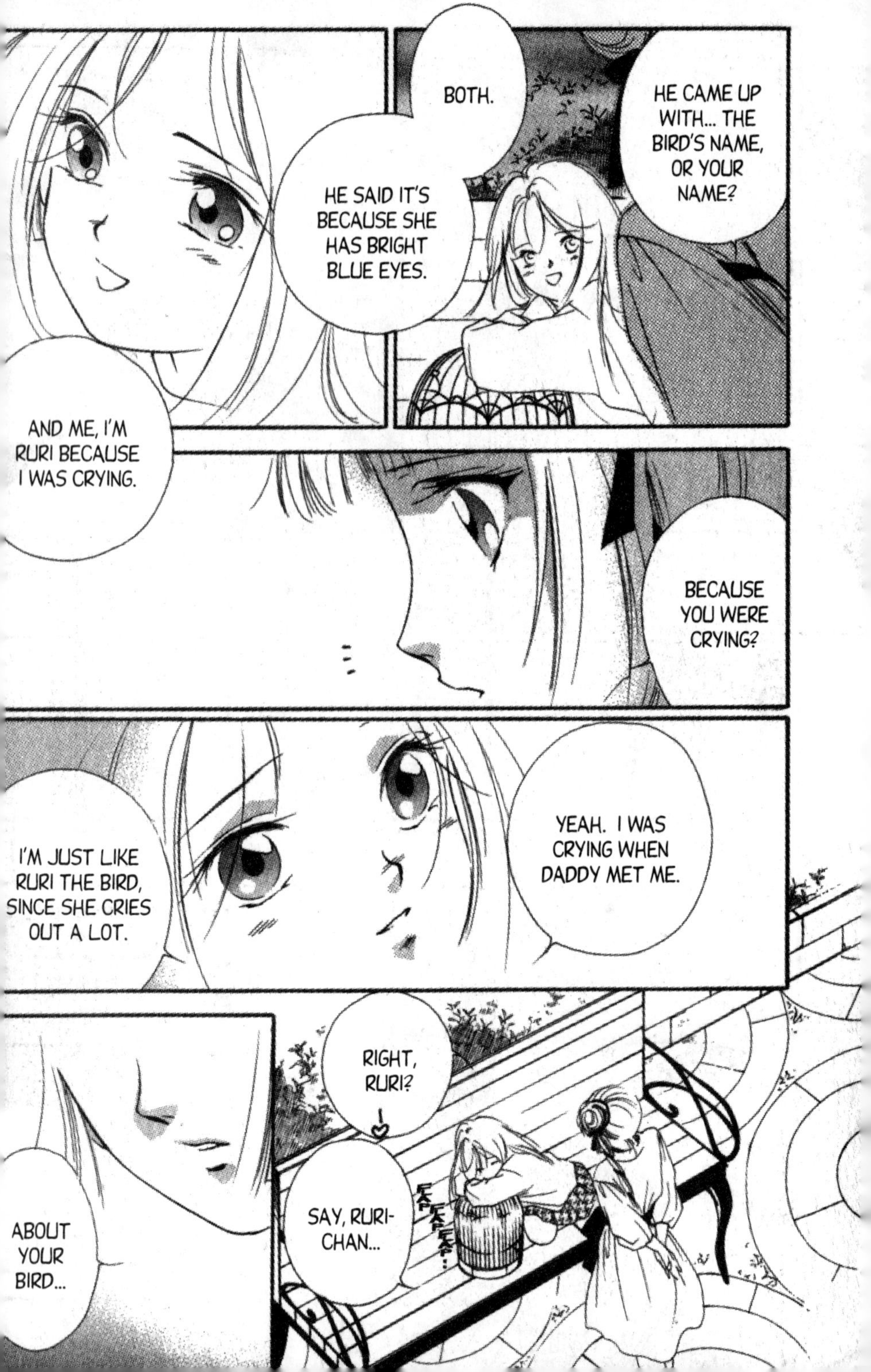
HE CAME UP WITH... THE BIRD'S NAME, OR YOUR NAME?
BOTH.
HE SAID IT'S BECAUSE SHE HAS BRIGHT BLUE EYES.
AND ME, I'M RURI BECAUSE I WAS CRYING.
BECAUSE YOU WERE CRYING?
...
YEAH. I WAS CRYING WHEN DADDY MET ME.
I'M JUST LIKE RURI THE BIRD, SINCE SHE CRIES OUT A LOT.
RIGHT, RURI?
SAY, RURI-CHAN...
ABOUT YOUR BIRD...

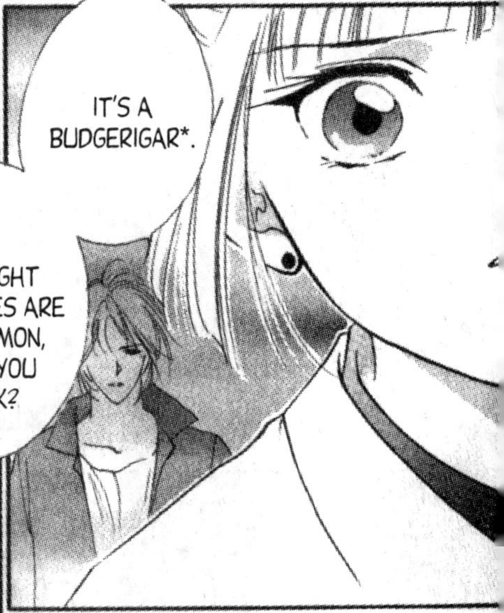
IT'S A BUDGERIGAR*.

*TRANSLATOR'S NOTE: A SMALL AUSTRALIAN PARROT, USUAL LIGHT GREEN WITH BLACK AND YELLOW MARKINGS IN THE WI BUT BRED UNDER DOMESTICATION IN MANY COLORS.

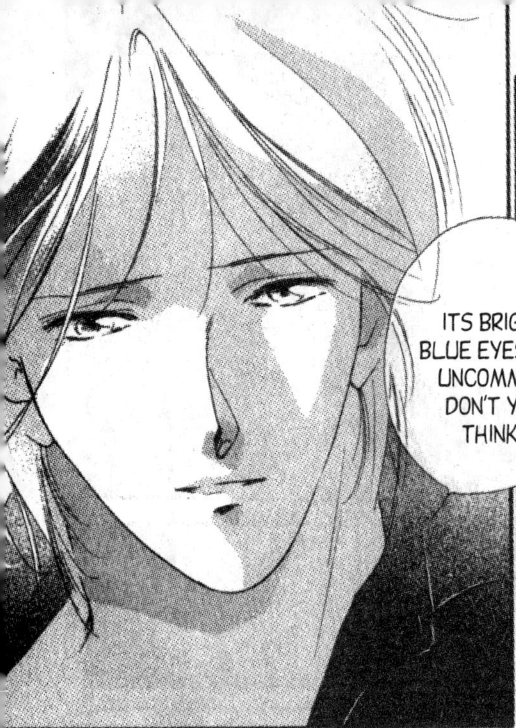
ITS BRIGHT BLUE EYES ARE UNCOMMON, DON'T YOU THINK?

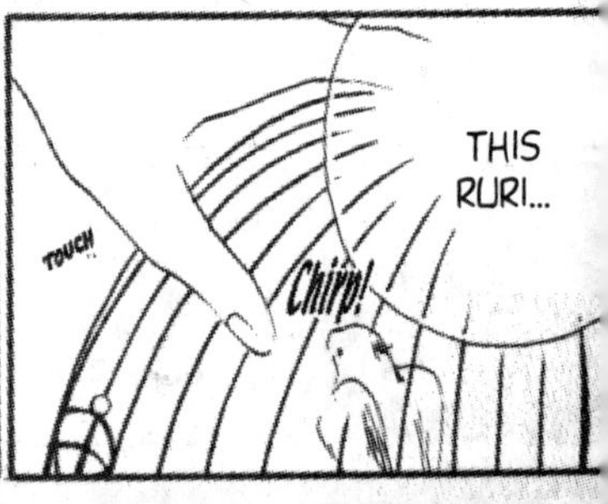
THIS RURI...
TOUCH
Chirp!

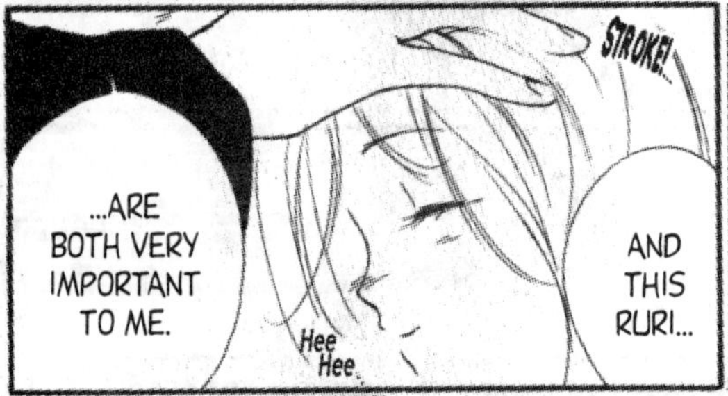
STROKE!
AND THIS RURI...
...ARE BOTH VERY IMPORTANT TO ME.
Hee Hee

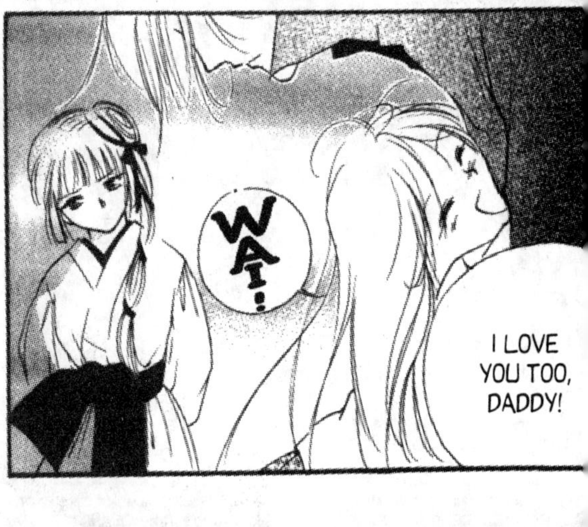
I LOVE YOU TOO, DADDY!
WAI!

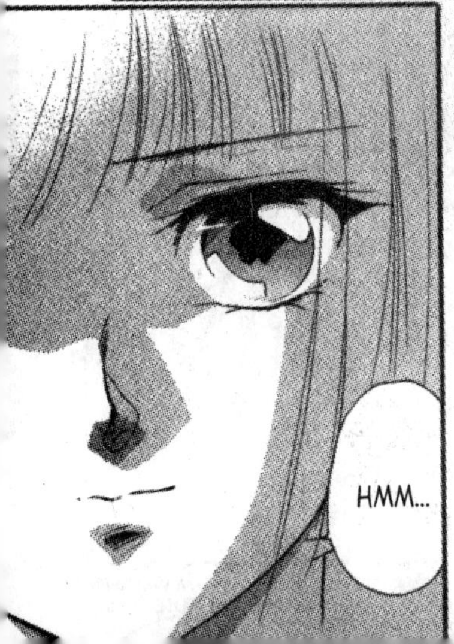
HMM...

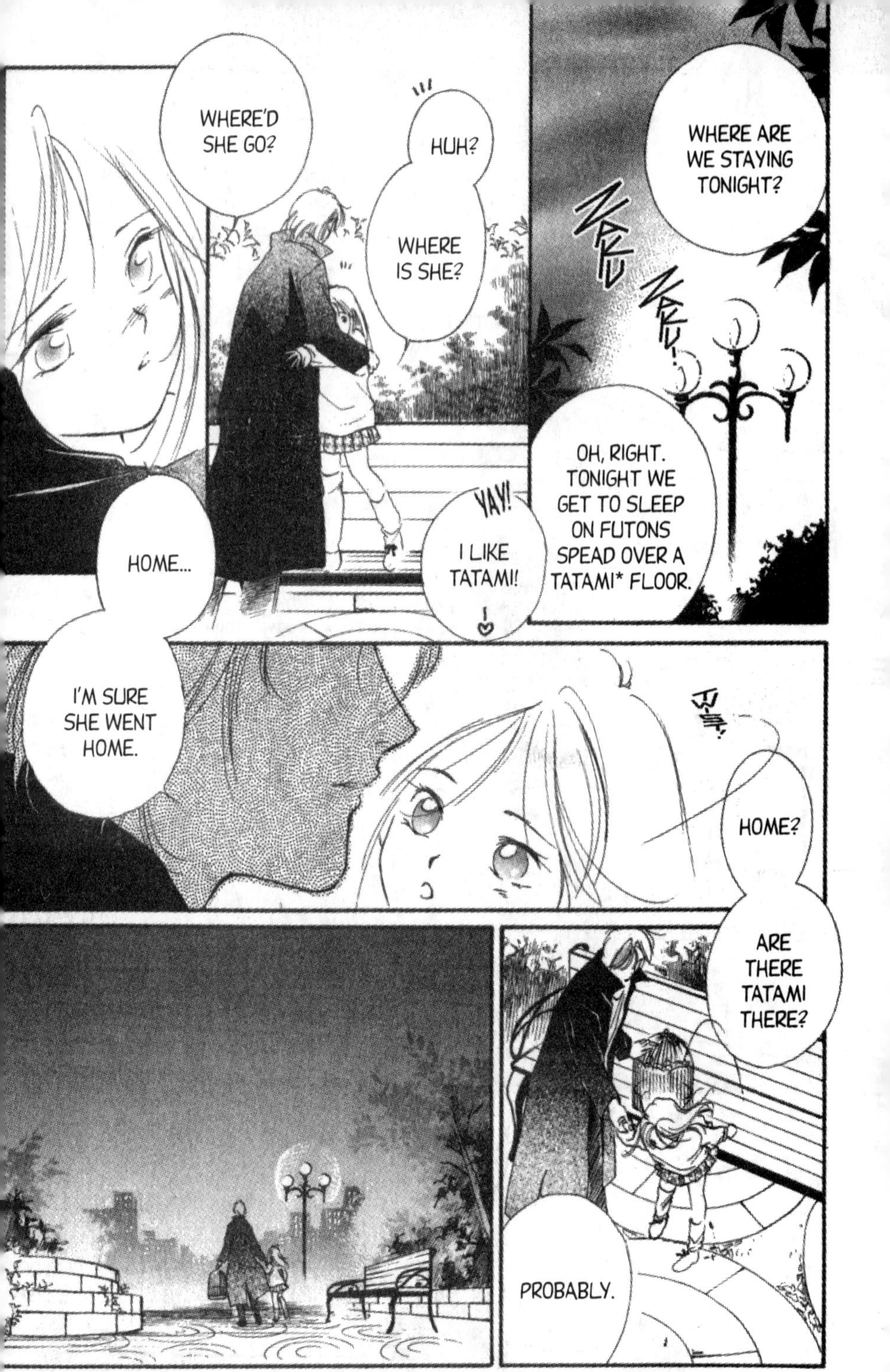
WHERE ARE WE STAYING TONIGHT?
NAKU NAKU-
OH, RIGHT. TONIGHT WE GET TO SLEEP ON FUTONS SPEAD OVER A TATAMI* FLOOR.
YAY!
I LIKE TATAMI!
HUH?
WHERE IS SHE?
WHERE'D SHE GO?
HOME...
I'M SURE SHE WENT HOME.
HOME?
ARE THERE TATAMI THERE?
PROBABLY.

TRANSLATOR'S NOTE: TATAMI ARE A TYPE OF FLOORING COMMON TO A TRADITIONAL JAPANESE HOME OR A ROOM IN A WESTERN-STYLE HOME; A RECTANGULAR MAT MADE FROM WOVEN RUSHES AND RICE STALKS AFTER HARVEST (CHEAPER ONES USE STYROFOAM OR SYNTHETIC FIBERS); TYPICALLY 180 X 90 CM.

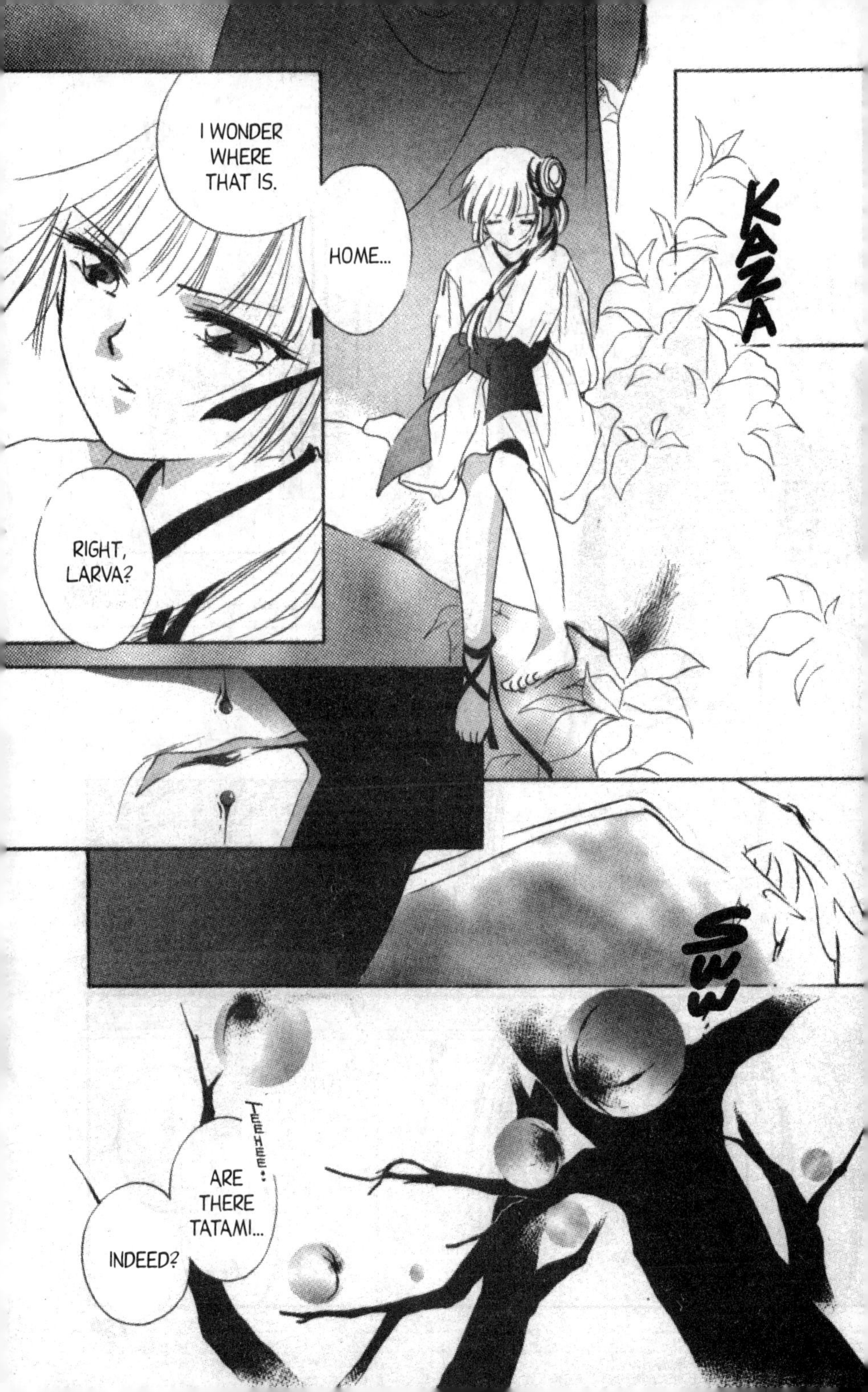
KAZA
HOME...
I WONDER WHERE THAT IS.
RIGHT, LARVA?
SWW
TEEHEE
ARE THERE TATAMI...
INDEED?

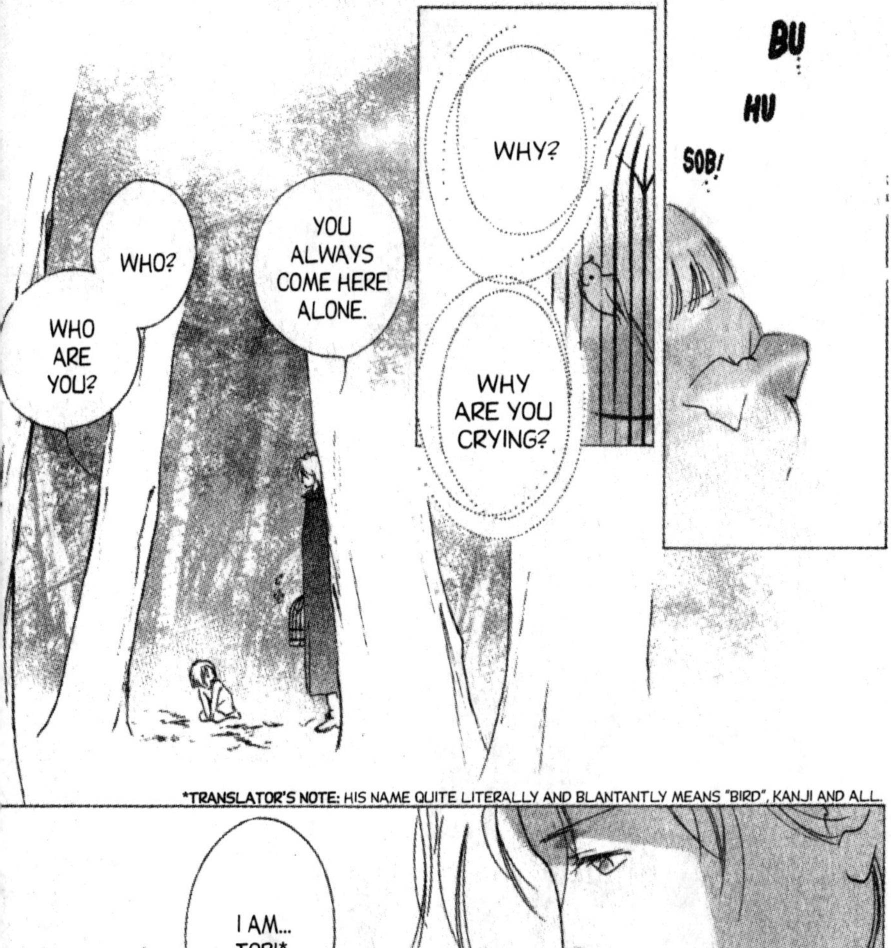
BU
HU
SOB!
WHY?
WHY ARE YOU CRYING?
YOU ALWAYS COME HERE ALONE.
WHO?
WHO ARE YOU?

*TRANSLATOR'S NOTE: HIS NAME QUITE LITERALLY AND BLANTANTLY MEANS "BIRD", KANJI AND ALL.

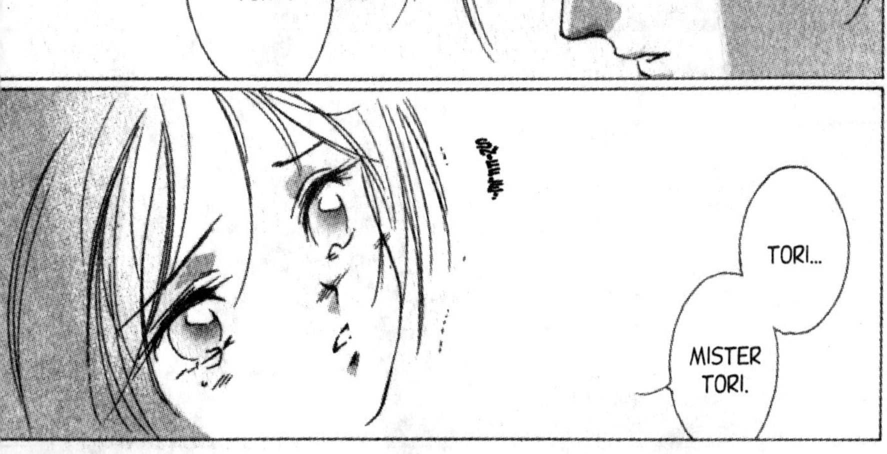
I AM... TORI*.
TORI...
MISTER TORI.

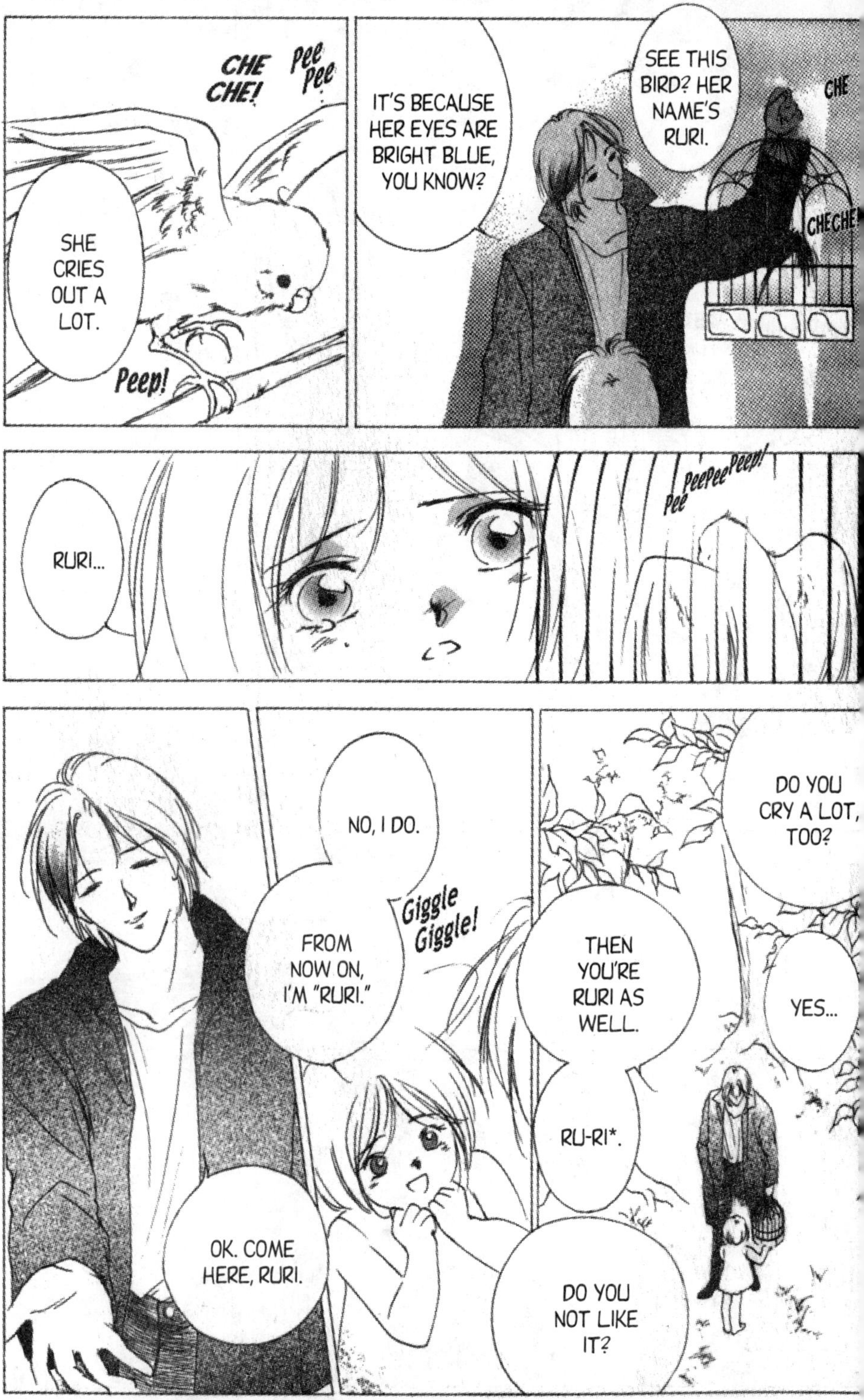
CHE
SEE THIS BIRD? HER NAME'S RURI.
CHECHE
IT'S BECAUSE HER EYES ARE BRIGHT BLUE, YOU KNOW?
CHE CHE!
Pee Pee
SHE CRIES OUT A LOT.
Peep!
Pee PeePeePeep!
RURI...
DO YOU CRY A LOT, TOO?
YES...
THEN YOU'RE RURI AS WELL.
RU-RI*.
DO YOU NOT LIKE IT?
NO, I DO.
FROM NOW ON, I'M "RURI."
Giggle Giggle!
OK. COME HERE, RURI.

*NOTE: IN JAPANESE THIS IS JUST A RESTATEMENT OF HER NAME USING KA

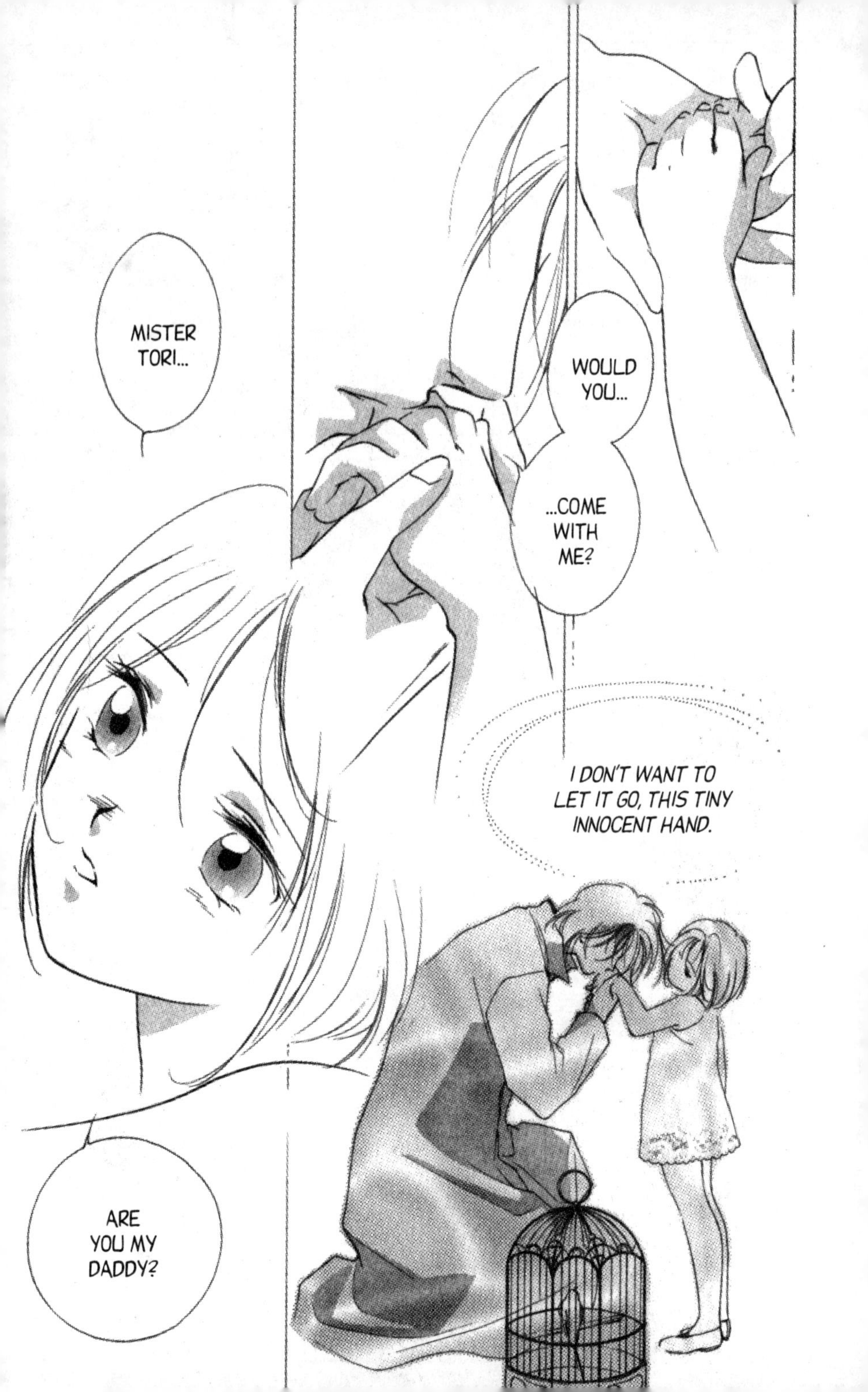
WOULD YOU...
...COME WITH ME?
I DON'T WANT TO LET IT GO, THIS TINY INNOCENT HAND.
MISTER TORI...
ARE YOU MY DADDY?

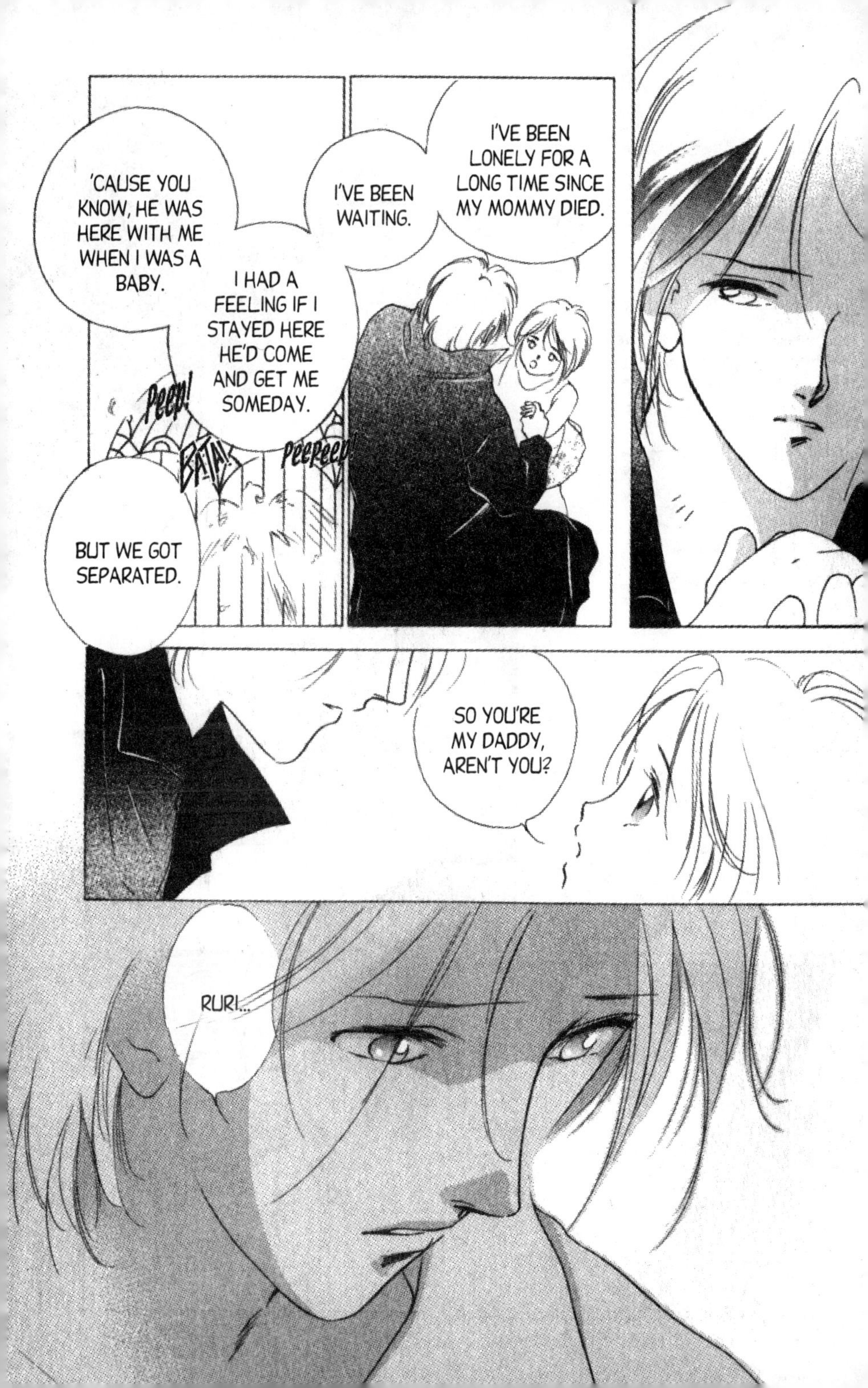
I'VE BEEN LONELY FOR A LONG TIME SINCE MY MOMMY DIED.
I'VE BEEN WAITING.
I HAD A FEELING IF I STAYED HERE HE'D COME AND GET ME SOMEDAY.
'CAUSE YOU KNOW, HE WAS HERE WITH ME WHEN I WAS A BABY.
Peepeep!
BATA!
Peep!
BUT WE GOT SEPARATED.
SO YOU'RE MY DADDY, AREN'T YOU?
RURI...

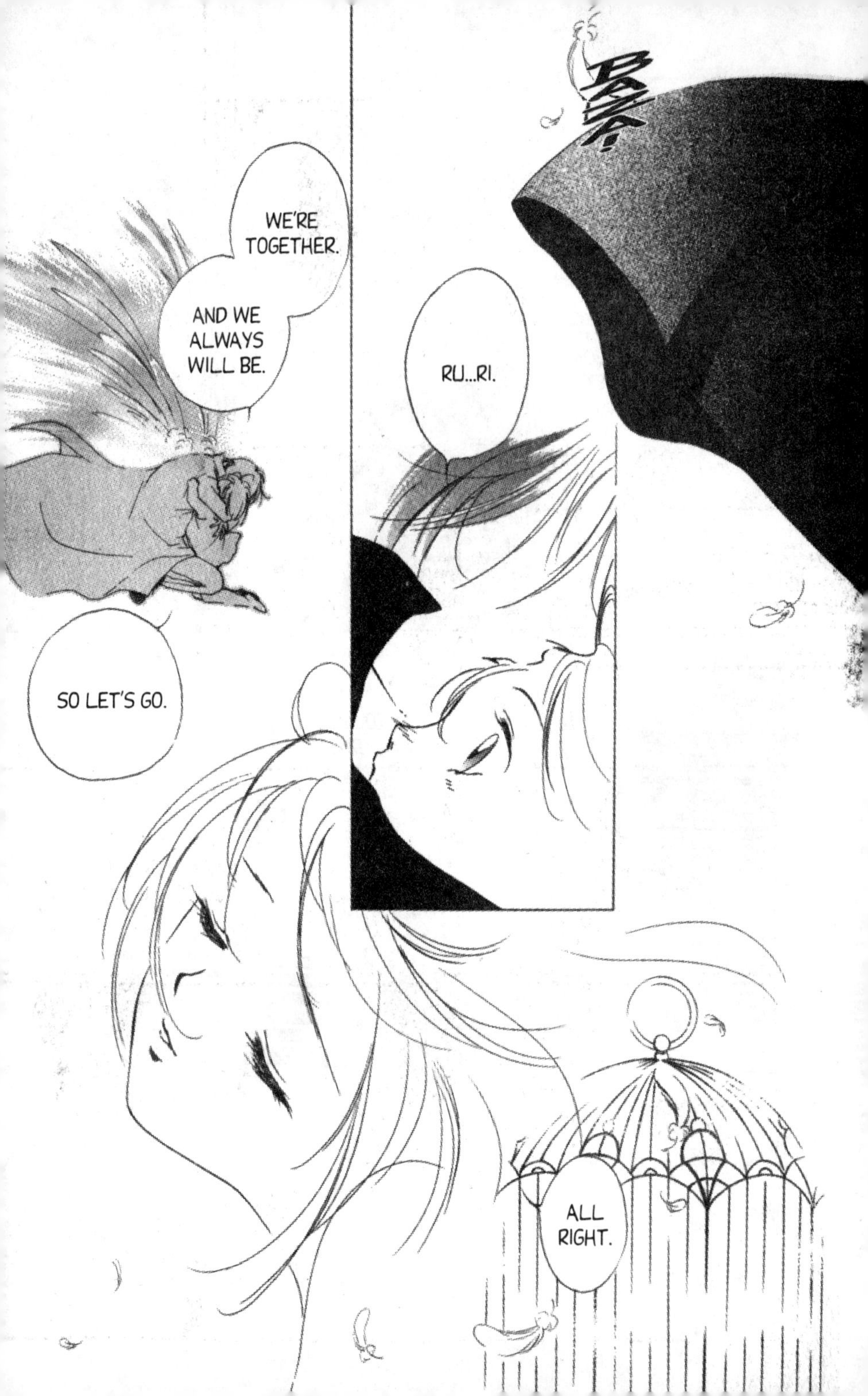
BASA!
RU...RI.
WE'RE TOGETHER.
AND WE ALWAYS WILL BE.
SO LET'S GO.
ALL RIGHT.

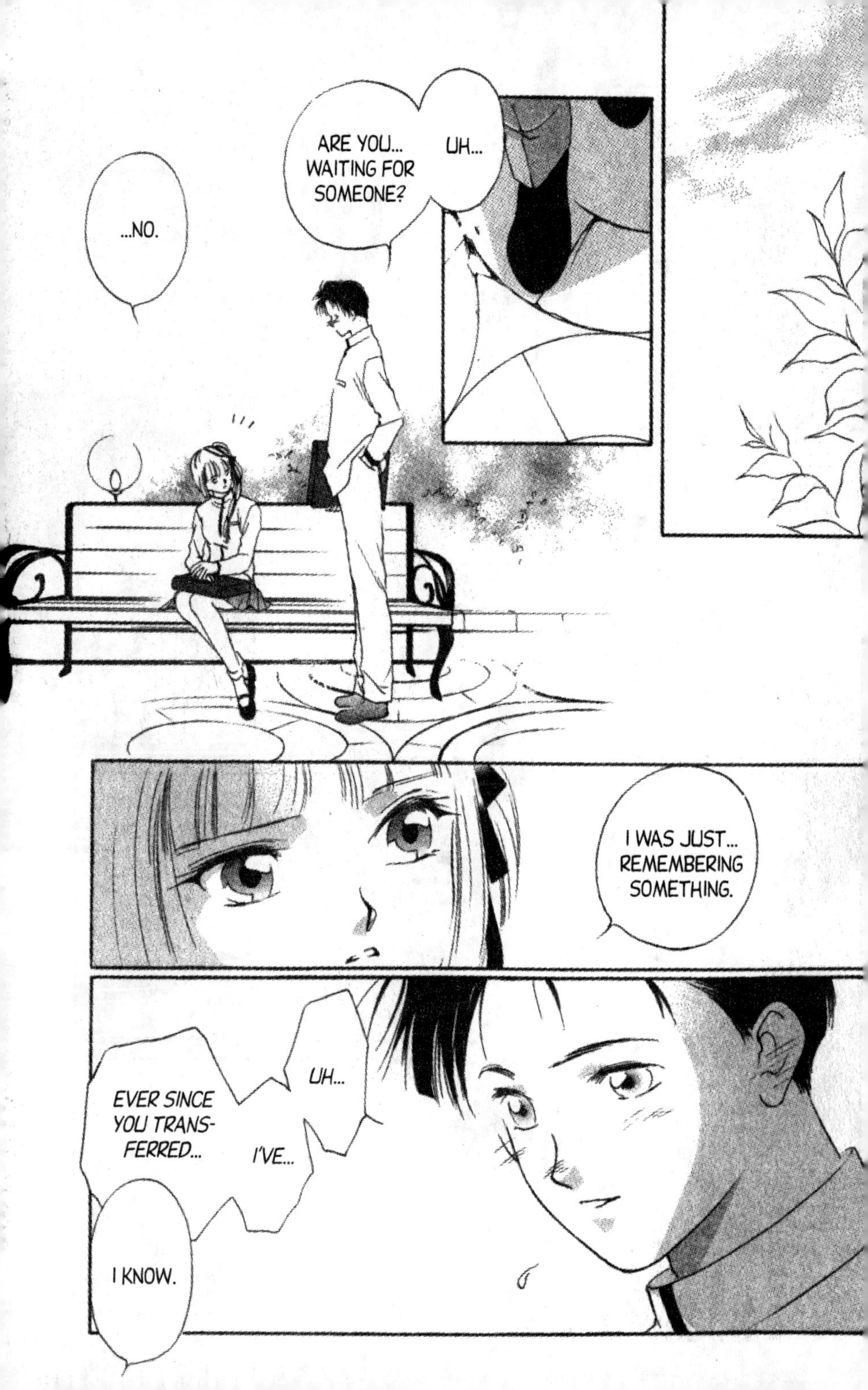
UH...
ARE YOU... WAITING FOR SOMEONE?
...NO.
I WAS JUST... REMEMBERING SOMETHING.
UH...
I'VE...
EVER SINCE YOU TRANS-FERRED...
I KNOW.

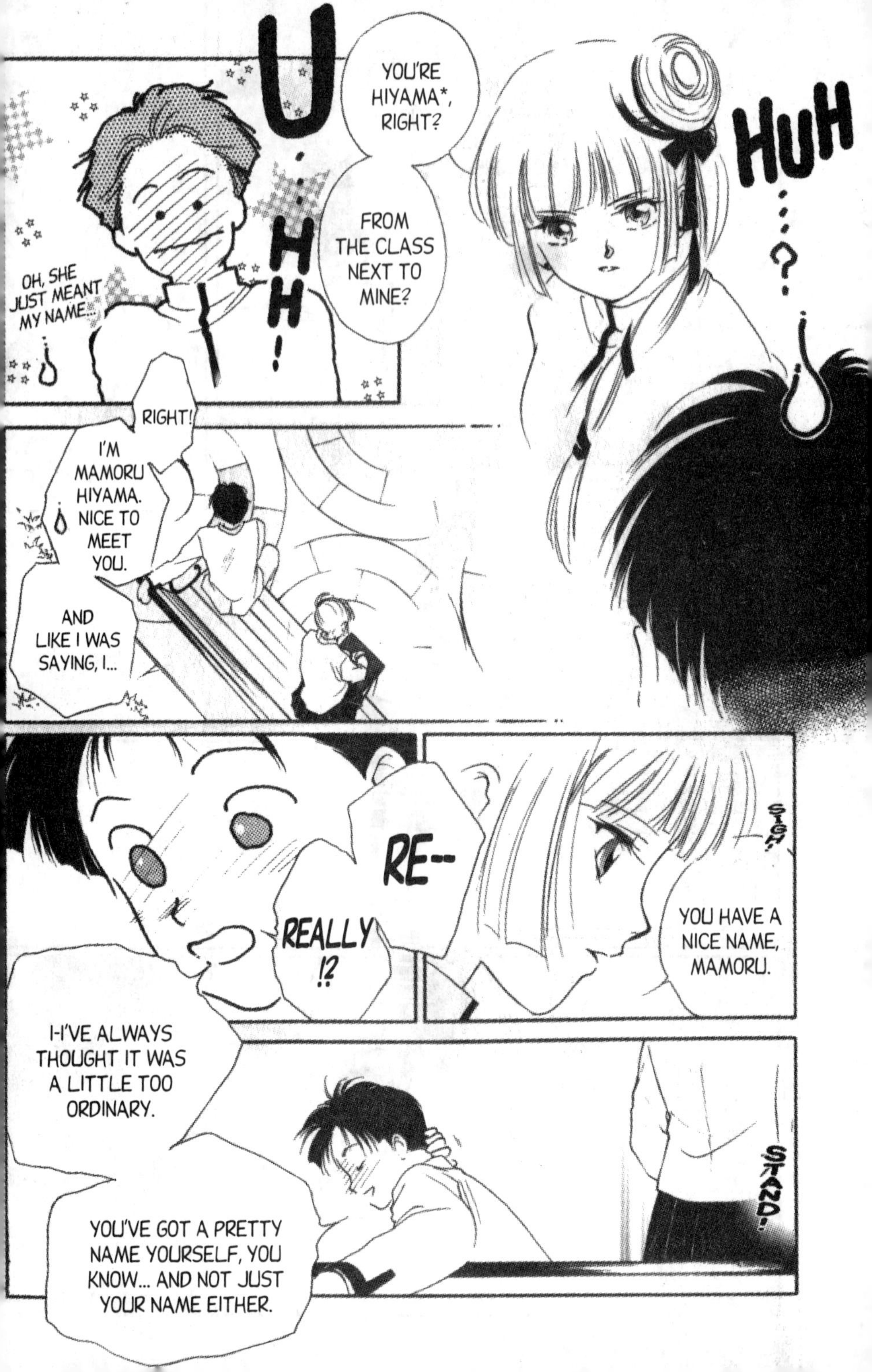
HUH...?
YOU'RE HIYAMA*, RIGHT?
FROM THE CLASS NEXT TO MINE?
UHH!
OH, SHE JUST MEANT MY NAME...
RIGHT!
I'M MAMORU HIYAMA. NICE TO MEET YOU.
AND LIKE I WAS SAYING, I...
SIGH!
YOU HAVE A NICE NAME, MAMORU.
RE--
REALLY!?
I-I'VE ALWAYS THOUGHT IT WAS A LITTLE TOO ORDINARY.
STAND!
YOU'VE GOT A PRETTY NAME YOURSELF, YOU KNOW... AND NOT JUST YOUR NAME EITHER.

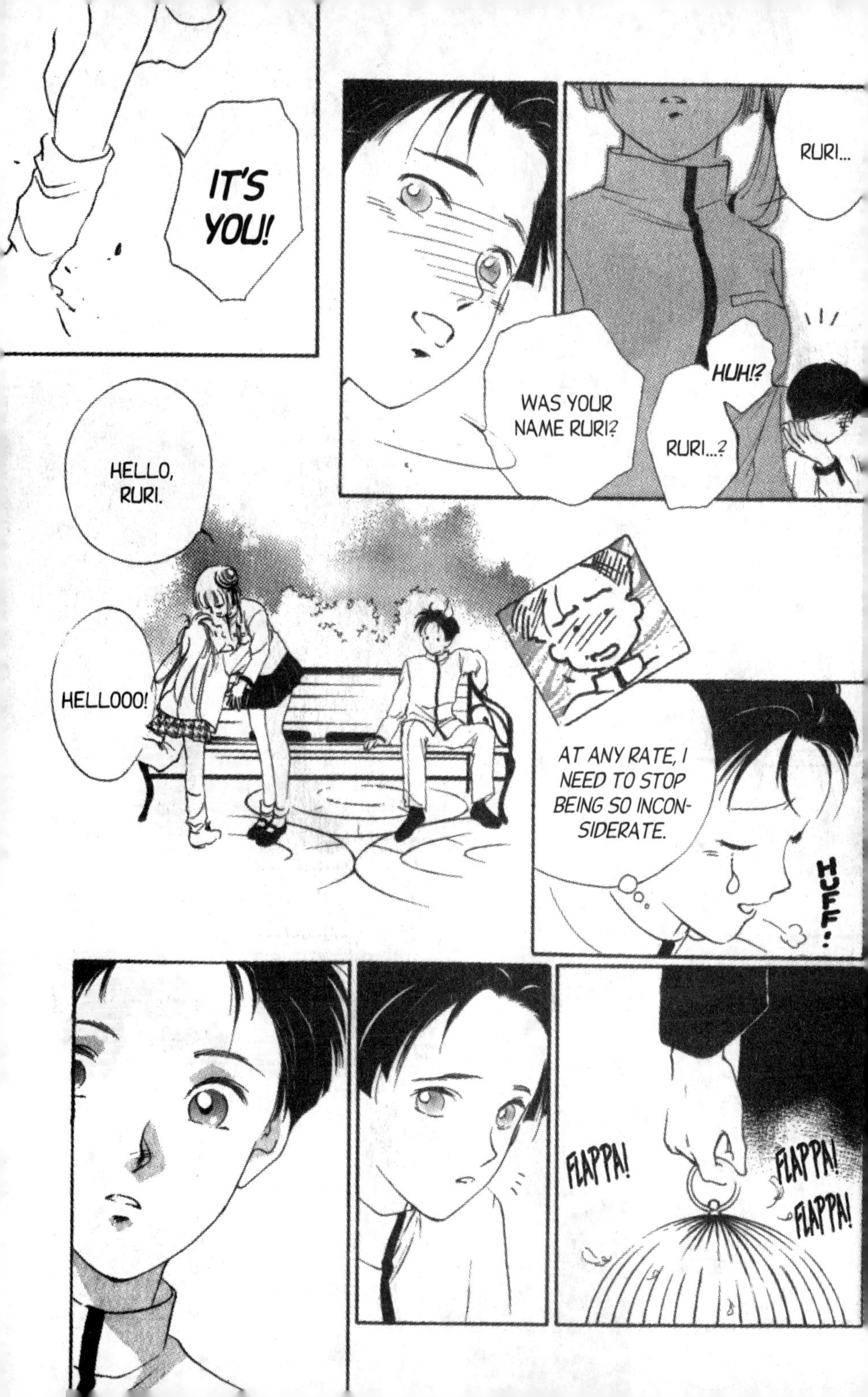
RURI...
HUH!?
RURI...?
WAS YOUR NAME RURI?
IT'S YOU!
AT ANY RATE, I NEED TO STOP BEING SO INCON-SIDERATE.
HUFF!
HELLO, RURI.
HELLOOO!
FLAPPA!
FLAPPA!
FLAPPA!

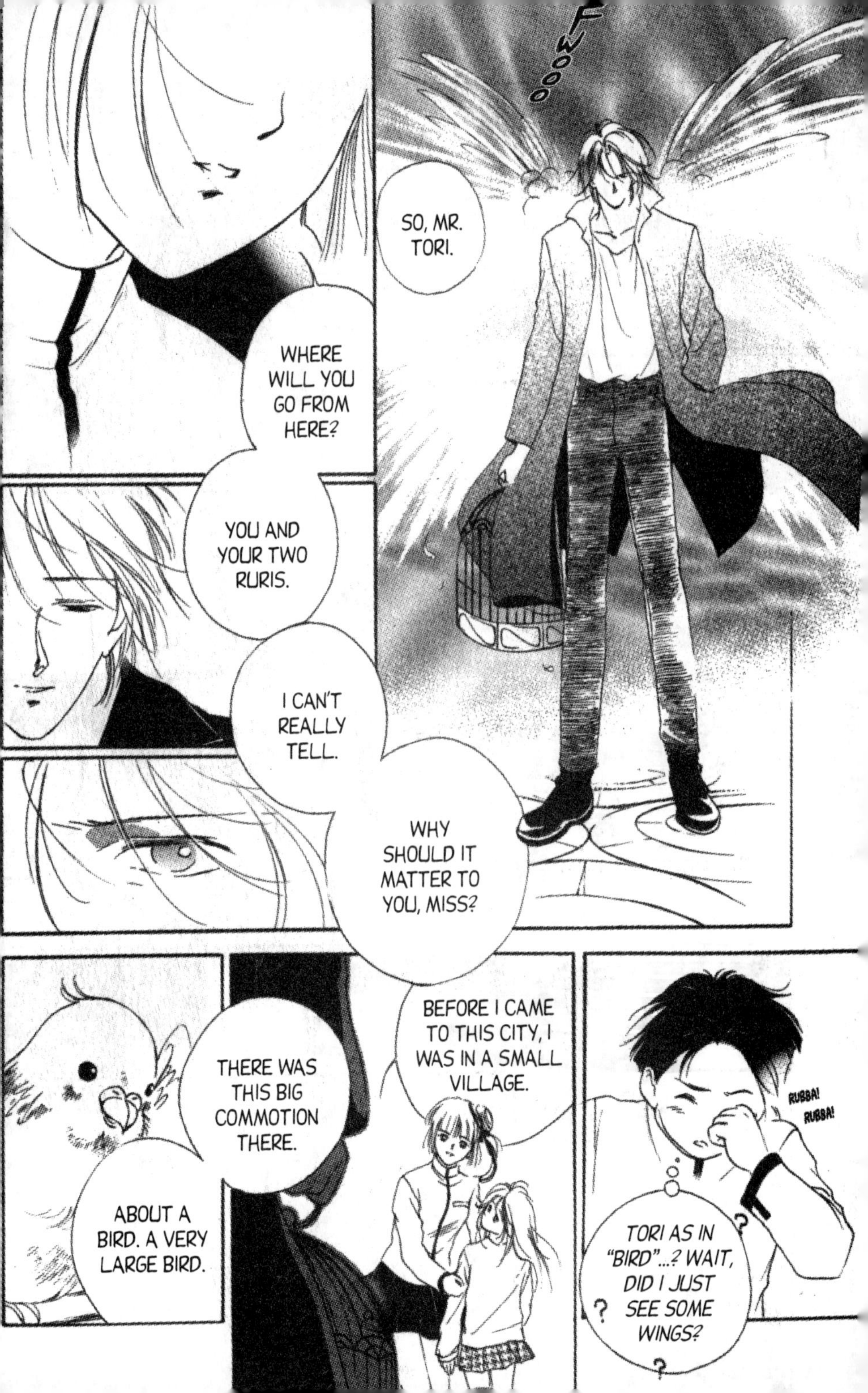
FWOOO
SO, MR. TORI.
WHERE WILL YOU GO FROM HERE?
YOU AND YOUR TWO RURIS.
I CAN'T REALLY TELL.
WHY SHOULD IT MATTER TO YOU, MISS?
RUBBA! RUBBA!
TORI AS IN "BIRD"...? WAIT, DID I JUST SEE SOME WINGS?
BEFORE I CAME TO THIS CITY, I WAS IN A SMALL VILLAGE.
THERE WAS THIS BIG COMMOTION THERE.
ABOUT A BIRD. A VERY LARGE BIRD.

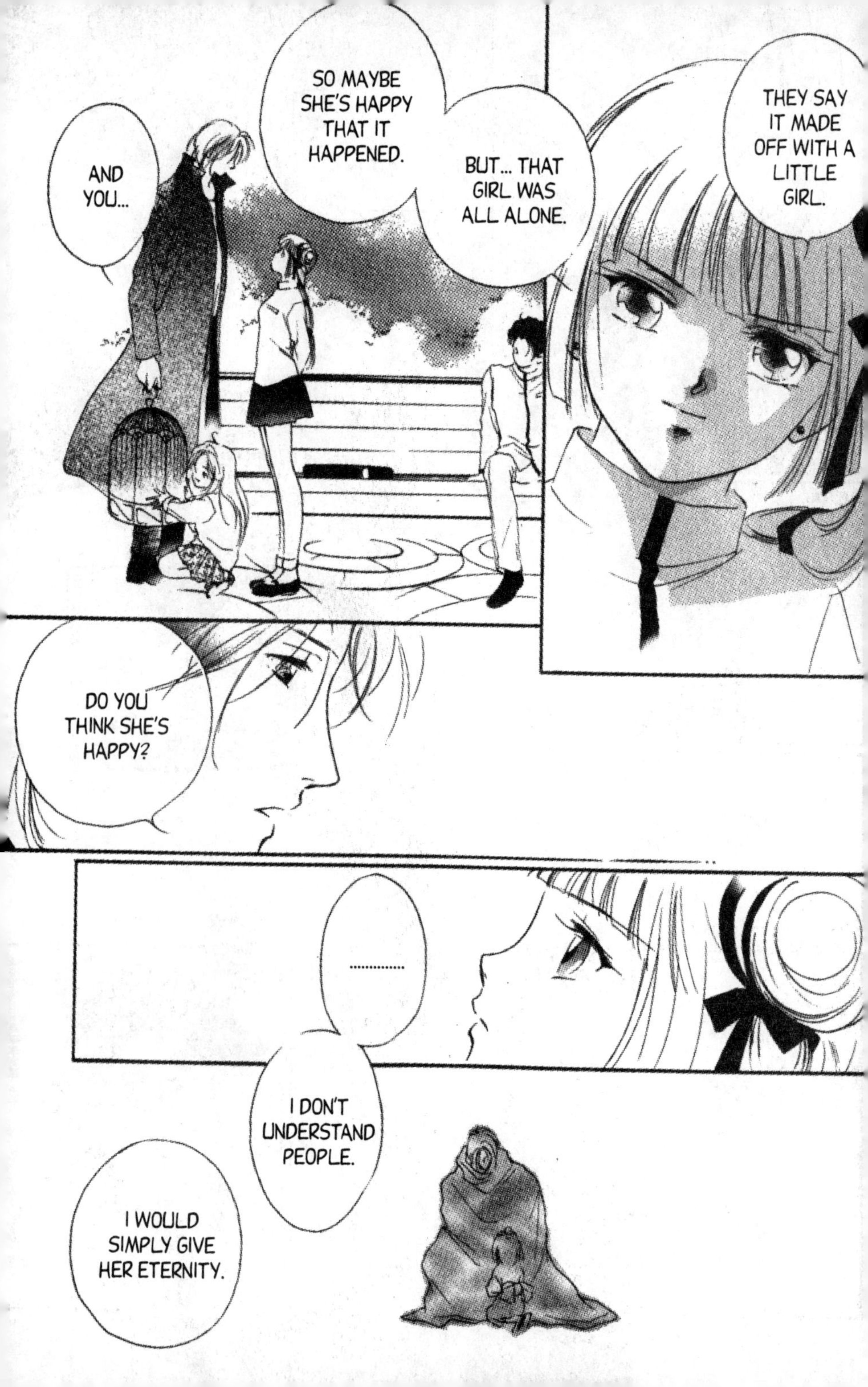
THEY SAY IT MADE OFF WITH A LITTLE GIRL.
BUT... THAT GIRL WAS ALL ALONE.
SO MAYBE SHE'S HAPPY THAT IT HAPPENED.
AND YOU...
DO YOU THINK SHE'S HAPPY?
....
I DON'T UNDERSTAND PEOPLE.
I WOULD SIMPLY GIVE HER ETERNITY.

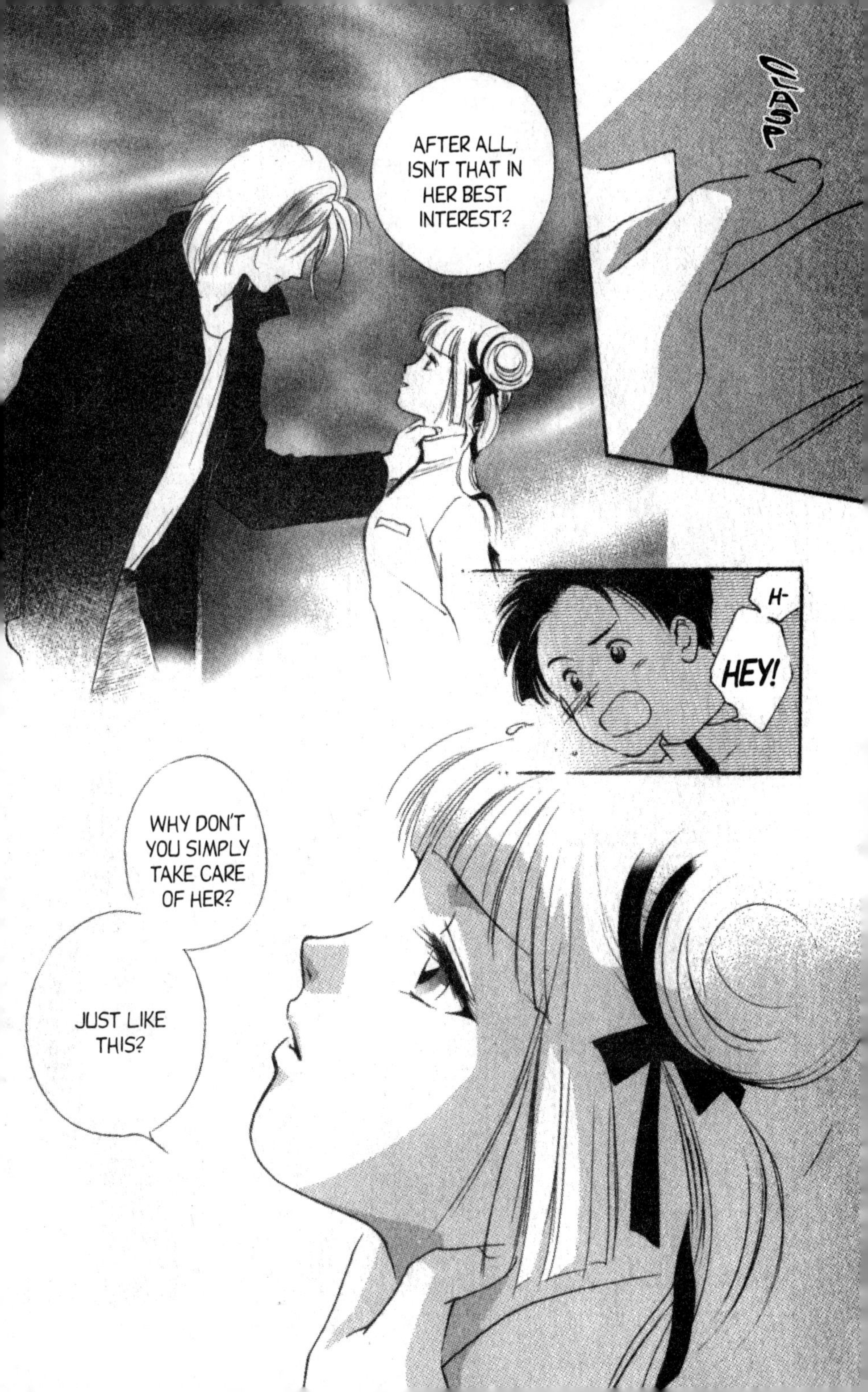
CLASP
AFTER ALL, ISN'T THAT IN HER BEST INTEREST?
H-
HEY!
WHY DON'T YOU SIMPLY TAKE CARE OF HER?
JUST LIKE THIS?

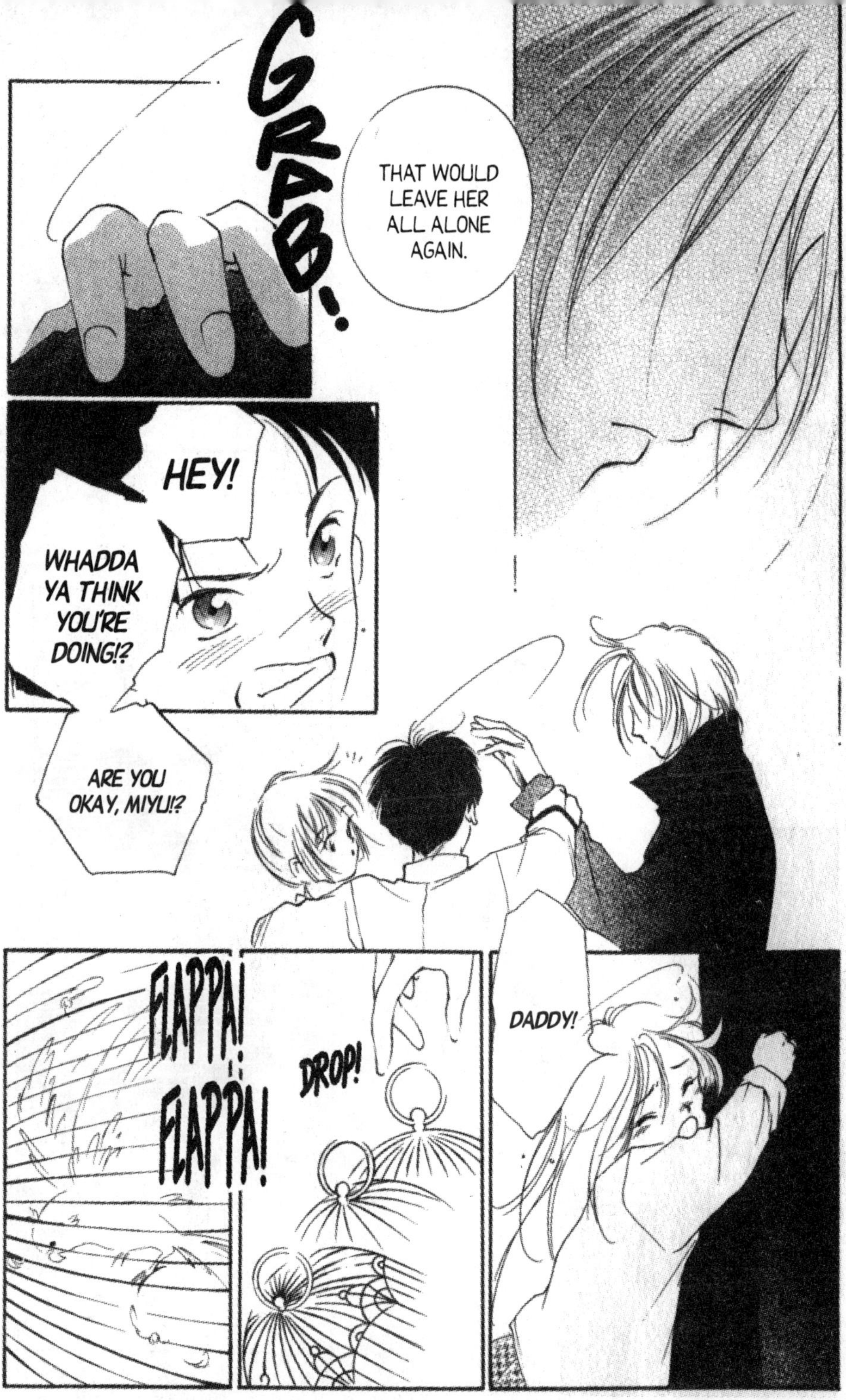
THAT WOULD LEAVE HER ALL ALONE AGAIN.
GRAB!!
HEY!
WHADDA YA THINK YOU'RE DOING!?
ARE YOU OKAY, MIYU!?
DADDY!
DROP!
FLAPPA! FLAPPA!

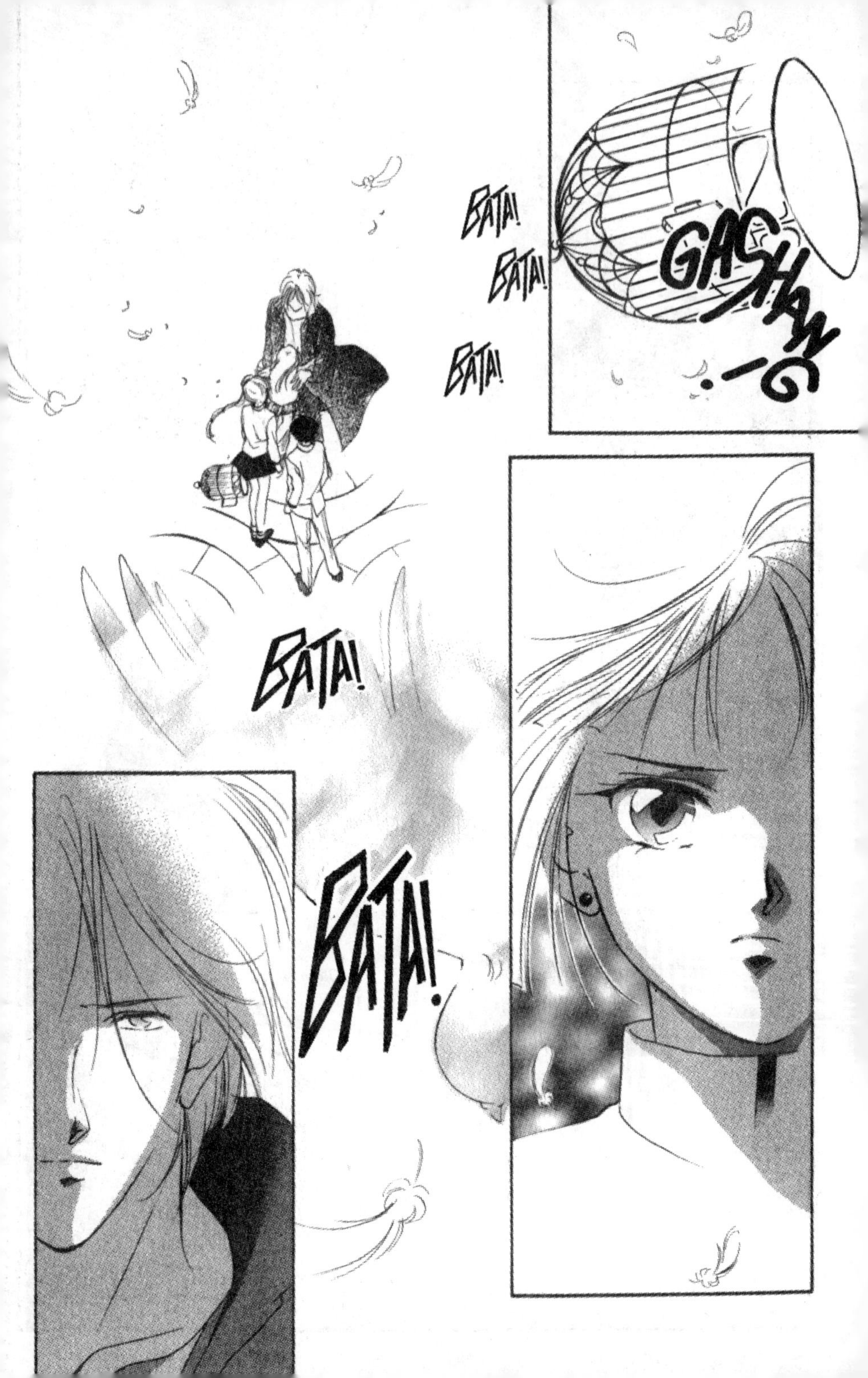
GASHAN!
BATA!
BATA!
BATA!
BATA!
BATA!

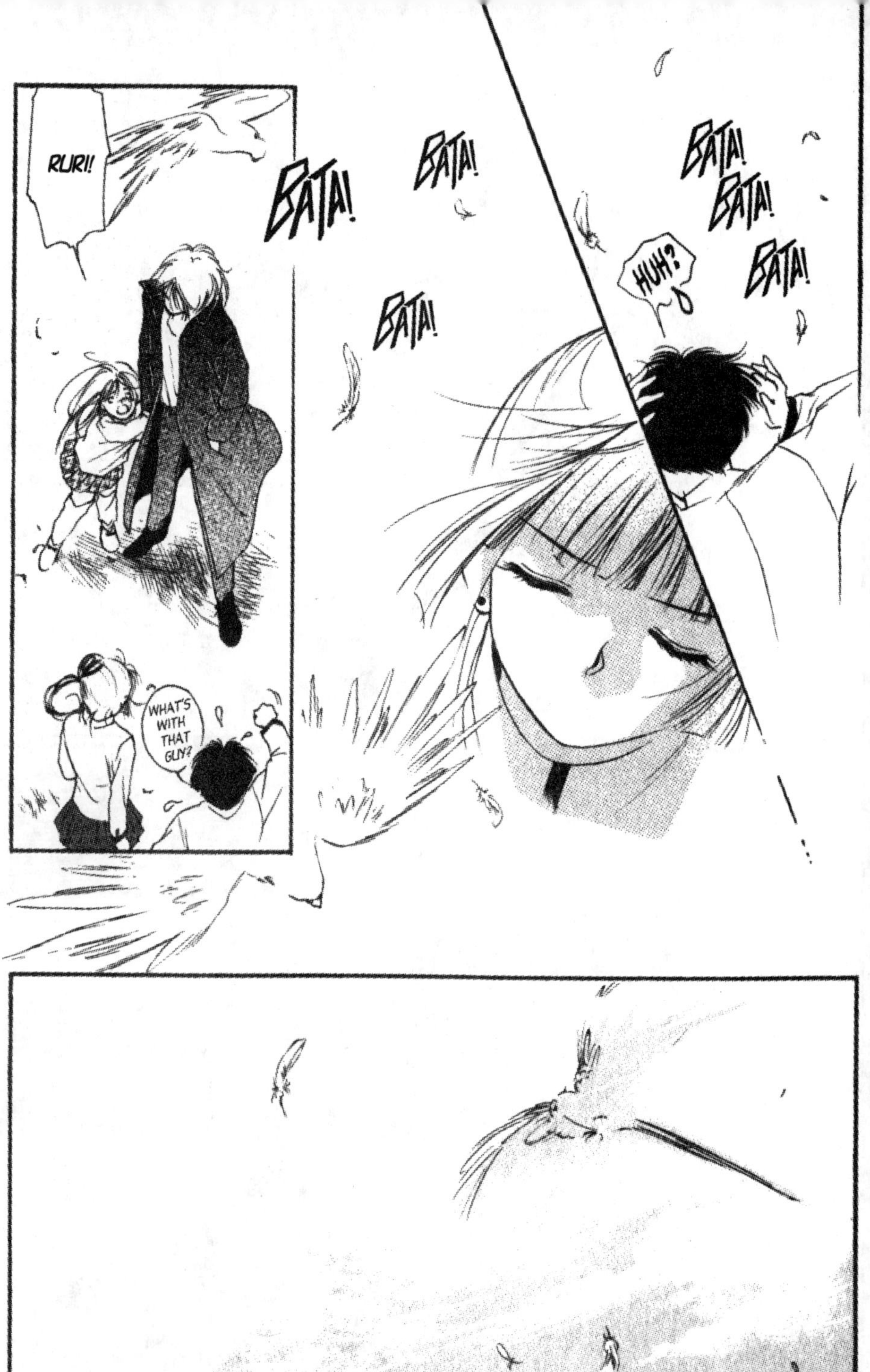
BATA!
BATA!
BATA!
HUH?
BATA!
BATA!
BATA!
RURI!!
WHAT'S WITH THAT GUY?

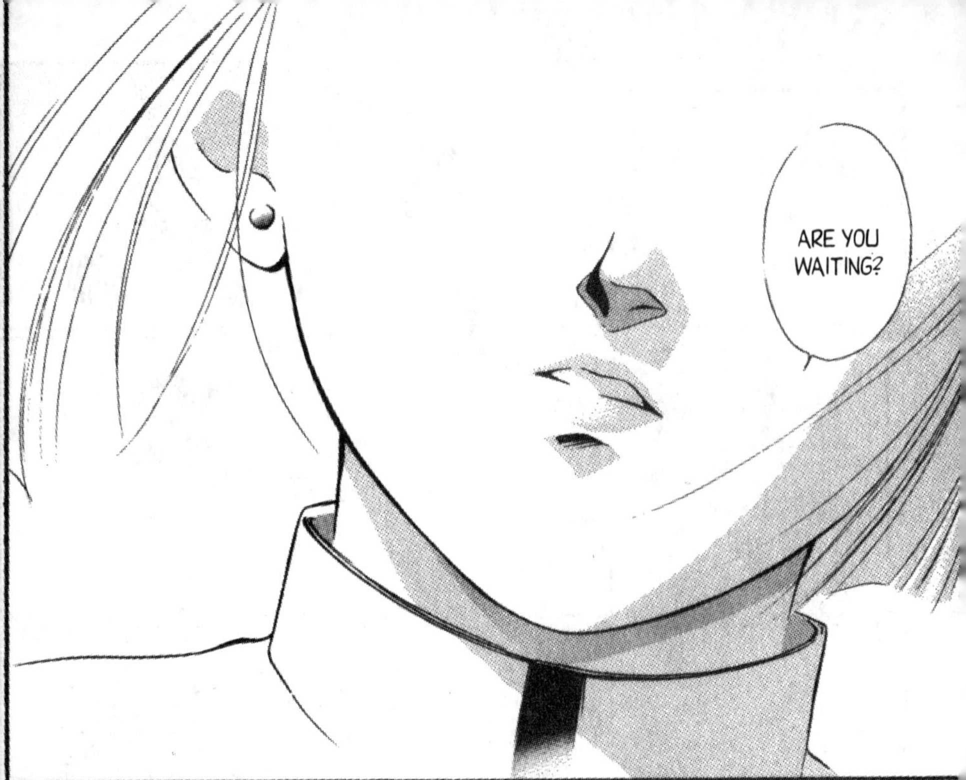
ARE YOU WAITING?
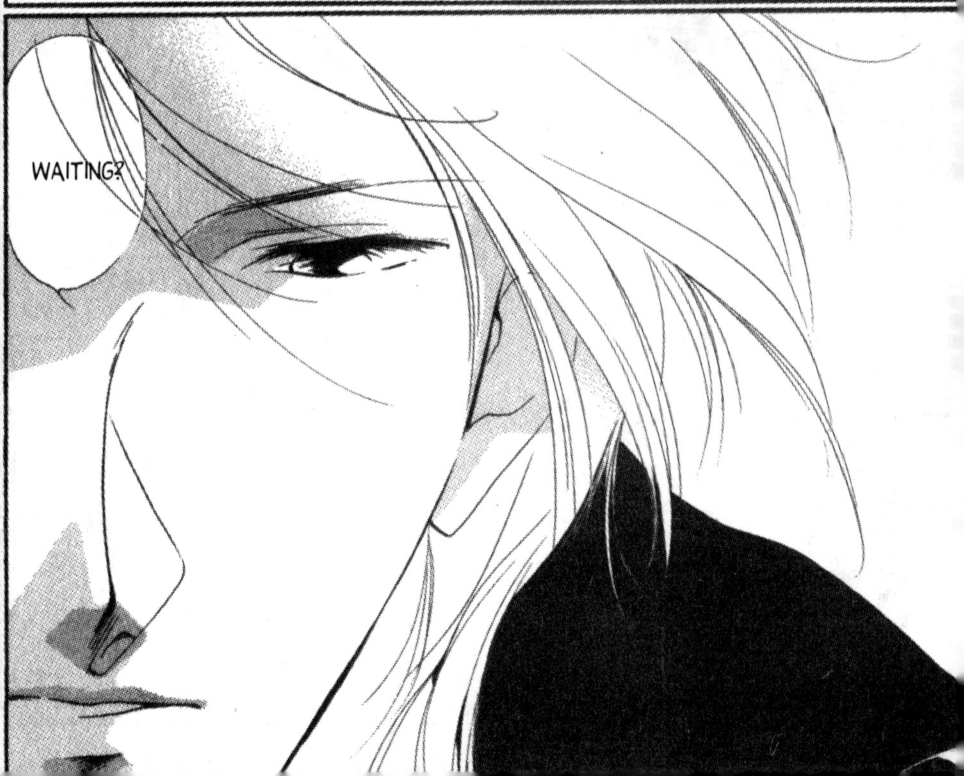
WAITING?

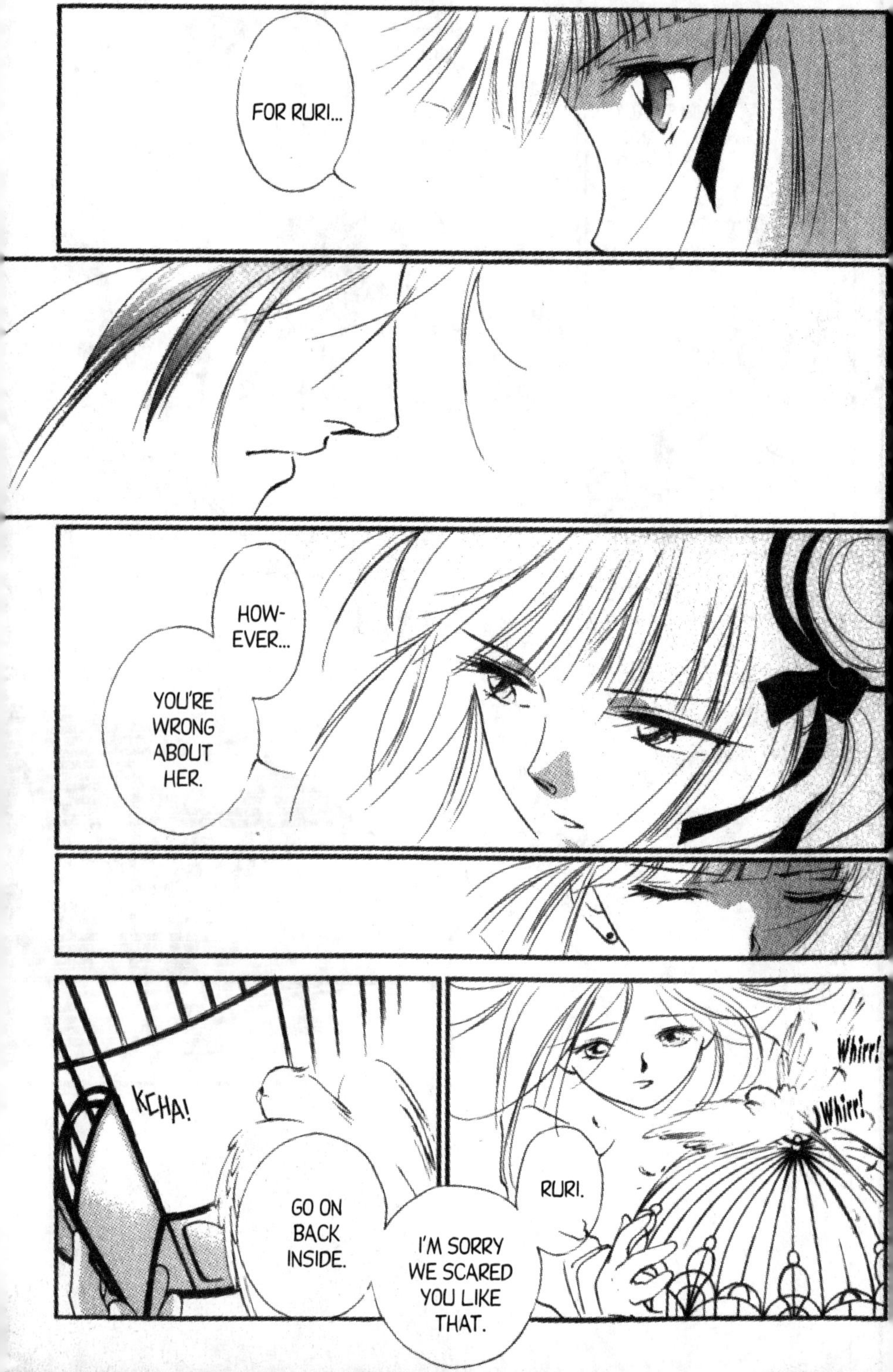
FOR RURI...
HOW-EVER...
YOU'RE WRONG ABOUT HER.
Whirr!
Whirr!
RURI.
I'M SORRY WE SCARED YOU LIKE THAT.
KCHA!
GO ON BACK INSIDE.

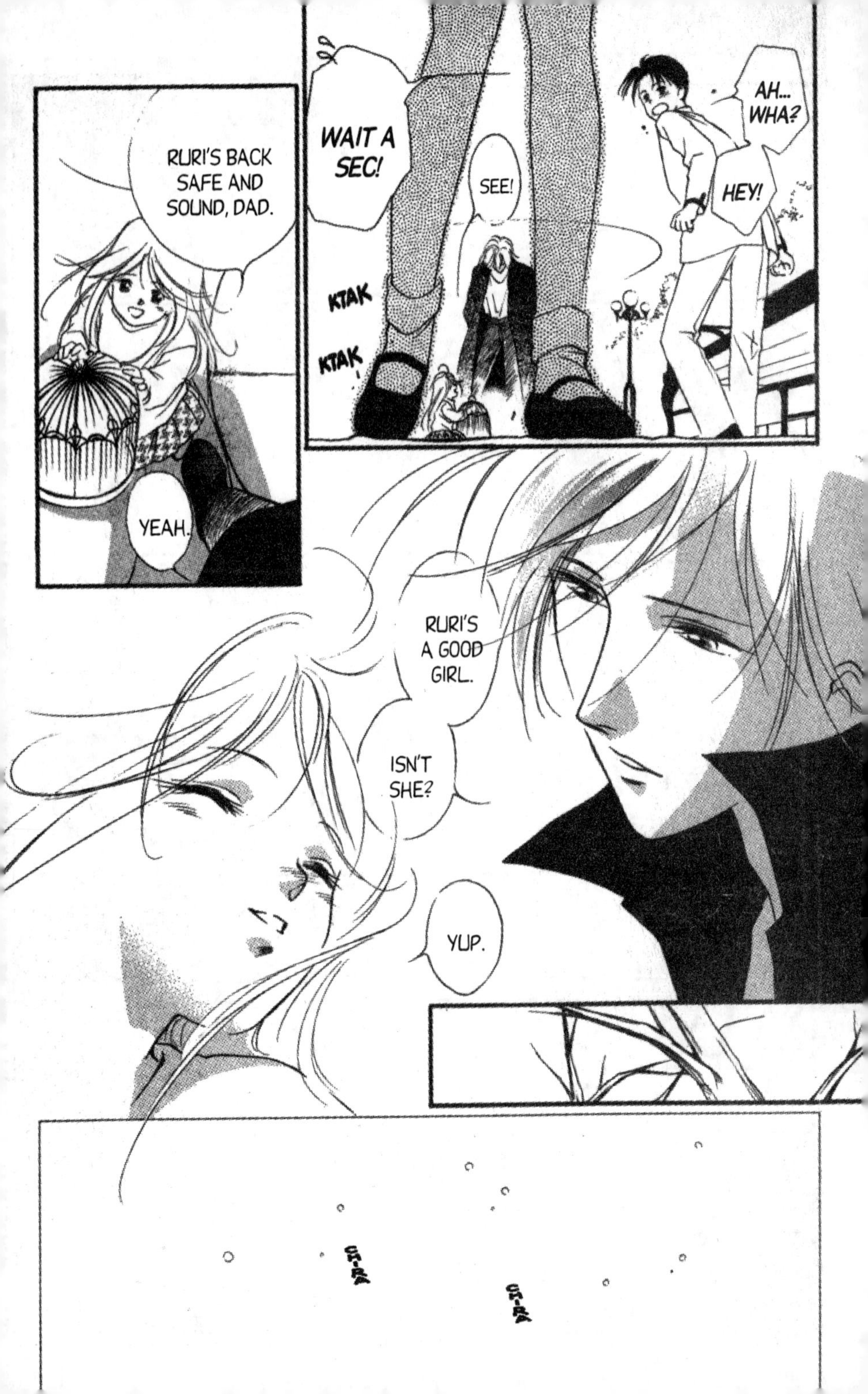
AH... WHA?
HEY!
SEE!
WAIT A SEC!
KTAK
KTAK
RURI'S BACK SAFE AND SOUND, DAD.
YEAH.
RURI'S A GOOD GIRL.
ISN'T SHE?
YUP.
CHIRA
CHIRA

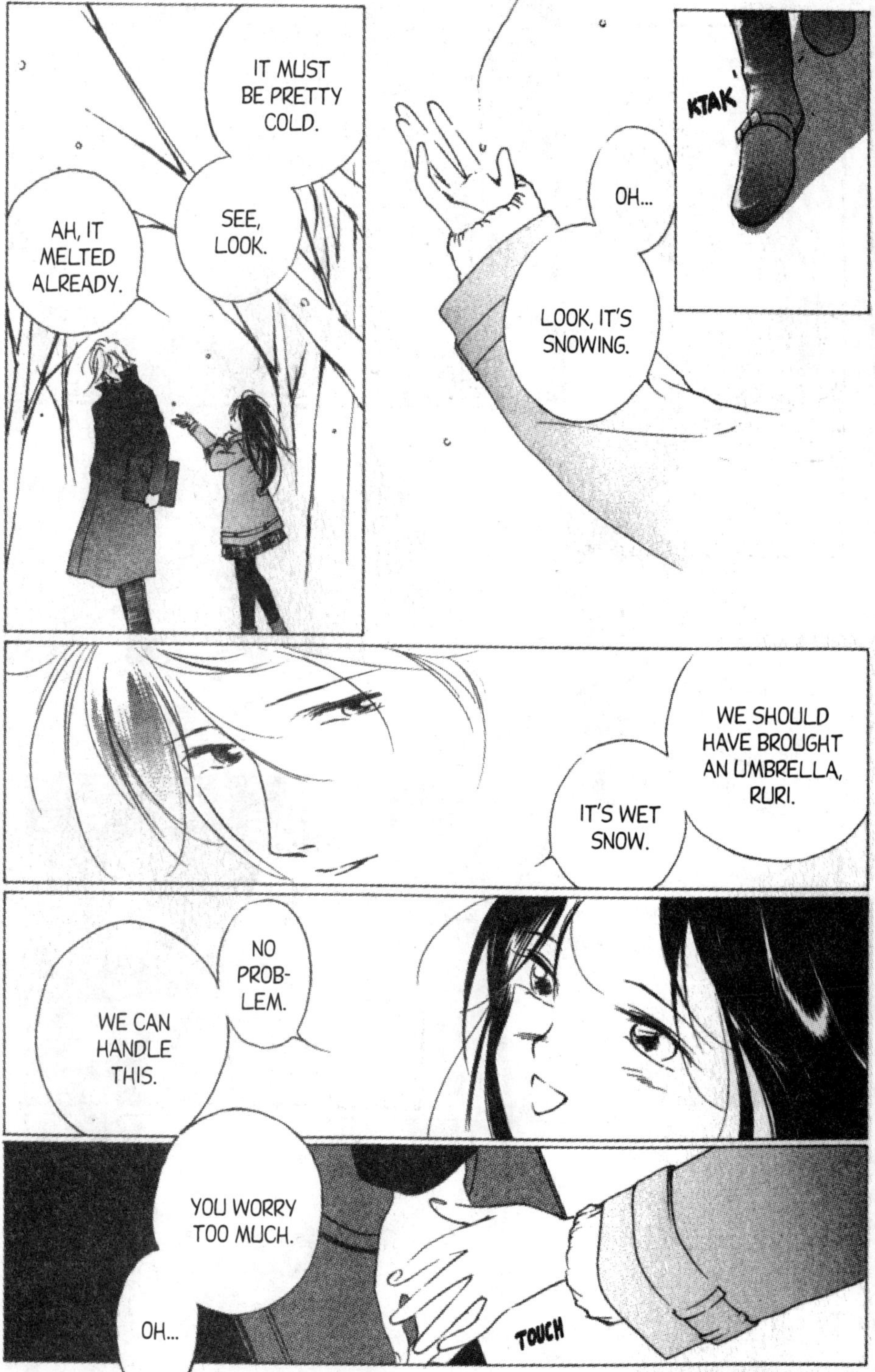
KTAK
OH...
LOOK, IT'S SNOWING.
IT MUST BE PRETTY COLD.
SEE, LOOK.
AH, IT MELTED ALREADY.
WE SHOULD HAVE BROUGHT AN UMBRELLA, RURI.
IT'S WET SNOW.
NO PROB-LEM.
WE CAN HANDLE THIS.
YOU WORRY TOO MUCH.
TOUCH
OH...

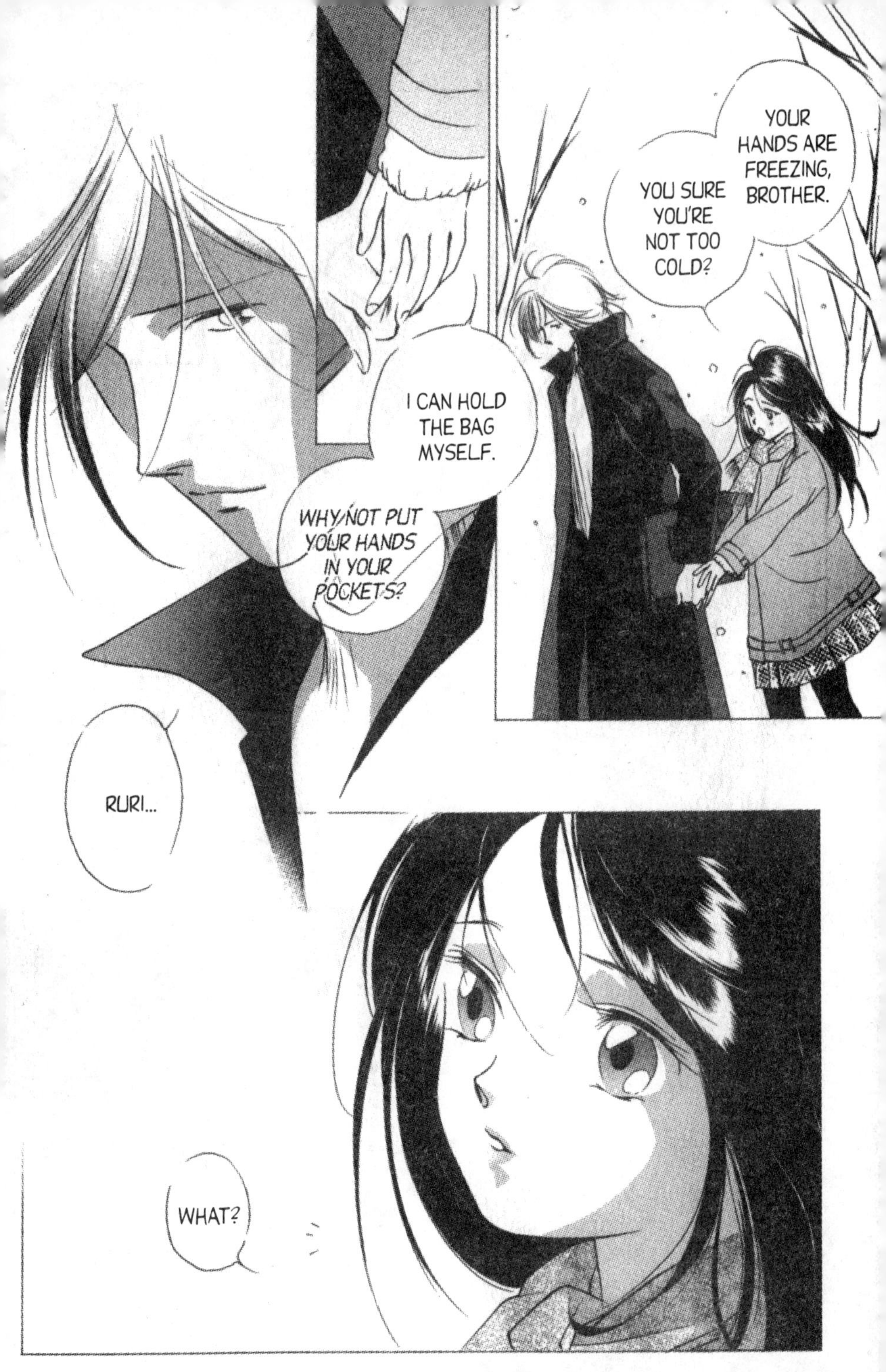
YOUR HANDS ARE FREEZING, BROTHER.
YOU SURE YOU'RE NOT TOO COLD?
I CAN HOLD THE BAG MYSELF.
WHY NOT PUT YOUR HANDS IN YOUR POCKETS?
RURI...
WHAT?

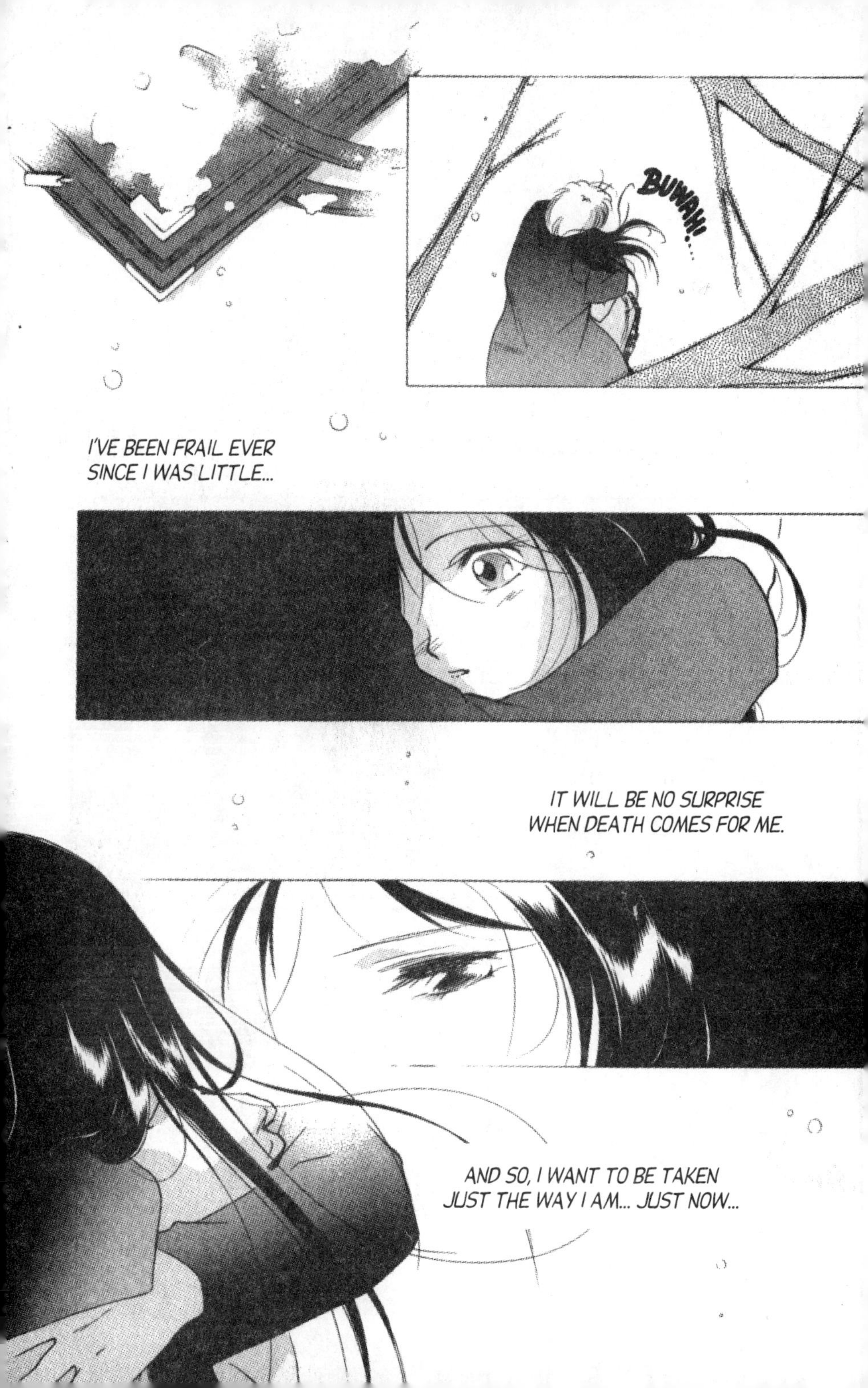
BUWAH!!...
I'VE BEEN FRAIL EVER SINCE I WAS LITTLE...
IT WILL BE NO SURPRISE WHEN DEATH COMES FOR ME.
AND SO, I WANT TO BE TAKEN JUST THE WAY I AM... JUST NOW...

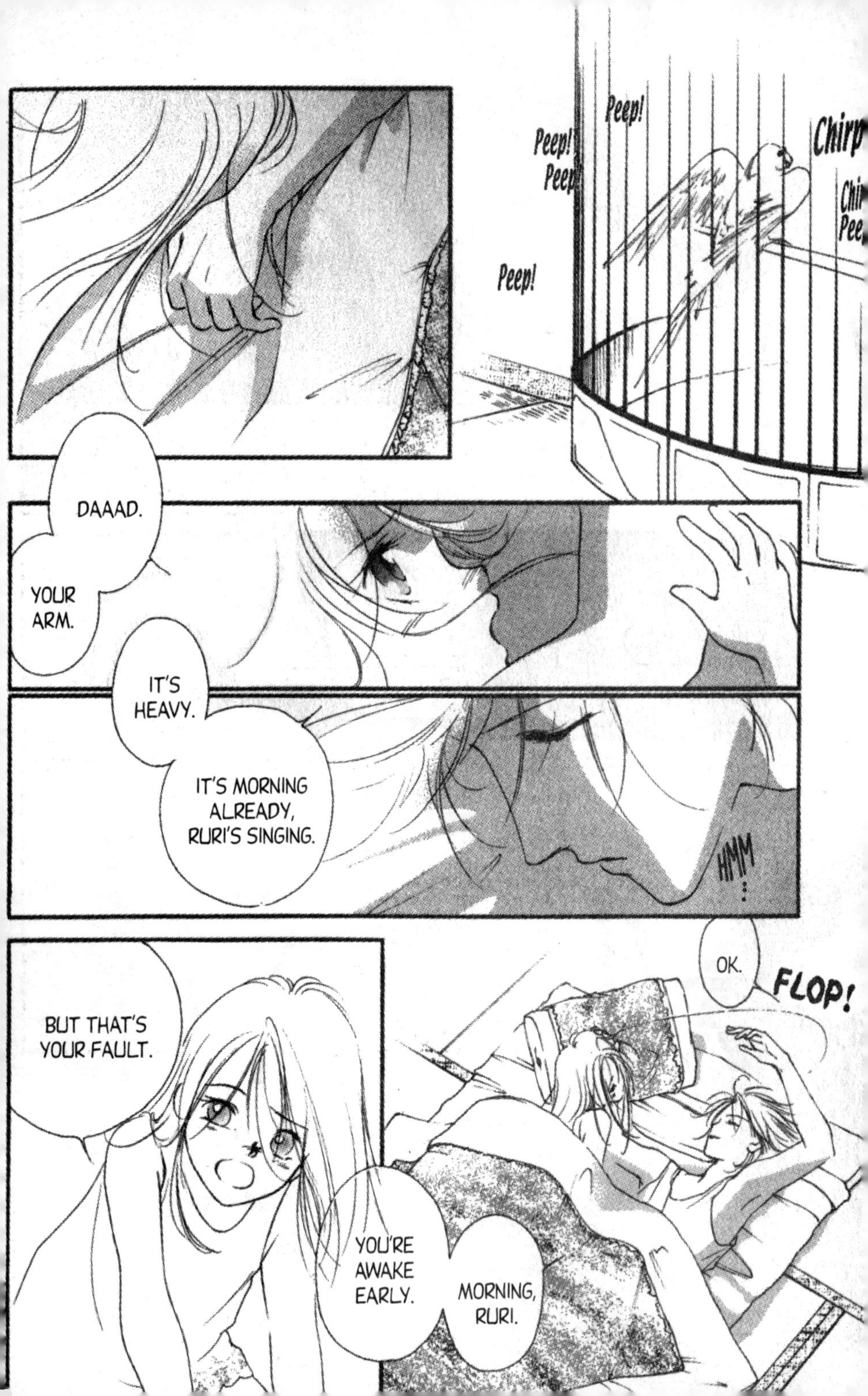
Chirp
Peep!
Peep! Peep!
Peep!
DAAAD.
YOUR ARM.
IT'S HEAVY.
IT'S MORNING ALREADY, RURI'S SINGING.
HMM...
OK.
FLOP!
MORNING, RURI.
YOU'RE AWAKE EARLY.
BUT THAT'S YOUR FAULT.

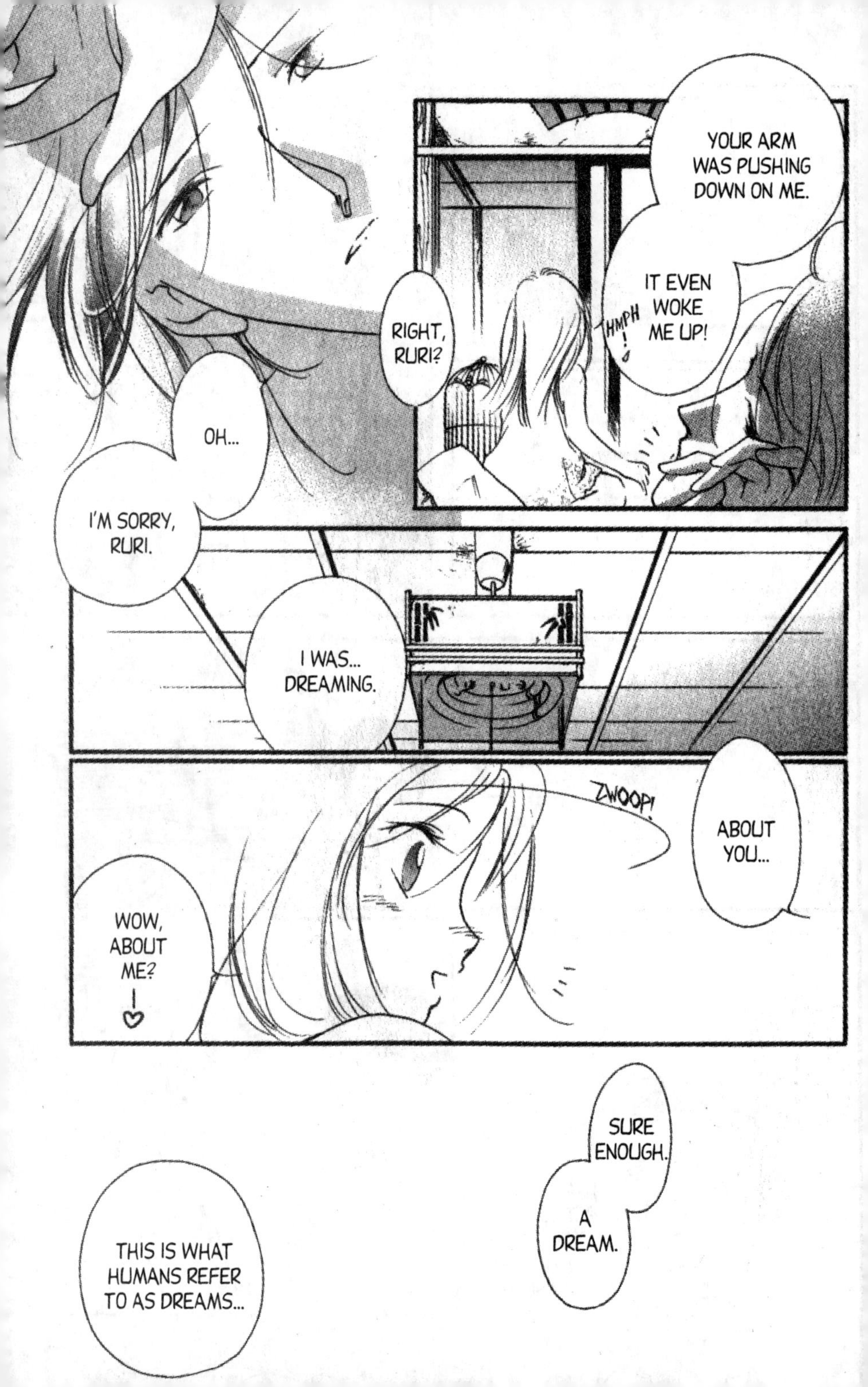
YOUR ARM WAS PUSHING DOWN ON ME.
IT EVEN WOKE ME UP!
HMPH!
RIGHT, RURI?
OH...
I'M SORRY, RURI.
I WAS... DREAMING.
ABOUT YOU...
ZWOOP!
WOW, ABOUT ME?
SURE ENOUGH.
A DREAM.
THIS IS WHAT HUMANS REFER TO AS DREAMS...

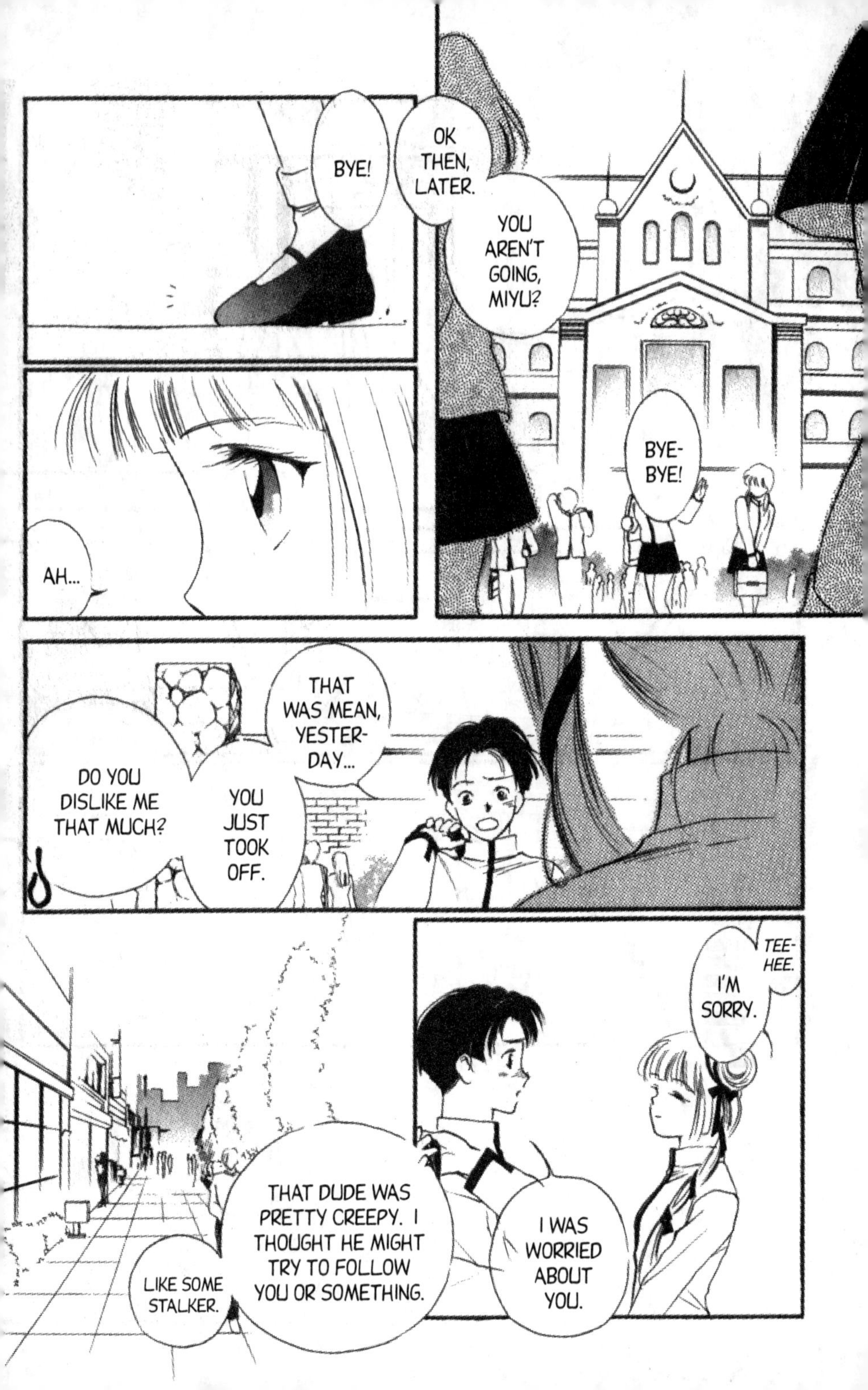
OK THEN, LATER.
YOU AREN'T GOING, MIYU?
BYE-BYE!
BYE!
AH...
THAT WAS MEAN, YESTER-DAY...
YOU JUST TOOK OFF.
DO YOU DISLIKE ME THAT MUCH?
TEE-HEE.
I'M SORRY.
I WAS WORRIED ABOUT YOU.
THAT DUDE WAS PRETTY CREEPY. I THOUGHT HE MIGHT TRY TO FOLLOW YOU OR SOMETHING.
LIKE SOME STALKER.

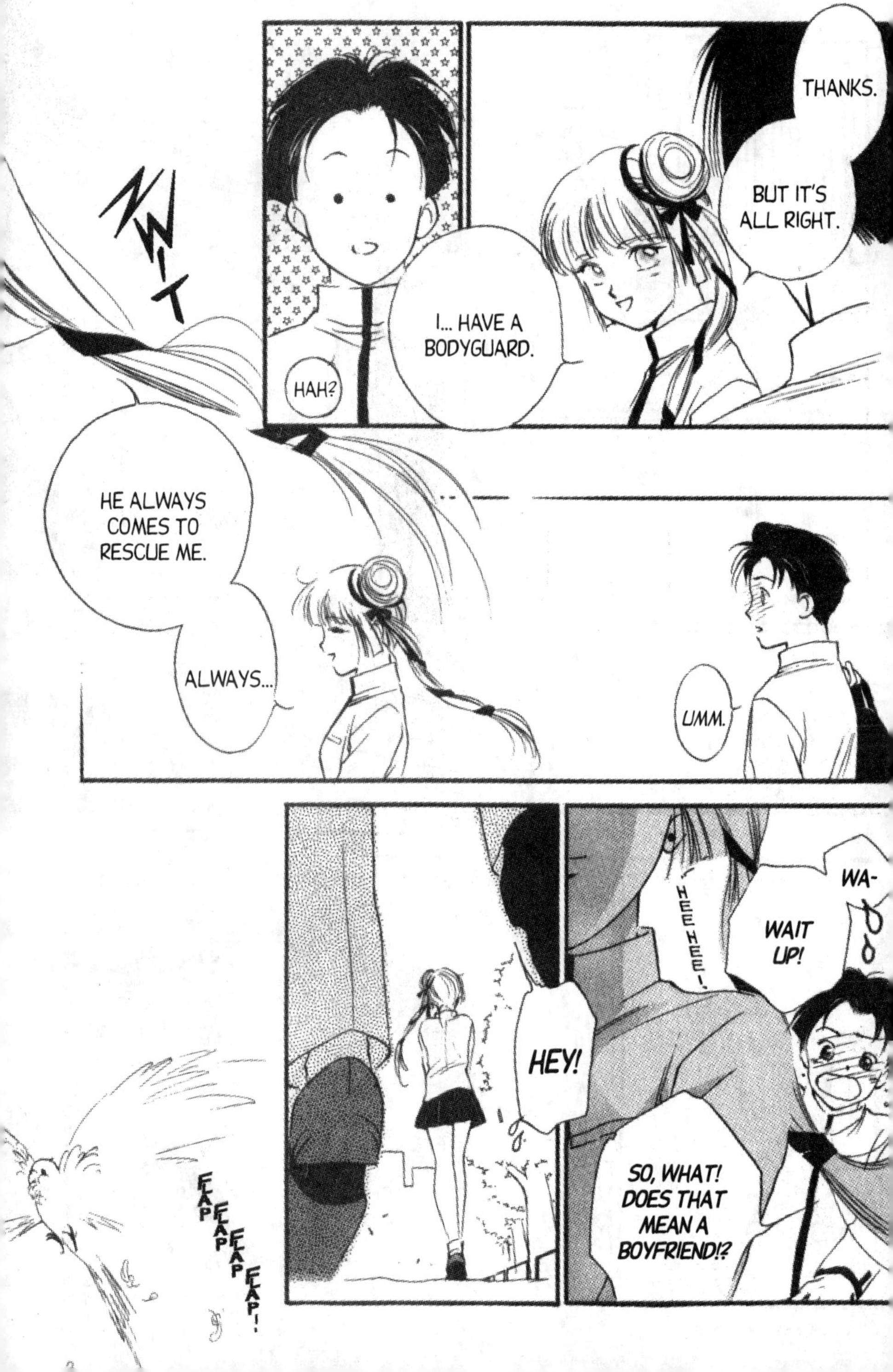
THANKS.
BUT IT'S ALL RIGHT.
I... HAVE A BODYGUARD.
HAH?
NWIT
HE ALWAYS COMES TO RESCUE ME.
ALWAYS...
UMM.
WA-
WAIT UP!
HEE HEE!
SO, WHAT! DOES THAT MEAN A BOYFRIEND!?
HEY!
FLAP FLAP FLAP FLAP!

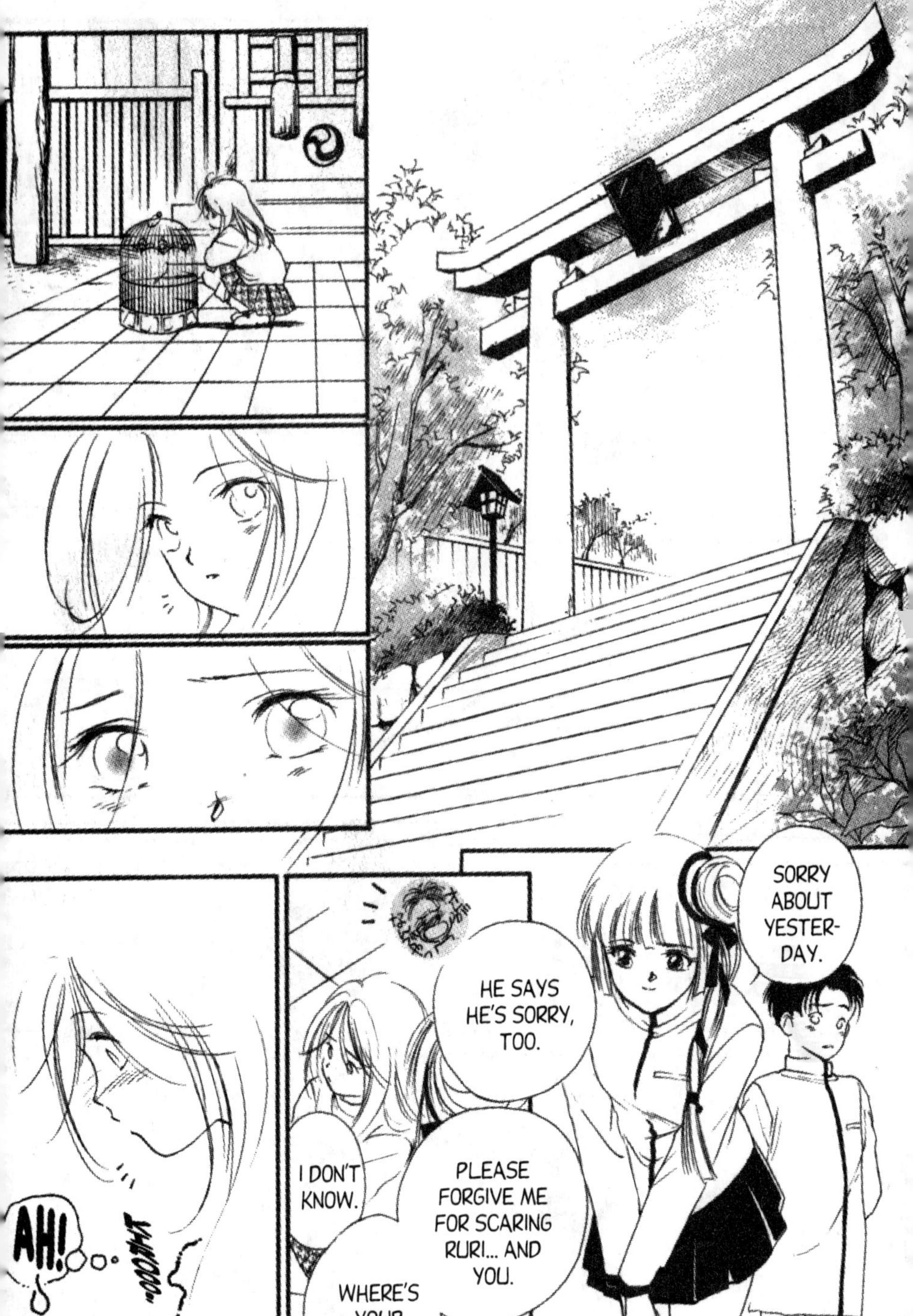
SORRY ABOUT YESTER-DAY.
HE SAYS HE'S SORRY, TOO.
PLEASE FORGIVE ME FOR SCARING RURI... AND YOU.
WHERE'S YOUR FATHER?
I DON'T KNOW.
AH!
WHOOO...

"EXT AROUND HEAD: "WHY ME!?"

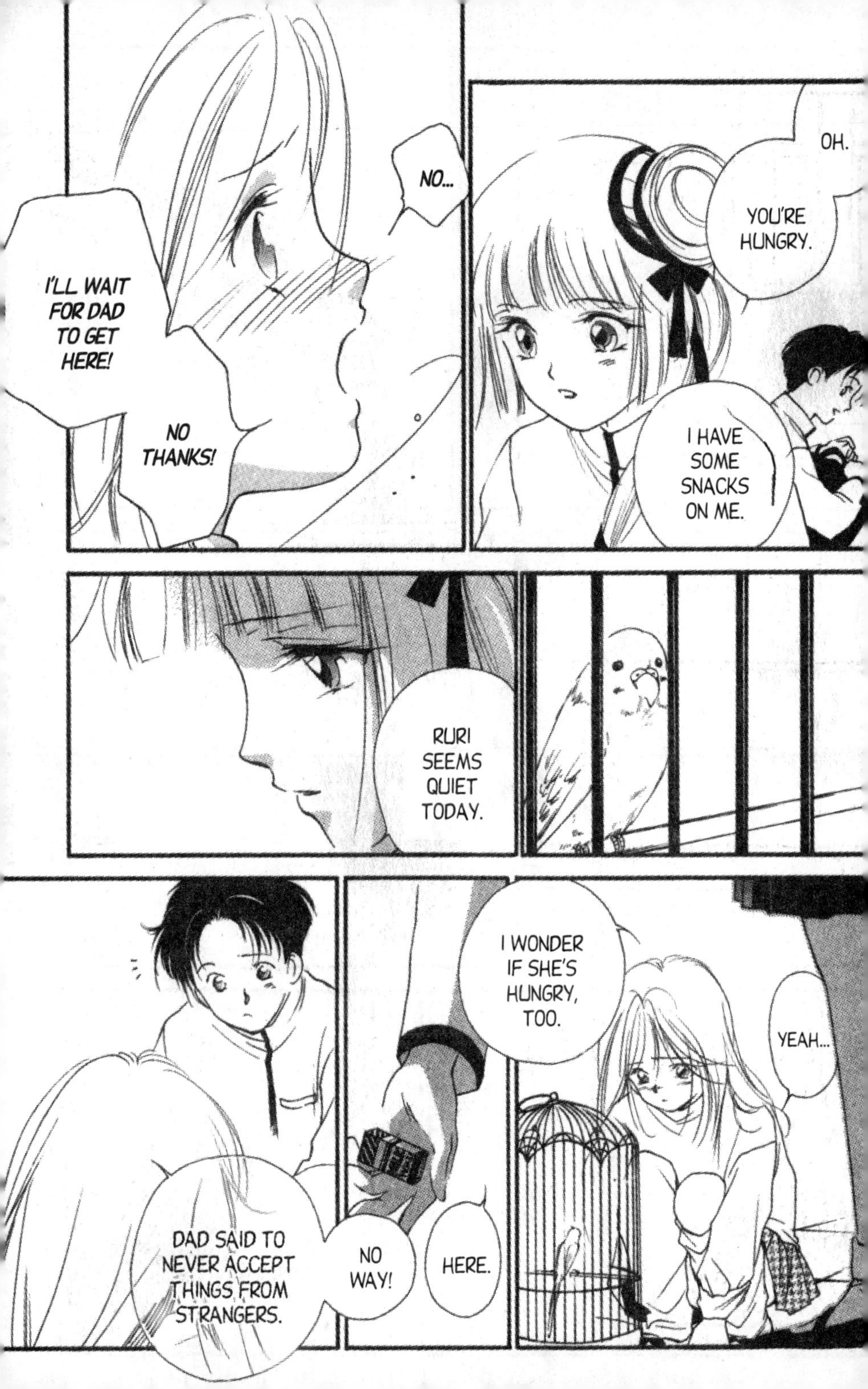
OH.
YOU'RE HUNGRY.
I HAVE SOME SNACKS ON ME.
NO...
I'LL WAIT FOR DAD TO GET HERE!
NO THANKS!
RURI SEEMS QUIET TODAY.
YEAH...
I WONDER IF SHE'S HUNGRY, TOO.
HERE.
NO WAY!
DAD SAID TO NEVER ACCEPT THINGS FROM STRANGERS.

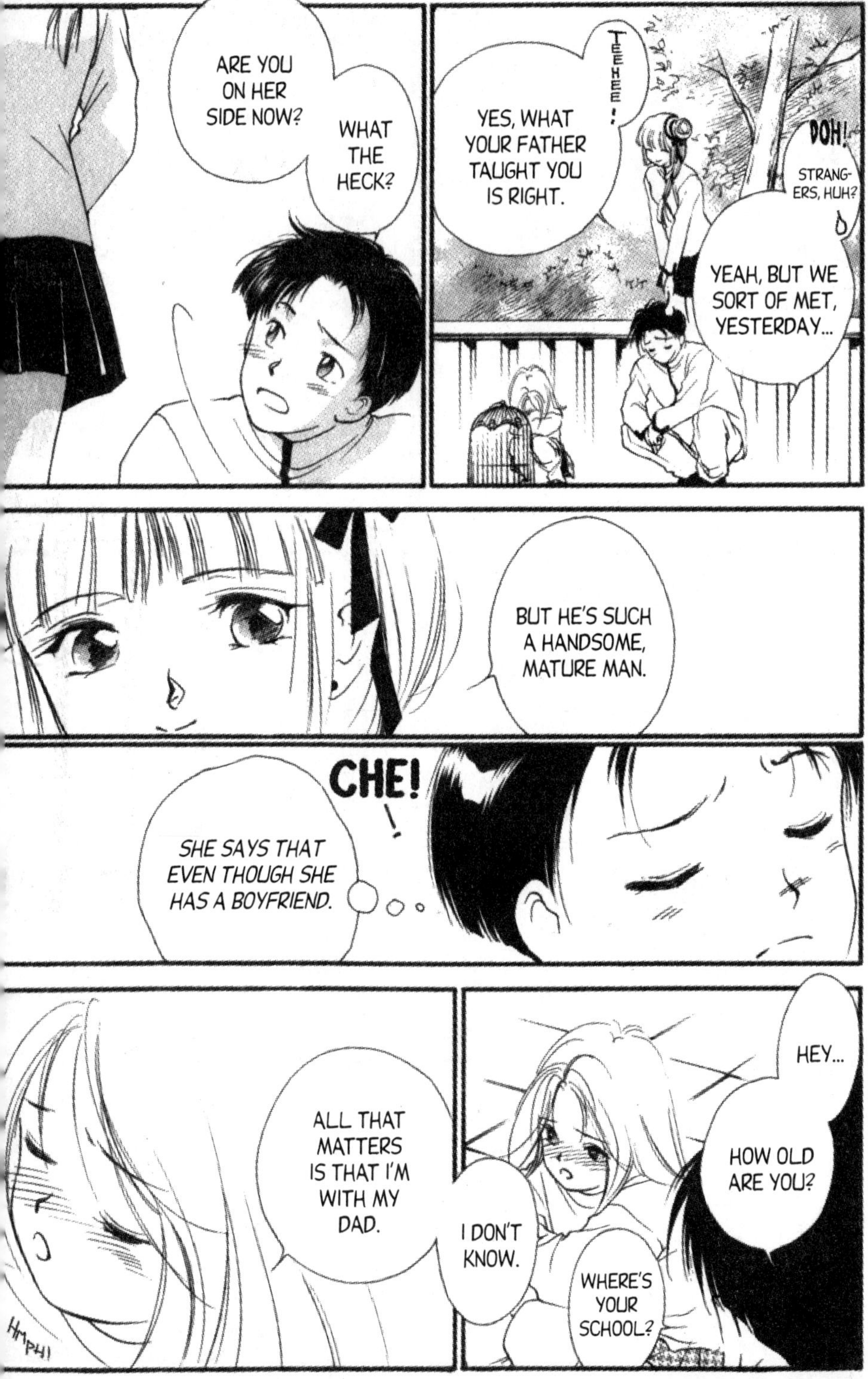
DOH!
STRANGERS, HUH?
YEAH, BUT WE SORT OF MET, YESTERDAY...
TEEHEE!
YES, WHAT YOUR FATHER TAUGHT YOU IS RIGHT.
ARE YOU ON HER SIDE NOW?
WHAT THE HECK?
BUT HE'S SUCH A HANDSOME, MATURE MAN.
CHE!
SHE SAYS THAT EVEN THOUGH SHE HAS A BOYFRIEND.
HEY...
HOW OLD ARE YOU?
WHERE'S YOUR SCHOOL?
I DON'T KNOW.
ALL THAT MATTERS IS THAT I'M WITH MY DAD.
HMPH!

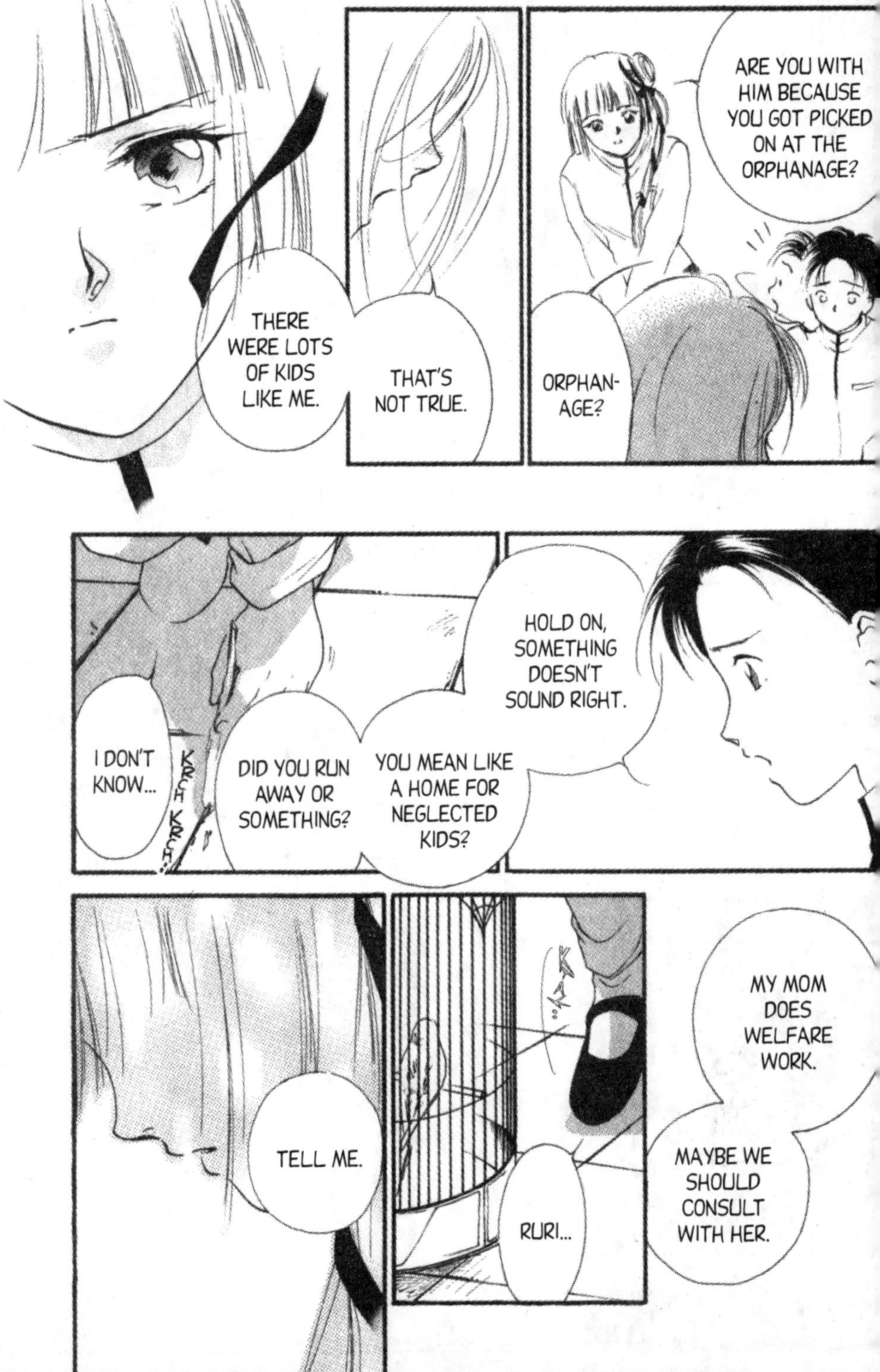
ARE YOU WITH HIM BECAUSE YOU GOT PICKED ON AT THE ORPHANAGE?
ORPHAN-AGE?
THAT'S NOT TRUE.
THERE WERE LOTS OF KIDS LIKE ME.
HOLD ON, SOMETHING DOESN'T SOUND RIGHT.
YOU MEAN LIKE A HOME FOR NEGLECTED KIDS?
DID YOU RUN AWAY OR SOMETHING?
KRCH KRCH...
I DON'T KNOW...
MY MOM DOES WELFARE WORK.
MAYBE WE SHOULD CONSULT WITH HER.
RURI...
TELL ME.

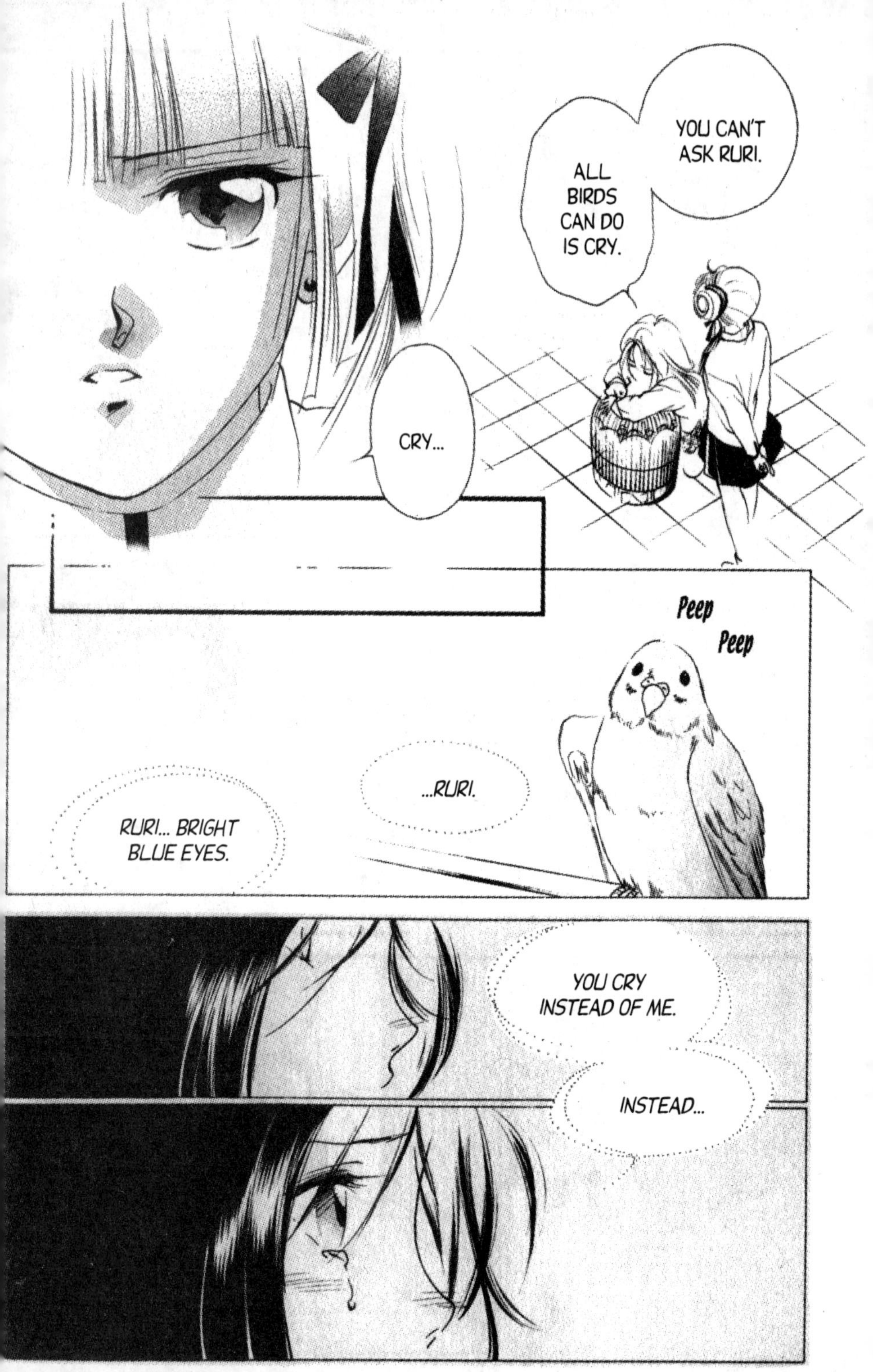
YOU CAN'T ASK RURI.
ALL BIRDS CAN DO IS CRY.
CRY...
Peep
Peep
...RURI.
RURI... BRIGHT BLUE EYES.
YOU CRY INSTEAD OF ME.
INSTEAD...

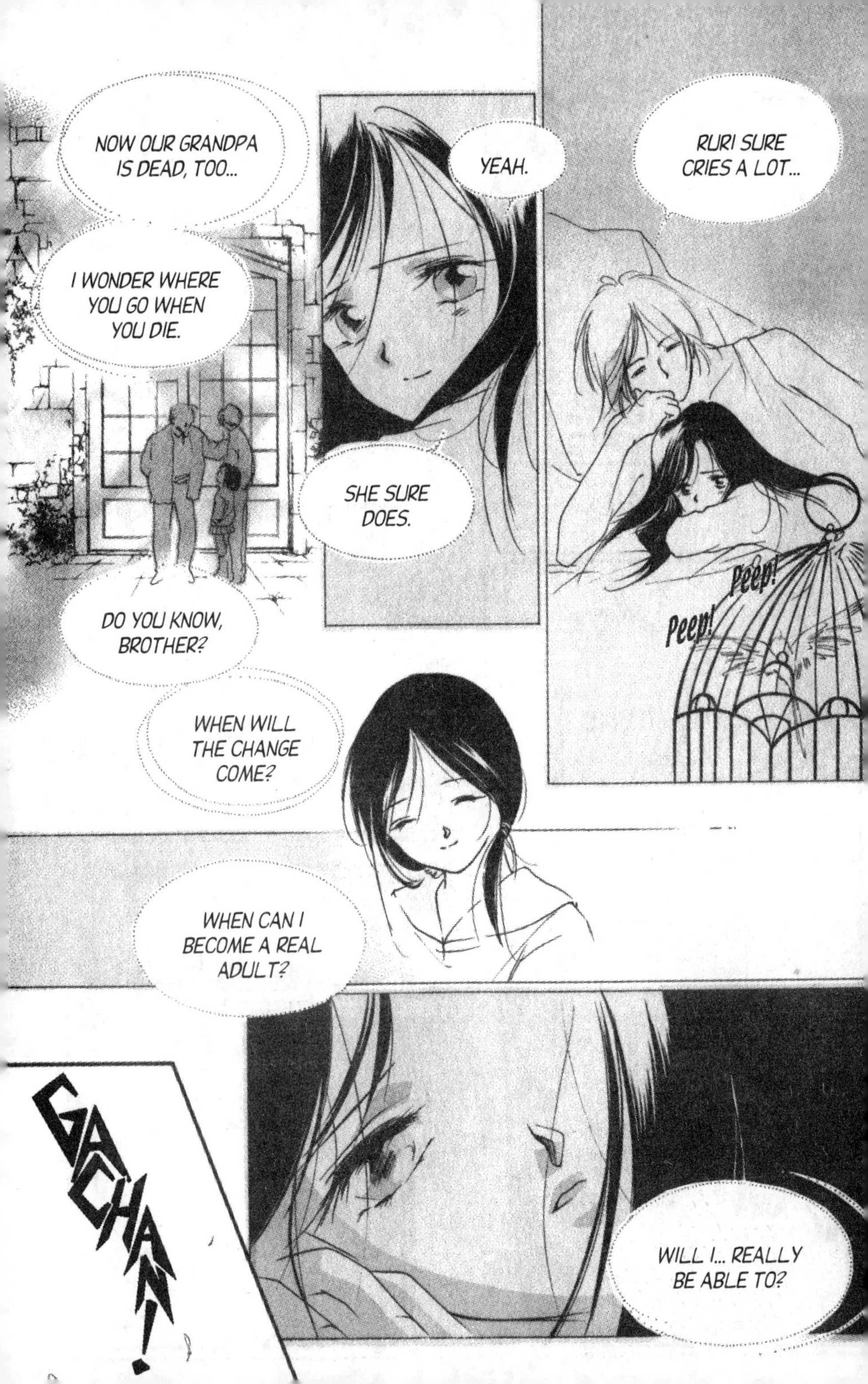
RURI SURE CRIES A LOT...
Peep!
Peep!
YEAH.
SHE SURE DOES.
NOW OUR GRANDPA IS DEAD, TOO...
I WONDER WHERE YOU GO WHEN YOU DIE.
DO YOU KNOW, BROTHER?
WHEN WILL THE CHANGE COME?
WHEN CAN I BECOME A REAL ADULT?
WILL I... REALLY BE ABLE TO?
GACHAN!

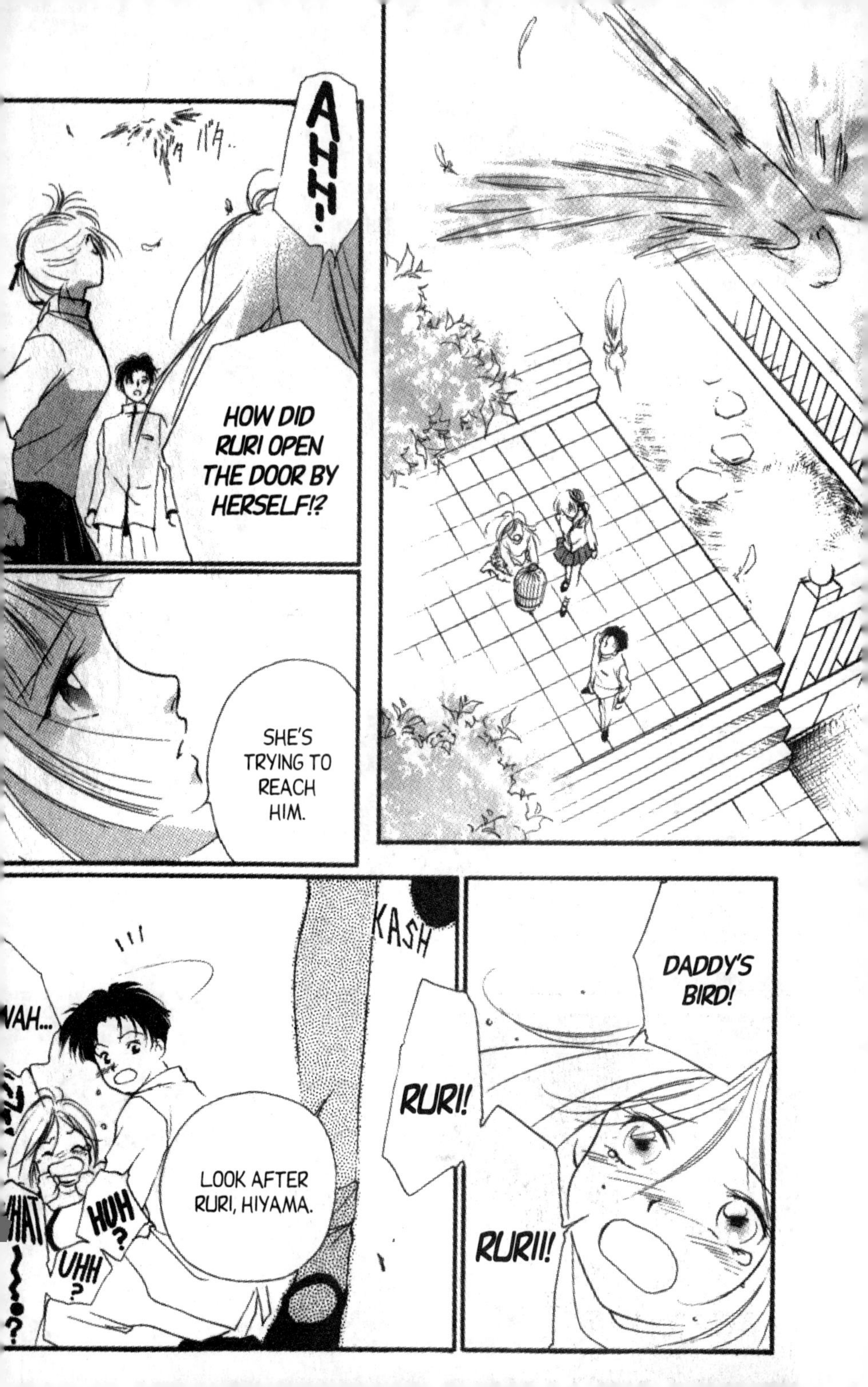
AHH!
HOW DID RURI OPEN THE DOOR BY HERSELF!?
SHE'S TRYING TO REACH HIM.
DADDY'S BIRD!
RURI!
RURII!
KASH
LOOK AFTER RURI, HIYAMA.
HUH?
UHH?
WAH...

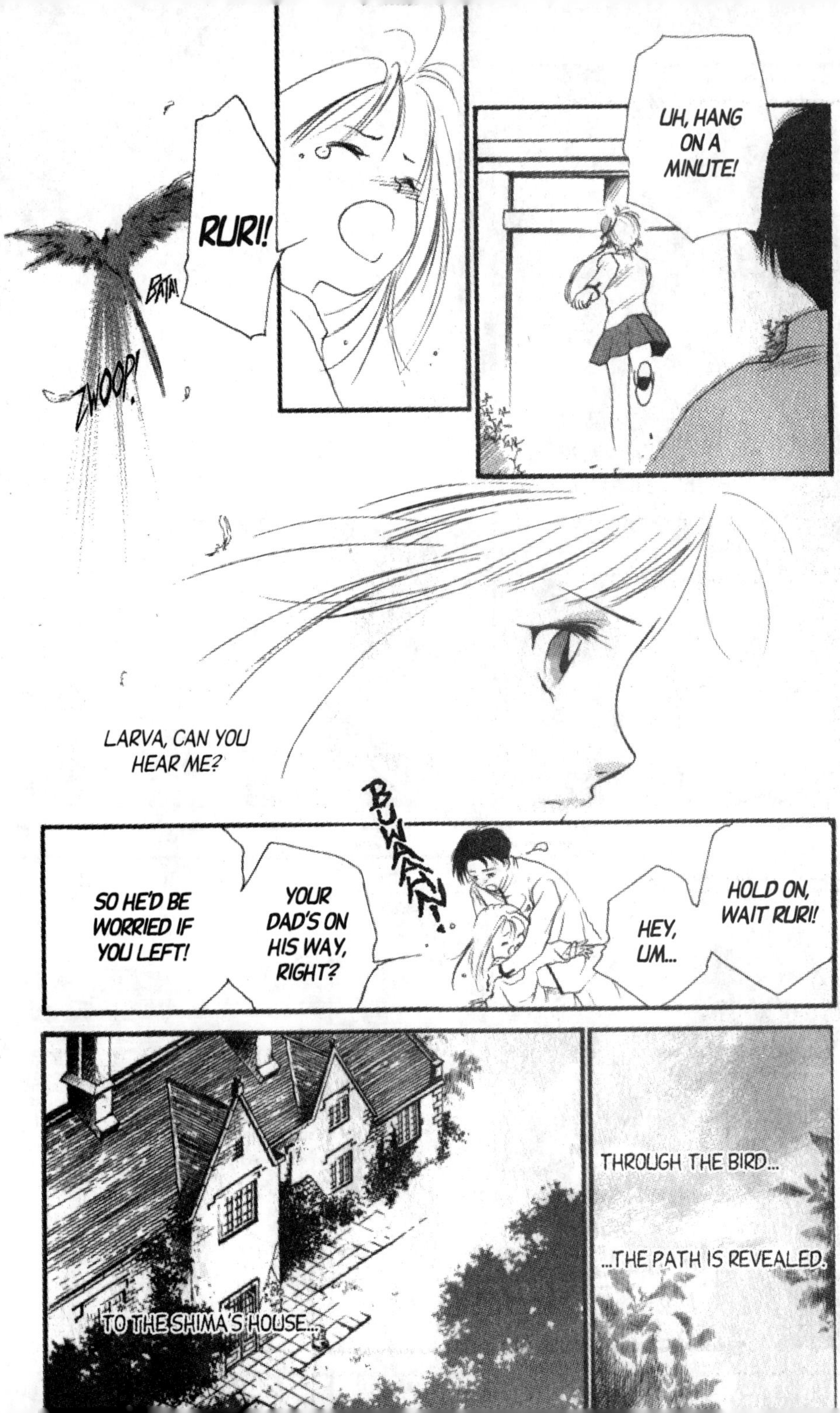
UH, HANG ON A MINUTE!
RURI!
BATA!
ZWOOP!
LARVA, CAN YOU HEAR ME?
BUWAAN!
HOLD ON, WAIT RURI!
HEY, UM...
YOUR DAD'S ON HIS WAY, RIGHT?
SO HE'D BE WORRIED IF YOU LEFT!
THROUGH THE BIRD...
...THE PATH IS REVEALED.
TO THE SHIMA'S HOUSE...

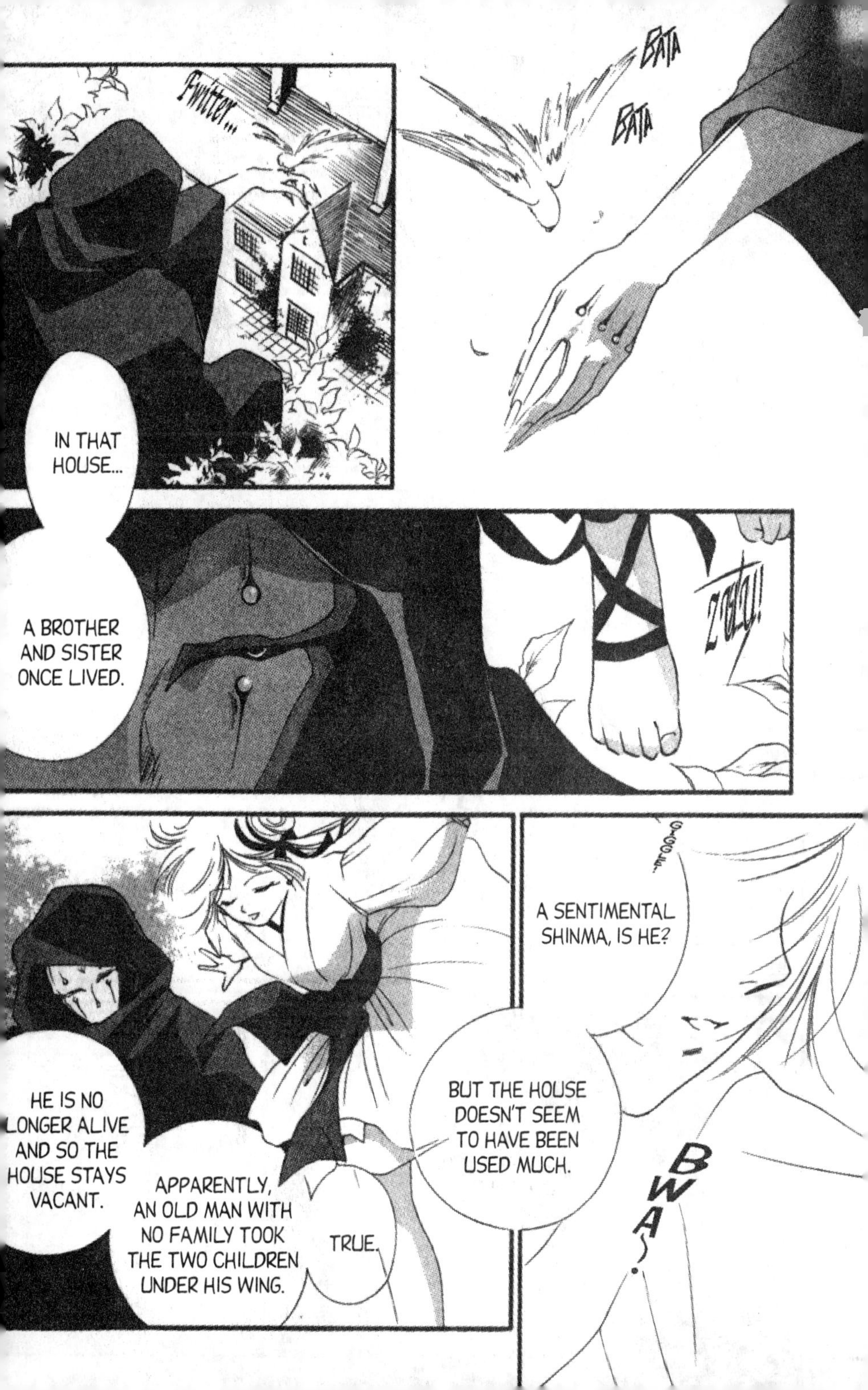
BATA
BATA
Twitter...
IN THAT HOUSE...
A BROTHER AND SISTER ONCE LIVED.
A SENTIMENTAL SHINMA, IS HE?
BUT THE HOUSE DOESN'T SEEM TO HAVE BEEN USED MUCH.
BWA~.
HE IS NO LONGER ALIVE AND SO THE HOUSE STAYS VACANT.
APPARENTLY, AN OLD MAN WITH NO FAMILY TOOK THE TWO CHILDREN UNDER HIS WING.
TRUE.

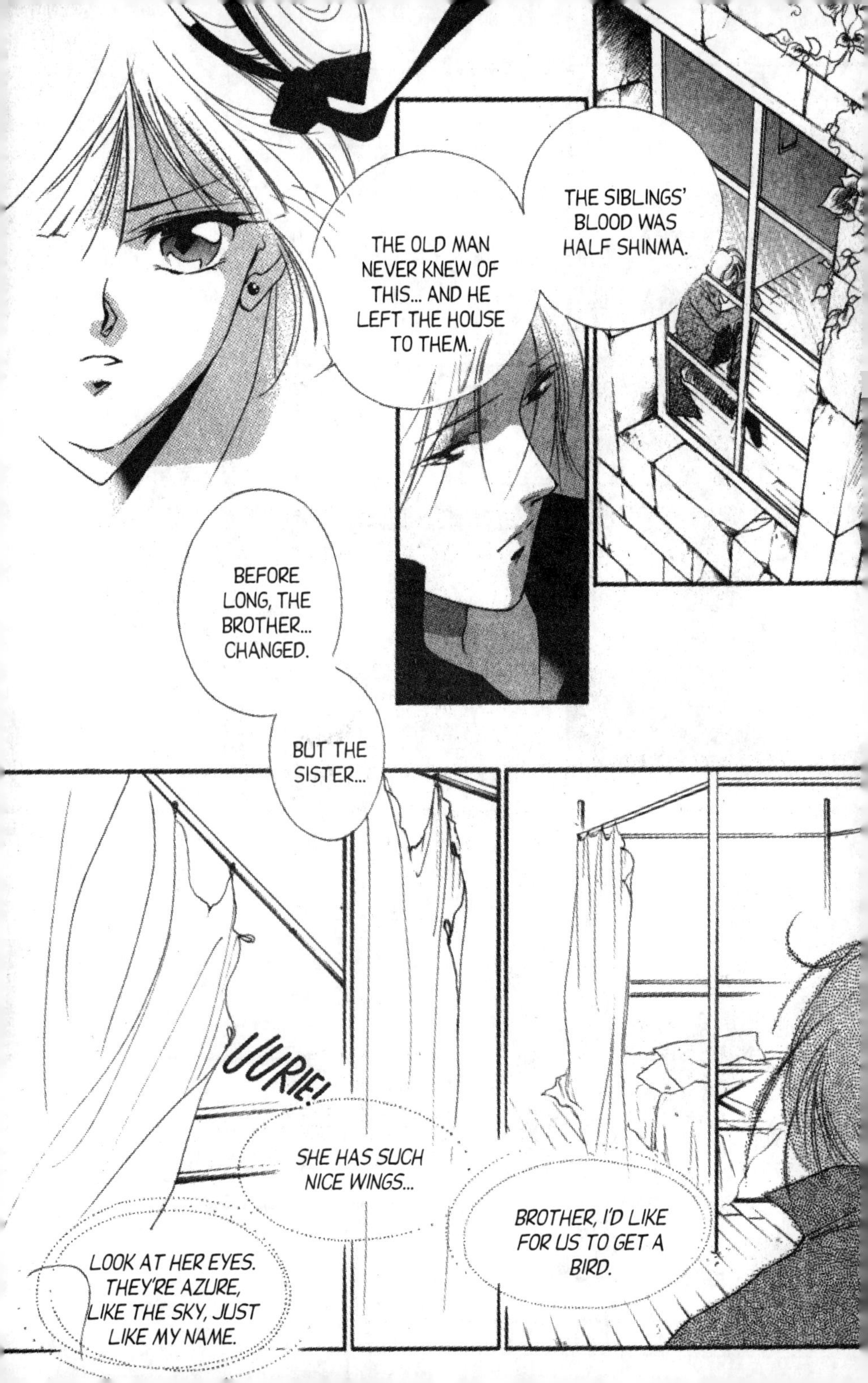
THE SIBLINGS' BLOOD WAS HALF SHINMA.
THE OLD MAN NEVER KNEW OF THIS... AND HE LEFT THE HOUSE TO THEM.
BEFORE LONG, THE BROTHER... CHANGED.
BUT THE SISTER...
BROTHER, I'D LIKE FOR US TO GET A BIRD.
SHE HAS SUCH NICE WINGS...
UURIE!
LOOK AT HER EYES. THEY'RE AZURE, LIKE THE SKY, JUST LIKE MY NAME.

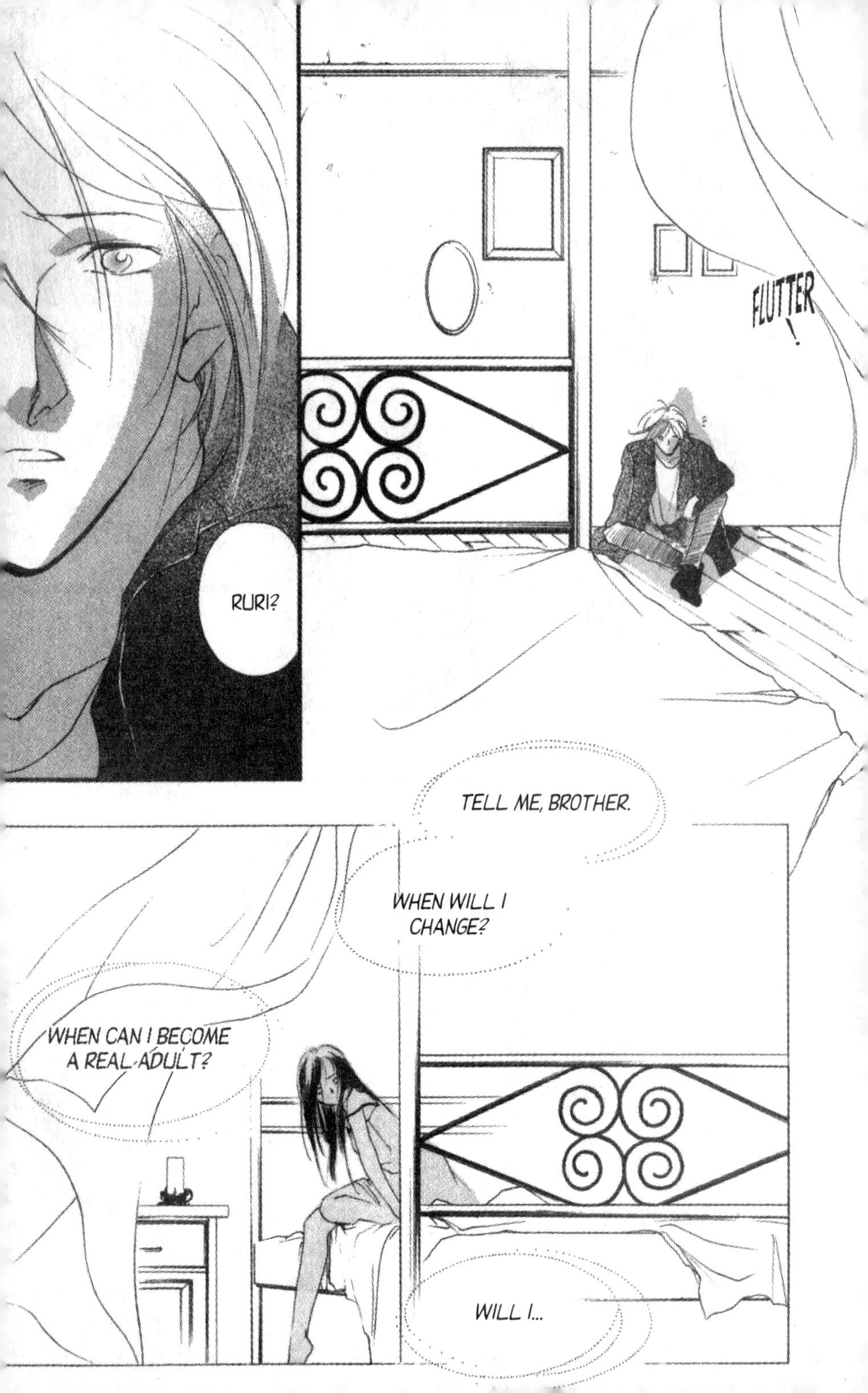
FLUTTER!
RURI?
TELL ME, BROTHER.
WHEN WILL I CHANGE?
WHEN CAN I BECOME A REAL ADULT?
WILL I...

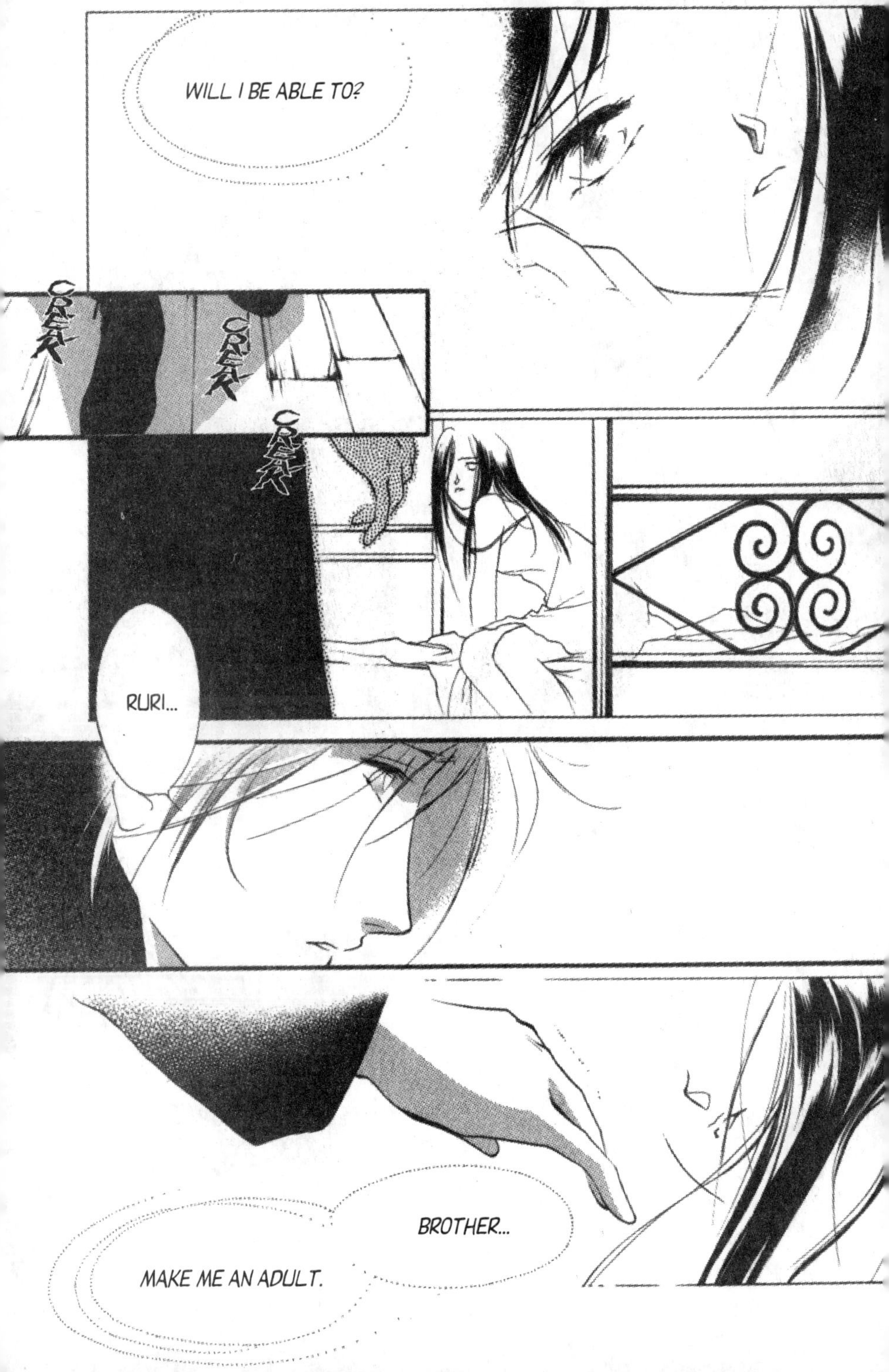
WILL I BE ABLE TO?
CREAK
CREAK
CREAK
RURI...
BROTHER...
MAKE ME AN ADULT.

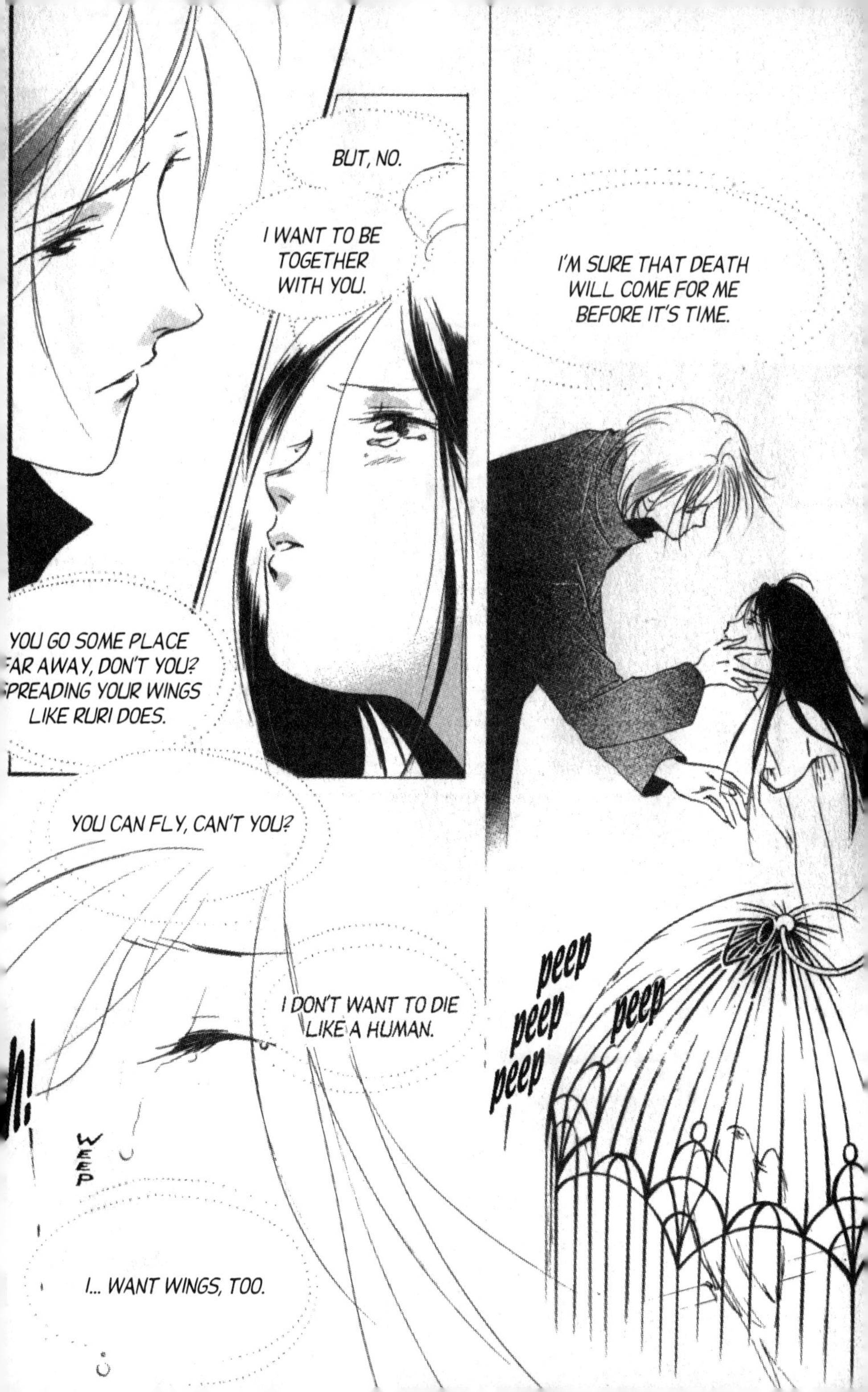
I'M SURE THAT DEATH WILL COME FOR ME BEFORE IT'S TIME.
peep peep peep peep
BUT, NO.
I WANT TO BE TOGETHER WITH YOU.
YOU GO SOME PLACE FAR AWAY, DON'T YOU? SPREADING YOUR WINGS LIKE RURI DOES.
YOU CAN FLY, CAN'T YOU?
I DON'T WANT TO DIE LIKE A HUMAN.
WEEP
I... WANT WINGS, TOO.

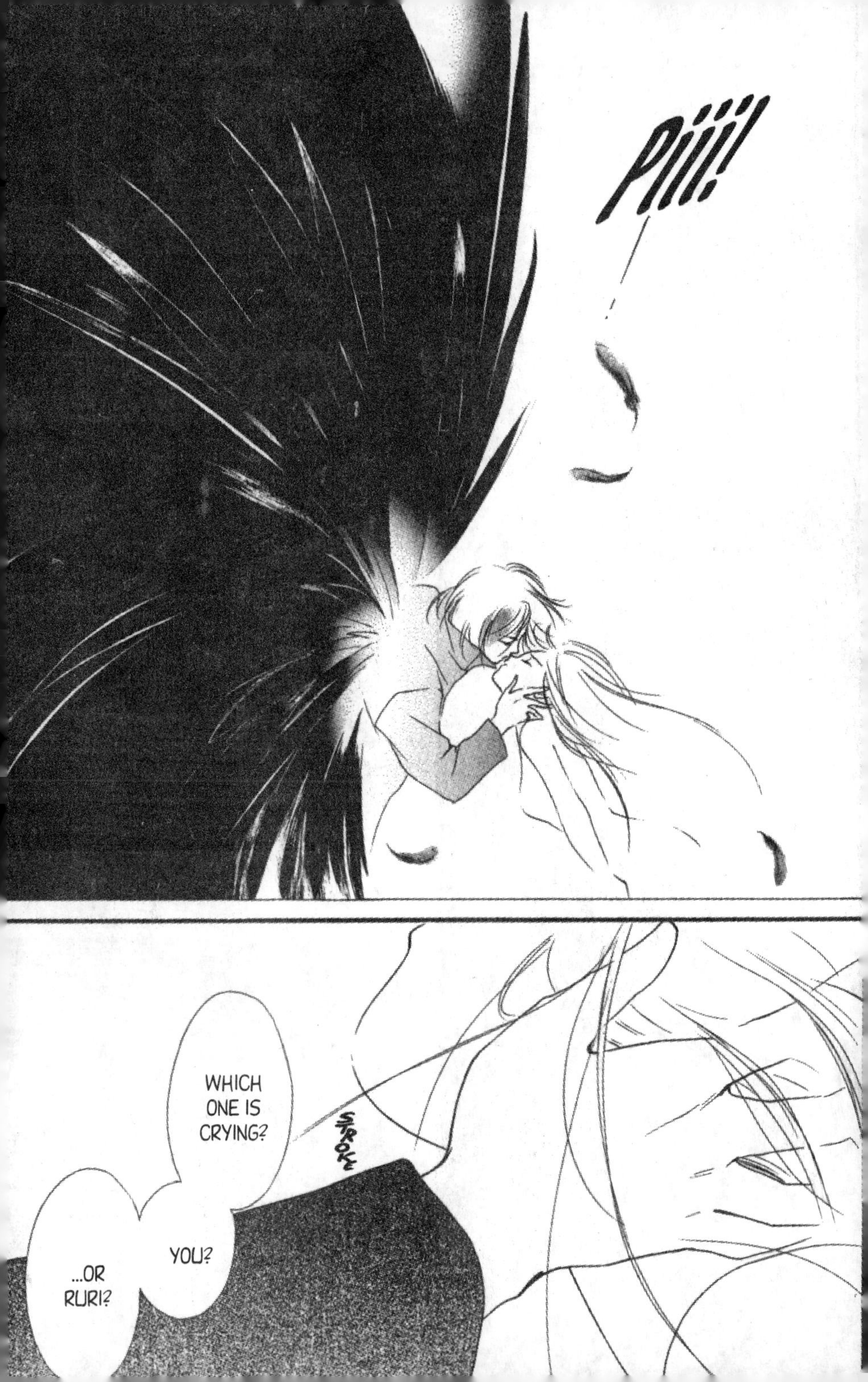
Piii!
STROKE
WHICH ONE IS CRYING?
YOU?
...OR RURI?

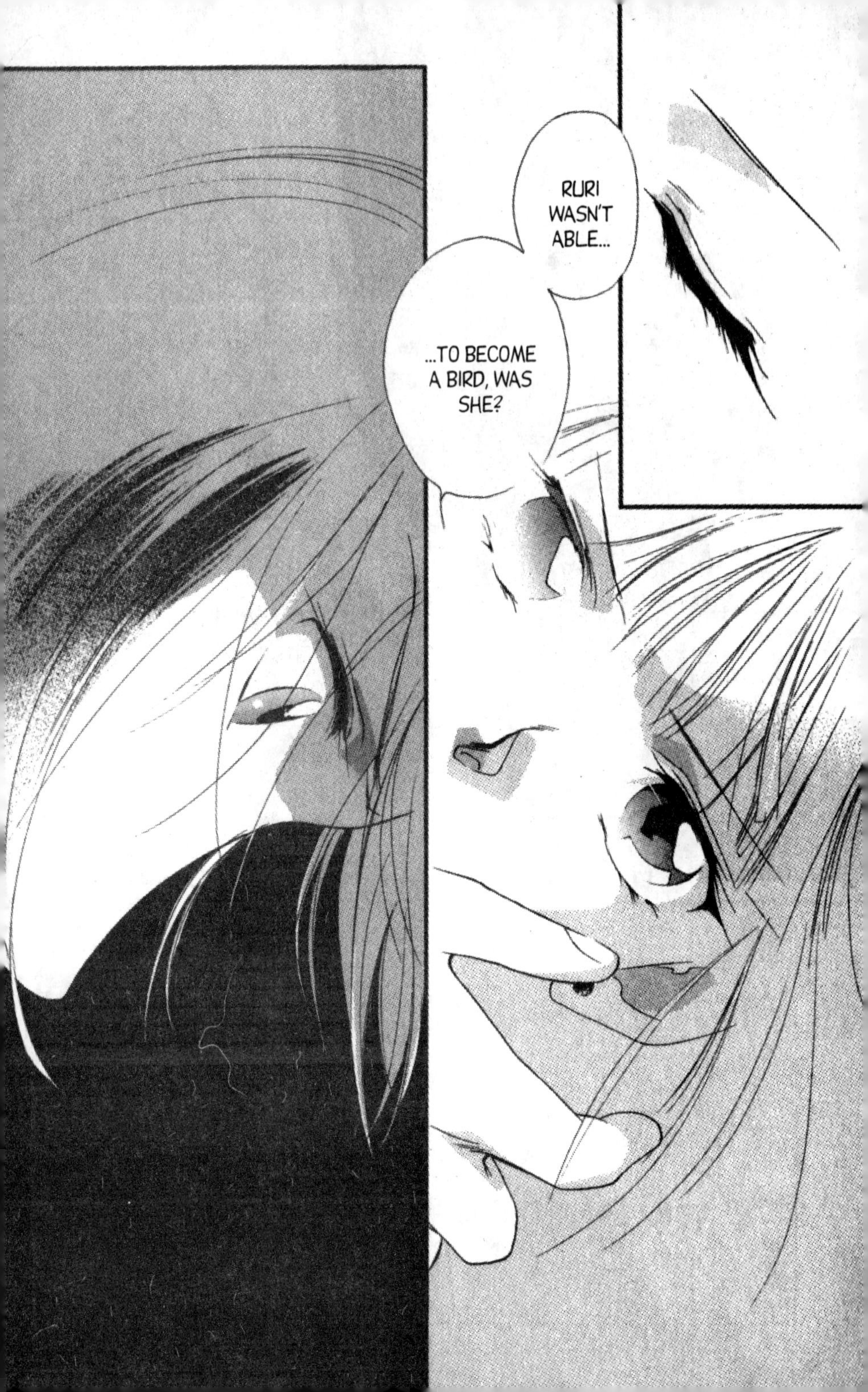
RURI WASN'T ABLE...
...TO BECOME A BIRD, WAS SHE?

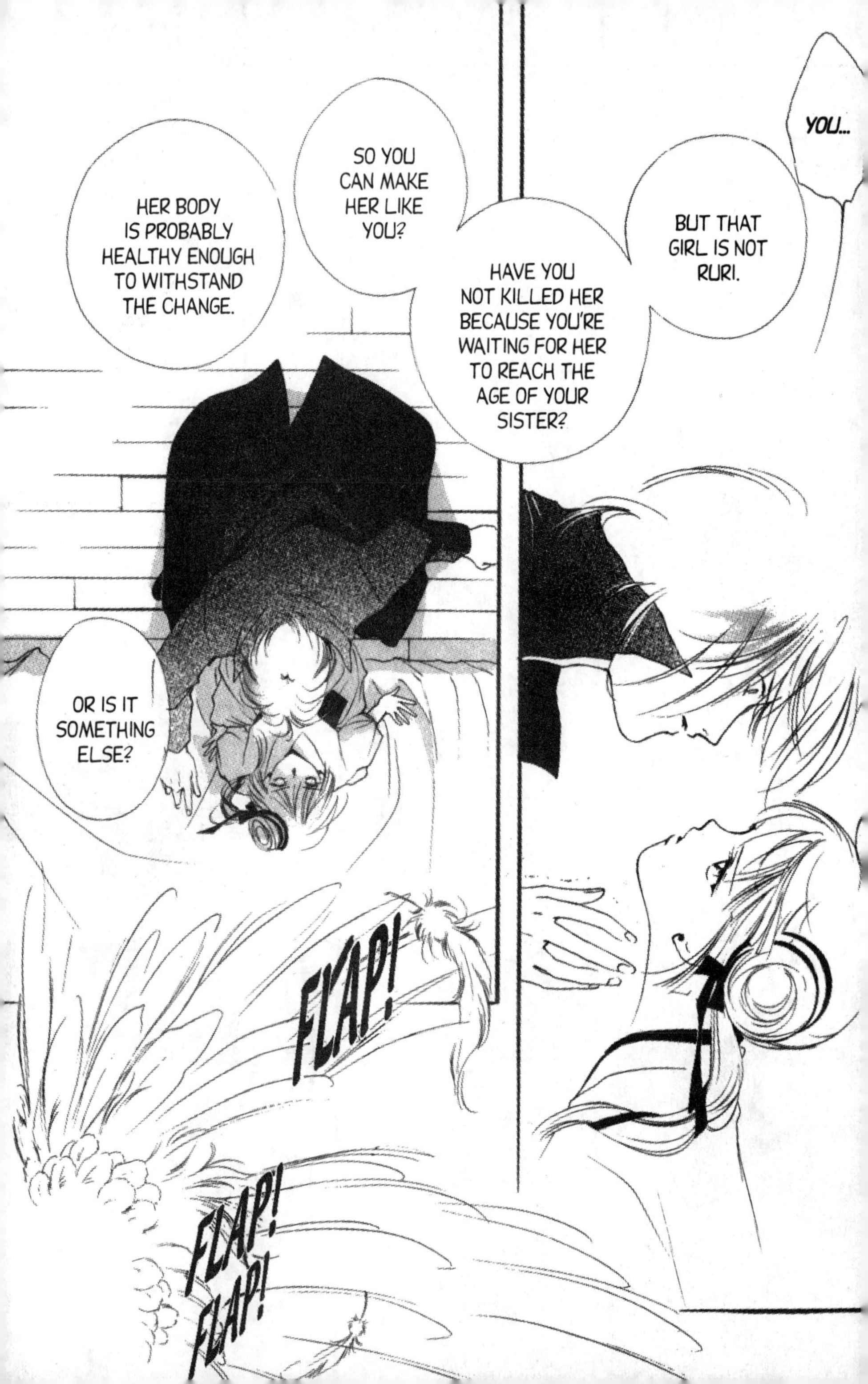
YOU...
BUT THAT GIRL IS NOT RURI.
HAVE YOU NOT KILLED HER BECAUSE YOU'RE WAITING FOR HER TO REACH THE AGE OF YOUR SISTER?
SO YOU CAN MAKE HER LIKE YOU?
HER BODY IS PROBABLY HEALTHY ENOUGH TO WITHSTAND THE CHANGE.
OR IS IT SOMETHING ELSE?
FLAP!
FLAP! FLAP!

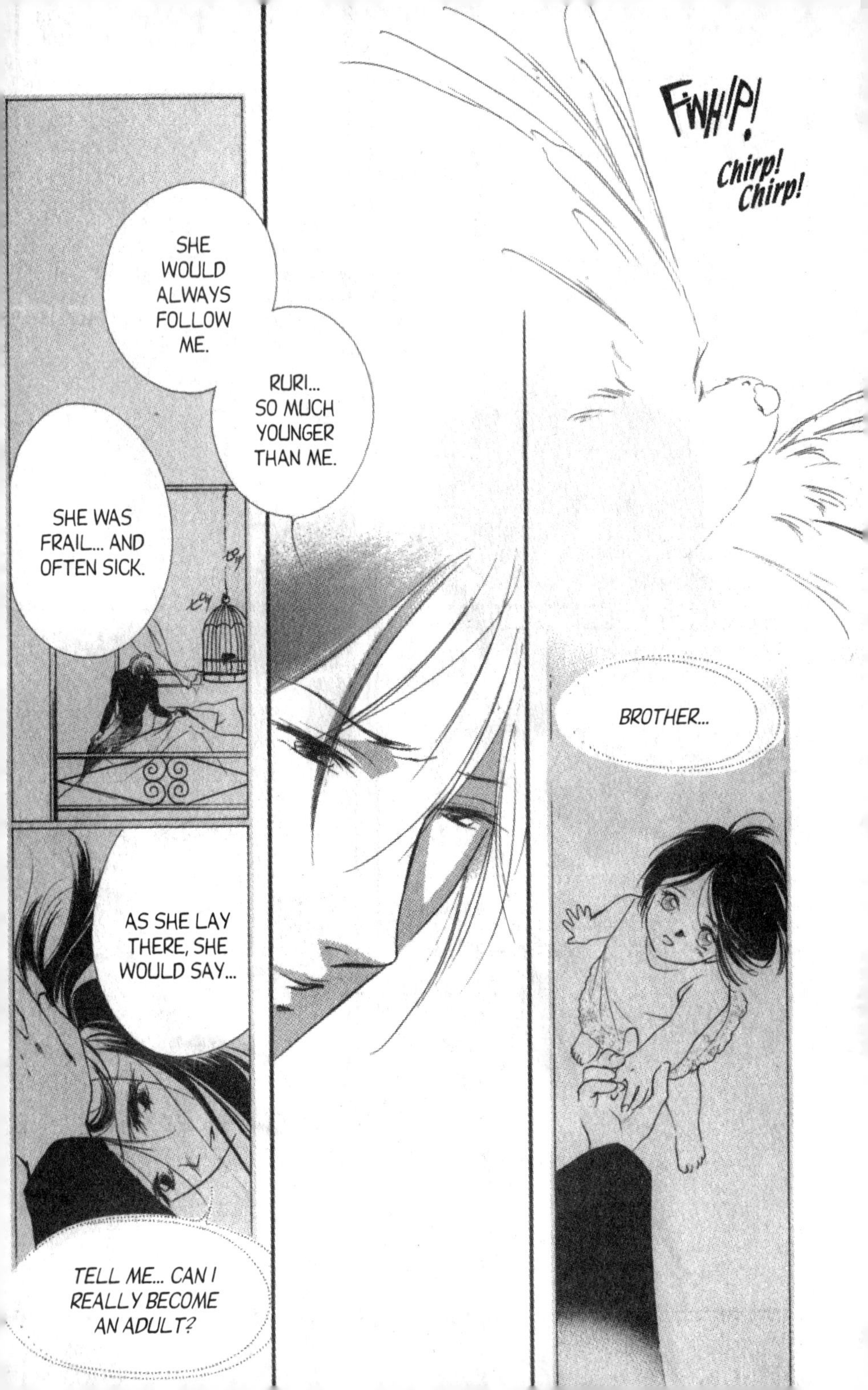
FWHIP!
Chirp! Chirp!
BROTHER...
SHE WOULD ALWAYS FOLLOW ME.
RURI... SO MUCH YOUNGER THAN ME.
SHE WAS FRAIL... AND OFTEN SICK.
AS SHE LAY THERE, SHE WOULD SAY...
TELL ME... CAN I REALLY BECOME AN ADULT?

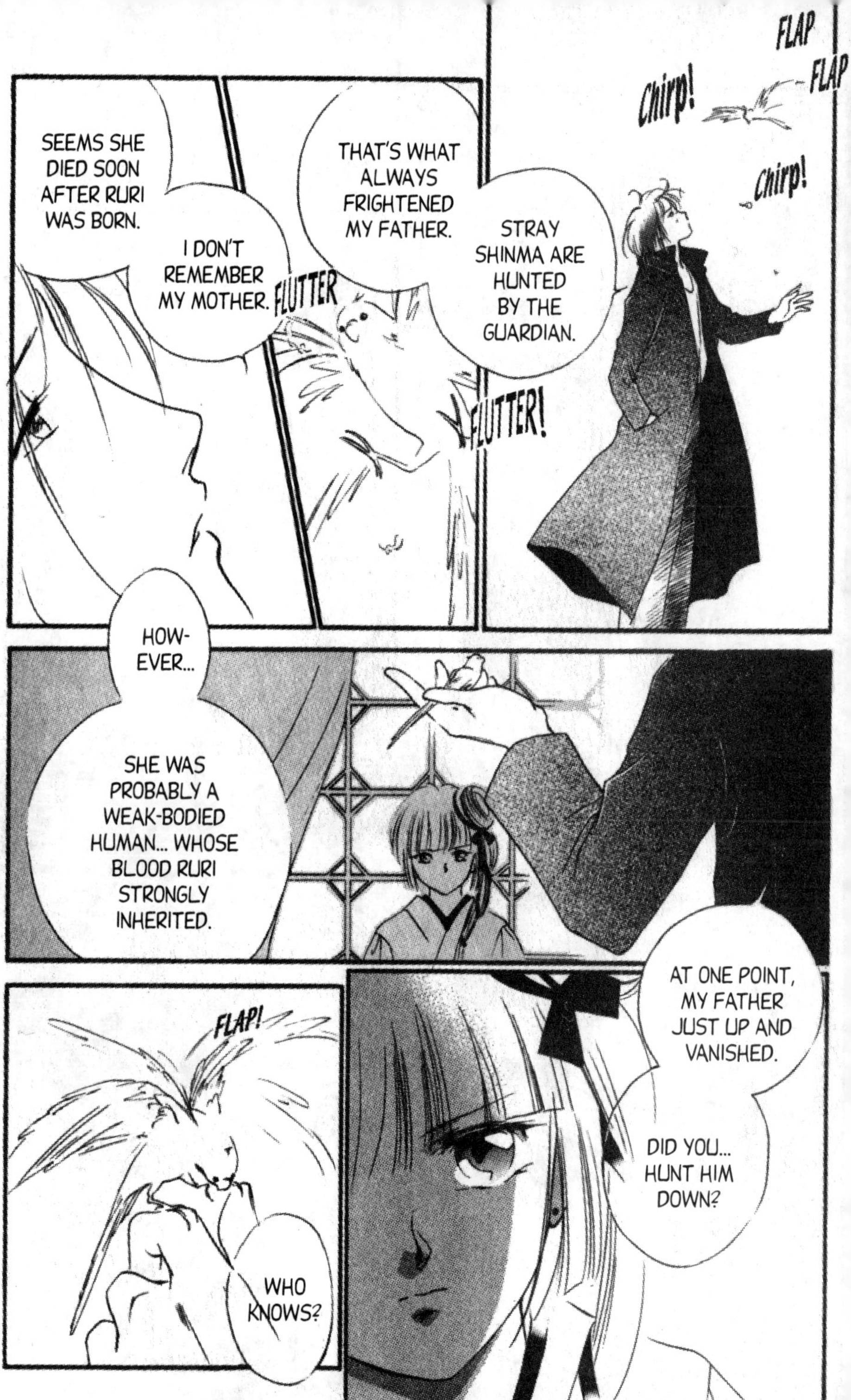
FLAP
FLAP
Chirp!
Chirp!
STRAY SHINMA ARE HUNTED BY THE GUARDIAN.
THAT'S WHAT ALWAYS FRIGHTENED MY FATHER.
FLUTTER!
FLUTTER
SEEMS SHE DIED SOON AFTER RURI WAS BORN.
I DON'T REMEMBER MY MOTHER.
HOW-EVER...
SHE WAS PROBABLY A WEAK-BODIED HUMAN... WHOSE BLOOD RURI STRONGLY INHERITED.
AT ONE POINT, MY FATHER JUST UP AND VANISHED.
DID YOU... HUNT HIM DOWN?
FLAP!
WHO KNOWS?

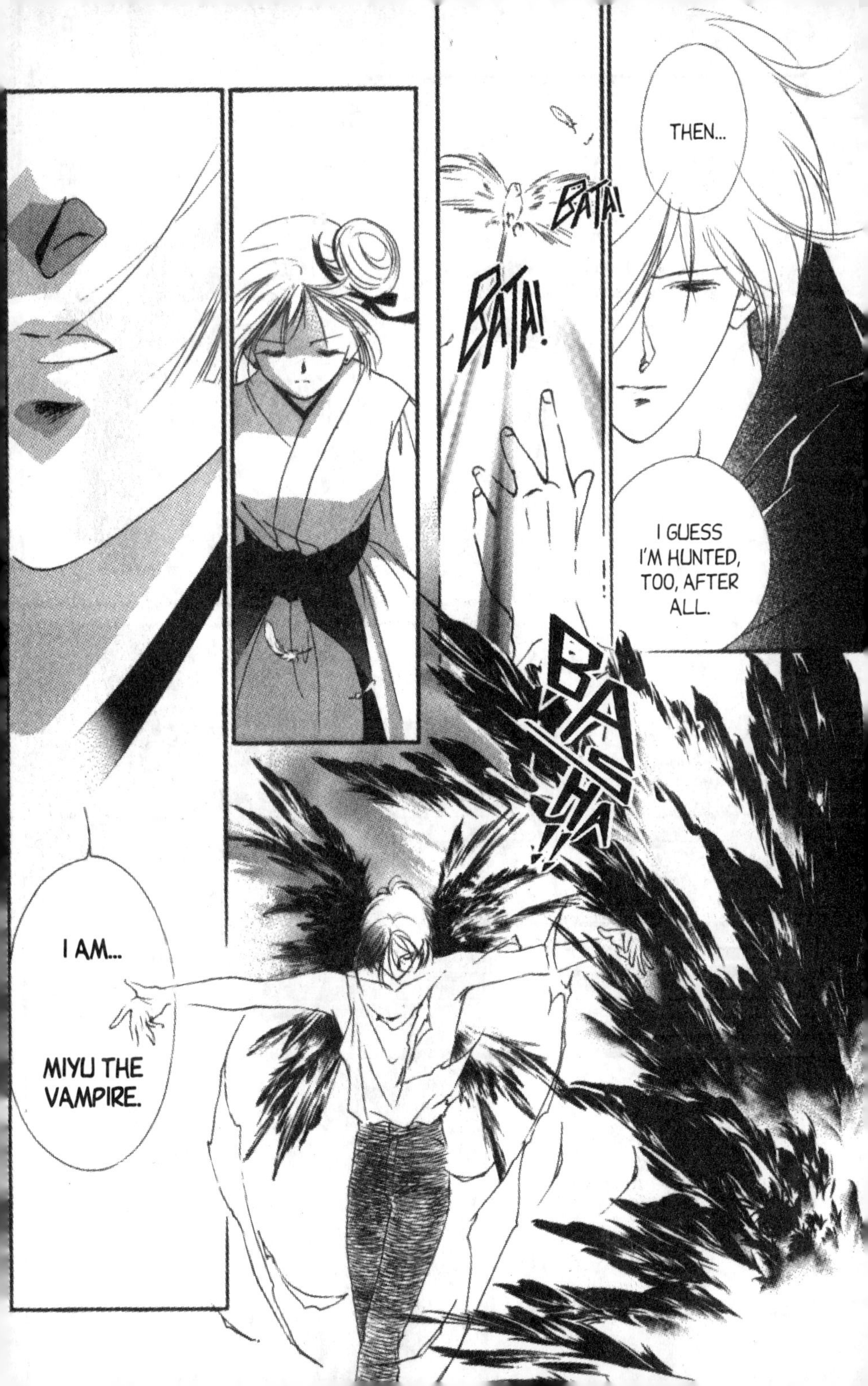
THEN...
I GUESS I'M HUNTED, TOO, AFTER ALL.
BATA!
BATA!
BASHA!!
I AM...
MIYU THE VAMPIRE.

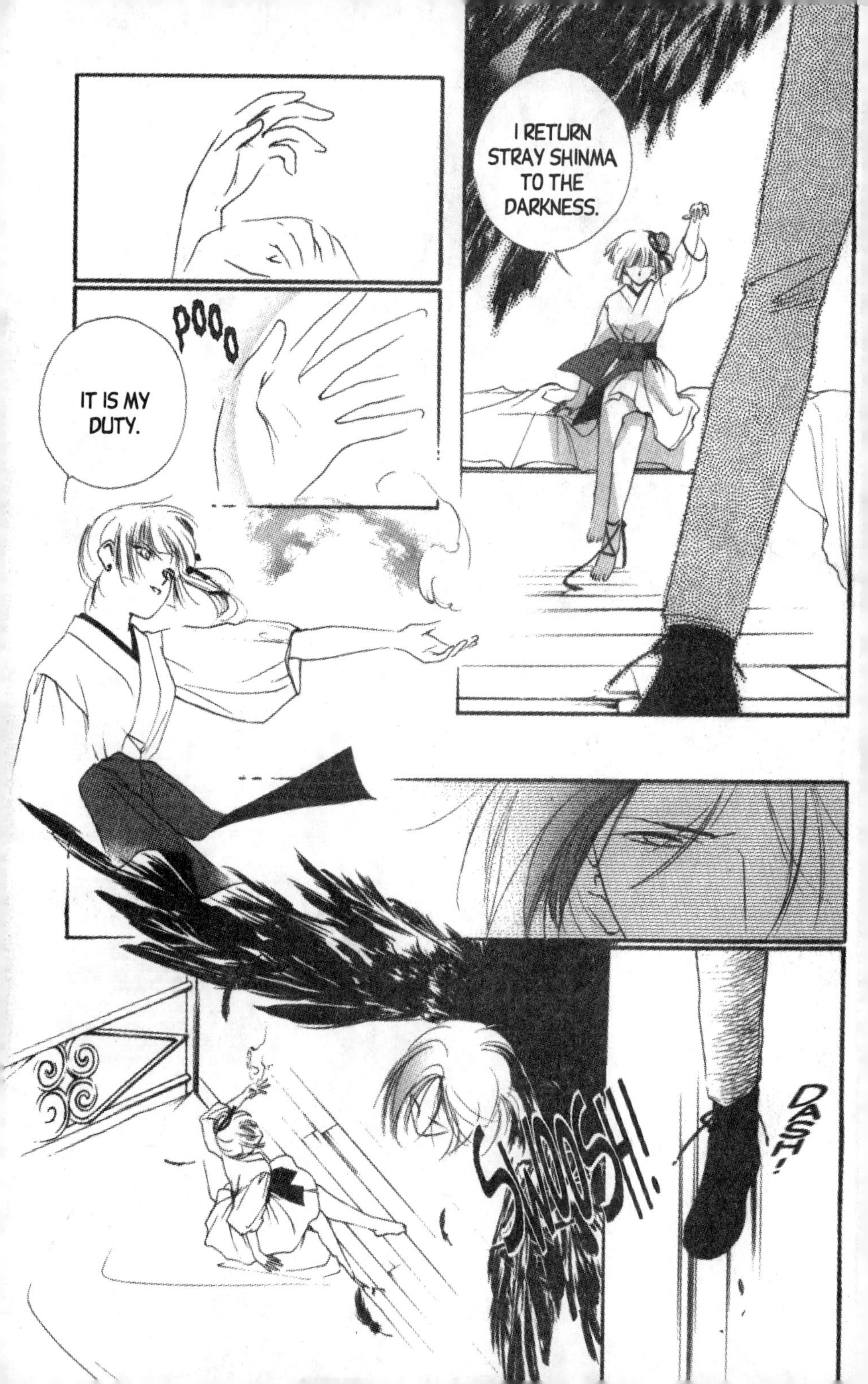
I RETURN STRAY SHINMA TO THE DARKNESS.
POOO
IT IS MY DUTY.
SHOOSH!!
CRUNT...

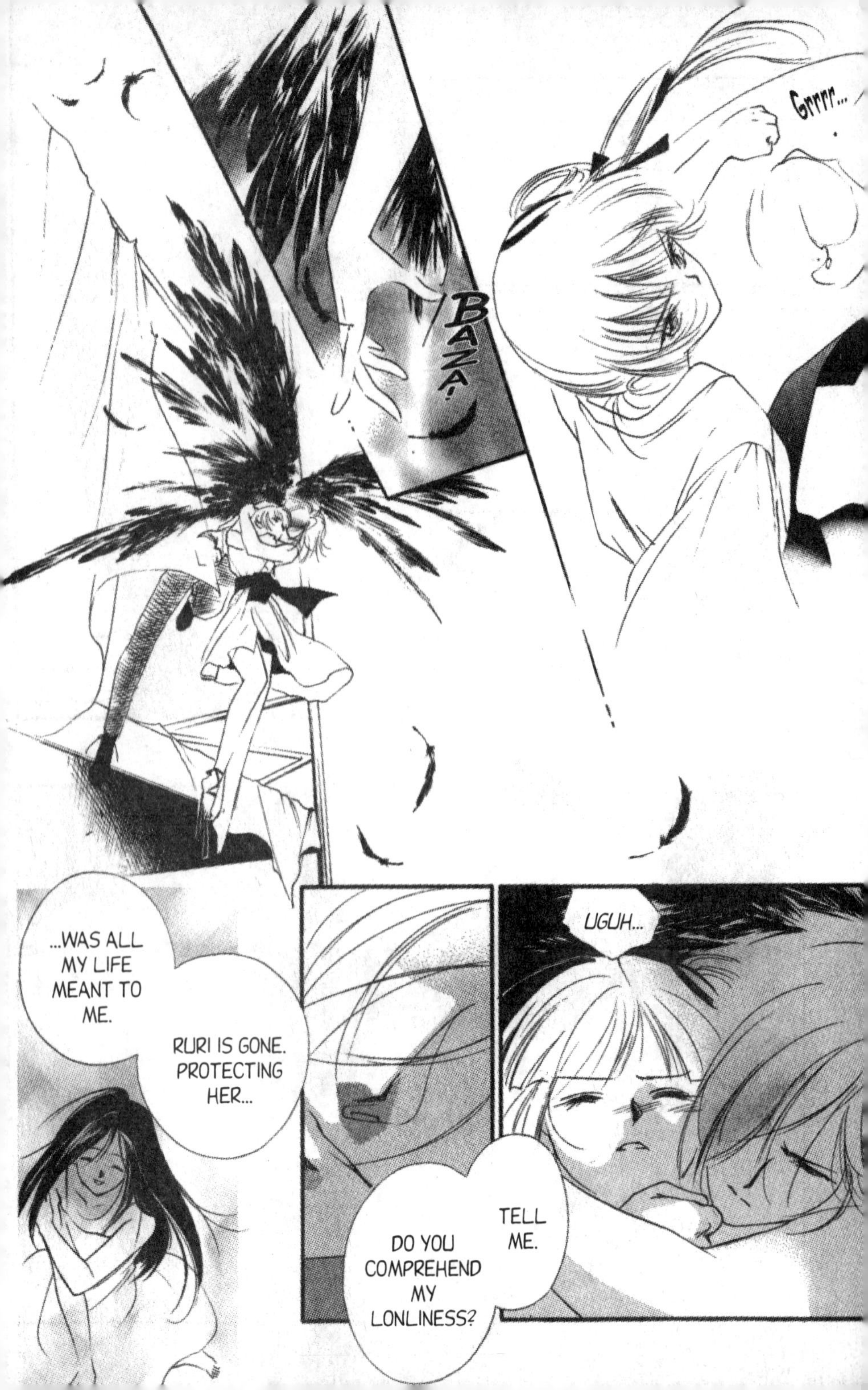
Grrrr...
BAZA!
UGUH...
TELL ME.
DO YOU COMPREHEND MY LONLINESS?
RURI IS GONE. PROTECTING HER...
...WAS ALL MY LIFE MEANT TO ME.

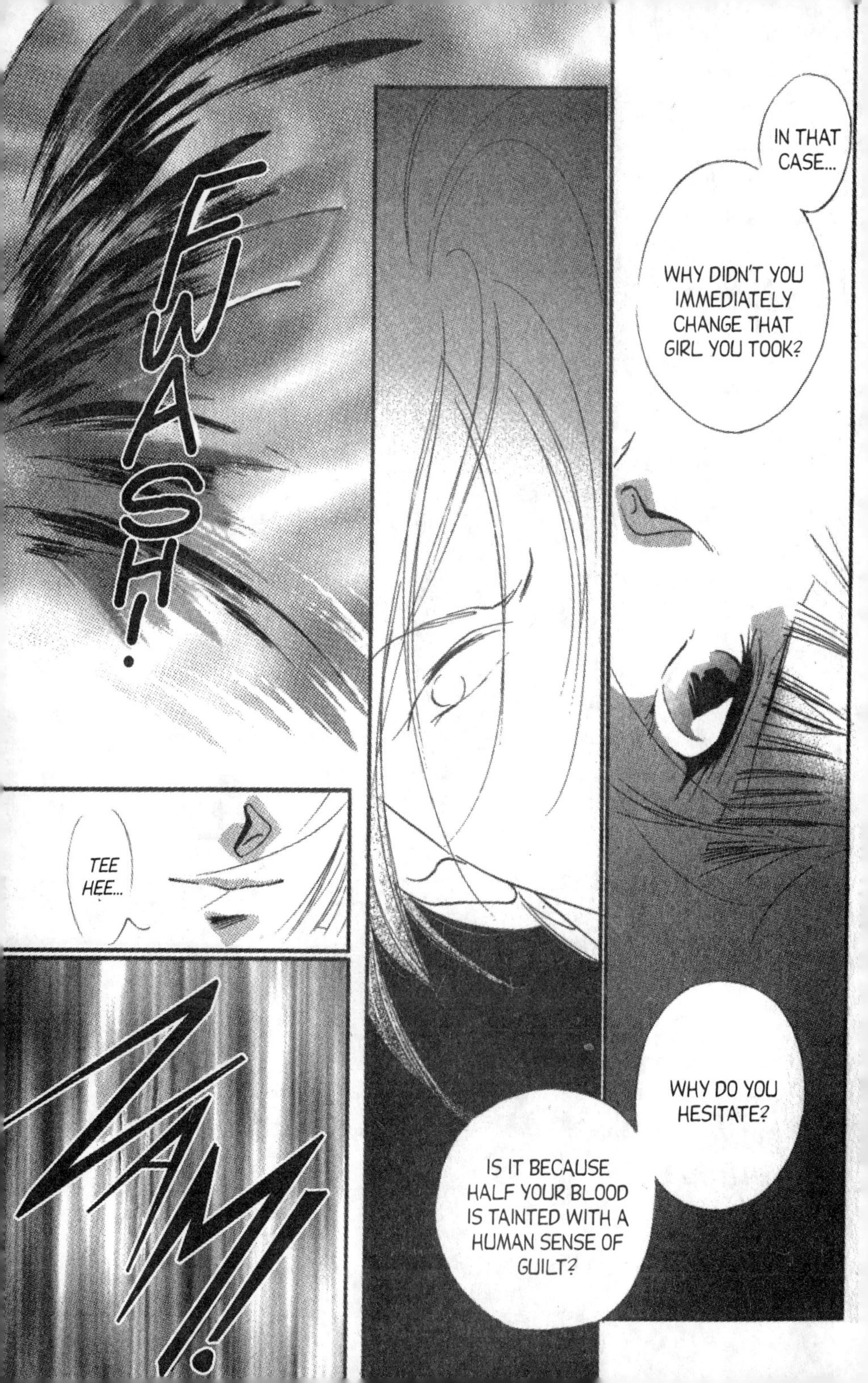
IN THAT CASE...
WHY DIDN'T YOU IMMEDIATELY CHANGE THAT GIRL YOU TOOK?
WHY DO YOU HESITATE?
IS IT BECAUSE HALF YOUR BLOOD IS TAINTED WITH A HUMAN SENSE OF GUILT?
FWASH!
TEE HEE...
ZAM!

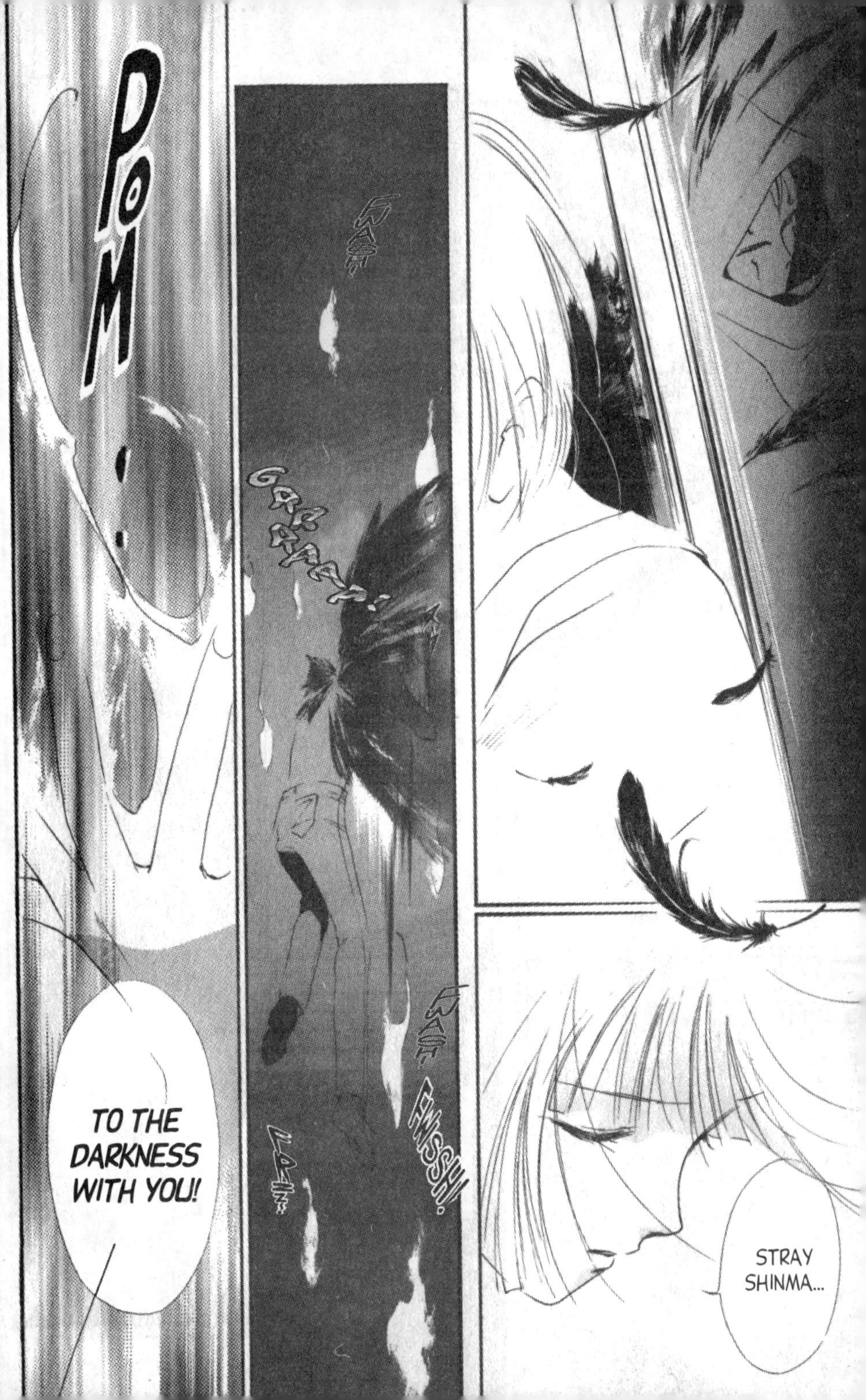
STRAY SHINMA...
FWOH!
GRRRAAAA!
FWOH!
FWISSH!
TO THE DARKNESS WITH YOU!
POM

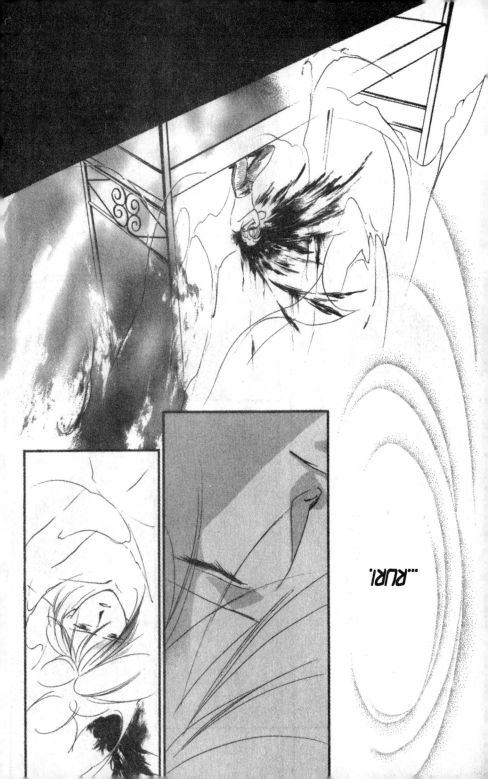

...RURI!

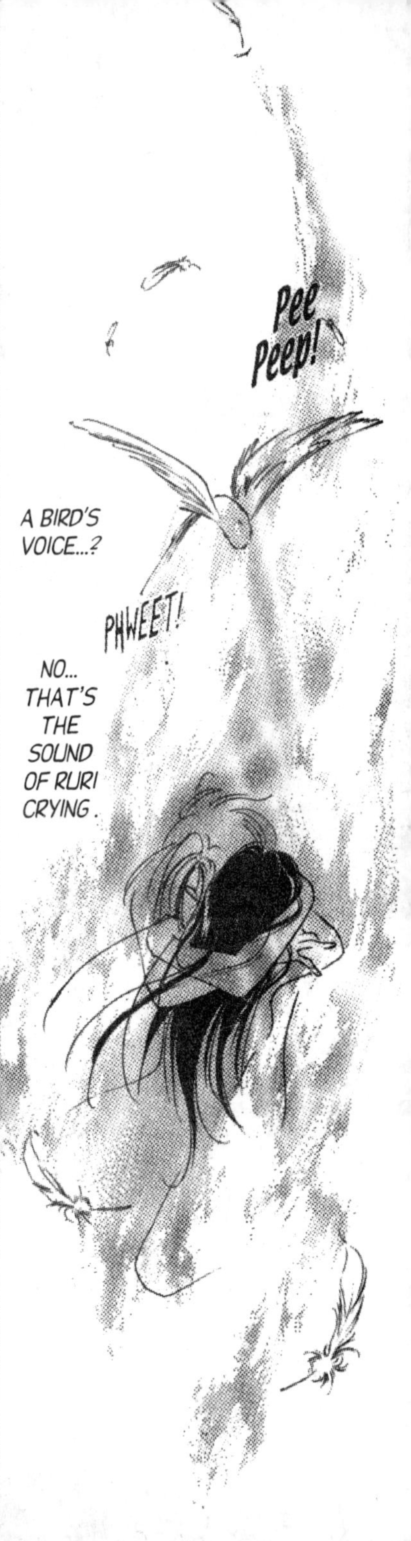
Pee Peep!
A BIRD'S VOICE...?
PHWEET!
NO... THAT'S THE SOUND OF RURI CRYING.
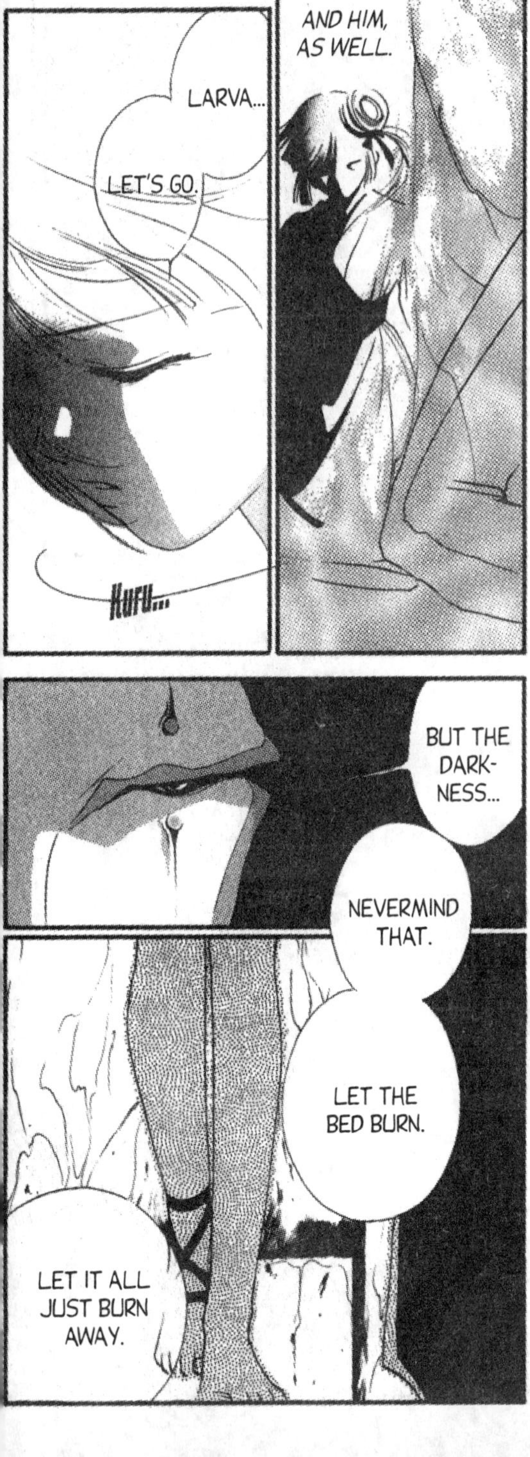
AND HIM, AS WELL.
LARVA...
LET'S GO.
Kuru...
BUT THE DARK-NESS...
NEVERMIND THAT.
LET THE BED BURN.
LET IT ALL JUST BURN AWAY.

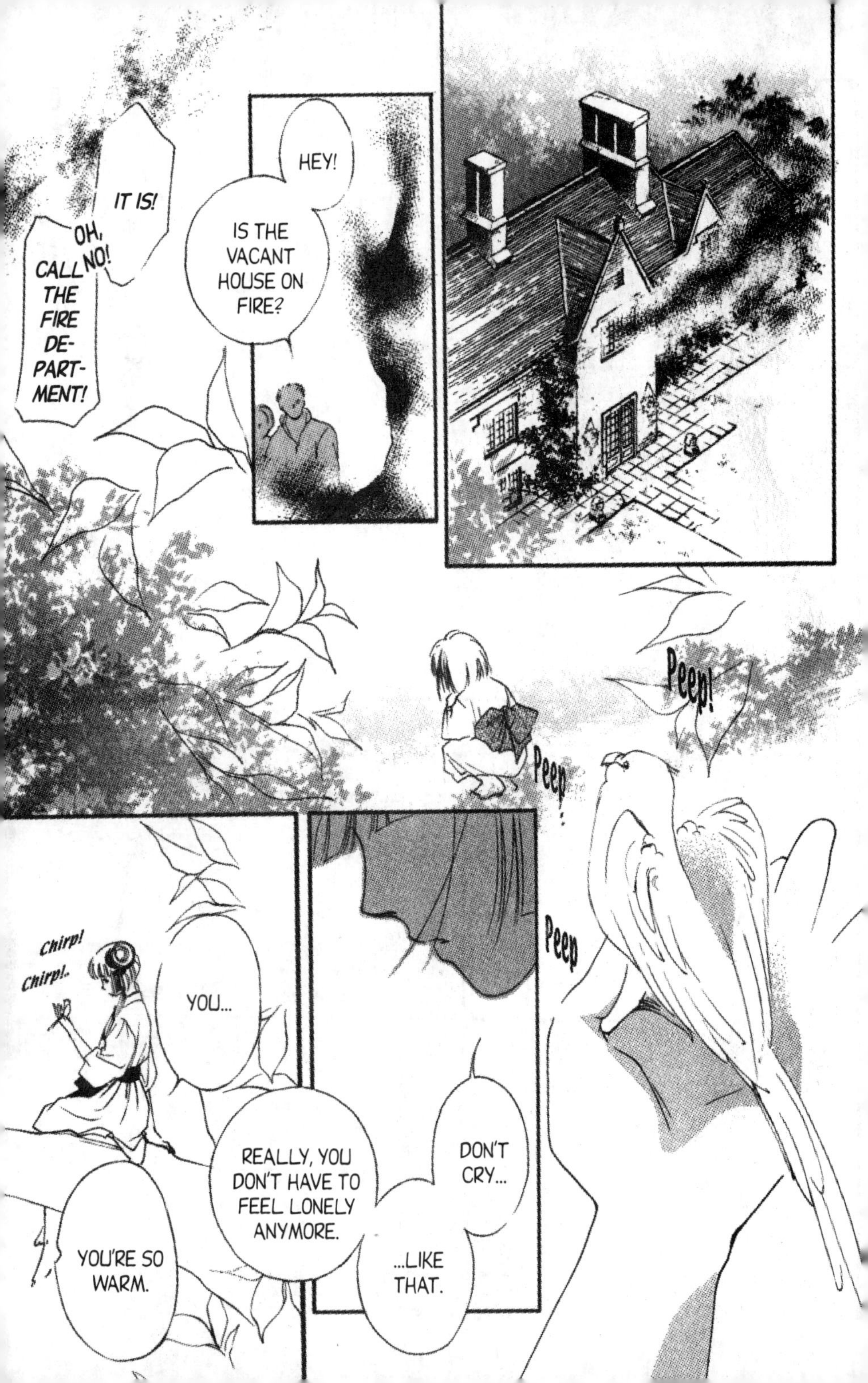
HEY!
IS THE VACANT HOUSE ON FIRE?
IT IS!
OH, NO!
CALL THE FIRE DE-PART-MENT!
Peep!
Peep
Peep
DON'T CRY...
...LIKE THAT.
REALLY, YOU DON'T HAVE TO FEEL LONELY ANYMORE.
Chirp!
Chirp!..
YOU...
YOU'RE SO WARM.

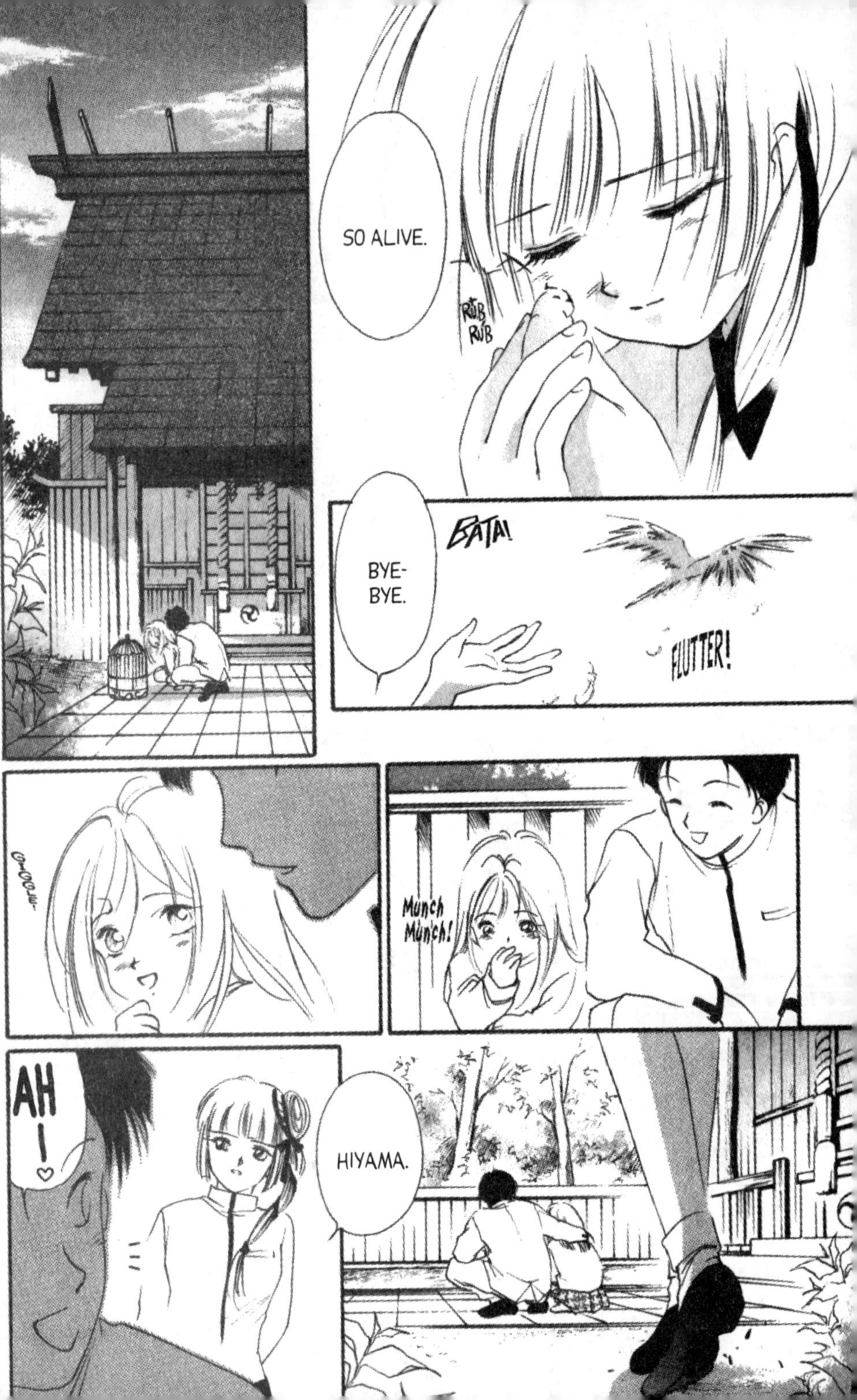
SO ALIVE.
RUB RUB
BYE-BYE.
BATA!
FLUTTER!
Munch Munch!
GIGGLE
HIYAMA.
AH!♡

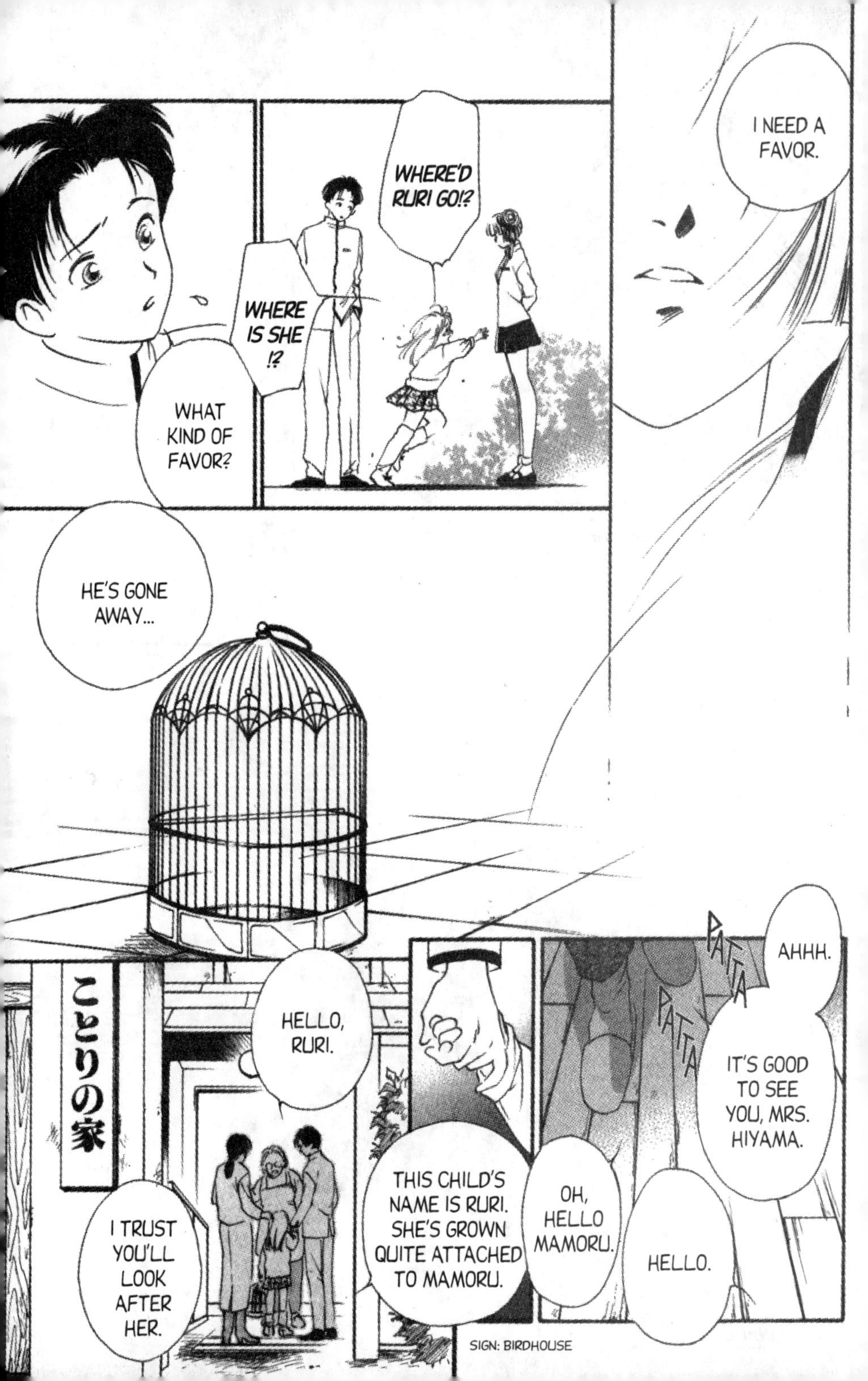
I NEED A FAVOR.
WHERE'D RURI GO!?
WHERE IS SHE !?
WHAT KIND OF FAVOR?
HE'S GONE AWAY...
AHHH.
PATTA
PATTA
IT'S GOOD TO SEE YOU, MRS. HIYAMA.
HELLO.
OH, HELLO MAMORU.
THIS CHILD'S NAME IS RURI. SHE'S GROWN QUITE ATTACHED TO MAMORU.
HELLO, RURI.
ことりの家
I TRUST YOU'LL LOOK AFTER HER.
SIGN: BIRDHOUSE

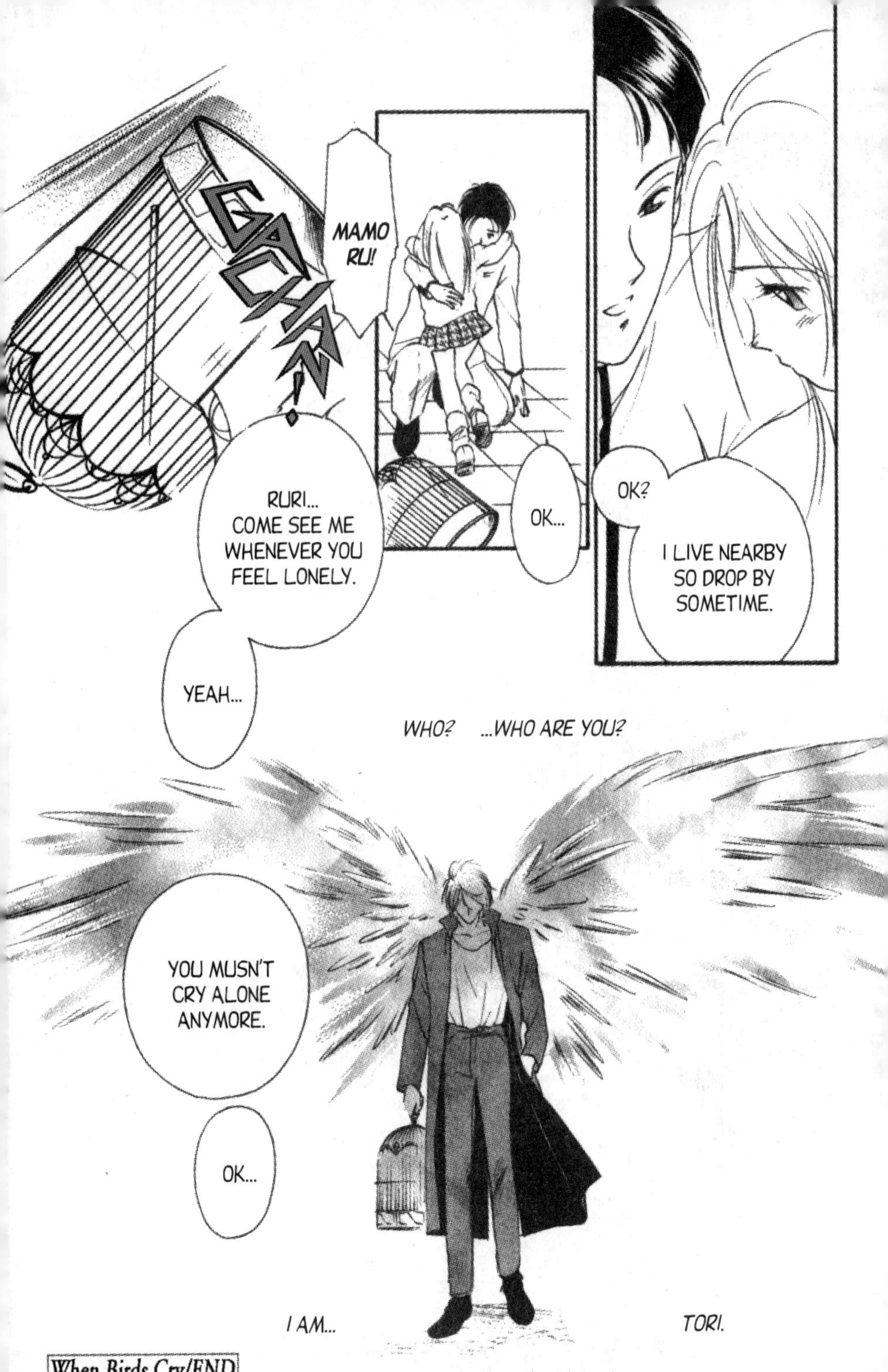
OK?
I LIVE NEARBY SO DROP BY SOMETIME.
OK...
MAMO RU!
GACHAN!
RURI... COME SEE ME WHENEVER YOU FEEL LONELY.
YEAH...
WHO? ...WHO ARE YOU?
YOU MUSN'T CRY ALONE ANYMORE.
OK...
I AM...
TORI.

When Birds Cry/END

Afterword

By Narumi Kakinouchi

*Thanks to everyone's fervent requests, Miyu is back! This, along with the TV animation, makes me extremely happy. However, Director Hirano is so busy that he's at about his wits' end. *Laugh* They broadcast every week, so it's like he has to finish a weekly homework assignment. Something else, too! My illustration collection is also being published and while I'm kind of nervous, I'm happy about it, too. Ashi Publishing gave it a good review. Be sure to check it out!*

*In an afterword of New Vampire Miyu, I wrote something about wanting to go back to working on the original Miyu... and sure enough here I am. She's such a deep character that even after writing the manuscript, there were various times when I thought that maybe I should have named her differently or drawn her from different angles. *Laugh**

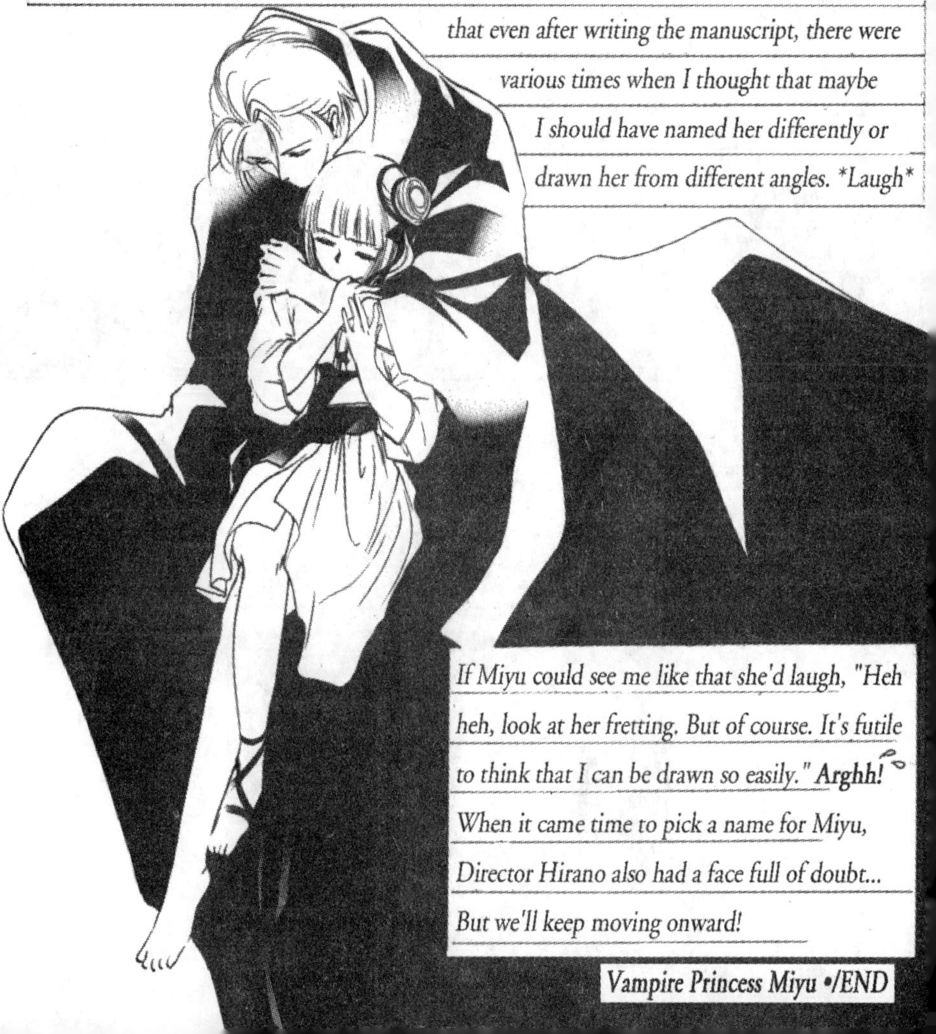

If Miyu could see me like that she'd laugh, "Heh heh, look at her fretting. But of course. It's futile to think that I can be drawn so easily." ***Arghh!*** *When it came time to pick a name for Miyu, Director Hirano also had a face full of doubt... But we'll keep moving onward!*

Vampire Princess Miyu •/END

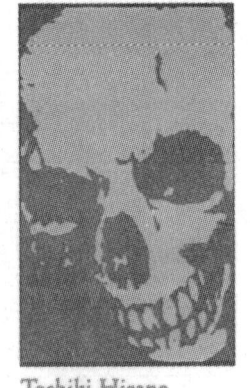

Narumi Kakinouchi

垣野内成美

Toshiki Hirano

平野俊貴

A dark, cold dimension... in this land of night which knows no rest, they are sleeping.

Miyu of the Vampire Clan is the guardian who watches over these slumbering Shinma even as she hunts stray Shinma which have slipped from the darkness into the human world.

Miyu takes flight so she can find the Shinma who have been lured by the call of human souls in chaos!

Attention Readers!!!

In order to preserve the original artwork, this volume of Vampire Princess Miyu has been printed in its Japanese format, reading right to left! This is the back of the book! Please begin reading from the other end of this novel... Thank you and enjoy!

HORROR
COMICS SPECIAL

ホラー コミックス スペシャル

吸血姫美夕□

平成10年4月5日　初版発行

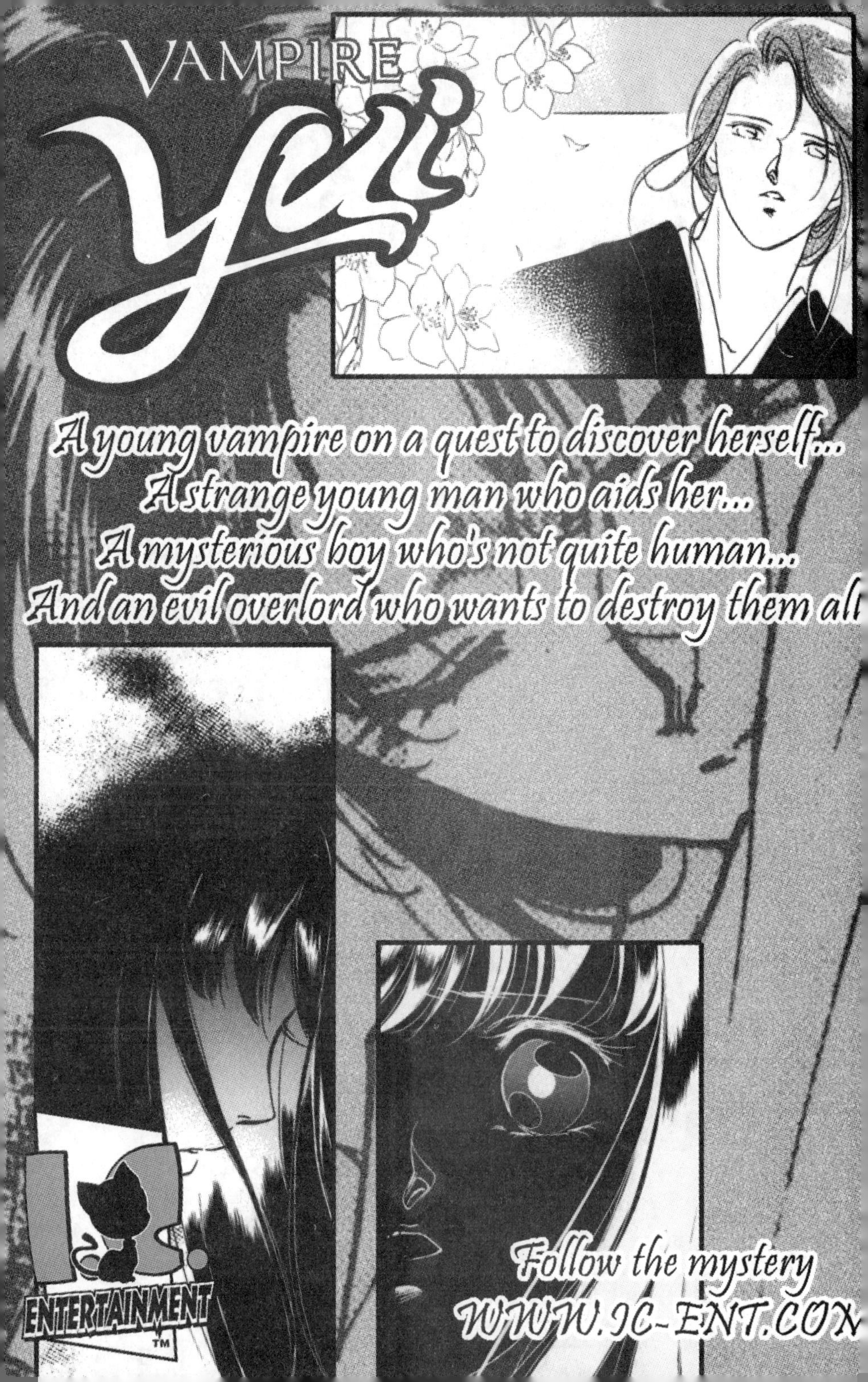
VAMPIRE
Yui
A young vampire on a quest to discover herself...
A strange young man who aids her...
A mysterious boy who's not quite human...
And an evil overlord who wants to destroy them all
ENTERTAINMENT
Follow the mystery
WWW.IC-ENT.COM

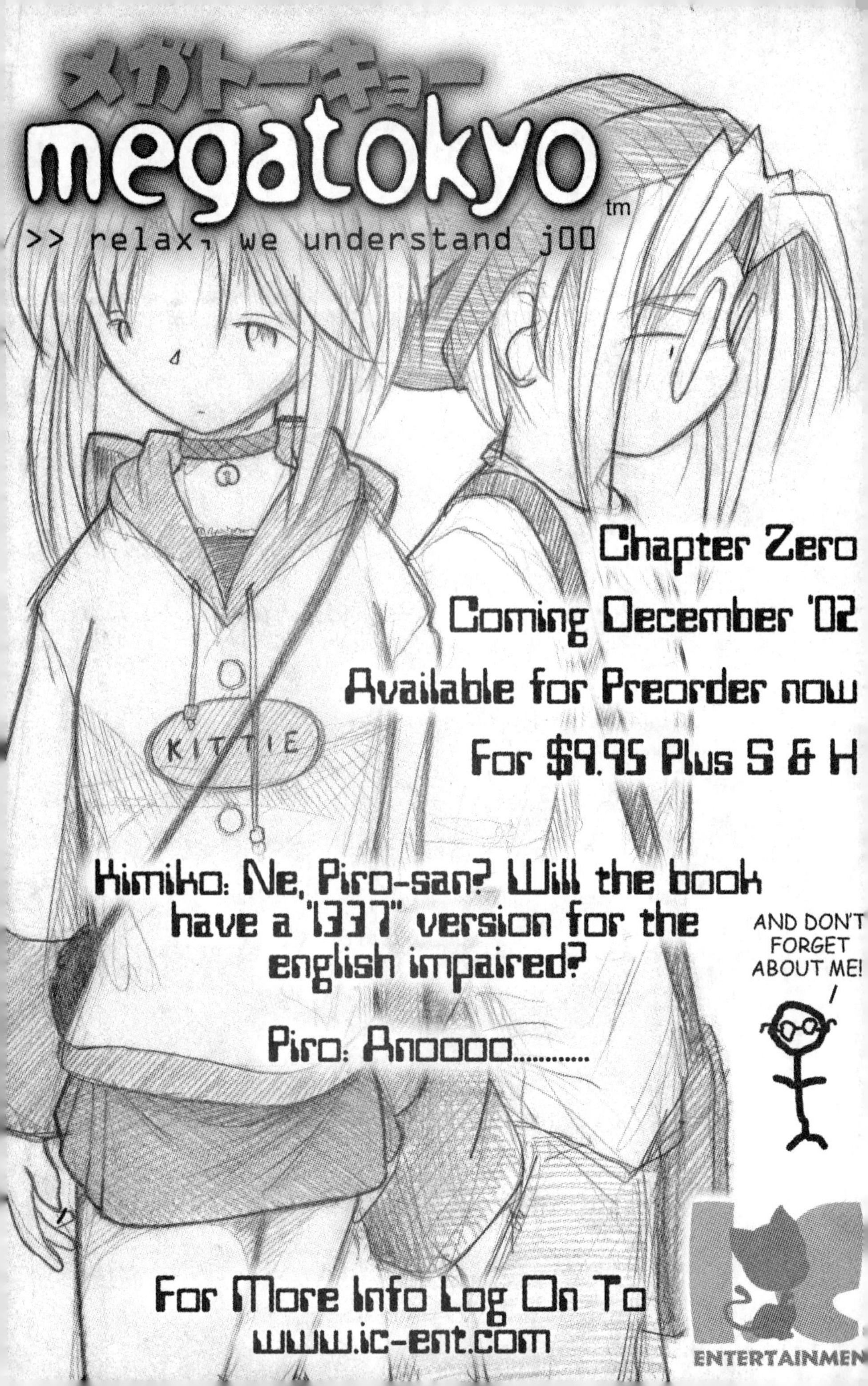

メガトーキョー
megatokyo tm
>> relax, we understand j00
KITTIE
Chapter Zero
Coming December '02
Available for Preorder now
For $9.95 Plus S & H
Kimiko: Ne, Piro-san? Will the book have a '1337" version for the english impaired?
Piro: Anoooo...........
AND DON'T FORGET ABOUT ME!
For More Info Log On To
www.ic-ent.com
ENTERTAINMEN

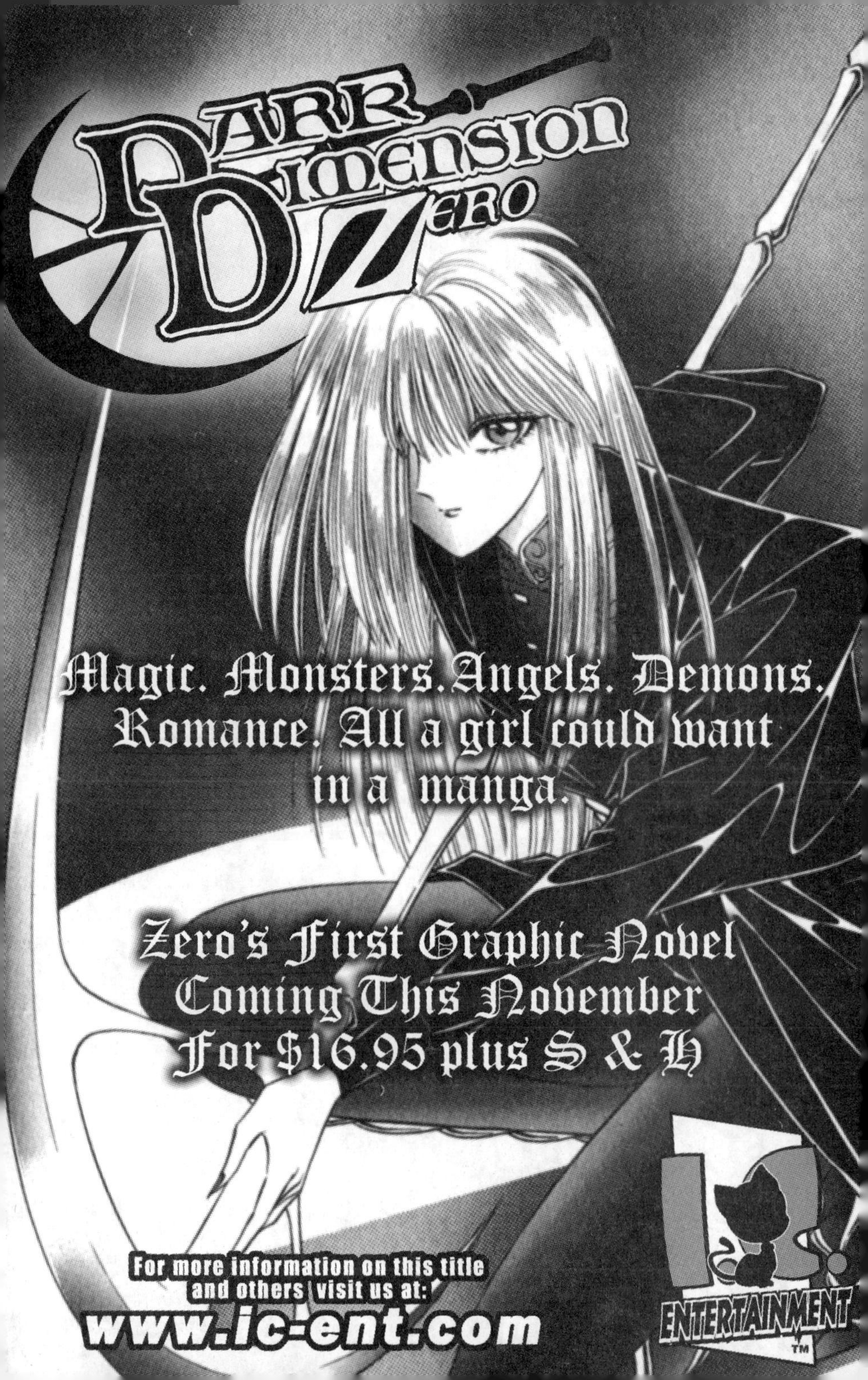
DARK DIMENSION ZERO
Magic. Monsters. Angels. Demons. Romance. All a girl could want in a manga.
Zero's First Graphic Novel Coming This November For $16.95 plus S & H
For more information on this title and others visit us at:
www.ic-ent.com
IC ENTERTAINMENT TM